Unitarianism in America

George Willis Cooke

Table of Contents

Unitarianism in America

George Willis Cooke

Kessinger Publishing reprints thousands of hard–to–find books!

Visit us at http://www.kessinger.net

UNITARIANISM IN AMERICA
A History of its Origin and Development

BY

GEORGE WILLIS COOKE

MEMBER OF THE AMERICAN HISTORICAL ASSOCIATION, AMERICAN ASSOCIATION FOR THE ADVANCEMENT OF SCIENCE, AMERICAN ACADEMY OF POLITICAL AND SOCIAL SCIENCE, ETC.

PREFACE.

The aim I have had in view in writing this book has been to give a history of the origin of Unitarianism in the United States, how it has organized itself, and what it has accomplished. It seemed desirable to deal more fully than has been done hitherto with the obscure beginnings of the Unitarian movement in New England; but limits of space have made it impossible to treat this phase of the subject in other than a cursory manner. It deserves an exhaustive treatment, which will amply repay the necessary labor to this end. The theological controversies that led to the separation of the Unitarians from the older Congregational body have been only briefly alluded to, the design of my work not requiring an ampler treatment. It was not thought best to cover the ground so ably traversed by Rev. George E. Ellis, in his Half-century of the Unitarian Controversy; Rev. Joseph Henry Allen, in his Our Liberal Movement in Theology; Rev. William Channing Gannett, in his Memoir of Dr. Ezra Stiles Gannett; and by Rev. John White Chadwick, in his Old and New Unitarian Beliefs. The attempt here made has been to supplement these works, and to treat of the practical side of Unitarianism,—its organizations, charities, philanthropies, and reforms.

With the theological problems involved in the history of Unitarianism this volume deals only so far as they have affected its general development. I have endeavored to treat of them fairly and without prejudice, to state the position of each side to the various controversies in the words of those who have accepted its point of view, and to judge of them as phases of a larger religious growth. I have not thought it wise to attempt anything approaching an exhaustive treatment of the controversies produced by the transcendental movement and by "the Western issue." If they are to be dealt with in the true spirit of the historical method, it must be at a period more remote from these discussions than that of one who participated in them, however slightly. I have endeavored to treat of all phases of Unitarianism without reference to local interests and without sectional preferences. If my book does not indicate such regard to what is national rather than to what is provincial, as some of my readers may desire, it is due to inability to secure information that would have given a broader character to my treatment of the subject.

The present work may appear to some of its readers to have been written in a sectarian spirit, with a purpose to magnify the excellences of Unitarianism, and to ignore its limitations. Such has not been the purpose I have kept before me; but, rather, my aim has been to present the facts candidly and justly, and to treat of them from the standpoint of a student of the religious evolution of mankind. Unitarianism in this country presents an attempt to bring religion into harmony with philosophy and science, and to reconcile Christianity with the modern spirit. Its effort in this direction is one that deserves careful consideration, especially in view of the unity and harmony it has developed in the body of believers who accept its teachings. The Unitarian body is a small one, but it has a history of great significance with reference to the future development of Christianity.

The names of those who accept Unitarianism have not been given in this book in any boastful spirit. A faith that is often spoken against may justify itself by what it has accomplished, and its best fruits are the men and women who have lived in the spirit of its teachings. In presenting the names of those who are not in any way identified with Unitarian churches, the purpose has been to suggest the wide and inclusive character of the Unitarian movement, and to indicate that it is not represented merely by a body of churches, but that it is an individual way of looking at the facts of life and its problems.

In writing the following pages, I have had constantly in mind those who have not been educated as Unitarians, and who have come into this inheritance through struggle and search. Not having been to the manner born myself, I have sought to provide such persons with the kind of information that would have been helpful to me in my endeavors to know the Unitarian life and temper. Something of what appears in these pages is due to this desire to help those who wish to know concretely what Unitarianism is, and what it has said and done to justify its existence. This will account for the manner of treatment and for some of the topics selected.

When this work was begun, the design was that it should form a part of the exhibit of Unitarianism in this country presented at the seventy–fifth anniversary of the formation of the American Unitarian Association. The time required for a careful verification of facts made it impossible to have the book ready at that date. The delay in its publication has not freed the work from all errors and defects, but it has given the opportunity for a more adequate treatment of many phases of the subject. Much of the work required in its preparation does not show itself in the following pages; but it has involved an extended examination of manuscript journals and records, as well as printed reports of societies, newspapers, magazines, pamphlets, and books. Many of the subjects dealt with, not having been touched upon in any previous historical work, have demanded a first–hand study of records, often difficult to find access to, and even more difficult to summarize in an interesting and adequate manner.

I wish here to warmly thank all those persons, many in number and too numerous to give all their names, who have generously aided me with their letters and manuscripts, and by the loan of books, magazines, pamphlets, and newspapers. Without their aid the book would have been much less adequate in its treatment of many subjects than it is at present. Though I am responsible for the book as it presents itself to the reader, much of its value is due to those who have thus labored with me in its preparation. In manuscript and in proof–sheet it has been read by several persons, who have kindly aided in securing accuracy to names, dates, and historic facts.

G.W.C.

BOSTON, October 1, 1902.

I. INTRODUCTION.—ENGLISH SOURCES OF AMERICAN UNITARIANISM.

The sources of American Unitarianism are to be found in the spirit of individualism developed by the Renaissance, the tendency to free inquiry that manifested itself in the Protestant Reformation, and the general movement of the English churches of the seventeenth century toward toleration and rationalism. The individualism of modern thought and life first found distinct expression in the Renaissance; and it was essentially a new creation, and not a revival. Hitherto the tribe, the city, the nation, the guild, or the church, had been the source of authority, the centre of power, and the giver of life. Although Greece showed a desire for freedom of thought, and a tendency to recognize the worth of the individual and his capacity as a discoverer and transmitter of truth, it did not set the individual mind free from bondage to the social and political power of the city. Socrates and Plato saw somewhat of the real worth of the individual, but the great mass of the people were never emancipated from the old tribal authority as inherited by the city–state; and not one of the great dramatists had conceived of the significance of a genuine individualism.[1]

[Sidenote: Renaissance.]

The Renaissance advanced to a new conception of the worth and the capacity of the individual mind, and for the first time in history recognized the full social meaning of personality in man. It sanctioned and authenticated the right of the individual to think for himself, and it developed clearly the idea that he may become the transmitter of valid revelations of spiritual truth. That God may speak through individual intuition and reason, and that this inward revelation may be of the highest authority and worth, was a conception first brought to distinct acceptance by the Renaissance.

A marked tendency of the Reformation which it received from the Renaissance was its acceptance of the free spirit of individualism. The Roman Church had taught that all valid religious truth comes to mankind through its own corporate existence, but the Reformers insisted that truth is the result of individual insight and investigation. The Reformation magnified the worth of personality, and made it the central force in all human effort.[2] To gain a positive personal life, one of free initiative power, that may in itself become creative, and capable of bringing truth and life to larger issues, was the chief motive of the Protestant leaders in their work of reformation. The result was that, wherever genuine Protestantism appeared, it manifested itself by its attitude of free inquiry, its tendency to emphasize individual life and thought, and its break with the traditions of the past, whether in literature or in religion. The Reformation did not, however, bring the principle of individuality to full maturity; and it retained many of the old institutional methods, as well as a large degree of their social motive. The Reformed churches were often as autocratic as the Catholic Church had been, and as little inclined to approve of individual departures from their creeds and disciplines; but the motive of individualism they had adopted in theory, and could not wholly depart from in practice. Their merit was that they had recognized and made a place for the principle of individuality; and it proved to be a developing social power, however much they might ignore or try to suppress it.

[Sidenote: Reformation.]

In its earliest phases Protestantism magnified the importance of reason in religious investigations, although it used an imperfect method in so doing. All doctrines were subjected more or less faithfully to this test, every rite was criticised and reinterpreted, and the Bible itself was handled in the freest manner. The individualism of the movement showed itself in Luther's doctrine of justification by faith, and his confidence in the validity of personal insight into spiritual realities. Most of all this tendency manifested itself in the assertion of the right of every believer to read the Bible for himself, and to interpret it according to his own needs. The vigorous assertion of the right to the free interpretation of the Word of God, and to personal insight into spiritual truth, led their followers much farther than the first reformers had anticipated. Individualism showed itself in an endless diversity of personal opinions, and in the creation of many little groups of believers, who were drawn together by an interest in individual leaders or by a common acceptance of hair-splitting interpretations of religious truths.[3]

The Protestant Church inculcated the law of individual fidelity to God, and declared that the highest obligation is that of personal faith and purity. What separated the Catholic and the Protestant was not merely a question of socialism as against individualism,[4] but it was also a problem of outward or inward law, of environment or intuition as the source of wholesome teaching, of ritualism or belief as the higher form of religious expression. The Protestants held that belief is better than ritual, faith than sacraments, inward authority than external force. They insisted that the individual has a right to think his own thoughts and to pray his own prayer, and that the revelation of the Supreme Good Will is to all who inwardly bear God's image and to every one whose will is a centre of new creative force in the world of conduct. They affirmed that the individual is of more worth than the social organism, the soul than the church, the motive than the conduct, the search for truth than the truth attained.

These tendencies of Protestantism found expression in the rationalism that appeared in England at the time of the Commonwealth, and especially at the Restoration. All the men of broader temper proclaimed the use of reason in the discussion of theological problems. In their opinion the Bible was to be interpreted as other books are, while with regard to doctrines there must be compromise and latitude. We find such a theologian as

Chillingworth recognizing "the free right of the individual reason to interpret the Bible."[5] To such men as Milton, Jeremy Taylor, and Locke the free spirit was essential, even though they had not become rationalists in the modern philosophical sense. They were slow to discard tradition, and they desired to establish the validity of the Bible; but they would not accept any authority until it had borne the test of as thorough an investigation as they could give it. The methods of rationalism were not yet understood, but the rational spirit had been accepted with a clear apprehension of its significance.

[Sidenote: Toleration.]

Toleration had two classes of advocates in the seventeenth century,—on the one hand, the minor and persecuted sects, and, on the other, such of the great leaders of religious opinion as Milton and Locke. The first clear assertion of the modern idea of toleration was made by the Anabaptists of Holland, who in 1611 put into their Confession of Faith this declaration of the freedom of religion from all state regulation: "The magistrate is not to meddle with religion, or matters of conscience, nor compel men to this or that form of religion, because Christ is King, and Lawgiver of the church and conscience." When the Baptists appeared in England, they advocated this principle as the one which ought to control in the relations of church and state. In 1614 there was published in London a little tract, written by one Leonard Busher, a poor laborer, and a member of the Baptist church that had recently been organized there. The writer addressed the King and Parliament with a statement of his conviction "that by fire and sword to constrain princes and peoples to receive that one true religion of the Gospel is wholly against the mind and merciful law of Christ."[6] He went on to say that no king or bishop is able to command faith, that it is monstrous for Christians to vex and destroy each other on account of religious differences. The leading Protestant bodies, especially the established churches, still held to the corporate idea of the nature of religious institutions; and, although they had rejected the domination of the Roman Church, they accepted the control of the state as essential to the purity of the church. This half–way retention of the corporate spirit made it impossible for any of the leading churches to give recognition to the full meaning of the Protestant idea of the worth of the individual soul, and its right to communicate directly with God. It remained for the persecuted Baptists and Independents, too feeble and despised to aspire to state influence, to work out the Protestant principle to its full expression in the spirit of toleration, to declare for liberty of conscience, the voluntary maintenance of worship, and the separation of church and state.

After the Restoration, and again after the enthronement of William and Mary, it became a serious practical problem to establish satisfactory relations between the various sects. All who were not sectarian fanatics saw that some kind of compromise was desirable, and the more liberal wished to include all but the most extreme phases of belief within the national church. When that national church was finally established on the lines which it has since retained, and numerous bodies of dissenters found themselves compelled to remain outside, toleration became more and more essential, in order that the nation might live at peace with itself. From generation to generation the dissenters were able to secure for themselves a larger recognition, disabilities were removed as men of all sects saw that restrictions were useless, and toleration became the established law in the relations of the various religious bodies to each other.

[Sidenote: Arminianism.]

The conditions which led to toleration also developed a liberal interpretation of the relations of the church to the people, a broader explanation of doctrines, and a rational insight into the problems of the religious life. One phase of this more comprehensive religious spirit was shown in Arminianism, which was nothing more than an assertion of individualism in the sphere of man's relations to God. Calvinism maintained that man cannot act freely for himself, that he is strictly under the sovereignty of the Divine Will. The democratic tendency in Holland, where Arminianism had its origin, expressed itself in the declaration that every man is free to accept or to reject religious truth, that the will is individual and self–assertive, and that the conscience is not bound. Arminius and his coworkers accepted what the early Protestant movement had regarded as essential, that religion should be always obedient to the rational spirit, that nature should be the test in regard to all which affects human conduct, and that the critical spirit ought to be applied to dogma and Bible. Arminius reasserted this freedom of the human spirit, and vindicated the right of the individual mind to seek God and his truth wherever they may be found.

As Protestantism became firmly established in England, and the nation accepted its mental and moral attitude without reserve, what is known as Arminianism came to be more and more prevalent. This was not a body of doctrines, and it was in no sense a sectarian movement: it was rather a mental temper of openness and freedom. In a word, Arminianism became a method of religious inquiry that appealed to reason, nature, and the needs of man. It put new emphasis on the intellectual side of religion, and it developed as a moral protest against the harsher features of Calvinism. It gave to human feelings the right to express themselves as elements in the problem of man's relations to God, and vindicated for God the right to be deemed as sympathetic and loving as the men who worship him.

While the Arminians accepted the Bible as an authoritative standard as fully as did the Calvinists, they were more critical in its study: they applied literary and historical standards in its interpretation, and they submitted it to the vindication of reason. They sought to escape from the tyranny of the Bible, and yet to make it a living force in the world of conduct and character. They not only declared anew the right of private judgment, but they wished to make the Bible the source of inward spiritual illumination,—not a standard and a test, but an awakener of the divine life in the soul. They sought for what is really essential in religious truth, limited the number of dogmas that may be regarded as requisite to the Christian life, and took the position that only what is of prime importance is to be required of the believer. The result was that Arminianism became a positive aid to the growth of toleration in England; for it became what was called latitudinarian,—that is, broad in temper, inclusive in spirit, and desirous of bringing all the nation within the limits of one harmonizing and noble–minded church.

[Sidenote: English Rationalists.]

It was in such tendencies as these, as they were developed in Holland and England, that American Unitarianism had its origin. To show how true this is, it may be desirable to speak of a few of the men whose books were most frequently read in New England during the eighteenth century. The prose writings of Milton exerted great influence in favor of toleration and in vindication of reason. Without doubt he became in his later years a believer in free will and the subordinate nature of Christ, and he was true to the Protestant ideal of an open Bible and a free spirit in man. Known as a Puritan, his pleas for toleration must have been read with confidence by his coreligionists of New England; while his rational temper could not have failed to have its effect.

His vindication of the Bible as the religion of Protestants must have commended Chillingworth to the liberal minds in New England; and there is evidence that he was read with acceptance, although he was of the established church. Chillingworth was of the noblest type of the latitudinarians in the Church of England during the first half of the seventeenth century; for he was generously tolerant, his mind was broad and liberal, and he knew the true value of a really comprehensive and inclusive church, which he

9

earnestly desired should be established in England. He wished to have the creed reduced to the most limited proportions by giving emphasis to what is fundamental, and by the extrusion of all else. It was his desire to maintain what is essential that caused him to say: "I am fully assured that God does not, and therefore that man ought not, to require any more of any man than this—to believe the Scripture to be God's word, to endeavor to find the true sense of it, and to live according to it."[7]

He would therefore leave every man free to interpret the Bible for himself, and he would make no dogmatic test to deprive any man of this right. The chief fact in the Bible being Christ, he insisted that Christianity is loyalty to his spirit. "To believe only in Christ" is his definition of Christianity, and he would add nothing to this standard. He would put no church or creed or council between the individual soul and God; and he would direct every believer to the Bible as the free and open way of the soul's access to divine truth. He found that the religion of Protestants consisted in the rational use of that book, and not in the teachings of the Reformers or in the confessions they devised. It is the great merit of Chillingworth that he vindicated the spirit of toleration in a broad and noble manner, that he was without sectarian prejudice or narrowness in his desire for an inclusive church, and that he spoke and wrote in a truly rational temper. He applied reason to all religious problems, and he regarded it as the final judge and arbiter. Religious freedom received from him the fullest recognition, and no one has more clearly indicated the scope and purpose of toleration.

Another English religious leader, much read in New England, was Archbishop Tillotson. It has been said of him that "for the first time since the Reformation the voice of reason was now clearly heard in the high places of the church."[8] He was an Arminian in his sympathies, and held that the way of salvation is open to all who choose to accept its opportunities. He expressed himself as being as certain that the doctrine of eternal decrees is not of God as he was sure that God is good and just. His ground for this opinion was that it is repugnant to the convictions of justice and goodness natural to men. He maintained that we shall be justified before God by means of the reformation that is wrought in our own lives. We have an intuition of what is right, and a natural capacity for living justly and righteously. Experience and reason he made concomitant spiritual forces with the Bible, and he held that revelation is but a republication of the truths of natural religion. Tillotson was truly a broad churchman, who was desirous of making the national church as comprehensive as possible; and he was one who practised as well as preached toleration.

Not less liberal was Jeremy Taylor, who was numbered among the dissenters. In the introduction to his Liberty of Prophesying he said, "So long as men have such variety of principles, such several constitutions, educations, tempers, and distempers, hopes, interests, and weaknesses, degrees of light and degrees of understanding, it was impossible all should be of one mind." Taylor justly said that in heaven there is room for all faiths. His Liberty of Prophesying, Chillingworth's Religion of Protestants, and Milton's Liberty of Unlicensed Printing are the great expressions of the spirit of toleration in the seventeenth century. Each was broad, comprehensive, and noble in its plea for religious freedom. It has been said of Taylor that "he sets a higher value on a good life than on an orthodox creed. He estimates every doctrine by its capacity to do men good."[9]

Another advocate of toleration was John Locke, whose chief influence was as a rationalist in philosophy and religion. While accepting Christianity with simple confidence, he subjected it to the careful scrutiny of reason. His philosophy awakened the rationalistic spirit in all who accepted it, so that many of his disciples went much farther than he did himself. While accepting revelation, he maintained that natural knowledge is more certain in its character. He taught that the conclusions of reason are more important than anything given men in the name of revelation. He did not himself widely depart from the orthodoxy of his day, though he did not accept the doctrine of the Trinity in the most approved form.

One of the rationalistic followers of Locke was Samuel Clarke, who attempted to apply the scientific methods of Newton to the interpretation of Christianity. He tried to establish faith in God on a purely scientific basis. He declared that goodness does not exist because God commands it, but that he commands it because it is good. He interpreted the doctrine of the Trinity in a rationalistic manner, holding to its form, but rejecting its substance.

These men were widely read in New England during the eighteenth century. In England they were accounted orthodox, and they held high positions either in the national church or in the leading dissenting bodies. They were not sectarian or bigoted, they wished to give religion a basis in common sense and ethical integrity, and they approved of a Christianity that is practical and leads to noble living.

When we consider what were the relations of the colonies to England during the first half of the eighteenth century, and that the New England churches were constantly influenced by the religious attitude of the mother–country,[10] it is plain enough that toleration and rationalism were in large measure received from England. In the same school was learned the lesson of a return to the simplicity of Christ, of making him and his life the standard of Christian fellowship. The great leaders in England taught positively that loyalty to Christ is the only essential test of Christian duty; and it is not in the least surprising the same idea should have found noble advocacy in New England. That a good life and character are the true indications of the possession of a saving faith was a thought too often uttered in England not to find advocacy in the colonies.

In this way Unitarianism had its origin, in the teachings of men who were counted orthodox in England, but who favored submitting all theological problems to the test of reason. It was not a sectarian movement in its origin or at any time during the eighteenth century; but it was an effort to make religion practical, to give it a basis in reality, and to establish it as acceptable to the sound judgment and common sense of all men. It was an application to the interpretation of theological problems of that individualistic spirit which was at the very source of Protestantism. If the individual ought to interpret the Bible for himself, so ought he to accept his own explanation of the dogmas of the church. In so doing, he necessarily becomes a rationalist, which may lead him far from the traditions of the past. If he thinks for himself, there is an end to uniformity of faith—a conclusion which such men as Chillingworth and Jeremy Taylor were willing to accept; and, therefore, they desired an all–inclusive church, in order that freedom and unity of faith might be both maintained.

In its beginning the liberal movement in New England was not concerned with the Trinity. It was a demand for simplicity, rationality, and toleration. When it had proceeded far on its way, it was led to a consideration of the problem of the Trinity, because it did not find that doctrine distinctly taught in the New Testament. Accepting implicitly the words of Christ, it found him declaring positively his own subordination to the Father, and preferred his teaching to that of the creeds. To the early liberals this was simply a question of the nature of Christ, and did not lessen for them their implicit faith in his revelation or their recognition of the beauty and glory of his divine character.

[1] Paul Lafargue, The Evolution of Property from Savagery to
   Civilization, 18, 19. "If the savage is incapable of conceiving the
   idea of individual possession of objects not incorporated with his
   person, it is because he has no conception of his individuality as

12

distinct from the consanguine group in which he lives.... Savages, even
though individually completer beings, seeing that they are
self–sufficing, than are civilized persons, are so thoroughly
identified with their hordes and clans that their individuality does
not make itself felt either in the family or in property. The clan was
all in all: the clan was the family; it was the clan that was the owner
of property." Also W.M. Sloan, The French Revolution and Religious
Reform, 38. "In the Greek and Roman world the individual, body, mind,
and soul, had no place in reference to the state. It was only as a
member of family, gens, curia, phratry, or deme, and tribe, that the
ancient city–state knew the men and women which composed it. The same
was true of knowledge: every sensation, perception, and judgment fell
into the category of some abstraction, and, instead of concrete things,
men knew nothing but generalized ideals."

[2] Francesco S. Nitti, Catholic Socialism, 74, 85, 86. "If we consider
the teachings of the Gospel, the communistic origins of the church, the
socialistic tendencies of the early fathers, the traditions of the
Canon Law, we cannot wonder that at the present day Socialism should
count no small number of its adherents among Catholic writers.... The
Reformation was the triumph of Individualism. Catholicism, instead, is
communistic by its origin and traditions.... The Catholic Church, with
her powerful organization, dating back over many centuries, has
accustomed Catholic peoples to passive obedience, to a passive
renunciation of the greater part of individualistic tendencies."

[3] See David Masson, Life of John Milton, III. 136; John Tulloch, Rational
Theology and Christian Philosophy in England, II. 9; John Hunt,
Religious Thought in England, I. 234.

[4] The word socialism is not used here with any understanding that the
Catholic Church accepts the social theories implied by that name. It is
used to indicate that the Roman Church maintains that revelation is to
the church itself, and that it is now the visible representative of
Christ. The Protestant maintains that revelation is made through an
individual, and not to a church. See Otto Gierke, Political Theories of

the Middle Age, translated by F.W. Maitland, 10, 22. "In all centuries
of the Middle Age Christendom is set before us a single, universal
community, founded and governed by God himself. Mankind is one mystical
body; it is one single and internally connected people or fold; it is
an all–embracing corporation, which constitutes that Universal Realm,
spiritual, and temporal, which may be called the Universal Church, or,
with equal propriety, the Commonwealth of the Human Race.... Mediaeval
thought proceeded from the idea of a single whole. Therefore an organic
construction of human society was as familiar to it as a mechanical and
atomistic construction was originally alien. Under the influence of
biblical allegories and the models set by Greek and Roman writers, the
comparison of mankind at large and every smaller group to an animate
body was universally adopted and pressed. Mankind in its totality was
conceived as an Organism."

[5] Tulloch, Rational Theology in England, I. 339.

[6] David Masson, Life of Milton, III. 102.

[7] The Religion of Protestants, II. 411.

[8] John Hunt, Religious Thought in England, II. 99.

[9] John Hunt, Religious Thought in England, I. 340.

[10] John Hunt, Religious Thought in England, I. 340.

II. THE LIBERAL SIDE OF PURITANISM.

Unitarianism was brought to America with the Pilgrims and the Puritans. Its origins are
not to be found in the religious indifference and torpidity of the eighteenth century, but in
the individualism and the rational temper of the men who settled Plymouth, Salem, and
Boston. Its development is coextensive with the origin and growth of Congregationalism,
even with that of Protestantism itself. So long as New England has been in existence, so
long, at least, Unitarianism, in its motives and in its spirit, has been at work in the name

of toleration, liberty, and free inquiry.

The many and wide divergences of opinion which were an essential result of the spirit and methods of Protestantism were shown from the first by the Pilgrims and Puritans. In Massachusetts, stringent laws were adopted in order to secure uniformity of belief and practice; but it was never achieved, except in name. Antinomianism early presented itself in Boston, and it was quickly followed by the incursions of the Baptists and Friends. Hooker did not find himself in sympathy with the Massachusetts leaders, and led a considerable company to Connecticut from Cambridge, Watertown, and Dorchester. Sir Henry Vane could not always agree with those who guided the religion and the politics of Boston; Roger Williams had another ideal of church and state than that which had come to the Puritans; and Sir Richard Saltonstall would not submit himself to the aristocratic methods of the Boston preachers.

These are but a few of the many indications of the individualistic spirit that marked the first years of the Puritan colonies. It was a part of the Protestant inheritance, and was inherent in the very nature of Protestantism itself. Although the Puritans had only in part, and with faltering steps, come to the acceptance of the individualistic and rational spirit in religion, yet they were on the way to it, however long they might be hindered by an autocratic temper. In fact, the Puritans throughout the seventeenth century in New England were trying at one and the same time to use reason and yet to cling to authority, to accept the Protestant ideal and yet to employ the Catholic methods in state and church. In being Protestants, they were committed to the central motive of individualism; but they never consistently turned away from that conception of the church which is autocratic and authoritative.

[Sidenote: The Church of Authority and the Church of Freedom.]

Looked at from the modern sociological point of view, there are two types of church, the one socialistic or institutional and the other individualistic, the one making the corporate power of the church the source of spiritual life, the other making the personal insight of the individual man the fountain of religious truth. Such a church as that of Rome may be properly called socialistic because of its corporate nature, because it maintains that revelation is to, and by means of, an institution, an organic religious body.[1]

Catholicism, whether of Rome, Greece, or England, makes the church as a great religious corporation the organ of religious expression. Such a corporation is the source of authority, the test of truth, the creator of spiritual ideals. On the other hand, such a church as the Protestant may be called individualistic because it makes the individual the channel of revelation. It emphasizes personality as of supreme worth, and it makes religious institutions of little value in comparison.

Practically, the difference between the socialistic and the individualistic church is as wide as it is theoretically. In all Catholic churches the child is born into the church, with the right to full acceptance into it by methods of tuition and ritual, whatever his individual qualities or capacities. In all distinctly Protestant churches, membership must be sought by individual preference or supernatural process.[2] The way to it is through individual profession of its creed or inward miraculous transformation of character by the profoundest of personal experiences. In all socialistic or Catholic churches—whether heathen, ethnic, or Christian—young people are admitted to membership after a definite period of training and an initiation by means of an impressive ritual. In all Protestant churches, initiation takes place as the result of personal experiences and mature convictions, and is therefore usually deferred until adult life has been reached.

When we bring out thus distinctly the ideals and methods of the two churches, we are able to understand that the Puritans were theoretically Protestants, but that they practically used the methods of the Catholics. This will be seen more clearly when we take the individualistic tendencies of the Puritans into distinct recognition, and place them in contrast with their socialistic practices. The Puritan churches were thoroughly individualistic in their admission of members, none being accepted into full membership but those who had been converted by means of a personal experience. In theory every male church member was a priest and king, authorized to interpret spiritual truth and to exercise political authority. Therefore, in 1631 the General Court of Massachusetts (being the legislative body) established the rule that only church members should exercise the right of suffrage. This law was continued on the statute books until 1664, and was accepted in practice until 1691.

Because the individual Christian was accounted a priest, however humble in learning or social position, he had the right to join with others in ordaining and setting apart to the ministry of God the man who was to lead the church as its teacher or pastor, though this practice was abandoned as the state–church idea developed, as it did in New England by a process of reaction. Every man could read the Bible for himself, and give it such meaning as his own conscience and reason dictated. By virtue of his Christian experience he had the personal right to find in it his own creed and the law of his own conduct. It was not only his right to do this, but it was also his duty. Revivalism was therefore the distinct outgrowth of Puritanism, the expression of its individualistic spirit. It was the human means of bringing the individual soul within reach of the supernatural power of God, and of facilitating that choice of the Holy Spirit by which one was selected for this change rather than another. The means were social, it is true; but the end reached was absolutely individual, as an experience and as a result attained. What confirmation was to the Catholic, that was conversion to the Puritan.

The Puritans in New England, however, inherited the older socialism to so large an extent that they proceeded to establish what was a state church in method, if not in theory. Though they began with the idea that the churches were to be supported by voluntary contributions (and always continued that method in Boston), yet in a few years they resorted to taxation for their maintenance, and enacted stringent laws compelling attendance upon them by every resident of a town, whatever his beliefs or his personal interests. They forbade the utterance of opinions not approved by the authorities, and made use of fines, imprisonment, and death in support of arbitrary laws enacted for this purpose. These methods were the same as those used by the older socialistic and state churches to compel acceptance of their teachings and practices. They were based on the idea of the corporate nature of the church, and its right to control the individual in the name of the social whole.

The harshness of the Puritan methods was the result of this attempt to maintain a new idea in harmony with an old practice. The Baptists were consistently individualists in rejecting infant baptism, accepting conversion as essential to church membership, maintaining freedom of conscience, and practising toleration as a fundamental social law. The Puritans inconsistently combined conversion and infant baptism,—the Protestant right of private judgment with the Catholic methods of the state church,—a democratic theory of popular suffrage with a most aristocratic limitation of that suffrage to church members. As late as 1674 only 2,527 men in all had been admitted to the exercise of the franchise in Massachusetts. One–sixth or one–eighth of the men were voters, the rest were disfranchised. The church and the state were controlled by this small minority in a community that was theoretically democratic, both in religion and politics.

It is not surprising that there began to be mutterings against such restrictions. It shows the strength of character in the Puritan communities of Massachusetts and New Haven that a large majority of the men submitted as long as they did to conditions thoroughly undemocratic. As a political measure, when the grumblings became so loud as to be no longer ignored, what is called the half–way covenant was adopted, by means of which a semi–membership in the churches could be secured, that gave the right of suffrage, but permitted no action within the church itself.[3] Many writers on this period fail to understand the significance of the half–way covenant; for they attribute to that legislation the disintegrating results that followed. They forget that these half–members were not admitted to any part in church affairs; and they refuse to see that the methods employed by the Puritans were, because of their exclusiveness, of necessity demoralizing. In fact, the half–way covenant was a result of the disintegration that had already taken place as the issue of an attempted compromise between the institutional and the individualistic theories of church government.

[Sidenote: Seventeenth–century Liberals.]

By arbitrary methods the Puritans succeeded in controlling church and state until 1688, when the interference of the English authorities compelled them to practise toleration and to widen the suffrage. The words of Sir Richard Saltonstall to John Cotton and John Wilson show clearly that these methods were not accepted by all, and even Saltonstall returned to England to escape the restrictions he condemned. "It doth not a little grieve my spirit to hear what sad things are daily reported of your tyranny and persecutions in New England," he wrote, "as that you fine, whip, and imprison men for their consciences. First you compel such to come into your assemblies as you know will not join with you in your worship, and when they show their dislike thereof or witness against it, then you stir up your magistrates to punish them for such (as you conceive) their public affronts. Truly, friends, this your practice of compelling any in matters of worship to do that whereof they are not persuaded is to make them sin, and many are made hypocrites thereby, conforming in their outward man for fear of punishment. We pray for you and wish you prosperity in every way, hoped that the Lord would have given you so much light and love there, that you might have been eyes to God's people here, and not to practise those courses in wilderness which you went so far to prevent. These rigid ways have laid you very low in the hearts of the saints."[4]

Another man who withdrew to England from the narrow spirit of the Puritans was William Pynchon, of Springfield, one of the best trained and ablest of the early settlers of Massachusetts. In 1650 he published a book on the Meritorious Price of our Redemption, in which he denied that Christ was subject to the wrath of God or suffered torments in hell for the redemption of men or paid the penalty for all human sins; but such teachings were too liberal and modern for the leaders in church and state.[5] What is now orthodox, that Christ's sacrifice was voluntary, was then heretical and forbidden.

If during the first half–century of New England no liberalism found definite utterance, it was because of its repression. It was in the air, even then, and it would have found expression, had there been opportunity or invitation. There were other men than Williams, Saltonstall, Pynchon, and Henry Vane, who believed in toleration, liberty of conscience, and a rational interpretation of religion. In a limited way such men were Henry Dunster and Charles Chauncy, the first two presidents of Harvard College, who both rejected infant baptism because it was not consistent with a converted church membership. It was a small thing to protest against, and to suffer for as Dunster suffered; but the principle was great for which he contended, the principle of individual conviction in religion.

The better spirit of the Puritans appears in such a saying as that of Sir Henry Vane, the second governor of the Massachusetts Bay Colony, that "all magistrates are to fear or forbear intermeddling with giving rule or imposing their own beliefs in religious matters."[6] To a similar purport was the saying of Thomas Hooker, the founder of Connecticut, that "the foundation of authority is laid in the free consent of the people."[7] In the writings of John Robinson, the Pilgrim leader, a like greatness of purpose and thought appears, as where he says that "the meanest man's reason, specially in matter of faith and obedience to God, is to be preferred before all authority of all men."[8] Robinson was a very strict Calvinist in doctrine; but he was tolerant in large degree, and thoroughly convinced of the worth of liberty of conscience. His liberality comes out in such words as these: "The custom of the church is but the custom of men; the sentence of the fathers but the opinions of men; the determinations of councils but the judgments of men."[9] How strong a believer in individual reason he was appears in this statement: "God, who hath made two great lights for the bodily eye, hath also made two lights for the eye of the mind; the one the Scriptures for her supernatural light, and the other reason for her natural light. And, indeed, only these two are a man's own, and so is not the authority of other men. The Scriptures are as well mine as any other man's, and so is

19

reason as far as I can attain to it."[10] When he says that "the credit commending a testimony to others cannot be greater than is the authority in itself of him that gives it nor his authority greater than his person,"[11] he puts an end to all arbitrary authority of priest and church.

It will be seen from these quotations that the spirit of liberality existed even in the very beginnings of New England, and in the convictions of the men who were its chief prophets and leaders. It was hidden away for a time, it may be, though it never ceased to find utterance in some form. The breadth of the underlying spirit finds expression in the compacts by which local churches united their members. The liberality was incipient, a promise of the future rather than a realization in the present.

The earliest churches of New England were not organized with a creed, but with a covenant. Occasionally there was a confession of faith or a creedal statement; but it was regarded as quite unnecessary because it was implied in the general acceptance of the Calvinistic doctrines, and the use of the Cambridge platform or other similar document. The covenant of a church could not be a statement of beliefs, because it was a vow between Christ and his church, and a pledge of the individual members of the church with relation to each other. The creed was implied, but it was not expressed; and, although all the churches were Calvinist at first, the nature of the covenant was such that, when men grew liberal, there was no written creedal test by which they could be held to the old beliefs. When Calvinism was outgrown, it could be slowly and silently discarded, both by individual members of a church and by the church itself, because it was not explicitly contained in the covenant. The creed was rejected, but the covenant was retained.

As soon as authority was withdrawn from the Puritan leaders by the English crown, the spirit of liberty began to show itself in many directions. In a sermon preached in 1691, Samuel Willard, the minister of the Old South Church in Boston, and afterwards president of Harvard College, gave utterance to what was stirring in many minds at that time. He said that God "hath nowhere by any general indulgence given away this liberty of his to any other authority in the world to have dominion over the consciences of men or to give rules of worship, but hath, on the other hand, strongly prohibited it and severely threatened any that shall presume to do it." He earnestly asserted that no authority is to be accepted but that of the Bible, and that is to be free for each person's individual interpretation. "Hath there not," Willard questions, "been too much of a pinning our faith on the credit or practice of others, attended on with a woful neglect to know what is the mind of Christ?" Here was a spirit that not many years later was showing itself in the liberal movement that grew into Unitarianism. The effort to free the consciences of men, and to bring all appeals to the Bible and to Christ, was what gave significance to the liberal movement of the next century.

[Sidenote: Growth of Liberty in Church Methods.]

There also began a movement to bring church and state into harmonious relations with each other, and to overcome the inconsistency of being individualist and socialist at the same moment. The theory of conversion being retained, it was proposed to make the ordinances of religion free to all, in order that they might bring about the supernatural change that was desired. This is the real significance of the position taken by Solomon Stoddard, of Northampton, who taught that the Lord's Supper is a converting ordinance, and who in practice did not ask for a supernatural regeneration as preparatory to a limited church membership, though he regarded this as essential to full admission. The half–way covenant had been adopted before Mr. Stoddard became the pastor of the church; but soon after his settlement this limited form of admission was more clearly defined, and he admitted persons into what he described as a "state of education."[12] This "large congregationalism," as it was called, was in time accepted as meaning that those who have faith enough to justify the baptism of their children have enough to admit them to full communion in the church. Mr. Stoddard appealed to the English practice in his defence of the broader principle which he adopted. He also vindicated his position by reference to the practices of the leading Protestant countries in Europe. His methods, as outlined and interpreted in his Appeal to the Learned,[13] were based more or less explicitly on the corporate idea of the church.

Although Stoddard was a strict Calvinist, there can be no doubt that his method of open communion slowly led to theological modifications. Not only did it have a tendency to bring the state and church into closer relations with each other, by making the membership in the two more nearly the same, but it led the way to the acceptance of the doctrine of moral ability, and therefore to a modification of Calvinism. If it was a practical rather than a theological reason that caused Stoddard to adopt open communion, it almost inevitably led to Arminianism, because it implied, as he presented its conditions, that man is able of his own free will to accept the terms of salvation which Calvinism had confined to the operation of the sovereignty of God alone.

Another way in which the spirit of the time was showing itself may be seen in the fact that the parish, towards the end of the seventeenth century, on more than one occasion refused to the church the selection of the minister; and church and parish met together for that purpose. This was the case in the first church of Salem in 1672, and at Dedham in 1685. So long as church members only were given the right of suffrage, the selection of the minister was wholly in their hands. As soon as the suffrage was extended, there was a movement to include all tax-payers amongst those who could exercise this choice. In 1666 such a proposition was discussed in Connecticut, and not long after it became the law. In 1692 the Massachusetts laws gave the church the right to select the minister, but permitted the parish to concur in or to reject such choice. During the next century there was a growing tendency to enlarge the privileges of the parish, and to make that the controlling factor in calling the minister and in all that pertained to the outward life of the church and congregation. The result will be seen more and more in the influence of the parish in the selection of liberal men for the pulpit.

A notable instance of the more liberal tendencies is seen in the formation of the Brattle Street Church of Boston in 1699. Although this church accepted the Westminster Confession of Faith and adopted the practices common to the New England churches at this period, it insisted upon the reading of the Bible without comment as a part of the church service. The relation of religious experiences as preparatory to admission to the church was discarded, all were admitted to communion who were approved by the pastor, and women were permitted to take part in voting on all church questions. These and other innovations occasioned much discussion; and a controversy ensued between the pastor Benjamin Colman and Increase Mather.[14] The Salem pastors, Rev. John Higginson and Rev. Nicholas Noyes, addressed a letter to the Brattle Street congregation, in which they criticised the church because it did not consult with other churches in its formation, because it did not make a public profession of repentance on behalf of its members, because baptism was administered on less stringent terms than was customary and too lax admission was given to the sacraments, and because the admission of females to full church activity had a direct tendency "to subvert the order and liberty of the churches." Though the Brattle Street Church was for a time severely criticised, it soon came into intimate relations with the other churches of Boston, and it ceased to appear as in any way peculiar. That it was organized on a broader basis of membership indicates very clearly that the old methods were not satisfactory to all the people.[15]

[Sidenote: A Puritan Rationalist.]

Unitarianism in America

The influence of similar ideas is seen in the books of John Wise, of Ipswich, whose Churches' Quarrel Espoused was published in 1710, and his Vindication of the Government of the New England Churches in 1717. His first book was in answer to the proposition of a number of the ministers of Boston to bring the churches under the control of associations. By this remonstrance the plan was defeated, and the independence of the local church fully established. In republishing his book, he added the Vindication, in order to give his ideas a more systematic expression. The Vindication is the most thoroughly modern book published in America during the eighteenth century. It has a literary directness and power remarkable for the time. Wise gives no quotations indicating that he had read the great liberal writers of England, but he was familiar with Plato and Cicero.

In his first book he speaks of "the natural freedom of human beings,"[16] and says that "right reason is a ray of divine wisdom enstamped upon human nature."[17] Again, he says that "right reason, that great oracle in human affairs, is the soul of man so formed and endowed by creation with a certain sagacity or acumen whereby man's intellect is enabled to take up the true idea or perception of things agreeable with and according to their natures."[18] In such utterances as these Wise was putting himself into the company of the most liberal minds of England in his day, though he may not have read one of them. The considerations that were influencing Milton, Chillingworth, and Jeremy Taylor, in favor of toleration and a broad inclusiveness of spirit, evidently were having their effect upon this New England pastor.

It is not to be assumed that John Wise was a rationalist in the modern sense; but he gave to the use of reason a significance that is surprising and refreshing, coming from the time and circumstances of his writing. In his Vindication we find him accepting reason and revelation as of equal validity. He appeals to the "dictates of right reason"[19] and the "common reason of mankind"[20] with quite as much confidence as to the Bible. He says that all questions of government, religious as well as political, are to be brought to "the assizes of man's own intellectual powers, reason, and conscience."[21] He assumes that God has created man capable of obeying his will and living in conformity with his law; for he says that, "if God did not highly estimate man as a creature exalted by his reason, liberty, and nobleness of nature, he would not caress him as he does in order to his submission."[22]

Wise says that the characteristic of man which is of greatest importance is that he is "most properly the subject of the law of nature."[23] He uses this expression frequently and in a thoroughly modern sense.

The second great characteristic of man, according to Wise, "is an original liberty enstamped upon his rational nature."[24] He indicates that he is not inclined to discuss the merely theological problem of man's relations to God, but, considered physically, man is at the head of creation, "and as such is a creature of a very noble character." [24] All the lower world is subject to his command, "and his liberty under the conduct of right reason is equal with his trust." [24] "He that intrudes upon this liberty violates the law of nature." [24] The effect of such liberty is not to lead man into license, but to make him the rational master of his own conduct. Every man is therefore at liberty "to judge for himself what shall be most for his behoof, happiness, and well–being."[25]

The third great characteristic of man is found in "an equality amongst men," [25] which is to be respected and vindicated by governments that are just and humane. "By a natural right," he says, "all men are born free; and, nature having set all men upon a level and made them equals, no servitude or subjection can be conceived without inequality."[26] Again he says that it is "a fundamental principle relating to government that, under God, all power is originally in the people."[27] This is true of the church as well as of the state, and Wise says the Reformation was a cheat and a schism and a notorious rebellion if the people are not the source of power in the church.

Two other ideas presented by this leader show his modernness and his originality. He says that "the happiness of the people is the object of all government,"[28] and that the state should seek to promote "the peculiar good and benefit of the whole, and every particular member, fairly and sincerely."[29] "The end of all good government," he assures his readers, "is to cultivate humanity, and promote the happiness of all, and the good of every man in all his rights, his life, liberty, estate, and honor, without injury or abuse done to any." [29] That government will seek the good of all is likely to be the case, because man has it as a fundamental law of his nature that he "maintain a sociableness with others."[30] "From the principles of sociableness it follows as a fundamental law of nature that man is not so wedded to his own interest but that he can make the common good the mark of his aim, and hence he becomes capacitated to enter into a civil state by the law of nature."[31] This attraction of man to his kind enables him to yield so much of his freedom as is necessary to make the state an efficient social power, "in which covenant is included that submission and union of wills by which a state may be conceived to be but one person."[32] This thoroughly modern idea of the social body, as being analogous in its nature to the individual man, is nobly expressed by Wise, who says that "a civil state is a compound moral person, whose will is the will of all, to the end it may use and apply the strength and riches of private persons toward maintaining the common peace, security, and well–being of all, which may be conceived as though the whole state was now become but one man."[33]

It is not surprising that the writings of John Wise had no immediate effect upon the theological thinking of the time, but they must have had their influence. Just before the opening of the Revolution they were republished because of their vindication of the spirit of human liberty and democracy. What Wise wrote to promote was congregational independence, and this may have been the reason why his theological attitude was never called in question. It is true enough that he questioned none of the Calvinistic doctrines in his books; but his political views were certain to disturb the old beliefs, and to give incentives to free discussion in religion.

[Sidenote: Harvard College.]

The centre of the liberalizing tendencies of the last years of the seventeenth century was Harvard College. That institution was organized on a basis as broad as that of the early church covenants, with no creed or doctrinal requirements. The original seal bore the motto Veritas; but, as the state–church idea grew, this motto was succeeded by In Christi gloriam, and then by Christo et Ecclesiae, though neither of these later mottoes was authoritatively adopted. The early charters were thoroughly liberal in spirit and intent, so much so as to be fully in harmony with the present attitude of the university.[34] Under the Puritanic development, however, this liberality was discarded, only to be restored in 1691, when William and Mary gave to Massachusetts a new and broader charter. From that time a new life entered into the college, that put it uncompromisingly on the liberal side a century later. Even under the rule of Increase Mather, seconded by the influence of his son Cotton, a broader spirit declared itself in the culture imparted and in the method of free inquiry.[35]

Samuel Willard, the successor to Increase Mather in the presidency, was of the liberal party in his breadth of mind and in his sound judgment. He was followed in 1708 by John Leverett, one of the founders of the Brattle Street Church, a man in whom the liberal spirit became a controlling motive in his management of the college.[36] It is not strange that the men who had been shut out from the suffrage and from active participation in the management of the churches, should now come forward to claim their rights, and to make their influence felt in college, church, and state. It was the distinct beginning of the liberal movement in New England, the time from which Unitarianism really took its origin.

[1] Kuno Francke, Social Forces in German Literature, 105. "No mediaeval
    man ever thought of himself as a perfectly independent being founded
    only on himself, or without a most direct and definite relation to
    some larger organism, be it empire, church, city, or guild. No
    mediaeval man ever doubted that the institutions within which he lived
    were divinely established ordinances, far superior and quite
    inaccessible to his own individual reason and judgment. No mediaeval
    man would ever have admitted that he conceived nature to be other than
    the creation of an extramundane God, destined to glorify its creator
    and to please the eye of man. It was reserved for the eighteenth
    century to draw the last consequences of individualism; to see in man,
    in each individual man, an independent and complete entity; to derive
    the origin of state, church, and society from the spontaneous action
    of these independent individuals; and to consider nature as a system
    of forces sufficient unto themselves. When we speak of individualism
    in the declining centuries of the Middle Ages, we mean by it that
    these centuries initiated the movement which the eighteenth century
    brought to a climax."

[2] Williston Walker, the Creeds and Platforms of Congregationalism, 246.
    "From the first the fathers of New England insisted that the children
    of church members were themselves members, and as such were justly
    entitled to those church privileges which were adapted to their state
    of Christian development, of which the chief were baptism and the
    watchful discipline of the church. They did not enter the church by
    baptism; they were entitled to baptism because they were already
    members of the church. Here then was an inconsistency in the
    application of the Congregational theory of the constitution of a
    church. While affirming that a proper church consisted only of those
    possessed of personal Christian character, the fathers admitted to

membership, in some degree at least, those who had no claim but
Christian parentage." That is, in theory they were Protestants, but in
practice they were Catholics.

[3] The ecclesiastical historians say that the half−way covenant had no
effect on suffrage. Dexter, Congregationalism as Seen in its
Literature, 468, says: "I am aware of no proof that half−way covenant
members of the church by that relation did acquire any further
privileges in the state." Williston Walker, New Englander, cclxiii.,
93, February, 1892, takes ground that "added political privilege was
no consequence of the dispute." On the other hand, the secular
historians as strongly assert that the suffrage was widened. John
Fiske, Beginnings of New England, 250, says the half−way covenant
"entitled to the exercise of political rights those who were
unqualified for participation in the Lord's Supper." Alexander
Johnston, Connecticut, 227, says "it really gave every baptized person
voice in church government." J.A. Doyle, The Puritan Colonies, II.,
98, asserts that "it broke down the hard barrier which fenced in
political privileges." The true explanation is given by George H.
Haynes, Representation and Suffrage in Massachusetts, 1620−1691, 54,
published in Johns Hopkins University Studies in Historical and
Political Science, Vol. XII., Nos. VIII. and IX. Haynes says that the
half−way covenant, as first formulated in 1657, "virtually recognized
a partial church−membership in persons who had made no formal
profession and subscribed to no creed. In 1662 the same opinion was
reaffirmed by the clergy, and the General Court ordered the result of
the Synod to be printed and 'commended the same unto the consideration
of all the churches and people of this jurisdiction.' Here ended
legislative action on the matter. This was no statutory change of the
basis of the franchise; but, as individual churches gradually adopted
more liberal conditions of admission and were therein sanctioned by
the General Court, it resulted that the operation of the religious
test became less odious and the suffrage was not a little broadened."

[4] Henry Bond, Early Settlers of Watertown, II. 916; Convers Francis,
Historical Sketch of Watertown, 135.

[5] Mason A. Green, History of Springfield, 113; E.H. Byington, The Puritan in England and New England, 185.

[6] A Healing Question.

[7] Alexander Johnston, Connecticut: A Study of a Commonwealth–Democracy, 72, Hooker's sermon preparatory to forming a government.

[8] The Works of John Robinson, American edition of 1851, I., 53.

[9] Ibid., 47.

[10] Ibid., 54.

[11] Ibid., 56.

[12] J.R. Trumbull, History of Northampton, I. 213.

[13] An Appeal to the Learned, being a vindication of the right of visible saints to the Lord's Supper, though they be destitute of a saving work of God's Spirit in their hearts, Boston, 1709. See also his Doctrine of Instituted Churches, Boston, 1700.

[14] Dwight, Life of Edwards, 300.

[15] S.K. Lothrop, History of Brattle Street Church, 7–40; E. Turrell, Life of Benjamin Colman, D.D., 96, 125, 178, 180.

[16] The Churches' Quarrel Espoused, edition of 1860, 140.

[17] Ibid., 143.

[18] Ibid., 145

[19] The Churches' Quarrel Espoused, edition of 1860, 32.

[20] Ibid., 58.

[21] Ibid., 72.

[22] Ibid., 65.

[23] Ibid., 30.

[24] Ibid., 33.

[25] The Churches' Quarrel Espoused, edition of 1860, 34.

[26] Ibid., 37.

[27] Ibid., 64.

[28] Ibid., 54.

[29] Ibid., 55.

[30] Ibid., 32.

[31] The Churches' Quarrel Espoused, edition of 1860, 32.

[32] Ibid., 39.

[33] Ibid., 40.

[34] Josiah Quincy, History of Harvard University, i. 44–54.

[35] Ibid., 65, 200.

[36] Josiah Quincy, in the seventh chapter of his History, gives a detailed account of this movement. It is also dealt with by Brooks Adams in his chapter on the founding of the Brattle Street Church, in his Emancipation of Massachusetts, though he gives it a somewhat

exaggerated and biassed importance. Most of the facts appear in Lothrop's History of the Brattle Street Church.

III. THE GROWTH OF DEMOCRACY IN THE CHURCHES.

From the moment when the Puritan control of the church and state in New England was so far weakened as to permit of free intellectual and religious activity the democratic spirit began to manifest itself. The old regime had so fixed itself upon the people that the progress was slow, but none the less it was steady and sure. So far as the new spirit influenced doctrines, it was called Arminianism, the technical theological name for democracy in religion at this time.

[Sidenote: Arminianism.]

Arminianism is a dead issue at the present day, for the Calvinists have accepted all that it taught when the name first came into vogue. Every kind of reaction from Calvinism in the New England of the first half of the eighteenth century took this designation, however; and to the Calvinists it was a word of disapproval and contempt. Toleration, free inquiry, the use of reason, democratic methods in church and state, were all named by this condemning word. Vices, social depravities, love of freedom and the world, assertion of personal independence, had the same designation. It is now difficult to understand how bitter was the feeling thus produced, how keen the hurt that was given the men who tried to defend themselves and their beliefs from this odium.

What the word "Arminian" legitimately meant, then, is what we now mean by liberalism. Primarily theological and doctrinal, it meant much more than the rejection of the doctrine of decrees and the autocratic sovereignty of God or the acceptance of the freedom of the will and the spiritual capacity of man. First of all, it was faith in man; and then it was the assertion of human liberty and equality. In a theological sense it did not have so wide a purport, but in a practical and popular sense it grew into these meanings.

In order fully to comprehend what Arminianism was in the eighteenth century, the student must remember that it was the theological expression of the democratic spirit, as Calvinism was of the autocratic. The doctrine of the sovereignty of God is but the intellectual reflection of kingship and the belief that the king can do no evil. The doctrine of decrees, as taught by the Calvinist, was the spiritual side of the assertion of the divine right of kings. On the other hand, when the people claim the right to rule, they modify their theology into Arminianism. From an age of the absolute rule of the king comes the doctrine of human depravity; and with the establishment of democracy appears the doctrine of man's moral capacity.

[Sidenote: The Growth of Arminianism.]

As early as 1730 Arminianism had come to have an influence sufficient to secure its condemnation and to awaken the fears of the stricter Calvinists. Jonathan Edwards said of the year 1734 that "about this time began the great noise that was in this part of the country about Arminianism."[1] At Northampton the leader of the opposition to Jonathan Edwards was an open Arminian, a grandson of Solomon Stoddard, and a cousin of Edwards. He was a young man of talent and education, and well read in theology. In a letter written in 1750, Edwards said, "There seems to be the utmost danger that the younger generation will be carried away with Arminianism as with a flood." In another letter of the same year he said that "Arminianism and Pelagianism[2] have made a strange progress within a few years."[3] In his farewell sermon, Edwards spoke of the prevalence of Arminianism when he settled in Northampton, and of its rapid increase in the succeeding years. He said that Arminian views were creeping into almost all parts of the land, and that they were making a progress unknown before.[4] In a letter of 1752 Edwards said that the principles of John Taylor, of Norwich, one of the early English Unitarians, were gaining many converts in the colonies. Taylor's works were made use of by Solomon Williams in his reply to Edwards on the qualifications necessary to communion.[5]

It was owing to the rapid growth of Arminianism that Edwards undertook his work on free will. In the preface to that work he said that "the term Calvinistic is, in these days, among most, a term of greater reproach than the term Arminian." That Edwards exaggerated the extent of this defection from Calvinism is probable, and yet it is very plain that it was this more liberal attitude of the Northampton church which caused his dismissal. What Stoddard had taught and practised was as yet powerful there, and Edwards's opposition to his grandfather's teachings undoubtedly led to the failure of his local work.

[Sidenote: Robert Breck.]

The council which dismissed Edwards from Northampton decided against him by a majority of one; and that one vote may have been cast by Robert Breck, of Springfield. If this were the case, there was something of poetic justice in it; for only a few years earlier Edwards had used his influence against the settlement of Breck because the latter was an Arminian. In 1734 a fierce church quarrel took place in Springfield, that involved many of the ministers of Massachusetts and Connecticut, invoked the aid of the county court, and was finally settled by the legislature of Massachusetts, when Mr. Breck was ordained.[6] He was charged with denying the authenticity of parts of the Bible, with discarding the necessity of Christ's satisfaction to divine justice for sin, with maintaining that the heathen who live up to the light of nature would be saved, and that the contrary doctrine was harsh. Breck refused to admit that he held these opinions, as thus stated; but he was regarded by many as an Arminian and a heretic. It was said of him that he would read any book, orthodox or otherwise, that would clear up a subject. That he departed to any considerable extent from the generally accepted faith of the time there is no evidence, but he was probably what was often called "a moderate Calvinist." He did not favor the methods of Whitefield, and he thoroughly distrusted the revival introduced by him. Soon after Breck's settlement the Springfield church followed the Brattle Street Church of Boston in discarding the relation of religious experiences as preliminary to admission to the church. It voted that it "did not look upon the making a relation to be a necessary term of communion."[7] At the very time that Edwards was preaching of the awful fate of sinners in the hands of an angry God, Breck was teaching that God is good and loving, and that his salvation is freely open to all who may wish for it. It has been truly said of these two men that "one had the heart and the other the intellect of theology." With all his logic and power of thought and marvellous spiritual insight, Edwards failed at Northampton because of conditions beyond the control of his strenuous will. Robert Breck gained year by year in his personal influence in Springfield, his cheerful and progressive teaching made a deep impression on the community, and before he died he saw a great change for the better in the people for whom he diligently labored. Perhaps we could not have a plainer indication of the change that was going on than is found in the experiences of these two men.[8]

When Whitefield visited Harvard College in 1740, he was received in a most friendly manner; yet he afterwards criticised the teaching there on the ground that it was not sufficiently devout and earnest, and that the pupils were not examined as to their religious experiences.[9] These charges were denied by the president and tutors, and he was not again welcomed to the college.

That there was a substantial basis for some of Whitefield's criticisms of Harvard there can be no doubt. In 1737, when Edward Holyoke was proposed as a candidate for the presidency, he met with a strong opposition from the strict Calvinists. After the opposition had spent itself, he was elected unanimously; and this act was received with marked approval by the General Court, from which body his maintenance was obtained. President Quincy says of President Holyoke that his religious principles coincided with the mildness and catholicity which characterized the government of the college. This evidently refers to the growing liberality of the college, and its unwillingness to lend its aid to extreme theological opinions. That moderateness of temper and that attitude of toleration which characterized the leading men in England had shown themselves at Cambridge, and with a strength that could not be overcome. "In Boston and its vicinity and along the seaboard of Massachusetts, clergymen of great talent and religious zeal," says President Quincy, "openly avowed doctrines which were variously denounced by the Calvinistic party as Arminianism, Arianism, Pelagianism, Socinianism, and Deism. The most eminent of these clergymen were alumni of Harvard, active friends and advocates of the institution, and in habits of intimacy and professional intercourse with its government. Their religious views, indeed, received no public countenance from the college; but circumstances gave color for reports, which were assiduously circulated throughout New England, that the influences of the institution were not unfavorable to the extension of such doctrines."[10]

At the commencement of 1737 candidates for degrees proposed to prove that the doctrine of the Trinity was not contained in the Old Testament, that creation did not exist from eternity, and that religion is not mysterious in its nature. Much alarm was caused to the conservative party by the negative form given these questions, which, it was said, "had the plain face of Arianism." This criticism the faculty tried to quiet, but their sympathies were evidently on the side of the graduates.[11] In 1738, when a professor of mathematics was chosen, it was proposed to examine him as to "his principles of religion"; but, after a long debate, this proposition was rejected. After these and other efforts to control the religious position of the college the strict Calvinists for the time withdrew their efforts and concentrated them upon Yale College, in which institution the faculty were now required for the first time to accept the Assembly's Catechism and Confession of Faith.

When the legislature of Connecticut, during the great awakening, passed a law prohibiting ministers from preaching as itinerants, several of the members of the Senior

Class subscribed the money necessary for the publication of an edition of Locke's essay On Toleration. When this was known to the faculty, they forbade the publication; and all the students apologized but one, who learned a few days before commencement that his name was to be dropped from the roll of graduates. He went to the faculty with the statement that he was of age, that he possessed ample means, and that he would carry his case to a hearing before the crown in England. In a few days he was quietly informed that he would be permitted to graduate. This is but a straw, and yet it shows clearly enough the direction of the current at this time. A demand for toleration was made because it was felt that there was a need for it.

[Sidenote: Books Read by Liberal Men.]

The names of no less than thirty–three ministers have been given who, during the period from 1730 to 1750, did not teach the Calvinistic doctrines in their fulness, and who had adopted more or less distinctly some form of Arminianism or Arianism. These men were among the best known, most successful, and most scholarly men in Eastern Massachusetts, though they were not wholly confined to that neighborhood. We find here and there some hint of the books these men read; and in that way we not only ascertain the cause of their departure from Calvinism, but we also obtain some clew to the nature of their opinions. Among the charges brought by Whitefield against Harvard in 1740 was that "Tillotson and Clarke are read instead of Shepard and Stoddard, and such like evangelical writers."[12] Dr. Wigglesworth, the divinity professor at Harvard, said that Tillotson had not been taken out of the college library in nine years, and Clarke not in two; and he gave a long list of evangelical writers who were frequently read. In spite of this disclaimer, however, it is evident that the methods of the rationalistic writers were coming into vogue at Harvard, and that even Dr. Wigglesworth did not teach theology in the manner of the author of the Day of Doom.

Writing in 1759, Dr. Joseph Bellamy, one of the chief followers and expositors of the teachings of Jonathan Edwards, said that the teachings of the liberal men in England had crossed the Atlantic; "and too many in our churches, and even among our ministers, have fallen in with them. Books containing them have been imported; and the demand for them has been so great as to encourage new impressions of some of them. Others have been written on the same principles in this country, and even the doctrine of the Trinity has been publicly treated in such a manner as all who believe that doctrine must judge not only heretical, but highly blasphemous."[13]

34

It is said of Charles Chauncy, of the First Church in Boston, that his favorite authors were Tillotson and Baxter.[14] Far more suggestive is the account we have of the books read by Jonathan Mayhew of the West Church in Boston, the first open antagonist of Calvinism in New England. Soon after 1740 he was reading the works of the great Protestant theologians of the seventeenth century, including Milton, Chillingworth, and Tillotson; and the eighteenth–century works of Locke, Samuel Clarke, Taylor, Wollaston, and Whiston. He also probably read Cudworth, Butler, Hutcheson, Leland, and other authors of a like character, some of them deists. Not one of these writers was a Calvinist for they found the basis of religion either in idealism or in rationalism.

The biographer of Mayhew says it "is evident from some of his discourses that he was a great admirer of Samuel Clarke, whose voluminous works were in his day much read by the liberal clergy." Clarke's Boyle lectures, delivered in 1704–5, showed that natural and revealed religion were essentially one, that moral action in man is free, and that Christianity is the religion of reason and nature. At a later period he defended the two propositions, that "no article of Christian faith delivered in the holy Scriptures is disagreeable to right reason," and that "without liberty of human actions there can be no real religion or morality." Even if one such man as Jonathan Mayhew read Clarke's work in the Harvard Library, it justified the alarm felt by Whitefield lest the students should be led away from their Calvinist faith.[15]

[Sidenote: The Great Awakening.]

It was "the great awakening" that showed how marked had been the growth of liberal opinions throughout New England in the forty years preceding. Silently, a great change had gone on, with little open expression of dissent from Calvinism, and without a knowledge on the part of most of the liberal men that they had in any way departed from the faith of the fathers. It was only with the coming of Whitefield and the revival that this change came to have recognition, and that even the slightest separation into parties took place.

The revival was an attempt to reintroduce the stricter Calvinism of the earlier time, with its doctrines of justification by faith alone, supernatural regeneration, and predestination made known to the believer by the Holy Ghost. The liberal party objected to the revival because it was opposed to the good old customs of the Congregational churches of New England. The itinerant methods of the revivalists, the shriekings, faintings, and appeals to fear and terror, were condemned as not in harmony with the established methods of the churches. In his book against the revivalists, Dr. Chauncy said that "now is the time when we are particularly called to stand for the good old way, and bear testimony against everything that may tend to cast a blemish on true primitive Christianity."[16]

When the great awakening came to an end, the liberal party was far stronger than before, partly because the members of it had come to know each other and to feel their own power, partly because men had been led to declare themselves who had never before perceived their own position, and partly because the agitation had set men to thinking, and to making such scrutiny of their beliefs as they had never made before. The testimonies of Harvard College and various associations of ministers against the methods of the revivalists were signed by sixty–three men, while those in favor of the revival were signed by one hundred and ten. These numbers represent the comparative strength of the two parties. It must be said, however, that the leading men in nearly every part of New England were among those opposing the revival methods, while in Eastern Massachusetts at least two–thirds of the ministers were of the liberal party.[17]

The strong feeling caused by the revival soon subsided, and no division between the Calvinist and the Arminian parties took place. The progressive tendencies went quietly on, step by step the old beliefs were discarded; but it was by individuals, and not in any form as a sectarian movement. The relations of the church to the state at this time would have made such a result impossible.

[Sidenote: Cardinal Beliefs of the Liberals.]

Looking over the whole field of the theological advance from 1725 to 1760, we find that three conclusions had been arrived at by the men of the liberal movement. The first of these was that what they stood for as a body was a recovery and restoration of primitive Christianity in its simplicity and power. It was said of Dr. Mayhew by his biographer that he "was a great advocate of primitive Christianity, and zealously contended for the faith once delivered to the saints."

The second opinion, to which they gave frequent utterance, was that the Bible is a divine revelation, the true source of all religious teaching, and the one sufficient creed for all men. In his sermon against the enthusiasm of the revivalists, Chauncy said that a true test of all religious excitement, and of every kind of new teachings, was to be found in their "regard to the Bible, and its acknowledgment that the things therein contained are the commandments of God." "Keep close to the Scripture," was his admonition to his congregation, "and admit of nothing for an impression of the spirit but what agrees with that unerring rule. Fix it in your minds as a truth you will invariably abide by, that the Bible is the grand test by which everything in religion is to be tried."

The third position of the men of the liberal movement was that Christ is the only means of salvation, and they yielded to him unquestioning loyalty and faith. Turning away from the creeds of men, as they did in so far as they could see their way, they concentrated their convictions upon Christ, and found in him the spiritual and vital centre of all faith that lives with true power to help men. Mayhew held that God could not have forgiven men their sins without the atonement of Christ, for his life and his gospel are the means of the great reconciliation by which man and God are brought into harmony with each other.

[Sidenote: Publications defining the Liberal Beliefs.]

In three publications may be seen what the Arminians had to teach that was opposed to Calvinism. In 1744 appeared in Boston a book of two hundred and eight pages by Rev. Experience Mayhew, one of a devoted family of missionaries to the Indians of Martha's Vineyard. He called his book "Grace Defended, in a Modest Plea for an important Truth: namely, that the offer of Salvation made to sinners comprises in it an offer of the Grace given in Regeneration." Mr. Mayhew claimed that he was a Calvinist, yet he rejected the teaching that every act of the unregenerate person is equal in the sight of God to the worst sin, and claimed that even the sinner can live so well and so justly as to favor his being accepted of God. Mayhew maintained that Christ died for all men, not for the elect only.[18] He claimed that "God cannot be truly said to offer salvation to sinners without offering to them whatsoever is necessary on his part, in order to their salvation."[19] Mayhew was usually credited with being an Arminian; for he positively rejected the doctrine of election, and he defended the principle of human freedom in the most affirmative manner.

In 1749 Lemuel Briant (or Bryant), the minister in that part of Braintree which became the town of Quincy, published a sermon which he entitled The Absurdity and Blasphemy of Depreciating Moral Virtue. It condemned reliance on Christ's merits without effort to live his life, and showed that it is the duty of the Christian to live righteously. Briant said that to hold any other view was hurtful and blasphemous. He claimed that "the great rule the Scriptures lay down for men to go by in passing judgment on their spiritual state is the sincere, upright, steady, and universal practice of virtue." "To preach up chiefly what Christ himself laid the stress upon (and whether this was not moral virtue let every one judge from his discourses) must certainly, in the opinion of all sober men, be called truly and properly, and in the best sense, preaching of Christ."

A pamphlet of thirty pages appeared in 1757, written by Samuel Webster, the minister of Salisbury, with the title "A Winter Evening's Conversation upon the doctrine of Original Sin, wherein the notion of our having sinned in Adam, and being on that account only liable to eternal Damnation, is proved to be Unscriptural." It is in the form of a dialogue between a minister and three of his parishioners, and gives, as few other writings of the eighteenth century do, a clear and explicit statement of the author's opinions in a readable and interesting form. That all have sinned in Adam the minister pronounces "a very shocking doctrine." "What! make them first to open their eyes in torment, and all this for a sin which certainly they had no hand in,—a sin which, if it comes upon them at all, certainly is without any fault or blame on their parts, for they had no hand in receiving it!" That Adam is our federal head, and that we sinned because he sinned, he calls "a mere castle in the air." "Sin and guilt are personal things as much as knowledge. I can as easily conceive of one man's knowledge being imputed to another as of his sins being so. No imputation in either case can make the thing to be mine which is not mine any more than one person may be another person." He declares that this doctrine of imputation causes infidelity. "It naturally leads men into every dishonorable thought of God which gives a great and general blow to religion." It impeaches the holiness of God, "for it supposes him to make millions sinners by his decree of imputation, who would otherwise have been innocent." That it was his decree alone "that made all Adam's posterity sinners is the very essence of this doctrine." "And so Christians are guilty of holding what even heathen would blush at." That God "should pronounce a sentence by which myriads of infants, as blameless as helpless, were consigned over to blackness of darkness to be tormented with fire and brimstone forever, is not consistent with infinite goodness." "How dreadfully is God dishonored by such monstrous representations as these!" Such a being cannot be loved by us, for every heart rebels against it. "All descriptions of the Divine Being which represent him in an unamiable light do the greatest hurt to religion that can be, as they strike at love, which is the fulfilling of the law. I am persuaded that many of those who think they believe this doctrine do not really believe it, or else they do not consider how it represents their heavenly Father." The pamphlet concludes with the acceptance of this broader teaching by the parishioners, but it was the cause of controversy in pulpits and by means of pamphlets. Bellamy denied the teachings of Webster, and Chauncy defended them. So bold a pamphlet as this showed how men had come to reason without compromise about the old doctrines, and gave evidence that the growing spirit of humanity would no longer accept what was harsh and cruel.

[Sidenote: Phases of Religious Progress.]

The New England churches were thus not standing still as regards doctrines, moral conduct, the methods of worship, or the relations they held to the state; but step by step they were moving away from the methods and the ideas of the fathers. The "lining out" of hymns was slowly abandoned, and singing by note took its place. The agitation that followed this attempt at reform was great and wide-spread. The introduction of an organized and trained choir was also in the nature of a genuine reform. When the liberal Thomas Brattle offered an organ to the new church in Brattle Street, it was voted "that they do not think it proper to use the same in the public worship of God." The instrument was, however, accepted by King's Chapel; and an organist was secured from London. It was not until 1770 that the church in Providence procured an organ, the first used in a Congregational church in New England.

When Dr. Jonathan Mayhew died, in 1766, Dr. Chauncy prayed at his funeral; and this was said to have been the first prayer ever made at a funeral in Boston, so strong was the Puritan dislike of the customs of the Catholic Church.[20] In this way, as well as in others, the new liberalism broke down the old customs, and introduced those with which we are familiar. Perhaps the most marked tendency of this kind was the introduction of the reading of the Bible into the services of the churches as a part of the order of worship. This innovation was distinctly due to the liberal men and the high esteem in which they held the Scriptures as a means of giving sobriety and reasonableness to their religion. The First Church in Boston, in May, 1730, voted that the reading of the Scriptures, instead of the old Puritan way of expounding them, be thereafter discretionary with the ministers of that church, but "that the mind of the church is that larger portions should be publicly read than has been used."[21] As we have seen, the Brattle Street Church had already led in this reform, having adopted this practice in 1699. This custom of reading the Bible as a part of the service of worship came slowly into general acceptance, for there was a strong feeling against it. When a Bible was presented to the parish in Mendon, in 1767, a serious commotion resulted because of the strong feeling against the Church of England then prevalent; and the donor gave it to the minister until such time as the church might wish to use it. It was as late as 1785 that a copy of the Bible was given to the First Church in Dedham, with the request that the reading of it should be made a part of the exercises of the Lord's day; and the parish instructed the minister to read such portions of it as he thought "most desirable" and of "such length as the several seasons of the year and other circumstances" might render proper. In the West Church of Medway it was not until 1806 that this practice was established, and two of the Salem churches began it the same year. The reading of the Bible at ordination services did not become customary until an even later date.[22]

Such are some of the practical innovations which accompanied the doctrinal development that was taking place. Liberality in one direction brought toleration and progress in others. Some of these changes were due to the fact that the prejudices against the Catholic Church and the Church of England had, in a measure, disappeared, because there was nothing to keep them alive. Others were due to the intellectual influences that came into the colonies from England. Still others resulted from the shifting relations of church and state, and were the effect of attempts to adjust those relations more satisfactorily.

[1] Narrative of Surprising Conversions, edition of 1808, 13.

[2] Denial of original sin, from Pelagius, an ascetic preacher of the fifth century.

[3] Dwight, Life of Edwards, 307, 336, 410, 413.

[4] Ibid., 649.

[5] Ibid., 495.

[6] Green, History of Springfield.

[7] Ibid., 255.

[8] E.H. Byington, The Puritan in England and New England, devotes a chapter to the controversy over Breck's settlement; but he does not treat of the theological problems involved.

[9] Whitefield's Seventh Journal, 28.

[10] History of Harvard University, 52.

[11] History of Harvard University, 23, 26.

[12] Whitefield's Journal, seventh part, 28.

[13] Historical Magazine, new series, IX. 227, April, 1871.

[14] W.B. Sprague, Annals of the Unitarian Pulpit, II.

[15] Levi L. Paine, A Critical History of the Evolution of Trinitarianism,
99. "Samuel Clarke and others took the ground that God is unipersonal,
and hence that the Son is a distinct personal being, distinguishing
God the Father as the absolute Deity from the Son whom they regarded
as God in a relative or secondary sense, being derived from the
Father, and having his beginning from Him."

[16] Seasonable Thoughts, 337.

[17] Alden Bradford, in his Memoir of the Life and Writings of Rev.
Jonathan Mayhew, D.D., gives a list of "the clergymen who openly
opposed or did not teach and advocate the Calvinistic doctrines" at
the time of Mayhew's ordination, in 1747. These were: Dr. Appleton,
Cambridge; Dr. Gay, Hingham; Dr. Chauncy, Boston; William Rand,
Kingston; Nathaniel Eelles, Scituate; Edward Barnard, Haverhill;
Samuel Cooke, West Cambridge (now Arlington); Jeremiah Fogg,
Kensington, N.H.; Dr. A. Eliot, Boston; Dr. Samuel Webster, Salisbury;
Lemuel Briant, Braintree; Dr. Stevens, Kittery, Me.; Dr. Tucker,
Newbury; Timothy Harrington, Lancaster; Dr. Gad Hitchcock, Pembroke;
Josiah Smith, Pembroke; William Smith, Weymouth; Dr. Daniel Shute,
Hingham; Dr. Samuel Cooper, Boston; Dr. Mayhew, Boston; Abraham
Williams, Sandwich; Anthony Wibird, Braintree (now Quincy); Dr.
Cushing, Waltham; Professor Wigglesworth, Harvard College; Dr. Symmes,
Andover; Dr. John Willard, Connecticut; Amos Adams, Roxbury; Dr.

Barnes, Scituate; Charles Turner, Duxbury; Dr. Dana Wallingford, Conn.; Ebenezer Thayer, Hampton, N.H.; Dr. Fiske, Brookfield; Dr. Samuel West, Dartmouth (now New Bedford); Dr. Hemenway, Wells. Among those who took part in the ordination of Jonathan Mayhew, and therefore presumably of the same theological opinions, were Hancock, Lexington; Cotton, Newton; Cooke, Sudbury; Prescott, Danvers (now Salem). To these may be added, says Bradford, though of a somewhat later date: Dr. Coffin, Buxton; Drs. Howard, West, Lathrop, and Belknap, Boston; Dr. Henry Cummings, Billerica; Dr. Deane, Portland; Thomas Cary, Newburyport; Dr. Fobes, Raynham; Timothy Hilliard, Cambridge; Thomas Haven, Reading; Dr. Willard, Beverly. Dr. Ezra Ripley added the names of Hedge, of Warwick, and Foster, of Stafford. This makes fifty-two in all, but probably as many more could be added by careful search.

[18] Grace Defended, 43.

[19] Ibid., 60.

[20] Alice Morse Earle, Customs and Fashions in Old New England, 364, 367. See H.M. Dexter, Congregationalism as seen in its Literature, 458.

[21] A.B. Ellis, History of the First Church in Boston, 199.

[22] New England Magazine, February, 1899. A.H. Coolidge on Scripture Reading in the Worship of the New England Churches.

IV. THE SILENT ADVANCE OF LIBERALISM.

The progressive tendencies went silently on; and step by step the old beliefs were discarded, but always by individuals and churches, and not by associations or general official action. Even before the middle of the eighteenth century there was not only a questioning of the doctrine of divine decrees, the conception that God elects some to bliss and some to perdition in accordance with his own arbitrary will, but there was also developing a tendency to reject the tritheism[1] which in New England took the place of a philosophical conception of the Trinity, such as had been held by the great thinkers of the Christian ages. In part this doubt about the Trinity was the result of a more thoughtful study of the Bible, where the doctrine taught by the leading theologians of the old school in New England does not appear; and in part it was the result of the reading of the works of the English divines of the more liberal school. Something of this tendency was also due to the spirit of free inquiry, and the rational interpretation of religion, that were beginning to make themselves felt amongst those not wholly committed to the old ways of thinking.

It was characteristic of those who questioned the doctrine of the Trinity, as then taught, that they insisted on stating their beliefs in the language of the New Testament, especially in that of Jesus himself. They found him teaching his own dependence on his Father, claiming for himself only an inferior and subordinate position. Believing in his pre–existence, his supernatural character and mission, they held that he was the creator of the world or that creation took place by means of the spirit that was in him, and that every honor should be paid him except that of worshipping him as the Supreme Being. As in the ancient family the son was always subordinate to his father, so the Son of God presented in the New Testament is less exalted than his Father. This conception of Christ is technically called Arianism, from the Alexandrian presbyter of the fourth century who first brought it into prominence.

[Sidenote: Subordinate Nature of Christ.]

The Arian heresy did not necessarily follow the Arminian, but much the same causes led to its appearance. Many of the leading men in England had become Arians, including Milton, Locke, Taylor, Clarke, Watts, and others; and the reading of their books in New England led to an inquiry into the truthfulness of the doctrine of the Trinity. As early as 1720 the preachers of convention and election sermons were insisting upon a recognition of Christ in the old way, showing that they were suspicious of heresy.[2] Most of the Arians retained the other doctrines in which they had been educated, even putting a stronger emphasis upon them than before. Rarely was the subordinate nature of Christ made in any way prominent in preaching. It was held so strictly subsidiary to the cardinal doctrines of incarnation and atonement that only the most intelligent and watchful could detect any difference between those who were Arians and those who were strict Trinitarians. Now and then a man of more pronounced convictions and utterance was shunned by his ministerial neighbors, but this rarely occurred and had little practical effect. So long as a preacher gave satisfaction to his own congregation, and had behind him the voters and the tax−list of his town, his heresies were passed by with only comment and gossip.

We find here and there definite indications of the doctrinal changes that were taking place, as in the republication of Emlyn's Humble Inquiry into the Scripture Account of Jesus Christ, which appeared in Boston in 1756. Thomas Emlyn, the first English preacher who called himself a Unitarian, published his Humble Inquiry in 1702; and in 1705 he established a Unitarian congregation in London. This distinctively Unitarian book made an able defence of the doctrine of the subordinate nature of Christ. More significant than the republication of the book itself was the preface written for it by a Boston layman, addressed to the ministers of the town, in which he said that he found its teaching "to be the true, plain, unadulterated doctrine of the Gospel." He also intimated that "many of his brethren of the laity in the town and country were in sympathy with him and sincerely desirous of knowing the truth." "In New Hampshire Province," wrote Dr. Joseph Bellamy, in 1760, "this party have actually, three years ago, got things so ripe that they have ventured to new model our Shorter Catechism, to alter or entirely leave out the doctrine of the Trinity, of the decrees, of our first parents being created holy, of original sin, Christ satisfying divine justice, effectual calling, justification, etc."[3]

[Sidenote: Some of the Liberal Leaders.]

The farther advance in the liberal movement may be most easily traced in the lives and teachings of three or four men. Rev Ebenezer Gay, who was settled in Hingham in 1717, was the first man in New England to arrive at a clear statement of opinions quite outside of and distinct from Calvinism. Writing of the years from 1750 to 1755, John Adams said that at that time Lemuel Briant, of Braintree, Jonathan Mayhew, of the West Church in Boston, Daniel Shute, of Hingham, John Brown, of Cohasset, and perhaps equal to all, if not above all, Ebenezer Gay, of Hingham, were Unitarians.[4] The rapid sale of Emlyn's book would prove the truthfulness of this statement. It was not by any sudden process that these men had come to what may be called Unitarianism, though, more properly, Arianism; and not as a mere result of a reaction from Calvinism. A new time had come, and with it new hopes and thoughts. The burdening sense of the spiritual world that belonged to the men of the seventeenth century did not belong to those of the eighteenth. Men had come to see that God must manifest himself in reason, common sense, nature, and the facts of life.

In the life and teachings of such a man as Ebenezer Gay we catch a new insight into the spirit that was active in New England throughout the eighteenth century for the realization of a larger faith. He was a man of a strong, original, vigorous nature, a born leader of men, and one who impressed his own character upon those with whom he came into contact. He opposed the revival, and he made the men of his own association think with him in their opposition to it. Years before the revival, however, he was a liberal in theology, and had found his way into Arminianism. With the spirit of free inquiry he was in fullest sympathy. He was strongly opposed to creeds and to all written articles of faith. He condemned in the most forcible terms the young man who, on the occasion of his ordination, "engages to preach according to a rule of faith, creed, or confession which is merely of human prescription or imposition." In his convention sermon of 1746 he denounced those who "insist upon the offensive peculiarities of the party they espoused rather than upon the more mighty things in which we are all agreed." It has been said of him that, after the middle of the century, "his discourses will be searched in vain for any discussions of controversial theology, any advocacy of the peculiar doctrines regarded as orthodox, or the expression of any opinions at variance with those of his successor, Dr. Ware."[5]

The sermon on Natural Religion as distinguished from Revealed, which Dr. Gay delivered as the Dudleian lecture at Harvard, in 1759, showed the reasonable and progressive spirit of his preaching. He claimed that there is no antagonism between natural and revealed religion, and that, while revealed religion is an addition to the natural, it is not built on the ruins, but on the everlasting foundations of it. Revelation can teach nothing contrary to natural religion or to the dictates of reason. "No doctrine or scheme of religion," he said, "should be advanced or received as Scriptural and divine which is plainly and absolutely inconsistent with the perfections of God, and the possibility of things. Absurdities and contradictions, are not to be obtruded upon our faith. No pretence of revelation can be sufficient for the admission of them. The manifest absurdity of any doctrine is a stronger argument that it is not of God than any other evidence can be that it is."

Jonathan Mayhew, the son of Experience Mayhew, of Martha's Vineyard, was settled over the West Church of Boston in 1747. He was even then known as a heretic, who had read the most liberal books of the English philosophers and theologians, and who had boldly accepted their opinions as his own. On the occasion of his ordination not one of the Boston ministers was present, although a number of them were well known for their liberal opinions. The ordination was postponed, and later several men of remoter parishes joined in inducting this young independent into his pulpit. No Boston minister would exchange pulpits with him, and he was not invited to join the ministerial association. He was shunned by the ministers, and he was dreaded by the orthodox; but he was gladly heard by a large congregation, which grew in numbers and intelligence as the years went on. He had among his hearers many of the leading men of the town, and to him gathered those who were most thoughtful and progressive. Boston has never had in any of its pulpits a man of nobler, broader, more humane qualities, or one with a mind more completely committed to seeking and knowing the truth, or with a more unflinching purpose to speak his own mind without fear or favor. His influence was soon powerfully felt in the town, and his name came to stand for liberty in politics as well as in religion. His sermons were rapidly printed and distributed widely. They were read in every part of New England with great eagerness; they were reprinted in England, and brought him a large correspondence from those who admired and approved of his teaching. Though he died in 1766, at the age of forty–six, his work and his influence did not die with him.

The cardinal thought of Jonathan Mayhew with reference to religion was that of free inquiry. Diligent and free examination of all questions, he felt, was necessary to any acquisition of the truth. He believed in liberty and toleration everywhere, and this made him accept in the fullest sense the doctrine of the freedom of the will. In man he found a self–determining power, the source of his moral and intellectual freedom. He said that we are more certain of the fact that we are free than we are of the truth of Christianity. This belief led him to the rejection of the Calvinistic doctrine of inability, and to a strong faith in the moral and spiritual possibilities of human nature. He described Christianity as "a practical science, the art of living piously and virtuously."[6] He had quite freed his mind from bondage to creeds when he said that, "how much soever any man may be mistaken in opinion concerning the terms of salvation, yet if he is practically in the right there is no doubt but he will be accepted of God."[7] He held that no speculative error, however great, is sufficient to exclude a good and upright man from the kingdom of heaven, who lives according to the genuine spirit of the gospel. To him the principle of grace was always a principle of goodness and holiness; and he held that grace can never be operative as a saving power without obedience to that righteousness and love which Christ taught as essential.[8] He declared that "the doctrine that men may obtain salvation without ceasing to do evil and learning to do well, without yielding a sincere obedience to the laws of Christianity, is not so properly called a doctrine of grace as it is a doctrine of devils."[9] He said, again, that we cannot be justified by a faith that is without obedience;

for it is obedience and good works that give to faith all its life, efficacy, and perfection.[10]

[Sidenote: The First Unitarian.]

Dr. Mayhew accepted without equivocation the right of private judgment in religion, and he practised it judicially and with wise insight. He unhesitatingly applied the rational method to all theological problems, and to him reason was the final court of appeal for everything connected with religion. His love of freedom was enthusiastic and persistent, and he was zealously committed to the principle of individuality. He believed in the essential goodness of human nature, and in the doctrine of the Divine Unity. He was the first outspoken Unitarian in New England, not merely because he rejected the doctrine of the Trinity, but because he accepted all the cardinal principles developed by that movement since his day. He was a rationalist, an individualist, a defender of personal freedom, and tested religious practices by the standard of common sense. His sermons were plain, direct, vigorous, and modern. A truly religious man, Mayhew taught a practical and humanitarian religion, genuinely ethical, and faithful in inculcating the motive of civic duty.

Dr. Mayhew's words may be quoted in regard to some of the religious beliefs commonly accepted in his day. "The doctrine of a total ignorance and incapacity to judge of moral and religious truths brought upon mankind by the disobedience of our first parents," he wrote, "is without foundation."[11] "I hope it appears," he says, "that the love of God and of our neighbor, that sincere piety of heart, and a righteous, holy and charitable life, are the weightier matters of the gospel, as well as of the law."[12] "Although Christianity cannot," he asserts, "with any propriety or justice be said to be the same with natural religion, or merely a republication of the laws of nature, yet the principal, the most important and fundamental duties required by Christianity are, nevertheless, the same which were enjoined under the legal dispensation of Moses, and the same which are dictated by the light of nature."[13] His great love of intellectual and spiritual freedom finds utterance in such a statement as this: "Nor has any order or body of men authority to enjoin any particular article of faith, nor the use of any modes of worship not expressly pointed out in the Scriptures; nor has the enjoining of such articles a tendency to preserve the peace and harmony of the church, but directly the contrary."[14] Such sentences as the following are frequent on Mayhew's pages, and they show clearly the trend of his mind: "Free examination, weighing arguments for and against with care and impartiality,

Unitarianism in America

is the way to find truth." "True religion flourishes the more, the more people exercise their right of private judgment."[15] "There is nothing more foolish and superstitious than a veneration for ancient creeds and doctrines as such, and nothing is more unworthy a reasonable creature than to value principles by their age, as some men do their wines."[16]

Mayhew insisted upon the strict unity of God, "who is without rival or competitor." "The dominion and sovereignty of the universe is necessarily one and in one, the only living and true God, who delegates such measures of power and authority to other beings as seemeth good in his sight." He declared that the not preserving of such unity and supremacy of God on the part of Christians "has long been just matter of reproach to them"; and he said the authority of Christ is always "exercised in subordination to God's will."[17] His position was that "the faith of Christians does not terminate in Christ as the ultimate object of it, but it is extended through him to the one God."[18] The very idea of a mediator implies subordination as essential to it.[19] His biographer says he did not accept the notion of vicarious suffering, and, that he was an Arian in his views of the nature of Christ. "He was the first clergyman in New England who expressly and openly opposed the scholastic doctrine of the Trinity. Several others declined pressing the Athanasian Creed, and believed strictly in the unity of God. They also probably found it difficult to explain their views on the subject, and the great danger of losing their good name served to prevent their speaking out. But Dr. Mayhew did not conceal or disguise his sentiments on this point any more than on others, such as the peculiar tenets of Calvinism. He explicitly and boldly declared the doctrine irrational, unscriptural, and directly contradictory."[20] He taught the strict unity of God as early as 1753, "in the most unequivocal and plain manner, in his sermons of that year."[21] What most excited comment and objection was that, in a foot-note to the volume of his sermons published in 1755, Mayhew said that a Catholic Council had elevated the Virgin Mary to the position of a fourth person in the Godhead, and added, by way of comment: "Neither Papists nor Protestants should imagine that they will be understood by others if they do not understand themselves. Nor should they think that nonsense and contradictions can ever be too sacred to be ridiculous." The ridicule here was not directed against the doctrine of the Trinity, as has been maintained, but the foolish defences of it made by men who accepted its "mysteries" as too wonderful for reason to deal with in a serious manner. This boldness of comment on the part of Mayhew was in harmony with his strong disapproval of creed-making in all its forms. He condemned creeds because they set up "human tests of orthodoxy instead of the infallible word of God, and make other

48

terms of Christian communion than those explicitly pointed out by the Gospel."[22]

Dr. Mayhew was succeeded in the West Church by Rev. Simeon Howard in 1767, who, though he was received in a more friendly spirit by the ministers of the town, was not less radical in his theology than his predecessor. Dr. Howard was both an Arminian and an Arian, and he was "a believer neither in the Trinity, nor in the divine predestination of total depravity, and necessary ruin to any human soul."[23] He was of a gentle and conciliatory temper, but his preaching was quite as thorough–going in its intellectual earnestness as was Dr. Mayhew's.

[Sidenote: A Pronounced Universalist.]

Another preacher on the liberal side was Dr. Charles Chauncy of the First Church in Boston, whose ministry lasted from 1727 to 1787. He was the most vigorous of the opponents of the great awakening, both in his pulpit and through the press. He wrote a book on certain French fanatics, with the purpose of showing what would be the natural results of the excesses of the revival; he preached a powerful sermon on enthusiasm, to indicate the dangers of religious excitement, when not controlled by common sense and reason; and he travelled throughout New England to gain all the information possible about the revival, its methods and results, and published his Seasonable Thoughts on the State of Religion in New England in 1743. He had been influenced by the reading of Taylor, Tillotson, Clarke, and the other latitudinarian and rationalistic writers of England; and he found the revival in its excesses repugnant to his every thought of what was true and devout in religion.

Dr. Chauncy was not an eloquent preacher; but he was clear, earnest, and honest. Many of his sermons were published, and his books numbered nearly a dozen. As early as 1739 he preached a sermon in favor of religious toleration. At a later period he said, "It is with me past all doubt that the religion of Jesus will never be restored to its primitive purity, simplicity, and glory, until religious establishments are so brought down as to be no more."[24] It was this conviction which made him oppose in his pulpit and in two or three books the effort that was made just before the Revolution to establish the English Church as the state form of religion in the colonies. He said, in 1767, that the American people would hazard everything dear to them—their estates, their lives—rather than suffer their necks to be put under the yoke of bondage to any foreign power in state or church.[25]

In his early life Dr. Chauncy was an Arminian, but slowly he grew to the acceptance of distinctly Unitarian and Universalist doctrines. Near the end of his life he Published four or five books in which he advanced very liberal opinions. One of these, published in Boston in 1784, was on The Benevolence of the Deity fairly and impartially Considered. This book followed the same method and purpose as Butler's Analogy, and aimed to show that God has manifested his goodness in creation and in the life of man. He said that our moral self–determination, or free will, is our one great gift from God. He discussed the moral problems of life in order to prove the benevolence of God, maintaining that the goodness we see in him is of the same nature with goodness in ourselves. The year following he published a book on the Scriptural account of the Fall and its Consequences, in which he rejected the doctrine of total depravity, and interpreted the new birth as a result of education rather than of supernatural change. Thus he brought to full statement the logical result of the half–way covenant and the teachings of Solomon Stoddard, as well as of the connection of church and state in New England. He saw that the method of education is the only one that can justly be followed in the preparation of the young for admission to a church that is sustained in any direct way by the state.

Dr. Chauncy's great work as a preacher and author[26] was brought to its close by his books in favor of universal salvation. In 1783–84 he published in Boston two anonymous pamphlets advocating the salvation of all men, and these pamphlets made no little stir. In 1784 he published in London a work which he called The Mystery hid from Ages and Generations, made manifest by the Gospel Revelation; or, The Salvation of All Men the Grand Thing aimed at in the Scheme of God: By One who wishes well to the whole Human Race. In this book Dr. Chauncy made an elaborate study of the New Testament, in order to prove that salvation is to be universal. Christ died for all, therefore all will be saved; because all have sinned in Adam, therefore all will be made alive in Christ. He looked to a future probation, to a long period after death, when the opportunity of salvation will be open to all. He maintained that the misery threatened against the wicked in Scripture is that of this intermediate state between the earthly life and the time when God shall be all in all. He held that sin will be punished hereafter in proportion to depravity, and that none will be saved until they come into willing harmony with Christ, who will finally be able to win all men to himself, otherwise the power of God will be set at naught and his good will towards men frustrated of its purpose. In the future state of discipline, punishment will be inflicted with salutary effect, and thus the moral recovery of mankind will be accomplished.

[Sidenote: Other Men of Mark.]

Another leader was Dr. Samuel West, of Dartmouth, now New Bedford, where he was settled in 1760, and where he preached for more than forty years.[27] He rejected the doctrines of fore–ordination, election, total depravity, and the Trinity. In preaching the election sermon of 1776, he took the ground of an undisguised rationalism. "A revelation," he said, "pretending to be from God, that contradicts any part of natural laws ought immediately to be rejected as imposture; for the deity cannot make a law contrary to the law of nature without acting contrary to himself,—a thing in the strictest sense impossible, for that which implies contradiction is not an object of Divine Power." The cardinal idea of West's; position, as of that of most of the liberal men of his time, was stated by him in one sentence, when he said, "To preach Christ is to preach the whole system of divinity, as it consists of both natural and revealed religion."[28]

In 1751 Rev. Thomas Barnard, of Newbury, was dismissed from his parish because he was regarded as unconverted by the revivalistic portion of his congregation; and in 1755 he was settled over the First Church in Salem. He was an Arminian, and at the same time an Arian of the school of Samuel Clarke. His son Thomas was settled over the North Church of Salem in 1773, which church was organized especially for him by his admirers in the First Church. He followed in the theological opinions of his father, but probably became somewhat more pronounced in his Arian views, so that, after his death, Dr. Channing called him a Unitarian. It is not surprising that the younger Barnard should have been liberal in his opinions and spirit, when we find his theological instructor, Rev. Samuel Williams, at his ordination, saying to him in the sermon preached on that occasion, "Be of no sect or party but that of good men, and to all such (whatever their differences among themselves) let your heart be opened." On another similar occasion Mr. Williams said that it had always been his advice to examine with caution and modesty, "but with the greatest freedom all religious matters."[29] It was said of the younger Barnard that he believed "the final salvation of no man depended upon the belief or disbelief of those speculative opinions about which men, equally learned and pious, differ." When it was said to him by one of his parishioners, "Dr. Barnard, I never heard you preach a sermon upon the Trinity," the reply was, "And you never will."[30]

In 1779 Rev. John Prince was settled over the First Church in Salem, as the colleague of the elder Barnard. He was an Arian, but in no combative or dogmatic manner. He was a student, a lover of science, and an advanced thinker and investigator for his time. In 1787 he invited the Universalist, Rev. John Murray, into his pulpit, then an act of the greatest liberality.[31] Another lover of science, Rev. William Bentley, was settled over the East Church of Salem, as colleague to Rev. James Diman, in 1782. The senior pastor was a strict Calvinist, but the parish called as his colleague this young man of pronounced liberal views in theology. As early as 1784 Mr. Bentley was interested in the teachings of the English Unitarian, William Hazlitt,[32] who at that time visited New England. And in 1786 he was reading Joseph Priestley's book against the Trinity with approval. He soon after commended Dr. Priestley's short tracts as giving a good statement of the simple doctrines of Christianity.[33] He insisted upon free inquiry in religion from the beginning of his ministry, and not long after he began preaching he became substantially a Unitarian.[34] In 1789 he maintained that "the full conviction of a future moral retribution" is "the great point of Christian faith."[35] It has been claimed that Mr. Bentley was the first minister in New England to take distinctly the Unitarian position, and there are good reasons for this understanding of his doctrinal attitude.[36] Dr. Bentley corresponded with scholars in Europe, as he also did with Arab chiefs in their own tongue. He knew of the religions of India, and he seems to have given them appreciative recognition. The shipmasters and foreign merchants of Salem, as they came in contact with the Oriental races and religions, discarded their dogmatic Christianity; and these men, almost without exception, were connected with the churches that became Unitarian. It may be accepted as a very interesting fact that "the two potent influences shaping the ancient Puritanism of Salem into Unitarianism were foreign commerce and contact with the Oriental religions."[37]

The formation of a second parish in Worcester, in 1785, was a significant step in the progress of liberal opinion. This was the first time when a town, outside of Boston, was divided into two parishes of the Congregational order on doctrinal grounds. On the death of the minister of the first parish several candidates were heard, and among them Rev. Aaron Bancroft, who was a pronounced Arminian and Arian. The majority preferred a Calvinist; but the more intelligent minority insisted upon the settlement of Mr. Bancroft,—a result they finally accomplished by the organization of a new parish. It was a severe struggle by which this result was brought about, every effort being made to defeat it; and for many years Mr. Bancroft was almost completely isolated in his religious opinions.[38]

[Sidenote: The Second Period of Revivals.]

52

Unitarianism in America

It must not be understood that there was any marked separation in the churches as yet on doctrinal grounds. Calvinism was mildly taught, and ministers of all shades of opinion exchanged pulpits freely with each other. They met in ministerial associations, and in various duties of ordinations, councils, and other ecclesiastical gatherings. The preaching was practical, not doctrinal; and controverted subjects were for the most part not touched upon in the pulpits. About 1780, however, began a revival of Calvinism on the part of Drs. Bellamy, Emmons, Hopkins, and others; and especially did it take a strenuous form in the works of Samuel Hopkins. The New Divinity, as it was sometimes called, taught that unconditional submission to God is the duty of every human being, that we should be willing to be damned for the glory of God, and that the attitude of God towards men is one of unbounded benevolence. This newer Calvinism was full of incentives to missionary enterprise, and was zealous for the making of converts. Under the impulse of its greater enthusiasm there began, about 1790, a series of revivals which continued to the middle of the nineteenth century. This was the second great period of revivalism in New England. It was far better organized than the first one, while its methods were more systematic and under better guidance; and the results were great in the building of churches, in establishing missionary outposts, and in awakening an active religious life amongst the people. It aroused much opposition to the liberals, and it made the orthodox party more aggressive. Just as the great awakening developed opposition to the liberals of that day, and served to bring into view the two tendencies in the Congregational churches, so this new revival period accentuated the divergencies between those who believed in the deity of Christ and those who believed in his subordinate nature, and led to the first assuming of positions on both sides. There can be little doubt that it put a check upon the friendly spirit that had existed in the churches, and that it began a division which ultimately resulted in their separation into two denominations.[39]

Such details of individual and local opinion as have here been given are all the more necessary because there was at this time no consensus of belief on the part of the more liberal men. Each man thought for himself, but he was very reluctant to depart from the old ways in ritual and doctrine; and if the ministers consulted with each other, and gave each other confidential assistance, there was certainly nothing in the way of public conference or of party assimilation and encouragement. A visitor to Boston in 1791 wrote of the ministers there that "they are so diverse in their sentiments that they cannot agree on any point in theology. Some are Calvinists, some Universalists, some Arminians, and one, at least, is a Socinian."[40] Another visitor, this time in 1801, found the range of opinions much wider. In all the ministers of Boston he found only one rigid Trinitarian;

one was a follower of Edwards, several were Arminians, two were Socinians, one a Universalist, and one a Unitarian.[41] This writer says it was not difficult to find out what men did not believe, but there was as yet no public line of demarcation among the clergy. There being no outward pressure to bring men into uniformity, no institution or body of men with authority to require assent to a standard of orthodoxy, little attention was given to merely doctrinal interests. The position taken was that presented by Rev. John Tucker of Newbury, in the convention sermon of 1768, when he said that no one has any right whatever to legislate in behalf of Christ, who alone has authority to fix the terms of the Gospel. He said that, as all believers and teachers of Christianity are "perfectly upon a level with one another, none of them can have any authority even to interpret the laws of this kingdom for others, so as to require their assent to such interpretation." He also declared that as "every Christian has and must have a right to judge for himself of the true sense and meaning of all gospel truths, no doctrines, therefore, no laws, no religious rites, no terms of acceptance with God or of admission to Christian privileges not found in the gospel, are to be looked upon by him as any part of this divine system, nor to be received and submitted to as the doctrines and laws of Christ."[42] Of Rev. John Prince, the minister of the First Church in Salem during the last years of the century, it was said that he never "preached distinctly upon any of the points of controversy which, in his day, agitated the New England churches."[43] The minister of Roxbury, Rev. Eliphalet Porter, said of the Calvinistic beliefs, that there was not one of them he considered "essential to the Christian faith or character."[44]

[Sidenote: King's Chapel becomes Unitarian.]

These quotations will indicate the liberty of spirit that existed in the New England churches of the later years of the eighteenth century, especially in the neighborhood of Boston, and along the seacoast; and also the diversity of opinion on doctrinal subjects among the ministers. It is impossible here to follow minutely the stages of doctrinal evolution, but a few dates and incidents will serve to indicate the several steps that were taken. The first of these was the settlement of Rev. James Freeman over King's Chapel in 1782, and his ordination by the congregation in 1787, the liturgy having been revised two years earlier to conform to the liberal opinions of the minister and people. These changes were brought about largely through the influence of Rev. William Hazlitt, the father of the essayist and critic of the same name, who had been settled over several of the smaller Unitarian churches in Great Britain. In the spring of 1783 he visited the United States, and spent several months in Philadelphia. He gave a course of lectures on the Evidences of Christianity in the college there, which were largely attended. He preached for several weeks in a country parish in Maryland, he had invitations to settle in Charleston and Pittsburg, and he had an opportunity to become the president of a college by subscribing to the doctrinal tests required, which he would not do; for "he would sooner die in a ditch than submit to human authority in matters of faith."[45] In June, 1784, he preached in the Brattle Street Church of Boston, and he anticipated becoming its minister; but his pronounced doctrinal position seems to have made that impossible. He also preached in Hingham, and some of the people there desired his settlement; but the aged Dr. Gay would not resign. It would appear that he preached for Dr. Chauncy, for Mr. Barnes in Salem, and also in several pulpits on Cape Cod. He gave in Boston his course of lectures on the Evidences of Christianity, and it was received with much favor by large audiences. The winter of 1784–85 was spent by Mr. Hazlitt in Hallowell, Me., in which place was a small group of wealthy English Unitarians, led by Samuel Vaughan, by whom Mr. Hazlitt had been entertained in Philadelphia. Mr. Hazlitt returned to Boston in the spring of 1785, and had some hope of settling in Roxbury. In the autumn, however, finding no definite promise of employment, he returned to England. He afterward corresponded with Dr. Howard, of the West Church in Boston, and with Dr. Lathrop, of West Springfield. The volumes of sermons he published in 1786 and 1790 were sold in this country, and one or two of them republished.

It would appear that Mr. Hazlitt's positive Unitarianism made it impossible for him to settle over any church in Boston or its neighborhood. In 1784 he assisted Dr. Freeman in revising the Prayer Book, the form of prayer used by Dr. Lindsey[46] in the Essex Street Chapel in London being adapted to the new conditions at King's Chapel. He also republished in Philadelphia and Boston many of Dr. Priestley's Unitarian tracts, while writing much himself for publication.[47] In his correspondence with Theophilus Lindsey, Dr. Freeman wrote of Mr. Hazlitt as a pious, zealous, and intelligent minister, to whose instructions and conversation he was particularly indebted.[48] "Before Mr. Hazlitt came to Boston", Dr. Freeman wrote, "the Trinitarian doxology was almost universally used. That honest, good man prevailed upon several respectable ministers to omit it. Since his departure the number of those who repeat only Scriptural doxologies has greatly increased, so that there are now many churches in which the worship is strictly Unitarian."[49]

Beginning with the year 1786, several of the liberal men in Boston were in correspondence with the leading Unitarian ministers in London, and their letters were afterward published by Thomas Belsham in his Life of Theophilus Lindsey. From this work we learn that Dr. Lindsey presented his own theological works and those of Dr. Priestley to Harvard College, and that they were read with great avidity by the students.[50] One of the Boston correspondents, writing in 1783, names James Bowdoin, governor of Massachusetts in 1785 and 1786, General Benjamin Lincoln, and General Henry Knox as among the liberal men. He said: "There are many others besides, in our legislature, of similar sentiments. While so many of our great men are thus on the side of truth and free inquiry, they will necessarily influence many of the common people."[51] He also said that people were less frightened at the Socinian name than formerly, and that this form of Christianity was beginning to have some public advocates. The only minister who preached in favor of it was Mr. Bentley, of Salem, who was described as "a young man of a bold, independent mind, of strong, natural powers, and of more skill in the learned languages than any person of his years in the state." Mr. Bentley's congregation was spoken of as uncommonly liberal, not alarmed at any improvements, and pleased with his introduction into the pulpit of various modern translations of the Scriptures, especially of the prophecies.[52]

[Sidenote: Other Unitarian Movements.]

In March, 1792, a Unitarian congregation was formed in Portland under the leadership of Thomas Oxnard, who had been an Episcopalian. Having been supplied with the works of Priestley and Lindsey through the generosity of Dr. Freeman, he became a Unitarian; and his personal intercourse with Dr. Freeman gave strength to his changed convictions. A number of persons of property and respectability of character joined him in accepting his new faith. In writing to his friend in November, 1788, Mr. Oxnard said: "I cannot express to you the avidity with which these Unitarian publications are sought after. Our friends here are clearly convinced that the Unitarian doctrine will soon become the prevailing opinion in this country. Three years ago I did not know a single Unitarian in this part of the country besides myself; and now, entirely from the various publications you have furnished, a decent society might be collected in this and the neighboring towns."[53] In 1792 an attempt was made to introduce a revised liturgy into the Episcopal church of Portland; and, when this was resisted, a majority of the congregation seceded and formed a Unitarian society, with Mr. Oxnard as the minister. This society was continued for a few years, and then ceased to exist. The members joined the first Congregational church, which in 1809, became Unitarian.[54] Also in 1792 was organized a Unitarian congregation in Saco, under the auspices of Hon. Samuel Thatcher, a member of

Congress and a Massachusetts judge.[55] Mr. Thatcher had been an unbeliever, but through the reading of Priestley's works he became a sincere and rational Christian. He met with much opposition from his neighbors, and an effort was made to prevent his re–election to Congress; but it did not succeed. The Saco congregation was at first connected with that at Portland, and it seems to have ceased its existence at the same time.[56]

In 1794 Dr. Freeman wrote that Unitarianism was making considerable progress in the southern counties of Massachusetts. In Barnstable he reported "a very large body of Unitarians."[57] Writing in May, 1796, he states that Unitarianism is on the increase in Maine, that it is making a considerable increase in the southern part of Massachusetts, and that a few seeds have been sown in Vermont. He thinks it may be losing ground in some places, but that it is growing in others. "I consider it," he writes, "as one of the most happy effects which have resulted from my feeble exertions in the Unitarian cause, that they have introduced me to the knowledge and friendship of some of the most valuable characters of the present age, men of enlightened heads and benevolent hearts. Though it is a standing article of most of our social libraries, that nothing of a controversial character should be purchased, yet any book which is presented is freely accepted. I have found means, therefore, of introducing into them some of the Unitarian Tracts with which you have kindly furnished me. There are few persons who have not read them with avidity; and when read they cannot fail to make an impression upon the minds of many. From these and other causes the Unitarian doctrine appears to be still upon the increase. I am acquainted with a number of ministers, particularly in the southern part of this state, who avow and publicly preach this sentiment. There are others more cautious, who content themselves with leading their hearers by a course of rational but prudent sermons gradually and insensibly to embrace it. Though this latter mode is not what I entirely approve, yet it produces good effects. For the people are thus kept out of the reach of false opinions, and are prepared for the impressions which will be made on them by more bold and ardent successors, who will probably be raised up when these timid characters are removed off the stage. The clergy are generally the first who begin to speculate; but the people soon follow, where they are so much accustomed to read and enquire."[58]

In 1793 was published Jeremy Belknap's biography of Samuel Watts, who was an Arian, or, at least, held to the subordinate nature of Christ. This book had a very considerable influence in directing attention to the doctrine of the Trinity, and in inducing inquiring men to study the subject critically for themselves. In 1797 Dr. Belknap became the minister of the Federal Street Church in Boston, and his preaching was from that time distinctly Unitarian. Dr. Joseph Priestley removed to Philadelphia in 1794, and he was at first listened to by large congregations. His humanitarian theology—that is, his denial of divinity as well as deity to Christ—probably had the effect of limiting the interest in his teachings. However, a small congregation was established in Philadelphia in 1796, formed mostly of English Unitarians. A congregation was gathered at Northumberland in 1794, to which place Priestley removed in that year.

In the year 1800 a division took place in the church at Plymouth, owing to the growth there of liberal sentiments. These began to manifest themselves as early as 1742, as a reaction from the intense revivalism of that Period.[59] Rev. Chandler Bobbins, who was strictly Calvinistic in his theology, was the minister from 1760 until his death in 1799. In 1794 a considerable number of persons in the parish discussed the desirability of organizing another church, in order to secure more liberal preaching. It was recognized that Mr. Robbins was an old man, that he was very much beloved, and that in a few years the opportunity desired would be presented without needless agitation; and the effort was therefore deferred. In November, 1799, at a meeting held for the election of a new pastor, twenty–three members of the church were in favor of Rev. James Kendall, the only candidate, while fifteen were in opposition. When the parish voted, two hundred and fifty–three favored Mr. Kendall, and fifteen were opposed. In September, 1800, the conservative minority, numbering eighteen males and thirty–five females, withdrew; and two years later they organized the society now called the Church of the Pilgrimage. The settlement of Mr. Kendall, a pronounced Arminian,[60] was an instance of the almost complete abandonment of Calvinism on the part of a congregation, in opposition to the preaching from the pulpit. In spite of the strict confession of faith which Dr. Robbins had persuaded the church to adopt, the parish outgrew the old teachings. Mr. Kendall, with the approval of his church, soon grew into a Unitarian; and it was fitting that the church of the Mayflower, the church of Robinson and Brewster, should lead the way in this advance.

As yet there was no controversy, except in a quiet way. Occasionally sharp criticism was uttered, especially in convention and election sermons; but there was no thought of separation or exclusion. The liberal men showed a tendency to magnify the work of charity; and they were, in a limited degree, zealous in every kind of philanthropic effort. More distinctly, however, they showed their position in their enthusiasm for the Bible and in their summing up of Christianity in loyalty to Christ. Towards all creeds and dogmas they were indifferent and silent, except as they occasionally spoke plainly out to condemn them. They believed in and preached toleration, and their whole movement stood more distinctly for comprehensiveness and latitudinarianism than for aught else. They were not greatly concerned about theological problems; but they thoroughly believed in a broad, generous, sympathetic, and practical Christianity, that would exemplify the teachings of Christ, and that would lead men to a pure and noble moral life.

[Sidenote: Growth of Toleration.]

That toleration was not as yet fully accepted in Massachusetts is seen in the fact that the proposed Constitution of 1778 was defeated because it provided for freedom of worship on the part of all Protestant denominations. The dominant religious body was not yet ready to put itself on a level with the other sects. In the Constitutional Convention of 1779 the more liberal men worked with the Baptists to secure a separation of state and church. Such men as Drs. Chauncy, Mayhew, West, and Shute were desirous of the broadest toleration; and they did what they could to secure it. As early as 1768, Dr. Chauncy spoke in plainest terms in opposition to the state support of religion. "We are in principle," he wrote, "against all civil establishments in religion. It does not appear to us that God has entrusted, the state with a right to make religious establishments. But let it be heedfully minded we claim no right to desire the interposition of the state to establish the mode of worship, government or discipline, we apprehend is most agreeable to the mind of Christ. We desire no other liberty than to be left unrestrained in the exercise of our principles, in so far as we are good members of society.... The plain truth is, by the gospel charter, all professed Christians are vested with precisely the same rights; nor has our denomination any more a right to the interposition of the civil magistrate in their favor than any other; and whenever this difference takes place, it is beside the rule of Scripture, and the genuine dictates, of uncorrupted reason."[61] All persons throughout the state, of whatever religious connection, who had become emancipated from the Puritan spirit, supported him in this opinion. They were in the minority as yet, and they were not organized. Therefore, their efforts were unsuccessful.

Another testing of public sentiment on this subject was had in the Massachusetts convention which, in 1788, ratified the Constitution of the United States. The sixth article, which provides that "no religious tests shall ever be required as a qualification to any office," was the occasion of a prolonged debate and much opposition. Hon. Theophilus Parsons took the liberal side, and declared that "the only evidence we can have of the sincerity and excellency of a man's religion is a good life," precisely the position of the liberal men. By several members it was urged, however, that this article was a departure from the principles of our forefathers, who came here for the preservation of their religion, and that it would admit deists and atheists into the general government.

In these efforts to secure religious toleration as a fundamental law of the state and nation the Baptist denomination took an active and a leading part. Not less faithful to this cause were the liberal men among the Congregationalists, while the opposition came almost wholly from the Calvinistic and orthodox churches. Such leaders on the liberal side as Dr. David Shute of the South Parish in Hingham, Rev. Thomas Thatcher of the West Parish in Dedham, and Dr. Samuel West of New Bedford, were loyally devoted in the convention to the support of the toleration act of the Constitution. In the membership of the convention there were seventeen ministers, and fourteen of them voted for the Constitution. The opinions of the fourteen were expressed by Rev. Phillips Payson, the minister of Chelsea, who held that a religious test would be a great blemish on the Constitution. He also said that God is the God of the conscience, and for human tribunals to encroach upon the consciences of men is impious.[62] As the Constitution was ratified by only a small majority of the convention, and as at the opening of its sessions the opposition seemed almost overwhelming, the position taken by the more liberal ministers was a sure indication of growing liberality. The great majority of the people, however, were still strongly in favor of the old religious tests and restrictions, as was fully indicated by subsequent events. The Revolution operated as a liberalizing influence, because of the breaking of old customs and the discussion of the principles of liberty attendant upon the adoption of the state and national constitutions. The growth of democratic sentiment made a strong opposition to the churches and their privileges, and it caused a diminution of reverence for the authority of the clergy. The twenty years following the Revolution showed a notable growth in liberal opinions.

Universalism presented itself as a new form of Calvinism, its advocates claiming that God decreed that all should be saved, and that his will would be triumphant. In many parts of the country the doctrine of universal salvation began to be heard during the last two decades of the eighteenth century, and the growth of interest in it was rapid from the beginning of the nineteenth. This movement began in the Baptist churches, but it soon appeared in others. At first it was undefined, a protest against the harsh teaching of future punishment. It was a part of the humanitarian awakening of the time, the new faith in man, the recognition that love is diviner than wrath. Many persons found escape from creeds that were hateful to them into this new and more hopeful interpretation of religion. Persons of every shade of protest, and "infidelity," and free thinking, found their way into this new body; and great was the condemnation and hatred with which it was received on the part of the other sects. In time this movement clarified itself, and it has had a positive influence for piety and for nobler views of God and the future.

Of much the same nature was the movement within the fellowship of the Friends led by Thomas Hicks. It was Unitarian and reformatory, influenced by the growing democracy and zeal for humanity the age was everywhere manifesting.

In the border states between north and south began, during the last decade of the eighteenth century, a movement in favor of discarding all creeds and confessions. It favored a return to the Bible itself as the great Protestant book, and as the one revealed word of God. Without learning or culture, these persons sought to make their faith in Christ more real by an evangelical obedience to his teachings. Some of them called themselves Disciples, holding that to follow Christ is quite enough. Others said that no other name than Christian is required. They were Biblical in their theology, and unsectarian in their attitude towards the forms and rituals of the church. In time these scattered groups of earnest seekers for a better Christian way, from Maine to Georgia, came to know each other and to organize for the common good.

With the rapid growth of Methodism the Arminian view of man was widely adopted. The Baptists received into their fellowship in all parts of New England, at least, many who were not deeply in sympathy with their strict rules, but who found with them a means of protesting against the harsher methods of the "standing order" of Congregationalists. Their demand for toleration and liberty of conscience began to receive recognition after the Revolution, and their influence was a powerful one in bringing about the separation of state and church. Those who were dissatisfied with a church that taxed all the people, and that was upheld by state authority, found with the Baptists a means of making their protest heard and felt.

In all directions the democratic spirit was being manifested, and conditions which had been upheld by the restrictive authority of England had to give way. The people were now speaking, and not the ministers only. It was an age of individualism, and of the reassertion of the tendency that had characterized New England from the first, but that

61

had been held in check by autocratic power. There was no outbreak, no rapid change, no iconoclastic overturning of old institutions and customs, but the people were coming to their own, thinking for themselves. In reality, the people were conservative, especially in New England; and they moved slowly, there was little infidelity, and steadily were the old ideals maintained. Yet the individualism would assert itself. Men held the old creeds in distinctly personal ways, and the churches grew into more and more of independency.

The theological development of the eighteenth century took two directions: that of rationalism and a demand for free inquiry, as represented by Jonathan Mayhew and William Bentley; and that of a philanthropic protest against the harsh features of Calvinism, as represented by Charles Chauncy and the Universalists. The demand that all theological problems should be submitted to reason for vindication or readjustment was not widely urged; but a few men recognized the worth of this claim, and applied this method without hesitation. A larger number followed them with hesitating steps, but with a growing confidence in reason as God's method for man's finding and maintaining the truth. The other tendency grew out of a benevolent desire to justify the ways of God to man, and was the expression of a deepening faith that the Divine Being deals with his children in a fatherly manner. That God is generous and loving was the faith of Dr. Chauncy, as it was of the Universalists and of the more liberal party among the Calvinists. Their philanthropic feelings toward their fellow–men seemed to them representative of God's ways of dealing with his creatures.

[1] Levi L. Paine, A Critical History of the Evolution of Trinitarianism, 105. "Nathaniel Emmons held tenaciously to three real persons. He said, 'It is as easy to conceive of God existing in three persons as in one person.' This language shows that Emmons employed the term 'person' in the strict literal sense. The three are absolutely equal, this involving the metaphysical assumption that in the Trinity being and person are not coincident. Emmons is the first theologian who asserts that, though we cannot conceive that three persons should be one person, we may conceive that three persons may be one Being, 'if we only suppose that being may signify something different from person in respect to Deity.'"

[2] E.H. Gillett, History and Literature of the Unitarian Controversy. Historical Magazine, April 1871; second series, IX. 222.

[3] Letter to Scripturista by Paulinus, 18.

[4] William S. Pattee, A History of Old Braintree and Quincy, 222. When a copy of Dr. Jedediah Morse's little book on American Unitarianism was sent to John Adams, he acknowledged its receipt in the following letter:—

QUINCY, May 15, 1815.

Dear Doctor,—I thank you for your favor of the 10th, and the pamphlet enclosed, entitled American Unitarianism. I have turned over its leaves, and found nothing that was not familiarly known to me. In the preface Unitarianism is represented as only thirty years old in New England. I can testify as a witness to its old age. Sixty–five years ago my own minister, the Rev. Lemuel Briant; Dr. Jonathan Mayhew, of the West Church in Boston; the Rev. Mr. Shute, of Hingham; the Rev. John Brown, of Cohasset; and perhaps equal to all, if not above all, the, Rev. Mr. Gay, of Hingham, were Unitarians. Among the laity how many could I name, lawyers, physicians, tradesmen, farmers! But at present I will name only one, Richard Cranch, a man who had studied divinity, and Jewish and Christian antiquities, more than any clergyman now existing in New England.

JOHN ADAMS.

Also see C.F. Adams, Three Episodes of Massachusetts History, 643; and J.H. Allen, An Historical Sketch of the Unitarian Movement since the Reformation, 175.

[5] History of Hingham, I., Part II., 24, Memoir of Ebenezer Gay, by Solomon Lincoln.

[6] Sermons, 1755, 83.

[7] Ibid., 103.

[8] Ibid., 119.

[9] Ibid., 125.

[10] Ibid., 245.

[11] Sermons, 1755, 50.

[12] Ibid., 82.

[13] Sermons, 1755, 83.

[14] Ibid., 65.

[15] Ibid., 62.

[16] Ibid., 63.

[17] Ibid, 268, 269.

[18] Sermons, 1755, 275, 276.

[19] A. Bradford, Memoir of the Life and Writings of Rev. Jonathan Mayhew, D.D., 36.

[20] Ibid., 464.

[21] Letter from his daughter, quoted by Bartol, The West Church and its Ministers, 129.

[22] Sermons, 293

[23] C.A. Bartol, The West Church and its Ministers.

[24] Reply to Dr. Chandler, quoted in Sprague's Annals of the Unitarian Pulpit, 9.

[25] Remarks upon a Sermon of the Bishop of Landaff, quoted by Sprague.

[26] Chauncy's many published sermons and volumes are carefully enumerated by Paul Leicester Ford in his Bibliotheca Chaunciana, a List of the Writings of Charles Chauncy. He gives the titles of sixty–one books and pamphlets published by Chauncy, and of eighty–eight about him or in reply to him.

[27] Sprague's Annals, 49; W.J. Potter, History of the First Congregational Society, New Bedford.

[28] Sprague's Annals. 42.

[29] George Batchelor, Social Equilibrium, 263, 264.

[30] Ibid., 265.

[31] Sprague's Annals, 131.

[32] Father of the essayist of the same name.

[33] Joseph Priestley, 1733–1804, was one of the ablest of English Unitarians. Educated in non–conformist schools, in 1755 he became a Presbyterian minister. In 1761 he became a tutor in a non–conformist academy, and in 1767 he was settled over a congregation in Leeds. He was the librarian of Lord Shelburne from 1774 until he was settled in Birmingham as minister, in 1780. In 1791 a mob destroyed his house, his manuscripts, and his scientific apparatus, because of his liberal political views. After three years as a preacher in Hackney, he removed to the United States in 1794, and settled at Northumberland in Pennsylvania, where the remainder of his life was spent. He published one hundred and thirty distinct works, of which those best remembered are his Institutes of Natural and Revealed Religion, A History of the Corruptions of Christianity, and A General History of the Christian Church to the Fall of the Western Empire. He was the discoverer of oxygen, and holds a high place in the history of

science. He was a materialist, but believed in immortality; and he believed that Christ was a man in his nature.

[34] C.S. Osgood and H.M. Batchelder, Historical Sketch of Salem, 86. "He took strong Arminian grounds; and under his lead the church became practically Unitarian in 1785, and was one of the first churches in America to adopt that faith."

[35] George Batchelor, Social Equilibrium, 270.

[36] Ibid., 267.

[37] Ibid., 283.

[38] E. Smalley, The Worcester Pulpit, 226, 232.

[39] See the Unitarian Advocate and Religious Miscellany, January, 1831, new series, III. 27, for Aaron Bancroft's recollections of this period. In the same volume was published Ezra Ripley's reminiscences, contained in the March, April, and May numbers. They are both of much importance for the history of this period. Also the third volume of first series, June, 1829, gives an important letter from Francis Parkman concerning Unitarianism in Boston in 1812.

[40] Life of Ashbel Green, President of Princeton College, 236.

[41] Life of Archibald Alexander, 252.

[42] Convention Sermon, 12, 13.

[43] Sprague, Annals of Unitarian Pulpit, 131.

[44] Ibid., 159.

[45] This is the statement of his daughter.

[46] Theophilus Lindsey, 1723–1808, was a curate in London, then the tutor
of the Duke of Northumberland, and afterward a rector in Yorkshire
and Dorsetshire. In 1763 he was settled at Catterick, in Yorkshire,
where his study of the Bible led him to doubt the truth of the
doctrine of the Trinity. In 1771 he joined with others in a petition
to Parliament asking that clergymen might not be required to
subscribe to the thirty–nine articles. When it was rejected a second
time he resigned, went to London, and opened in a room in Essex
Street, April 1774, the first permanent Unitarian meeting in England.
A chapel was built for him in 1778, and he preached there until 1793.
He published, in 1783, An Historical View of the State of the
Unitarian Doctrine and Worship from the Reformation to our own Times,
two volumes of sermons, and other works. In 1774 he published a
revised Prayer Book according to the plan suggested by Dr. Samuel
Clarke, which was used in the Essex Street Chapel.

[47] Four Generations of a Literary Family: The Hazlitts in England,
Ireland, and America, 23, 26, 30, 40, 43, 50; Lamb and Hazlitt:
Further Letters and Records, 11–15.

[48] Monthly Repository, III., 305. Mr. Hazlitt "arrived at Boston May 15,
1784; and, having a letter to Mr. Eliot, who received him with great
kindness, he was introduced on that very day to the Boston
Association of Ministers. The venerable Chauncy, at whose house it
happened to be held, entered into a familiar conversation with him,
and showed him every possible respect as he learned that he had been
acquainted with Dr. Price. Without knowing at the time anything of
the occasion which led to it, ordination happened to be the general
subject of discussion. After the different gentlemen had severally
delivered their opinions, the stranger was requested to declare his
sentiments, who unhesitatingly replied that the people or the
congregation who chose any man to be their minister were his proper
ordainers. Mr. Freeman, upon hearing this, jumped from his seat in a
kind of transport, saying, 'I wish you could prove that, Sir,' The
gentleman answered that 'few things could admit of an easier proof.'
And from that moment a thorough intimacy commenced between him and

Mr. Freeman. Soon after, the Boston prints being under no *imprimatur*, he published several letters in supporting the cause of Mr. Freeman. At the solicitation of Mr. Freeman he also published a Scriptural Confutation of the Thirty–nine Articles. Notice being circulated that this publication would appear on a particular day, the printer, apprised of this circumstance, threw off a hundred papers beyond his usual number, and had not one paper remaining upon his hands at noon. This publication in its consequences converted Mr. Freeman's congregation into a Unitarian church, which, as Mr. Freeman acknowledged, could never have been done without the labors of this gentleman."

[49] American Unitarianism, from Belsham's Life of Lindsey, 12, *note.*

[50] American Unitarianism, 16.

[51] American Unitarianism, note.

[52] Ibid., 20.

[53] American Unitarianism, 17.

[54] "Oxnard was a merchant, born in Boston in 1740, but settled in Portland, where he married the daughter of General Preble, in 1787. He was a loyalist, and fled from the country at the outbreak of the war. He returned to Portland in 1787. A few years later, 1792, the Episcopal church being destitute of a minister, he was engaged as lay reader, with the intention of taking orders. His Unitarianism put a sudden end to his Episcopacy, but not to his preaching. He gathered a small congregation in the school–house, and preached sometimes sermons of his own, but more often of other men. He died in 1799." John C. Perkins, How the First Parish became Unitarian,—historical sermon preached in Portland.

[55] American Unitarianism, 18.

[56] Ibid., 17, 20.

[57] American Unitarianism, 24.

[58] American Unitarianism, 22.

[59] Church Records, in MS., II. 7.

[60] Rev. Thomas Robbins, Diary for October 13, 1799, I. 97, heard Mr. Kendall, and said: "He appears to be an Arminian in full. I fear be will lead many souls astray." See John Cuckson, A Brief History of the First Church in Plymouth, eighth chapter.

[61] Chauncy against Chandler, 152.

[62] These particulars are taken from the Debates and Proceedings in the Convention of the Commonwealth of Massachusetts held in the year 1788, and which finally ratified the Constitution of the United States, Boston, 1856.

V. THE PERIOD OF CONTROVERSY.

In the spring of 1805 Rev. Henry Ware, who had been for nearly twenty years pastor of the first church in the town of Hingham, was inaugurated as the Hollis Professor of Divinity at Harvard College. The place had been made vacant by the death of Professor David Tappan, who was a moderate Calvinist; that is, one who recognized the sovereignty of God, but allowed to man a limited opportunity for personal effort in the process of salvation. It was assumed by the conservative party that a Calvinist would be appointed, because the founder of this important professorship, it was claimed, was of that way of thinking, and so conditioned his gift as to require that no one but a Calvinist should hold the position. This was strenuously denied by the liberals, who maintained that Hollis was not only liberal and catholic in his own theology, but that he made no such restrictions as were claimed.[1] When the nomination of Mr. Ware was presented to the overseers, it was strongly opposed; but he was elected by a considerable majority. A pamphlet soon appeared in opposition to him, and this was the beginning of a controversy that lasted for a quarter of a century.[2]

This war of pamphlets was made more furious by Rev. John Sherman's One God in One Person Only, and Rev. Hosea Ballou's Treatise on the Atonement, both of which appeared in 1805. Mr. Sherman's book was described in The Monthly Anthology as "one of the first acts of direct hostility against the orthodox committed on these western shores."[3] The little book by Hosea Ballou had small influence on the current of religious thinking outside the Universalist body, to which he belonged, and probably did not at all enter into the controversy between the orthodox and the liberal Congregationalists. It was, however, the first positive statement of the doctrine of the atonement in a rational form, not as expiatory, but as reconciling man to the loving authority of God. Within a decade it brought the leading Universalists to the Unitarian position.[4] These works were followed, in 1810, by Rev. Noah Worcester's Bible News of the Father, Son, and Holy Ghost, which presented clearly and forcibly an Arian view of the Trinity, or the subordination of Christ to God. These definitions of their position on the part of the liberals were met by the publication of The Panoplist, which was begun by Dr. Jedidiah Morse, of Charlestown, Mass., in 1805. This magazine interpreted the orthodox positions, and devoted itself zealously to the defence of the old ideas, as understood by its editors. It was not vehemently aggressive, but was largely devoted to general religious interests, and to the promotion of a higher spirit of devotion. It was followed by The Spirit of the Pilgrims, which was more combative, and in some degree intolerant. In the year 1808 the Andover Theological School was founded, the result of a reconciliation between the Hopkinsians and the Calvinists of the old type, affording an opportunity for theological training on the part of those who could not accept the liberal attitude of Harvard.

Most of the liberal men of this time refused to bring their beliefs to the test of exact definition. It was their opinion that no theological statement can have high value in relation to Christian attainments. Under these conditions were trained the men who became the leaders in the early Unitarian movement. William Ellery Channing, who was settled over the Federal Street Church in June, 1803, was distinctly evangelical, and of a profound and earnest piety. Slowly he grew to accept the liberal attitude, as the result of his love of freedom, his lofty spirituality of nature, and his tolerant and generous cast of mind. He gave spiritual and intellectual direction to the new movement, guided its philanthropic efforts, and brought to noble issue its spiritual philosophy. Early in the year 1804, Joseph Stevens Buckminster was settled over the Brattle Street Church; and,

70

though he preached but a little over six years before a blighting disease took him away, yet he left behind a tradition of great pulpit gifts and a wonderfully attractive personality. Another to die in early manhood was Samuel Cooper Thacher, who was settled at the New South in 1811, and who was long remembered for his scholarship and his zeal in the work which he had undertaken. Charles Lowell went to the West Church in 1806, and he nobly sustained the traditions for liberality and spiritual freedom that had gathered about that place of worship. In 1814 appeared Edward Everett, at the age of twenty (which had been that of Buckminster when he entered the pulpit), as the minister of the Brattle Street Church, to charm with his eloquence, learning, grace, and power. Francis Parkman began his career at the New North in 1812,—"a man of various information, a kind spirit, singular benevolence, polished yet simple manners, fine literary taste."[5] A few years later John Gorham Palfrey became the minister of the Brattle Street Church, and James Walker was settled over the Harvard Church in Charlestown. Among the laymen in the churches to which these men preached were many persons of distinction. The liberal fellowship, therefore, was of the highest social and intellectual standing. The piety of the churches was serious, if not profound; and the religion presented was simple, sincere, intellectual, and earnestly spiritual.

[Sidenote: The Monthly Anthology.]

The practical and tolerant aims of the liberals were shown by the manner in which they began to give expression publicly to their position. In The Monthly Anthology they first found voice, although that publication was started without the slightest controversial purpose. Begun by a young man as a monthly literary journal in 1803, when he found it would not support him, he abandoned it;[6] and the publishers asked Rev. William Emerson, the minister of the First Church in Boston, to take charge of it. He consented to do so, and gathered about him a company of friends to aid him in its management. Their meetings finally grew into The Anthology Club, which continued the publication through ten volumes. Among the members were William Emerson, Samuel Cooper Thacher, Joseph S. Buckminster, and Joseph Tuckerman, pastors of churches in Boston and vicinity of the liberal school. There was also John S.J. Gardiner, the rector of Trinity Church, who was the president of the club throughout the whole period of its existence, and one of the most frequent contributors to the periodical. The members were not drawn together by any sectarian spirit, but by a common aim of doing something for literature, and for the advancement of culture. The Monthly Anthology was the first distinctly literary journal published in this country. It had an important influence in developing the intellectual tastes of New England, and of giving initiative to its literary capacities. The spirit of The Monthly Anthology was broad and catholic. Naturally, therefore, in its pages the liberals made their first protest against party aims and methods. In a few instances theological problems were discussed, the extreme Trinitarian doctrines were criticised, and the liberal attitude was defended.

[Sidenote: Society for Promoting Christian Knowledge, Piety, and Charity.]

In the year 1806 Rev. William Emerson began the publication of The Christian Monitor, in his capacity as the secretary of the Society for promoting Christian Knowledge, Piety, and Charity, a society then newly founded by residents of Boston and its vicinity for the purpose of publishing enlightened and practical tracts and books. This series of small books, each containing one hundred and fifty or two hundred pages, and issued quarterly, was begun for the purpose of publishing devotional works of a practical and liberal type. The first number contained prayers and devotional exercises for personal or family use, and there followed Bishop Newcombe's Life and Character of Christ, a condensed reproduction of Law's Serious Call, Bishop Hall's Contemplations, Erskine's Letters to the Bereaved, and two or three volumes of sermons on religious duties and the education of children.

Besides The Christian Monitor this society issued a series of Religious Tracts which had a considerable circulation. Then it undertook the publication of books for children, and for family reading. In aiming to publish works of pure morality and practical piety, its methods were thoroughly catholic and liberal; for it was unsectarian, and yet earnestly Christian. The spirit and methods of this society were thoroughly characteristic of the time when it was organized, and of the men who gave it life and purpose. Not dogma, but piety, was what they desired. In the truest sense they were unsectarian Christians, zealous for good works and a devout life.[7]

[Sidenote: General Repository.]

The Monthly Anthology and The Christian Monitor represented the mild and undogmatic attitude of the liberals, their shrinking from all controversy, and their desire to devote their labors wholly to the promotion of a tolerant and catholic Christianity. The beginning of the controversial spirit on the liberal side found expression in The General Repository and Review, which was begun in Cambridge by Rev. Andrews Norton, in April, 1812. In the first number of this quarterly review the editor said that the discussion of the doctrine of the Trinity "in our own country has hitherto been chiefly confined to private circles," and cited the books of John Sherman and Noah Worcester as the only exceptions. The review opened, however, with a defence of liberal Christianity which was aggressive and outspoken. In later issues an energetic statement was made of the liberal position, the controversial articles were able and explicit, and in a manner hitherto quite unknown on the part of what the editor called "catholic Christians." One of the numbers contained a long and interesting survey of the religious interests of the country, and summed up in an admirable manner the prospects for the liberal churches. After the publication of the sixth number, Mr. Norton withdrew from the work to become the librarian of Harvard College; and it was continued through two more issues by "a society of gentlemen." To this journal Mr. Norton was by far the largest contributor; but other writers were Edward Everett, and his brother, Alexander H. Everett, Joseph S. Buckminster, John T. Kirkland, Sidney Willard, George Ticknor, Washington Allston, John Lowell, Noah Worcester, and James Freeman, most of them connected with Harvard College or with the liberal churches in Boston. It is evident, however, that the liberal public was not yet ready for so aggressive and out–spoken a journal.

[Sidenote: The Christian Disciple.]

What was desired was something milder, less aggressive, of a distinctly religious and conciliatory character. To this end Drs. Channing, Charles Lowell, and Tuckerman, and Rev. S.C. Thatcher, with whom was afterwards associated Rev. Francis Parkman, planned a monthly magazine that should be liberal in its character, but not sectarian or dogmatic. They invited Rev. Noah Worcester, whose Bible News had cost him his pulpit, to remove from New Hampshire to Boston to become its editor. Although Mr. Worcester's beliefs affiliated him with the Hopkinsians in everything except his attitude in regard to the inferiority of Christ to God, yet he was compelled to withdraw from his old connections, and to find new fields of activity. He began The Christian Disciple as a religious and family magazine, the first number being issued in May, 1813. It was not designed for theological discussion or distinctly for the defence of the liberal position. Its tone was conciliatory and moderate, while it zealously defended religious liberty and charity. Its aim was practical and humanitarian, to help men live the Christian life, as individuals, and in their social relations. When it touched upon controverted questions, it was in an expository manner, with the purpose of instructing its readers, and of leading them to a higher appreciation of true religion. As his biographer well said of Noah

Worcester, he made this work "distinguished for its unqualified devotedness to the individual rights of opinion, and the sacred duty of a liberal regard to them in other men."[8]

Dr. Worcester was not so much a theologian as a philanthropist; and, if he was drawn into controversy, it was accidentally, and much to his surprise and disappointment. It was not for the sake of defending his own positions that he replied to his critics, but in the name of truth, and from an exacting sense of duty. His gentle, loving, and sympathetic nature unfitted him for intellectual contentions; and he much preferred to devote himself to philanthropies and reforms. In the briefest way The Christian Disciple reported the doings of the liberal churches and men, but it gave much space to all kinds of organizations of a humanitarian character. It advocated the temperance reform with earnestness, and this at a time when there were few other voices speaking in its behalf. It devoted many pages to the condemnation of slavery, and to the approval of all efforts to secure its mitigation or its abolition. It gave large attention to the evils of war, a subject which more and more absorbed the interest of the editor. It condemned duelling in the most emphatic terms, as it did all forms of aggressiveness and inhumanity. In spirit Dr. Worcester was as much a non-resistant as Tolstoi, and for much the same reasons. More extended reports of Bible societies were given than of any other kind of organization, and these societies especially enlisted the interest of Dr. Worcester and his associates.

With the end of 1818 Dr. Worcester withdrew from the editorship of The Christian Disciple, to devote himself to the cause of peace, the interests of Christian amity and goodwill, and the exposition of his own theological convictions. The management of the magazine came into the hands of its original proprietors, who continued its publication.

Under the new management the circulation of the magazine increased. At first the younger Henry Ware became the editor, and he carried the work through the six volumes published before it took a new name. It became more distinctly theological in its purpose, and it undertook the task of presenting and defending the views of the liberals. In 1824 The Christian Disciple passed into the hands of Rev. John Gorham Palfrey, and he changed its name to The Christian Examiner without changing its general character. At the end of two years Mr. Francis Jenks became the editor, but in 1831 it came under the control of Rev. James Walker and Rev. Francis W.P. Greenwood. Gradually it became the organ of the higher intellectual life of the Unitarians, and gave expression to their interest in literature, general culture, and the philanthropies, as well as theological knowledge. The sub–title of Theological Review, which it bore during the first five volumes, indicated its preference for subjects of speculative religious interest; but during the half–century of its best influence it was the General Review or the Religious Miscellany, showing that it was theological only in the broadest spirit.

[Sidenote: Dr. Morse and American Unitarianism.]

Reluctant as the liberal men were, to take a denominational position, and to commit themselves to the interests of a party in religion, or even to withdraw themselves in any way from the churches with which they had been connected, they were compelled to do so by the force of conditions they could not control. One of the first distinct lines of separation was caused by the refusal of the more conservative men to exchange pulpits with their liberal neighbors. This tendency first began to show itself about the year 1810; and it received a decided impetus from the attitude taken by Rev. John Codman, who in 1808 became the minister of the Second Church in Dorchester. He refused to exchange with several of the liberal ministers of the Boston Association, although he was an intimate friend of Dr. Channing, who had directed his theological training, and also preached his ordination sermon. The more liberal members of his parish attempted to compel him to exchange with the Boston ministers without regard to theological beliefs; and a long contention followed, with the result that the more liberal part of his congregation withdrew in 1813, and formed the Third Religious Society in Dorchester.[9] The withdrawal of ministerial courtesies of this kind gradually increased, especially after the controversies that began in 1815, though it was not until many years later that exchanges between the two parties ceased.

In 1815 Dr. Jedidiah Morse, the editor of The Panoplist, and the author of various school books in geography and history, published in a little book of about one hundred pages, which bore the title of American Unitarianism, a chapter from Thomas Belsham's[10] biography of Theophilus Lindsey, in which Dr. Lindsey's American correspondents, including prominent ministers in Boston and other parts of New England, had declared their Unitarianism. Morse also published an article in The Panoplist, setting forth that these ministers had not the courage of their convictions, that, while they were Unitarians, they had withheld their opinions from open utterance. His object was to force them to declare themselves, and either to retract their heresies or else to state them and to withdraw from the churches with which they had been connected. In a letter addressed to Rev. Samuel C. Thacher, Dr. Channing gave to the public a reply to these charges of insincerity and want of open–mindedness. He said that, while many of the ministers and members of their congregations were Unitarians, they did not accept Dr. Belsham's type of Unitarianism, which made Christ a man. He declared that no open declaration of Unitarianism had been made, because they were not in love with the sectarian spirit, and because they were quite unwilling to indulge in any form of proselyting. "Accustomed as we are," he wrote, "to see genuine piety in all classes of Christians, in Trinitarians and Unitarians, in Calvinists and Arminians, in Episcopalians, Methodists, Baptists, and Congregationalists, and delighting in this character wherever it appears, we are little anxious to bring men over to our peculiar opinions."[11]

The publication of Dr. Morse's book, however, gave new emphasis to the spirit of separation which was soon to compel the formation of a new denomination. It was followed four years later by Dr. Channing's Baltimore sermon and by other positive declarations of theological opinion.[12] From that time the controversy raged fiercely, and any possibility of reconciliation was removed. Before this time those who were not orthodox had called themselves Catholic, Christians or Liberal Christians to designate their attitude of toleration and liberality. The orthodox had called them Unitarians; and especially was this attempted by Dr. Morse in the introduction to his American Unitarianism, in order to fasten upon them the objectionable name given to the English liberals. It was assumed that the American liberals must agree with the English in their materialism and in their conception of Christ as a man. Dr. Channing repudiated this assumption, and declared it unjust and untrue; but he accepted the word Unitarian and gave it a meaning of his own. Channing defined the word to mean only anti–Trinitarianism; and he accepted it because it seemed to him presumptuous to use the word liberal as applied to a party, whereas it may be applicable to men of all opinions.

[Sidenote: Evangelical Missionary Society.]

Of more interest than these contentions in behalf of theological opinions is the way in which the liberal party brought itself to the task of manifesting its own purposes. Its first organizations were tentative and inclusive, without theological purpose or bias. No distinct lines were drawn, and to them belonged orthodox and liberal alike. Their sole distinguishing attitude was a catholicity of temper that permitted the free activity of the liberals. One of the first organizations of this kind was the Evangelical Missionary Society, which was formed by several of the ministers resident in Worcester and Middlesex Counties. The first meeting was held in Lancaster, November 4, 1807, when a constitution was adopted and the society elected officers. "The great object of this Society," said the constitution, "is to furnish the means of Christian knowledge and moral improvement to those inhabitants of our own country who are destitute or poorly provided." The growth of the country, even in New England (for the operations of the society were confined to that region), developed many communities in which the population was scattered, and without adequate means of education and religion. To aid these communities in securing good teachers and ministers was the purpose of the society. It refused to send forth itinerants, but carefully selected such towns as gave promise of permanent growth, and sent to them ministers instructed to organize churches and to promote the building of meeting–houses. In this way it was the means of establishing a number of churches in Maine, New Hampshire, and Massachusetts. It also sent a number of teachers into new settlements in Maine, who were successful in training many of their pupils for teaching in the public schools. In several instances minister and teacher were combined in one person, but the work was none the less effective.

In 1816 this society was incorporated, its membership was broadened to include the state, and active aid and financial support were given it by the churches in Boston and Salem. It was not sectarian, though, after its incorporation, its membership was more largely recruited from liberals. In time it became distinctly Unitarian in its character, and such it has remained to the present day. Very slowly, however, did it permit itself to lose any of its marks of catholicity and inclusiveness. In the end its membership was confined to Unitarians because no one else wished to share in its unsectarian purposes. At the present time this society does a quiet and helpful work in the way of aiding churches that have ceased to be self–supporting because of the shifting conditions of population, and in affording friendly assistance to ministers in times of distress or when old age has come upon them.

[Sidenote: The Berry Street Conference.]

The first meeting of the liberal ministers for organization was held in the vestry of the Federal Street Church[13] on the evening of May 30, 1820, which immediately preceded election day, the time when anniversary meetings were usually held. The ministers of the state then gathered in Boston to hear the election sermon, and for such counselling of each other as their congregational methods made desirable. At this meeting Dr. Channing gave an address stating the objects that had brought those present together, and the desirability of their drawing near each other as liberal men for mutual aid and support. "It was thought by some of us," he said, "that the ministers of this commonwealth who are known to agree in what are called liberal and catholic views of Christianity needed a bond of union, a means of intercourse, and an opportunity of conference not as yet enjoyed. It was thought that by meeting to join their prayers and counsels, to report the state and prospects of religion in different parts of the commonwealth, to communicate the methods of advancing it which have been found most successful, to give warning of dangers not generally apprehended, to seek advice in difficulties, and to take a broad survey of our ecclesiastical affairs and of the wants of our churches, much light, strength, comfort, animation, zeal, would be spread through our body. The individuals who originated this plan were agreed that, whilst the meeting should be confined to those who harmonize generally in opinion, it should be considered as having for its object, not simply the advancement of their peculiar views, but the general diffusion of practical religion and of the spirit of Christianity."

As this address indicates in every word of it the liberal men were sensitively anxious to put no fetters on each other; and their reluctance to circumscribe their own personal freedom was extreme. This was the cause that had thus far prevented any effectual organization, and it now withheld the members from any but the most tentative methods. Having escaped from the bondage of sect, they were suspicious of everything that in any manner gave indication of denominational restrictions.

[Sidenote: The Publishing Fund Society.]

In May, 1821, a year later than the foundation of the Berry Street Conference, several gentlemen in Boston, "desirous of promoting the circulation of works adapted to improve the public mind in religion and morality," met and established a Publishing Fund. The publishing committee then appointed consisted of Dr. Joseph Tuckerman, Dr. John Gorham Palfrey, and Mr. George Ticknor. The Publishing Fund Society refused to print doctrinal tracts or those devoted in any way to sectarian interests. The members of the society made declaration that their publications had nothing to do with any of the isms in religion. Their great object was the increase of practical goodness, the improvement of men in all that truly exalts and ennobles them or that qualifies them for usefulness and happiness. Most of their tracts were in the form of stories of a didactic character, in which the writers assumed the broad principles of Christian theology and ethics which are common to all the followers of Christ, without meddling with sectarian prejudice or party views. In such statements as these the promoters of this work indicated their methods, their aim being to furnish good reading to youth, and to those in scattered communities who could not have access to books that were instructive. Besides the tracts of this kind the society also published a series for adults, which were of a more strictly devotional character, and yet did not omit to provide entertainment and instruction.[14] This society continued its work for many years, and it issued a considerable number of tracts and books that well served the purpose for which they were designed.

[Sidenote: Harvard Divinity School.]

One important result of the theological discussions of the time was the organization of the Divinity School in connection with Harvard College. The eighteenth–century method of preparation for the ministerial office was to study with some settled pastor, who directed the reading of the student, gave him practical acquaintance with the labors of a pastor, and initiated him into the profession by securing for him the "approbation" of the ministerial association with which he was connected. Another method was for the student to continue his residence in Cambridge, and follow his theological studies under the guidance of the president and the Hollis professor, making use of the library of the college. When Rev. Henry Ware was inducted into the Hollis professorship, it was seen that some more systematic method of theological study was desirable. He gradually enlarged the scope of his activities, and in 1811 he began a systematic courser of instruction for the resident students in theology. Ware "was one of those genuine lovers of reform and progress," as John Gorham Palfrey said, "who are always ready for any innovation for the better; who, in the pursuit of what is truly good and useful, are not only content to move on with the age, but desirous to move on before it."[15] This effort of his to improve the methods of theological study proved to be the germ of the existing Divinity School.

The Hollis professorship of divinity was founded by Thomas Hollis, of London, in 1721. Samuel Dexter, of Boston, established a lectureship of Biblical criticism in 1811. Both the professorship and the lectureship were designed for the undergraduates, and not primarily for students in theology. In 1815, however, it became apparent to some of the liberals that a school wholly devoted to the preparation of young men for the ministry was needed.

Those who subscribed to the $30,000 secured for this purpose were in 1816 formed into the Society for the Promotion of Theological Education in Harvard University. This society rendered efficient aid to the school for several years. At a meeting held at the Boston Athenaeum, July 17, 1816, Rev. John T. Kirkland became its president, Rev. Francis Parkman, recording secretary, Rev. Charles Lowell, corresponding secretary, and Jonathan Phillips, treasurer. The society was supported by annual subscriptions, life subscriptions, and donations. The school began its work in 1816, with Rev. Andrews Norton as the Dexter lecturer on Biblical criticism, Rev. J.T. Kirkland as instructor in systematic theology, Rev. Edward Everett in the criticism of the Septaugint, Professor Sidney Willard in Hebrew, and Professor Levi Frisbie in ethics. In 1819 Mr. Norton was advanced to a professorship, and thereafter devoted his whole time to the school; and during that year the school was divided into three classes. In 1824 the Society for the Promotion of Theological Education took the general direction of the school, arranging the course of study and otherwise assuming a supervision, which continued until 1831, when the school received a place as one of the departments of the University. In 1826 a building was erected for the school by the society, which has borne the name of Divinity Hall. In 1828 a professorship of pulpit eloquence and pastoral care was established by the society, and in 1830 the younger Henry Ware entered upon its duties.[16] He was succeeded in 1842 by Rev. Convers Francis. In 1830 Rev. John Gorham Palfrey became the professor of Biblical literature, and soon after the instructor in Hebrew. Rev. George Rapall Noyes, in 1840, took the Hancock professorship of Hebrew and the Dexter lectureship in Biblical criticism.

Though organized and conducted by the Unitarians, the Divinity School was from the first unsectarian in its purpose and methods; for the Society for the Promotion of Theological Education, on its organization, put into its constitution this fundamental law: "It being understood that every encouragement be given to the serious, impartial and unbiassed investigation of Christian truth, and that no assent to the peculiarities of any denomination, be required either of the students or professors or instructors."

[Sidenote: The Unitarian Miscellany.]

The first outspoken periodical on the liberal side that aimed at being distinctly denominational was published in Baltimore. Dr. Freeman preached in that city in 1816, with the result that during the following year a church was organized there. It was there in 1819, on the occasion of the ordination of Rev. Jared Sparks as the first minister of this church, that Dr. Channing gave utterance to the first great declaration of the Unitarian position, in a sermon that has never been surpassed in this country as an intellectual interpretation of the highest spiritual problems.

In January, 1821, Rev. Jared Sparks began the publication in Baltimore of The Unitarian Miscellany and Christian Monitor; and for three years he was its editor. For another three years it was conducted by his successor in the Baltimore pulpit, Rev. Francis W.P. Greenwood, who continued it until he became the minister of King's Chapel, when it ceased to exist. During the six years of its publication this magazine was ably edited. It was controversial in a liberal spirit, it was positively denominational, and it had a large and widely extended circulation. It reported all prominent Unitarian events, and those of a liberal tendency in all religious bodies. Attacks on Unitarianism were repelled, and the Unitarian position was explained and vindicated. Mr. Sparks was as aggressive as Andrews Norton had been, and was by no means willing to keep to the quiet and reticent manner of the Unitarians of Boston. When he was attacked, he replied with energy and skill; and he carried the war into the enemies' camp. His magazine was far more positive than anything the liberals had hitherto put forth, and its methods were viewed with something of suspicion in the conservative circles of Massachusetts. He published a series of letters on the Episcopal Church in The Unitarian Miscellany, which he enlarged and put into a book.[17] Another series of letters was on the comparative moral tendencies of Trinitarian and Unitarian doctrines, and these grew into a volume.[18] Both were in reply to attacks made upon him, and both were regarded with suspicion and doubt by the men about Cambridge; but, in time, they came to see that his method was sincere, learned, and honest.

In The Unitarian Miscellany, as in all their utterances of this time, the Unitarians manifested much anxiety to maintain their position as the true expounders of primitive Christianity. They did not covet a place outside the larger fellowship of the Christian faith. A favorite method of vindicating their right to Christian recognition was by the publication of the works of liberal orthodox writers of previous generations. Such an attempt was made by Jared Sparks in his Collection of Essays and Tracts in Theology, with Biographical and Critical Notices, issued in Boston from 1823 to 1826. In the general preface to these six volumes, Mr. Sparks said that "the only undeviating rule of selection will be that every article chosen shall be marked with rational and liberal views of Christianity, and suited to inform the mind or improve the temper and practice," and that the series was "designed to promote the cause of sacred learning, of truth and charity, of religious freedom and rational piety." In the first volume were included Turretin's essay on the fundamentals of religious truth, a number of short essays by Firmin Abauzit,

Francis Blackburne's discussion of the value of confessions of faith, and several essays by Bishop Hoadley. That these writings have now no significance, even to intelligent readers, does not detract from the value of their publication; for they had a living meaning and power. Other writers, drawn upon in the succeeding volumes were Isaac Newton, Jeremy Taylor, John Locke, Isaac Watts, William Penn, and Mrs. Barbauld. The catholicity of the editor was shown in the wide range of his authors, whose doctrinal connections covered the whole field of Christian theology.

In the publication of The Unitarian Miscellany, Mr. Sparks had the business aid of the Baltimore Unitarian Book Society, formed November 19, 1820, which was organized to carry on this work, and to disseminate other liberal books and tracts. This society distributed Bibles, "and such other books as contain rational and consistent views of Christian doctrines, and are calculated to promote a correct faith, sincere piety, and a holy practice." In the year 1821 was formed the Unitarian Library and Tract Society of New York; and similar societies were started in Philadelphia and Charleston soon after, as well as in other cities. Some of these societies published books, tracts, and periodicals, all of them distributed Unitarian publications, and libraries were formed of liberal works. The most successful of these societies, which soon numbered a score or two, was that in Baltimore. This society extended its missionary operations with the printed page widely, sending tracts into every part of the country, the demand for them having become very large. Its periodical had an extended circulation, its cheapness, its popular character, and its outspoken attitude on doctrinal questions serving to make it the most successful of the liberal publications of the time.[19]

[Sidenote: The Christian Register.]

On April 20, 1821, was issued the first number of The Christian Register, the regular weekly publication of which began with August 24 of that year. Its four pages contained four columns each, but the third of these pages was given to secular news and advertisements. The first page was devoted to general religious subjects, the second discussed those topics which were of special interest to Unitarians, while the fourth was given to literary miscellanies. Almost nothing of church news was reported, and only in a limited way was the paper denominational. It was a general religious newspaper of a kind that was acceptable to the liberals, and it defended and interpreted their cause when occasion demanded. The paper was started wholly as an individual enterprise by its publisher, Rev. David Reed, who acted for about five years as its editor. He had the encouragement of the leading Unitarians of Boston and its vicinity; and, when such men as Channing, Ware, and Norton wished to speak for the Unitarians, its columns were open to them. Among the other early contributors were Kirkland, Story, Edward Everett, Walker, Dewey, Furness, Palfrey, Gannett, Noah Worcester, Greenwood, Bancroft, Sparks, Alexander Young, Freeman, Burnap, Pierpont, Noyes, Lowell, Frothingham, and Pierce.

In his prospectus the publisher spoke of the growth of the spirit of free religious inquiry in the country; and he said that in all classes of the community there was an eagerness to understand theological questions, and to arrive at and practice the genuine principles of Christianity. His ideal was a periodical that should present the same doctrines and temper as The Christian Disciple, but that would be of a more popular character. "The great object of The Christian Register," he said to his readers, "will be to inculcate the principles of a rational faith, and to promote the practice of genuine piety. To accomplish this purpose it will aim to excite a spirit of free and independent religious inquiry, and to assist in ascertaining and bringing into use the true principles of interpreting the Scriptures."

For a number of years The Christian Register conformed to "the mild and amiable spirit" in which it began its career, rarely being aroused to an aggressive attitude, and seldom undertaking to speak for Unitarianism as a distinct form of Christianity. When the liberals were fiercely attacked, it spoke out, as, for instance, at the time when the Unitarians were charged with stealing churches from the orthodox.[20] Otherwise it was mild and placid enough, given to expressing its friendly interest in every kind of reform, from the education of women to the emancipation of slaves, thoroughly humanitarian in its attitude, not doctrinal or controversial, but faithfully catholic and tolerant. It was a well–conducted periodical, represented a wide range of interests, and was admirably suited to interpret the temper and spirit of a rational religion. It is now the oldest weekly religious newspaper published in this country. As the leading Unitarian periodical, it is still conducted with notable enterprise and ability.

Another periodical also deserves mention in this connection, and that is the North American Review, which was begun by William Tudor, one of the members of The Anthology Club, in May, 1815. While it was not religious in its character, it was from the first, and for more than sixty years, edited by Unitarians; and its contributors were very largely from that religious body. The same tendencies and conditions that led the liberals to establish The Monthly Anthology, The Christian Disciple, and The Christian Examiner, gave demand amongst them for a distinctly literary and critical journal. They had gained that form of liberated and catholic culture which made such works possible, and to a large extent they afforded the public necessary to their support. Mr. Tudor was succeeded as the editor of the review by Professor Edward T. Channing, and then followed in succession Edward Everett, Jared Sparks, Alexander H. Everett, John Gorham Palfrey, Francis Bowen, and Andrew P. Peabody, all Unitarians. Among the early Unitarian contributors were Nathan Hale, Joseph Story, Nathaniel Bowditch, W.H. Prescott, William Cullen Bryant, and Theophilus Parsons. For many years few of the regular contributors were from any other religious body, not because the editors put restrictions upon others, but because those who were interested in general literary, historical, and scientific subjects belonged almost exclusively to the churches of this faith.

[Sidenote: Results of the Division in Congregationalism.]

The controversy which began in 1805 continued for about twenty years. The pamphlets and books it brought forth are almost forgotten, and they would have little interest at the present time. They gradually widened the breach between the orthodox and the liberal Congregationalists. It would be difficult to name a decisive date for their actual separation. The organization of the societies, and the establishment of the periodicals already mentioned, were successive steps to that result. The most important event was undoubtedly the formation of the American Unitarian Association, in 1825; but even that important movement on the part of the Unitarians did not bring about a final separation. Individual churches and ministers continued to treat each other with the same courtesy and hospitality as before.

That the breach was inevitable seems to be the verdict of history; and yet it is not difficult to see to–day how it might have been avoided. The Unitarians were dealt with in such a manner that they could not continue the old connection without great discomfort and loss of self–respect. They were forced to organize for self–protection, and yet they did so reluctantly and with much misgiving. They would have preferred to remain as members of the united Congregational body, but the theological temper of the time made this impossible. It would not be just to say that there was actual persecution, but there could not be unity where there was not community of thought and faith.

When the division in the Congregational churches came, one hundred and twenty–five churches allied themselves with the Unitarians,—one hundred in Massachusetts, a score in other parts of New England, and a half–dozen west of the Hudson River. These churches numbered among them, however, many of the oldest and the strongest, including about twenty of the first twenty–five organized in Massachusetts, and among them Plymouth (organized in Scrooby), Salem, Dorchester, Boston, Watertown, Roxbury, Hingham, Concord, and Quincy. The ten Congregational churches in Boston, with the exception of the Old South, allied themselves with the Unitarians. Other first churches to take this action were those of Portsmouth, Kennebunk, and Portland.

Outside New England a beginning was made almost as soon as the Unitarian name came into recognition. At Charleston, S.C., the Congregational church, which had been very liberal, was divided in 1816 as the result of the preaching of Rev. Anthony Forster. He was led to read the works of Dr. Priestley, and became a Unitarian in consequence. Owing to ill–health, he was soon obliged to resign; and Rev. Samuel Gilman was installed in 1819. Rev. Robert Little, an English Unitarian, took up his residence in Washington in 1819, and began to preach there; and a church was organized in 1821. While chaplain of the House of Representatives, in 1821–22, Jared Sparks preached to this society fortnightly, and in the House Chamber on the alternate Sunday. When he went to Charleston, in 1819, to assist in the installation of Mr. Gilman, he preached to a very large congregation in the state–house in Raleigh; and the next year he spoke to large congregations in Virginia.[21] More than a decade earlier there were individual Unitarians in Kentucky.[22] On his journey to the ordination of Jared Sparks, Dr. Channing preached in a New York parlor; and on his return he occupied the lecture–hall of the Medical School. The result was the First Congregational Church (All Souls'), organized in 1819, which was followed by the Church of the Messiah in 1825. In fact, many of the more intelligent and thoughtful persons everywhere were inclined to accept a liberal interpretation of Christianity.

Although the Congregational body was divided into two distinct denominations, there were three organizations, formed prior to that event, which have remained intact to this day. In these societies Orthodox and Unitarian continue to unite as Congregationalists, and the sectarian lines are not recognized. The first of these organizations is the Massachusetts Congregational Charitable Society, which was formed early in the eighteenth century for the purpose of securing "support to the widows and children of deceased congregational ministers." The second is the Massachusetts Convention of

Congregational Ministers, also formed early in the eighteenth century, although its records begin only with the year 1748. It was formed for consultation, advice, and counsel, to aid orphans and widows of ministers, and to secure the general promotion of the interests of religion. The convention sermon has been one of the recognized institutions of Massachusetts, and since the beginning of the Unitarian controversy it has been preached alternately by ministers of the two denominations. The Society for Propagating the Gospel among the Indians and Others in North America was formed in 1787. The members, officers, and missionaries of this society have been of both denominations; and the work accomplished has been carried on in a spirit of amity and good–will. These societies indicate that co–operation may be secured without theological unity, and it is possible that they may become the basis in the future of a closer sympathy and fellowship between the severed Congregational churches.

[Sidenote: Final Separation of State and Church.]

From the beginning the liberal movement had been more or less intimately associated with that for the promotion of religious freedom and the separation of state and church. Many of the states withdrew religion from state control on the adoption of the Federal Constitution. In New England this was done in the first years of the century. Connecticut came to this result after an exciting agitation in 1818. Massachusetts was more tenacious of the old ways; but in 1811 its legislative body passed a "religious freedom act," that secured individuals from taxation for the support of churches with which they were not connected. The constitutional convention of 1820 proposed a bill of rights that aimed to secure religious freedom, but it was defeated by large majorities. It was only when church property was given by the courts to the parish in preference to the church, and when the "standing order" churches had been repeatedly foiled in their efforts to retain the old prerogatives, that a majority could be secured for religious freedom. In November, 1833, the legislature submitted to the people a revision of the bill of rights, which provided for the separation of state and church, and the voluntary support of churches. A majority was secured for this amendment, and it became the law in 1834. Massachusetts was the last of all the states to arrive at this result, and a far greater effort was required to bring it about than elsewhere. The support of the churches was now purely voluntary, the state no longer lending its aid to tax person and property for their maintenance.

Thus it came about that Massachusetts adopted the principle and method of Roger Williams after two centuries. For the first time she came to the full recognition of her own democratic ideals, and to the practical acceptance of the individualism for which she had contended from the beginning. She had fought stubbornly and zealously for the faith she prized above all other things, but by the logic of events and the greatness of the principle of liberty she was conquered. The minister and the meeting–house were by her so dearly loved that she could not endure the thought of having them shorn of any of their power and influence; but for the sake of their true life she at last found it wise and just to leave all the people free to worship God in their own way, without coercion and without restraint.

Although the liberal ministers and churches led the way in securing religious freedom, yet they were socially and intellectually conservative. Radical changes they would not accept, and they moved away from the old beliefs with great caution. The charge that they were timid was undoubtedly true, though there is no evidence that they attempted to conceal their real beliefs. Evangelical enthusiasm was not congenial to them, and they rejected fanaticism in every form. They had a deep, serious, and spiritual faith, that was intellectual without being rationalistic, marked by strong common sense, and vigorous with moral integrity. They permitted a wide latitude of opinion, and yet they were thoroughly Christian in their convictions. Most of them saw in the miracles of the New Testament the only positive evidence of the truth of Christianity, which was to them an external and supernatural revelation. They were quite willing to follow Andrews Norton, however, who was the chief defender of the miraculous, in his free criticism of the Old Testament and the birth–stories in the Gospels.

The liberal ministers fostered an intellectual and literary expression of religion, and yet their chief characteristic was their spirituality. They aimed at ethical insight and moral integrity in their influence upon men and women, and at cultivating purity of life and an inward probity. In large degree they developed the spirit of philanthropy and a fine regard for the rights and the welfare of others. They were not sectarian or zealous for bringing others to the acceptance of their own beliefs; but they were generous in behalf of all public interests, faithful to all civic duties, and known for their private generosity and faithful Christian living. Under the leadership of Dr. Channing the Catholic Christians, as they preferred to call themselves, cultivated a spirituality that was devout without being ritualistic, sincere without being fanatical. The churches around them, to a large degree, kept zealously to the externals of religion, and accepted physical evidences of the truthfulness of Christianity; but Channing sought for what is deeper and more permanent. His preference of rationality to the testimony of miracles, spiritual insight to external evidences, devoutness of life to the rites of the church, characterized him as a great religious leader, and developed for the Catholic Christians a new type of Christianity. Whatever Channing's limitations as a thinker and a reformer, he was a man of prophetic insight and lofty spiritual vision. In other ages he would have been canonized as a saint or called the beatific doctor; but in Boston he was a heretic and a reformer, who sought to lead men into a faith that is ethical, sincere, and humanitarian. He prized Christianity for what it is in itself, for its inwardness, its fidelity to human nature, and its ethical integrity. His mind was always open to truth, he was always young for liberty, and his soul dwelt in the serene atmosphere of a pure and lofty faith.

[1] Josiah Quincy, History of Harvard University, I. 230, Chapter XII; Christian Examiner, VII. 64; XXX. 70.

[2] Jedidiah Morse, True Reasons on which the Election of a Hollis Professor of Divinity in Harvard College were opposed at the Board of Overseers.

[3] III. 251, March, 1806.

[4] Richard Eddy, Universalism in America, II. 87; Oscar F. Safford, Hosea Ballou: A Marvellous Life Story, 71.

[5] O.B. Frothingham, Boston Unitarianism, 161.

[6] Josiah Quincy, History of the Boston Athenaeum, 1. "In the year 1803 Phineas Adams, a graduate of Harvard College, of the class of 1801, commenced in Boston, under the name of *Sylvanus Per−se*, a periodical work entitled The Monthly Anthology or Magazine of Polite Literature. He conducted it for six months, but not finding its proceeds sufficient for his support, he abandoned the undertaking. Mr. Adams, the son of a farmer in Lexington, manifested in early boyhood a passion for elegant learning. He adopted literature as a profession; but, after the failure of his attempt as editor of The Anthology, he taught school in different places, till, in 1811, he entered the Navy as chaplain and teacher of mathematics. Here he became distinguished for mathematical science in its relation to nautical affairs. In 1812 he accompanied

Commodore Porter in his eventful cruise in the Pacific, of which the published journal bears honorable testimony to Mr. Adams's zeal for promoting geographical and mathematical knowledge. He again joined Porter in the expedition for the suppression of piracy in the West Indies, and he died on that station in 1823, much respected in the service."

[7] In October, 1888, this society gave up its organization, and the sum of $1,265.10 was given to the American Unitarian Association for the establishment of a publishing fund.

[8] Unitarian Biography, I. 40, Memoir by Henry Ware, Jr.

[9] William Allen, Memoir of John Codman, 81.

[10] Thomas Belsham, 1750–1829, was a dissenting English preacher and teacher. In 1789 he became a Unitarian, and was settled in Birmingham. From 1805 to his death he preached to the Essex Street congregation in London. He wrote a popular work on the Evidences of Christianity, and he translated the Epistles of St. Paul. He was a vigorous and able writer.

[11] Memoir of W.E. Channing, by W.H. Channing, I. 380.

[12] Among the controversial works printed in Boston at this time was Yates's Vindication of Unitarianism, an English book, which was republished in 1816.

[13] The entrance to the vestry of Federal Street Church was on Berry Street, hence the name given the conference.

[14] Christian Examiner, I. 248.

[15] American Unitarian Biography, Life of Henry Ware, I. 241.

[16] James Walker, Christian Examiner, X. 129; John G. Palfrey, Christian Examiner, XI. 84; The Divinity School of Harvard University: Its History, Courses of Study, Aims and Advantages.

[17] Letters on the Ministry, Ritual, and Doctrines of the Protestant Episcopal Church, addressed to Rev. William E. Wyatt, D.D., in Reply to a Sermon, Baltimore, 1820.

[18] Comparative Moral Tendency of Trinitarian and Unitarian Doctrines, addressed to Rev. Samuel Miller, Boston, 1823.

[19] H.B. Adams, Life and Writings of Jared Sparks, I. 175.

[20] Dr. George E. Ellis, in Unitarianism: Its origin and History, 147. The most prominent instance was that of the First Church in Dedham, and this was decided by legal proceedings. "The question recognized by the court was simply this: whether the claimants had been lawfully appointed deacons of the First Church; that is, whether the body which had appointed them was by law the First Church. The decision of the court was as follows: 'When the majority of the members of a Congregational church separate from the majority of the parish, the members who remain, although a minority, constitute the church in such parish, and retain the rights and property belonging thereto.' This legal decision would have been regarded as a momentous one had it applied only to the single case then in hearing. But it was the establishment of a precedent which would dispose of all cases then to be expected to present themselves in the troubles of the time between parishes and the churches gathered within them. The full purport of this decision was that the law did not recognize a church independently of its connection with the parish in which it was gathered, from which it might sever itself and carry property with it." It was in accordance with the practice in New England for at least a century preceding the decision in the Dedham case, and the decision was rendered as the result of this practice.

[21] H.B. Adams, Life and Writings of Jared Sparks, gives a most interesting account in his earlier chapters of the origin of Unitarianism, especially of its beginnings in Baltimore and other places outside New England.

[22] James Garrard, governor of Kentucky from 1796 to 1802, was a Unitarian. Harry Toulmin, president of Transylvania Seminary and secretary of the state of Kentucky, was also a Unitarian.

VI. THE AMERICAN UNITARIAN ASSOCIATION.

The time had come for the liberals to organize in a more distinctive form, in order that they might secure permanently the results they had already attained. The demand for organization, however, came almost wholly from the younger men, those who had grown up under the influence of the freer life of the liberal churches or who had been trained in the independent spirit of the Divinity School at Harvard. The older men, for the most part, were bound by the traditions of "the standing order":[1] they could not bring themselves to desire new conditions and new methods.

The spirit of the older and leading laymen and ministers is admirably illustrated in Rev. O.B. Frothingham's account of his father in his book entitled Boston Unitarianism. They were interested in many, public–spirited enterprises, and the social circle in which they moved was cultivated and refined; but they were provincial, and little inclined to look beyond the limits of their own immediate interests. Dr. Nathaniel L. Frothingham, minister of the First Church in Boston, one of the earliest American students of German literature and philosophy, and a man of rational insight and progressive thinking, may be regarded as a representative of the best type of Boston minister in the first half of the nineteenth century. In a sermon preached in 1835, on the occasion of the twentieth anniversary of his settlement, Dr. Frothingham said that he had never before used the word "Unitarian", in his pulpit, though his church had been for thirty years counted as Unitarian. "We have," he said, "made more account of the religious sentiment than of theological opinions." In this attitude he was in harmony with the leading men of his day.[2]

Channing, for instance, was opposed to every phase of religious organization that put bonds upon men; and he would accept nothing in the form of a creed. He severely condemned "the guilt of a sectarian spirit," and said that "to bestow our affections on those who are ranged under the same human leader, or who belong to the same church with ourselves, and to withhold it from others who possess equal if not superior virtue, because they bear a different name, is to prefer a party to the church of Christ."[3] In 1831 he described Unitarianism as being "characterized by nothing more than by the spirit of freedom and individuality. It has no established creed or symbol," he wrote. "Its friends think each for himself, and differ much from each other."[4] Later he wrote to a friend: "I distrust sectarian influence more and more. I am more detached from a denomination, and strive to feel more my connection with the Universal Church, with all good and holy men. I am little of a Unitarian, and stand aloof from all but those who strive and pray for clearer light, who look for a purer and more effectual manifestation of Christian truth."[5]

Many of the Unitarians were in fullest sympathy with Channing as to the fundamental law of spiritual freedom and as to the evils of sectarianism. A considerable number of them were in agreement with him as to the course pursued by the Unitarian movement. Having escaped from one sect, they were not ready to commit themselves to the control of another. Therefore they withheld themselves from all definitely organized phases of Unitarianism, and would give no active support to those who sought to bring the liberals together for purposes of protection and forward movement. Under these circumstances it was difficult to secure concert of action or to make successful any definite missionary enterprise, however little of sectarianism it might manifest. Even to the present time Unitarianism has shown this independence on the part of local churches and this freedom on the part of individuals. Because of this attitude, unity of action has been difficult, and denominational loyalty never strong or assured.

However, a different spirit animated the younger men, who persisted in their effort to secure an organization that would represent distinctively the Unitarian thought and sentiment. The movement towards organization had its origin and impulse in a group of young ministers who had been trained at the Harvard Divinity School under Professor Andrews Norton. While Norton was conservative in theology and opposed to sectarian measures, his teaching was radical, progressive, and stimulating. His students accepted his spirit of intellectual progress, and often advanced beyond his more conservative teachings. In the years between 1817 and 1824 James Walker, John G. Palfrey, Jared Sparks, Alexander Young, John Pierpont, Ezra S. Gannett, Samuel Barrett, Thomas R.

Sullivan, Samuel J. May, Calvin Lincoln, and Edward B. Hall were students in the Divinity School; and all of these men were leaders in the movement to organize a Unitarian Association. Pierpont gave the name to the new organization, distinctly defining it as Unitarian. Gannett, Palfrey, and Hall served it as presidents; Gannett, Lincoln, and Young, as secretaries. Walker, Palfrey, and Barrett gave it faithful service as directors, and Lincoln as its active missionary agent. A number of young laymen in Boston and elsewhere, mostly graduates of Harvard College, were also interested in the formation of the new organization. Among them were Charles G. Loring, Robert Rantoul, Samuel A. Eliot, Leverett Salstonstall, George B. Emerson, and Alden Bradford. All these young men were afterwards prominent in the affairs of the city or state, and they were faithful to the interests of the Unitarian churches with which they were connected.

[Sidenote: Initial Meetings.]

The first proposition to form a Unitarian organization for missionary purposes was made in a meeting of the Anonymous Association, a club to which belonged thirty or forty of the leading men of Boston. They were all connected with Unitarian churches, and were actively interested in promoting the growth of a liberal form of Christianity. It appears from the journal of David Reed, for many years the editor and publisher of The Christian Register, that the members of this association were in the habit of meeting at each other's houses during the year 1824 for the purpose of discussing important subjects connected with religion, morals, and politics. At a meeting held at the house of Hon. Josiah Quincy in the autumn of that year, attention was called to certain articles that had been published in The Christian Register, and the importance was suggested of promoting the growth of liberal Christianity through the distribution of the printed word. A resolution was submitted, inquiring if measures could not be taken for uniting the efforts of liberal–minded persons to give greater efficiency to the attempt to extend a knowledge of Unitarian principles by means of the public press; and a committee was appointed to consider and report on the expediency of forming an organization for this purpose. This committee consisted of Rev. Henry Ware, the younger, Alden Bradford, and Richard Sullivan. Henry Ware was the beloved and devoted minister of the Second Church in Boston. His colleagues were older men, both graduates of Harvard College and prominent in the social and business life of Boston. The purpose which these men had in mind was well defined by Dr. Gannett, writing twenty years after the event: "We found ourselves," he said, "under the painful necessity of contributing our assistance to the propagation of tenets which we accounted false or of forming an association through which we might address the great truths of religion to our fellow–men without the adulteration of erroneous dogmas. To take one of these courses, or to do nothing in the way of Christian beneficence, was the only alternative permitted to us. The name which we adopted has a sectarian sound; but it was chosen to avoid equivocation on the one hand and misapprehension on the other."[6] The committee, under date of December 29, 1824, sent out a circular inviting a meeting of all interested, "in order to confer together on the expediency of appointing an annual meeting for the purpose of union, sympathy, and co–operation in the cause of Christian truth and Christian charity." In this circular will be found the origin of the clause in the present constitution of the Unitarian Association defining its purposes.

In response to this call a meeting was held in the vestry of the Federal Street Church on January 27, 1825. Dr. Channing opened the meeting with prayer. Richard Sullivan was chosen moderator, and James Walker secretary. There were present all those who have been hitherto named in connection with this movement, together with many others of the leading laymen and ministers of the liberal churches in New England.[7] The record of the meeting made by Rev. James Walker is preserved in the first volume of the correspondence of the Unitarian Association; and it enables us, in connection with the more confidential reminiscences of David Reed, to give a fairly complete record of, what was said and done. Henry Ware, the younger, in behalf of the committee, presented a statement of the objects proposed by those desirous of organizing a national Unitarian society; and he offered a resolution declaring it "desirable and expedient that provision should be made for future meetings of Unitarians and liberal Christians generally." The adoption of this resolution was moved by Stephen Higginson; and the discussion was opened by Dr. Aaron Bancroft, the learned and honored minister of the Second Church in Worcester. He was fearful that sufficient care might not be taken as to the manner of instituting the proposed organization, and he doubted its expediency. He was of the opinion that Unitarianism was to be propagated slowly and silently, for it had succeeded in his own parish because it had not been openly advocated. He did not wish to oppose the design generally, but he was convinced that it would do more harm than good.

Dr. Bancroft was followed by Professor Andrews Norton, the greatly respected teacher of most of the younger ministers, who defended the proposed organization, and said that its purpose was not to make proselytes. Then Dr. Charming arose, and gave to the proposition of the committee a guarded approval. He thought the object of the convention, as he wished to call it, should be to "spread our views of religion, not our mere opinions, for our religion is essentially practical." The friendly attitude of Channing gave added emphasis to the disapproval of the prominent laymen who spoke after him. Judge Charles Jackson, an eminent justice of the Supreme Court of Massachusetts, thought there was danger in the proposed plan, that it was not becoming to liberal Christians, that it, was inconsistent with their principles, and that it would not be beneficial to the community. He was ready to give his aid, to any specific work, but he thought that everything could be accomplished that was necessary, without a general–association of any kind. The same opinion was expressed by George Bond, a leading merchant of Boston, who was afraid that Unitarianism would become popular, and that, when it had gamed a majority of the people of the country to its side, it would become as intolerant as the other sects. For this reason he believed the measure inexpedient, and moved an adjournment of the meeting.

Three of the most widely known and respected of the older ministers also spoke in opposition to the proposition to form an association of liberal Christians. These men were typical pastors and preachers, whose parishes were limited only by the town in which they lived, and who preached the gospel without sectarian prejudice or doctrinal qualifications. Dr. John Pierce, of Brookline, thought the measure of the committee "very dangerous," and likely to do much harm in many of the parishes by arousing the sectarian spirit. He spoke three times in the course of the meeting, opposing with his accustomed vehemence all attempt at organization. Dr. Abiel Abbot, of Beverly, thought that presenting a distinct object for opposition would arrest the progress of Unitarianism, for in his neighborhood liberal Christianity owed everything to slow and silent progress. Dr. John Allyn, of Duxbury, one of the most original and learned ministers of his time in New England, was opposed to the use of any sectarian name, especially that of Unitarian or Liberal. He was willing to join in a general convention, and he desired to have a meeting of delegates from all sects. He expressed the opinion of several leading men who were present at this meeting, who favored an unsectarian organization, that should include all men of liberal opinions, of whatever name or denominational connection.

Those who were in favor of a Unitarian Association did not remain silent, and they spoke with clearness and vigor in approval of the proposition of the committee. Alden Bradford, who became the Secretary of State in Massachusetts, and wrote several valuable biographical and historical works, thought that Unitarians were too timid and did not wisely defend their position. He was followed by Andrews Norton in a vigorous declaration of the importance of the association, in the course of which he pointed out how inadequately Unitarians had protected and fostered the institutions under their care, and declared that closer union was necessary. Jared Sparks also earnestly favored the project, and said that what was proposed was not a plan of proselyting. It was his opinion that Unitarians ought to come forward in support of their views of truth, and that an association was necessary in order to promote sympathy among them throughout the country. Colonel Joseph May, who had been for thirty years a warden of King's Chapel, and a man held in high esteem in Boston, referred to the work already accomplished by the zeal and effort of the few Unitarians who had worked together to promote liberal interests. The most incisive word spoken, however, came from John Pierpont, who was just coming into his fame as an orator and a leader in reforms. "We have," he declared, "and we must have, the name Unitarian. It is not for us to shrink from it. Organization is necessary in order to maintain it, and organization there must be. The general interests of Unitarians will be promoted by using the name, and organizing in harmony with it."

In the long discussion at this meeting it appears that, of the ministers, Channing, Norton, Bancroft, Ware, Pierpont, Sparks, Edes, Nichols, Parker, Thayer, Willard, and Harding were in favor of organization; Pierce, Allyn, Abbot, Freeman, and Bigelow, against it. Of the laymen, Charles Jackson and George Bond were vigorously in opposition; and Judge Story, Judge White, Judge Howe, of Northampton, Alden Bradford, Leverett Salstonstall, Stephen Higginson, and Joseph May spoke in favor. The result of the meeting was the appointment of a committee, consisting of Sullivan, Bradford, Ware, Channing, Palfrey, Walker, Pierpont, and Higginson, which was empowered to call together a larger meeting at some time during the session of the General Court. But this committee seems never to have acted. At the end of his report of this preliminary meeting James Walker wrote: "The meeting proposed was never called. As there appeared to be so much difference of opinion as to the expediency and nature of the measure proposed, it was thought best to let it subside in silence."

The zeal of those favorable to organization, however, did not abate; and the discussion went on throughout the winter. On May 25, 1825, at the meeting of the Berry Street Conference of Ministers, Henry Ware, the younger, who had been chairman of the first committee, renewed the effort, and presented the following statement as a declaration of the purposes of the proposed organization:—

It is proposed to form a new association, to be called The American
Unitarian Society. The chief and ultimate object will be the promotion

of pure and undefiled religion by disseminating the knowledge of it where adequate means of religious instruction are not enjoyed. A secondary good which will follow from it is the union of all Unitarian Christians in this country, so that they would become mutually acquainted, and the concentration of their efforts would increase their efficiency. The society will embrace all Unitarian Christians in the United States. Its operations would extend themselves through the whole country. These operations would chiefly consist in the publication and distribution of tracts, and the support of missionaries.

It was announced that in the afternoon a meeting would be held for the further consideration of the subject. This meeting was held at four o'clock, and Dr. Henry Ware acted as moderator. The opponents of organization probably absented themselves, for action was promptly taken, and it was "*Voted*, that it is expedient to form a new society to be called the American Unitarian Association." All who were present expressed themselves as in favor of this action. Rev. James Walker, Mr. Lewis Tappan, and Rev. Ezra S. Gannett were appointed a committee to draft a form of organization. On the next morning, Thursday, May 26, 1825, this committee reported to a meeting, of which Dr. Nathaniel Thayer, of Lancaster, was moderator; and, with one or two amendments, the constitution prepared by the committee was adopted. This constitution, with slight modifications, is still in force. The object of the Association was declared to be "to diffuse the knowledge and promote the interests of pure Christianity." A committee to nominate officers selected Dr. Channing for president; Joseph Story, of Salem, Joseph Lyman, of Northampton, Stephen Longfellow, of Portland, Charles H. Atherton, of Amherst, N.H., Henry Wheaton, of New York, James Taylor, of Philadelphia, Henry Payson, of Baltimore, William Cranch, of Alexandria, Martin L. Hurlbut, of Charleston, as vice–presidents; Ezra S. Gannett, of Boston, for secretary; Lewis Tappan, of Boston, for treasurer; and Andrews Norton, Jared Sparks, and James Walker, for executive committee.

When Mr. Gannett wrote to his colleague, Dr. Channing, to notify him of his election as president, there came a letter declining the proffered office. "I was a little disappointed," Channing wrote, "at learning that the Unitarian Association is to commence operations immediately. I conversed with Mr. Norton on the subject before leaving Boston, and found him so indisposed to engage in it that I imagined that it would be let alone for the present. The office which in your kindness you have assigned to me I must beg to decline. As you have made a beginning, I truly rejoice in your success." Norton and Sparks also declined to serve as directors, ill–health and previous engagements being assigned by them for their inability to act with the other officers elected. The executive committee proceeded to fill these vacancies by the election of Dr. Aaron Bancroft, of Worcester, as president, and of the younger Henry Ware and Samuel Barrett to the executive committee; and the board of directors thus constituted administered the Association during its first year.

In the selection of Dr. Bancroft as the head of the new association a wise choice was made, for he had the executive and organizing ability that was eminently desirable at this juncture. He was an able preacher, and one of the strongest thinkers in the Unitarian body. His biography of Washington had made him widely known; and his volume of controversial sermons, published in 1822, had received the enthusiastic praise of John Adams and Thomas Jefferson. When he was settled, he was almost an outcast in Worcester County because of his liberalism; but such were the strength of his character and the power of his thought that gradually he secured a wide hearing, and became the most popular preacher in Central Massachusetts. After fifty years of his ministry he could count twenty–one vigorous Unitarian societies about him, all of which had profited by his influence.[8] Although he was seventy years of age at the time he accepted the presidency of the Unitarian Association, he was in the full enjoyment of his powers; and he filled the office for ten years, giving it and the cause which the Association represented the impetus and weight of his sound judgment and deserved reputation.

The executive work of the Association fell to the charge of the secretary, Ezra S. Gannett, who had been one of the most enthusiastic advocates of the new organization. Gannett was but twenty–four years old, and had been but one year in the active ministry, as the colleague of Dr. Channing. He had youth, zeal, and executive force. Writing of him after his death, Dr. Bellows said: "He had rare administrative qualities and a statesmanlike mind. He would have been a leader anywhere. He had the ambition, the faculties, and the impulsive temperament of an actor in affairs. He had the fervor, the concentration of will, the passionate enthusiasm of conviction, the love of martyrdom, which make men great in action."[9] Throughout his life Gannett labored assiduously for the Association, serving it in every capacity refusing no drudgery, travelling over the country in its interests, and giving himself, heart and soul, to the cause it represented. The Unitarian cause never had a more devoted friend or one who made greater sacrifices in its behalf. To him more than to any other man it owes its organized life and its missionary serviceableness.

Lewis Tappan, the treasurer, was a successful young business man. His term of service was brief; for two years after the organization of the Association he removed to New York, where he had an honorable career as one of the founders of the Journal of Commerce, and as the head of the first mercantile agency established in the country. He was later one of the anti–slavery leaders in New York, and an active and earnest member of Plymouth Church in Brooklyn.[10]

The executive committee was composed of the three devoted young ministers who had been foremost in organizing the Association. Barrett was thirty, Ware and Walker were thirty–one years of age; and all three had been in Harvard College and the Divinity School together. Samuel Barrett had just been chosen minister of the newly formed Twelfth Congregational Church of Boston, which he served throughout his life. He was identified with all good causes in Eastern Massachusetts, a founder of the Benevolent Fraternity, and an overseer of Harvard College. Henry Ware, the younger, was, at the time of his election, the minister of the Second Church in Boston. Five years later he became professor in the Harvard Divinity School, and his memory is still cherished as the teacher and exemplar of a generation of Unitarian ministers. James Walker was, in 1825, the minister of the Harvard Church in Charlestown, and already gave evidence of the sanity and catholicity of mind, the practical organizing power, the wide philosophic culture, and the dignity of character which afterward distinguished him as professor in Harvard College, and as its president.

Thus the organization started on its way, as the result of the determined purpose of a small company of the younger ministers and laymen. It took a name that separated it from all other religious organizations in this country, so far as its members then knew. The Unitarian name had been first definitely used in this country in 1815, to describe the liberal or Catholic Christians. They at first scornfully rejected it, but many of them had finally come to rejoice in its declaration of the simple unity of God. As a matter of history, it may be said that the word "Unitarian" was used in this doctrinal sense only; and it had none of the implications since given it by philosophy and science. Those who used it meant thereby to say that they accepted the doctrine of the absolute unity of God, and that the position of Christ was a subordinate though a very exalted one. No one can read their statements with historic apprehension, and arrive at any other conclusion. Yet these persons had no wish to cut themselves off from historic Christianity; rather was it

99

their intent to restore it to its primitive purity.

[Sidenote: Work of the First Year.]

If others were disinclined to action, the executive committee of the Unitarian Association was determined that something should be done. At their first, meeting, held in the secretary's study four days after their election, there were present Norton, Walker, Tappan, and Gannett. They commissioned Rev. Warren Burton to act as their agent in visiting neighboring towns to solicit funds, and a week later they voted to employ him as a general agent. The committee held six meetings during June; and at one of these an address was adopted, defining the purposes and methods of the Association. "They wish it to be understood," was their statement, "that its efforts will be directed to the promotion of true religion throughout our country; intending by this, not exclusively those views which distinguish the friends of this Association from other disciples of Christ; but those views in connection with the great doctrines and principles in which all Christians coincide, and which constitute the substance of our religion. We wish to diffuse the knowledge and influence of the gospel of our Lord and Saviour. Great good is anticipated from the co-operation of persons entertaining similar views, who are now strangers to each other's religious sentiments. Interest will be awakened, confidence inspired, efficiency produced by the concentration of labors. The spirit of inquiry will be fostered, and individuals at a distance will know where to apply for information and encouragement. Respectability and strength will be given to the class among us whom our fellow Christians have excluded from the control of their religious charities, and whom, by their exclusive treatment, they have compelled in some measure to act as a party." The objects of the Association were stated to be the collection of information about Unitarianism in various parts of the country; the securing of union, sympathy, and co-operation among liberal Christians; the publishing and distribution of books inculcating correct views of religion; the employment of missionaries, and the adoption of other measures that might promote the general purposes held in view.

At the end of the year the Association held its first anniversary meeting in Pantheon Hall, on the evening of June 30, 1826, when addresses were made by Hon. Joseph Story, Hon. Leverett Salstonstall, Rev. Ichabod Nichols, and Rev. Henry Coleman. The executive committee presented its report, which gave a detailed account of the operations during the year. They gave special attention to their discovery of "a body of Christians in the Western states who have for years been Unitarians, have encountered persecution on account of their faith, and have lived in ignorance of others east of the mountains who maintained many similar views of Christian doctrine." With this group of churches, which would consent to no other name than that of Christian, a correspondence had been opened; and, to secure a larger acquaintance with them, Rev. Moses G. Thomas[11] had visited several of the Western states. His tour carried him through Pennsylvania, Ohio, Kentucky, Indiana, Illinois, and as far as St. Louis. His account of his journey was published in connection with the second report of the Association, and is full of interest. He did not preach, but he carefully investigated the religious prospects of the states he journeyed through; and he sought the acquaintance of the Christian churches and ministers. He gave an enthusiastic account of his travels, and reported that the west was a promising field for the planting of Unitarian churches. He recommended Northumberland, Harrisburg, Pittsburg, Steubenville, Marietta, Paris, Lexington, Louisville, St. Louis, St. Charles, Indianapolis, and Cincinnati as promising places for the labors of Unitarian missionaries,—places "which will properly appreciate their talents and render them doubly useful in their day and generation."

During the first year of its existence the Unitarian Association endeavored to unite with itself, or to secure the co–operation of, the Society for the Promotion of Christian Knowledge, Piety, and Charity, the Evangelical Missionary Society, and the Publishing Fund Society; but these organizations were unwilling to come into close affiliation with it. The Evangelical Missionary Society has continued its separate existence to the present time, but the others were absorbed by the Unitarian Association after many years. This is one indication of how difficult it was to secure an active co–operation among Unitarians, and to bring them all into one vigorous working body. In concluding their first report, the officers of the Association alluded to the difficulties with which they had met the reluctance of the liberal churches to come into close affiliation with each other. "They have strenuously opposed the opinion," they said of the leaders of the Association, "that the object of the founders was to build up a party, to organize an opposition, to perpetuate pride and bigotry. Had they believed that such was its purpose or such would be its effect, they would have withdrawn themselves from any connection with so hateful a thing. They thought otherwise, and experience has proved they did not judge wrongly."

[Sidenote: Work of the First Quarter of a Century.]

Having thus organized itself and begun its work, the Association went quietly on its way. At no time during the first quarter of a century of its existence did it secure annual contributions from one-half the churches calling themselves Unitarian, and it did well when even one-third of them contributed to its treasury during any one year. The churches of Boston, for the most part, held aloof from it, and gave it only a feeble support, if any at all. They had so long accepted the spirit of congregational exclusiveness, had so great a dread of interference on the part of ecclesiastical organizations, and so keenly suspected every attempt at co-operation on the part of the churches as likely to lead to restrictions upon congregational independence, that it was nearly impossible to secure their aid for any kind of common work. Very slowly the contributions increased to the sum of $5,000 a year, and only once in the first quarter of a century did the total receipts of a year reach $15,000. With so small a treasury no great work could be undertaken; but the money given was husbanded to the utmost, and the salaries paid to clerks and the general secretary were kept to the lowest possible limit.

Dr. Bancroft was succeeded in the presidency of the Association, in 1836, by Dr. Channing, who nominally held the position for one year; but at the next annual meeting he declined to have his name presented as a candidate.[12] The office was then filled by Dr. Ichabod Nichols, of Portland, who served from 1837 to 1844. He was the minister of the First Church in Portland from 1809 to 1855, and then retired to Cambridge, where he wrote his Natural Theology and his Hours with the Evangelists. Joseph Story, the great jurist, who had been vice-president of the Association from 1826 to 1836, was elected president in 1844, and served for one year. He was followed by Dr. Orville Dewey, who was president from 1845 to 1847. He had been settled in New Bedford, and over the Church of the Messiah in New York; and subsequently he had short pastorates in Albany, in Washington, and over the New South Church in Boston. His lectures and his sermons have made him widely known. In intellectual and emotional power he was one of the greatest preachers the country has produced. Dr. Gannett served as the president from 1847 to 1851, being succeeded by Dr. Samuel K. Lothop, who continued to hold the office until 1856. Dr. Lothrop was first settled in Dover, N.H., but became the minister of the Brattle Street Church, Boston, in 1834, retaining that position until 1876.

The office of secretary was held by Rev. Ezra S, Gannett until 1831. He was succeeded in that year by Rev. Alexander Young, who held the position for two years. Dr. Young was the minister of the New South Church from 1825 until his death, in 1854. His Chronicles of the Pilgrim Fathers, and other works, have given him a reputation as a historian. In 1829 the office of foreign secretary was created; and it was held by the younger Henry Ware from 1830 to 1834, when it ceased to exist. Rev. Samuel Barnett was secretary in

1833 and 1834, and recording secretary until 1837. In 1834 the office of general secretary was established, in order to secure the services of an active missionary. Rev. Jason Whitman, who held this position for one year, had been the minister in Saco; and he was afterward settled in Portland and Lexington. Rev. Charles Briggs became the general secretary in 1835, and continued in office until the end of 1847. He had been settled in Lexington, but did not hold a pastorate subsequent to his connection with the Association. In the mean time Rev. Samuel K. Lothrop was the assistant or recording secretary from 1837 to 1847. In 1847 Rev. William G. Eliot was elected the general secretary; but he did not serve, owing to the claims of his parish in St. Louis. Rev. Frederick West Holland, who had been settled in Rochester, was made the general secretary in January, 1848; and he held the position until the annual meeting of 1860. Subsequently he was settled in East Cambridge, Neponset, North Cambridge, Rochester, and Newburg.

It was Charles Briggs who first gave definite purpose to the missionary work of the Association. The annual report of 1850 said of him that he "had led the institution forward to high ground as a missionary body, by unfailing patience prevailed over every discouragement, by inexhaustible hope surmounted serious obstacles, by the most persuasive gentleness conciliated opposition, and done perhaps as much as could be asked of sound judgment, knowledge of mankind, and devotion to the cause, with the drawback of a slender and failing frame." In 1845 Rev. George G. Channing entered upon a service as the travelling agent of the Association, which he continued for two years. His duties required him to take an active interest in missionary enterprises, revive drooping churches, secure information as to the founding of new churches, and to add to the income of the Association. He was a brother of Dr. Channing, held one or two pastorates, and was the founder and editor of The Christian World, which he published in Boston as a weekly Unitarian paper from January, 1843, to the end of 1848.

At a meeting of the Unitarian Association held on June 3, 1847, the final steps were taken that secured its incorporation under the laws of Massachusetts. In the revised constitution the fifteen vice-presidents were reduced to two, and the president and vice-presidents were made members of the executive committee, and so brought into intimate connection with the work of the Association. The directors and other officers were made an executive committee, by which all affairs of moment must be considered; and it was required to hold stated monthly meetings. These changes were conducive to an enlarged interest in the work of the Association, and also to the more thorough consideration of its activities on the part of a considerable body of judicious and experienced officers. They were made in recognition of the increasing missionary labors of the Association, and enabled it thenceforth to hold and to manage legally the moneys that came under its control.

[Sidenote: Publication of Tracts and Books.]

One of the first subjects to which the Association gave attention was the publication of tracts, six of which were issued during the first year. In connection with their publication a series of depositaries was established for their sale. David Reed of The Christian Register became the general agent, while there were ten county depositaries in Massachusetts, four in New Hampshire, three in Maine, and one each in Connecticut, New York City, Philadelphia, Charleston, and Washington.[13] For a number of years the tracts were devoted to doctrinal subjects. Several of Channing's ablest sermons and addresses were first printed in this form. Among the other contributors to the first series were the three Wares, Orville Dewey, Joseph Tuckerman, James Walker, George Ripley, Samuel J. May, John G. Palfrey, Ezra S. Gannett, Samuel Gilman, George R. Noyes, William G. Eliot, Andrew P. Peabody, F.A. Farley, James Freeman Clarke, S.G. Bulfinch, George Putnam, Joseph Allen, Frederic H. Hedge, Edward B. Hall, George E. Ellis, Thomas B. Fox, Charles T. Brooks, J.H. Morison, Henry W. Bellows, William H. Furness, John Cordner, Chandler Robbins, Augustus Woodbury, and William R. Alger. Ten or twelve tracts were issued yearly, those of the year having a consecutive page numbering, so that, in fact, they appeared in the form of a monthly periodical, each tract bearing the date of its publication, and being sent regularly to all subscribers to the Association. In all, three hundred tracts appeared in this form in the first series, making twenty−six volumes.

For nearly half a century none of the tracts of the Association were published for free distribution. They were issued at prices ranging from two to ten cents each, according to the size, some of them having not more than ten or twelve pages, while others had more than a hundred. So long as there was an eagerness for theological reading, and an earnest intellectual interest in the questions which divided the several religious bodies of the country from each other, it was not difficult to sell editions of from 3,000 to 10,000 copies of all the tracts published by the Association. From the first, however, there were many calls for tracts for free distribution. To meet this demand, there was formed in Boston, by a number of young men during the year 1827, The Unitarian Book and

Pamphlet Society, for "the gratuitous distribution of Unitarian publications of an approved character." It undertook especially to distribute "such publications as shall be issued by the American Unitarian Association or recommended by it." This society also circulated tracts printed by The Christian Register and The Christian World, the call for such publications having led the publishers of these periodicals to give their aid in meeting the demand for pamphlets on theological problems and on practical religious duties. The society also distributed Bibles to the poor of the city and in more distant country places, furnishing them to missionaries and others who would undertake work of this kind. In the same manner they gave away large numbers of books, their list for 1836 including Scougal's Life of God in the Soul of Man, Ware's Formation of the Christian Character, and works by Worcester, Channing Whitman, and Greenwood. The call for aid was considerable from the western and southern states; and books were sent to Havana, New Brunswick, and the Sandwich Islands. In the winter of 1840–41 this society was reorganized, an urgent appeal was made to the churches for an increase of funds, and during the next few years its work was large and important.

In the year 1848 was begun a special effort for the circulation of Unitarian books, on the part of The Book and Pamphlet Society, The Society for Promoting Christian Knowledge, Piety, and Charity, as well as by the Unitarian Association. In that year the second of these organizations sent out circulars to 263 colleges and theological schools, offering to give Unitarian books, to those desiring to receive them; and to 59 of these institutions assortments of books worth from two dollars to one hundred dollars were forwarded. The first request came from the Catholic College at Worcester, and the last from the Wisconsin University at Madison. At the same time the Association was pressing the sale and free distribution of the Works and the Memoir of Dr. Charming, as well as various books by Peabody, Livermore, Bartol, and others.

The Association began to make use of colporters about the year 1847. The next year it had two young ministers engaged in this work, and by 1850 this kind of missionary labor had increased to considerable proportions. Especially in the West was much use made of the colporter, and in this way in many of the states the works of Channing were sold in large numbers. By these agents, tracts were given away with a free hand, and books were given to ministers and those who especially needed them. The Western ministers, almost without exception, served as colporters, selling books and distributing them as important helps to their missionary labors. In many communities zealous laymen took part in this kind of service, and the several depositaries of books and tracts were used as centres from which colporters and others could draw their supplies. As early as 1835 a general depositary had been established in Cincinnati, and in 1849 one was opened in Chicago.

The Association could not have undertaken any work that would have brought in a larger or more immediate return in the way of religious education and spiritual growth than this of the publication of tracts and books. Previous to 1850 a doctrinal sermon was rarely preached in a Unitarian church, and the tracts were the most important means of giving to the members of established churches a knowledge of Unitarian theology. By the same means many other persons were made acquainted with the Unitarian beliefs, and the result was to be seen in the formation of churches where tracts and books had been largely distributed.[14]

[Sidenote: Domestic Missions.]

The work of domestic missions from the first largely claimed the attention of the Association, and it was one the chief objects in its formation. During the summer of 1826 the members of the Harvard Divinity School were sent throughout New England to gather information, and to preach where opportunity offered. The special object was to make ministers and congregations acquainted with the purposes of the Association. It was found that there was much opposition to it, and that in many parishes there existed no desire to have its mission extended.

Persons of all shades of belief were connected with many of the liberal parishes, some of the churches not having as yet ceased their relations with the towns in which they were located; and the ministers were not willing to have theological questions brought to the attention of their congregations. "The great objection everywhere seems to be," reported one of the young men, who had travelled through many of the towns of central Massachusetts, "that the clergymen do not like to awaken party spirit. People will go on quietly performing all external duties of religion without asking themselves if they are listening to the doctrine of the Trinity or not; but the moment you wish to act, they call up all their old prejudices, and take a very firm stand. This necessarily creates division and dissension, and renders the situation of the minister very uncomfortable."[15] The ministers did not preach on theological subjects; and, while they were liberal themselves, they had not instructed their parishioners in such a manner that they followed in the same path of thinking which their leaders had travelled.

It was evident, therefore, that there was work enough in New England for the Association to accomplish, and such as would fully tax its resources.[16] It had turned its eyes toward the West and South, however; and it was not willing to leave these fields unoccupied. In 1836 the general secretary, Charles Briggs, spent eight months in these regions; and he found everywhere large opportunities for the spread of Unitarianism. Promising openings were found at Erie, Cleveland, Toledo, Detroit, Marietta, Tremont, Jacksonville, Memphis, and Nashville, in which villages or cities churches were soon after formed. It was reported at this time that there was hardly a town in the West where there were not Unitarians, or in which it was not possible by the right kind of effort to establish a Unitarian church.

As a result of the interest awakened by the tour of the general secretary, fourteen missionaries were put into the field in 1837. In 1838 twenty–three missionaries visited eleven states, including New York, Pennsylvania, Ohio, Michigan, Illinois, Missouri, Kentucky Alabama, and Georgia.[17] They were men of experience in parish labors, but they did not go out to the new country to remain there permanently. They attracted large congregations, however, formed several societies which promised to be permanent, administered the ordinances, established Sunday–schools, and did much to strengthen the churches. In 1839 seven preachers were sent into the west, and at the next anniversary there was an urgent call made by the Association for funds with which to establish a permanent missionary agent in the field. Something more was needed than a few Massachusetts ministers preaching from town to town with no purpose of locating with any of the churches they helped to organize. Ministers for the new churches were urgently demanded, but few men from New England were willing to remove to the west; and, though recruits came from the orthodox churches, this source of supply was not sufficient.

The repeated calls made for larger resources with which to carry on the work of domestic missions resulted in meetings held in Boston during the year 1841, at which pledges were made to a fund of $10,000 yearly for five years, to be used for missionary purposes. This sum was secured in 1843 and the next four years, so that larger aid was given to missionary activities and to the building of churches. At the annual meeting of 1849 special attention was given to the subject of domestic missions, and plans were devised for largely extending all the activities in this direction. Much interest was taken in the western work during the following years, and slowly new churches came into existence. In 1849 Rev. Edward P. Bond was sent to San Francisco, where a number of New

England people had held lay services and formed a church, and in a few years a strong society had grown up in that city. Mr. Bond also went to the Sandwich Islands; but he was not able to open a mission there, owing to ill–health. In the South the work languished, largely owing to the growth of anti–slavery sentiment in the North, with which Unitarians were generally in sympathy.

From 1830 to 1850 the Unitarians were confronted by the greatest opportunity which has ever opened to them for missionary activities. The vast region of the middle west was in a formative state, the people were everywhere receptive to liberal influences, other churches had not been firmly established, and there was urgent demand for leadership of a progressive and rational kind. Here has come to be the controlling centre of American life,—in politics, education, and social power. A few of the leaders saw the opportunity, but the churches were not ready to respond to their appeals.

The work accomplished by the Association during the first twenty–five or thirty years of its existence, the period reviewed in this chapter, was small, compared with the opportunity and with the wishes of those who most had at heart the interests for the promotion of which it was established. Yet there was wanting in no year encouragement for its friends or something accomplished that cheered them to larger efforts. In 1850, at the twenty–fifth anniversary, historical addresses were delivered by Samuel Osgood, John G. Palfrey, Henry W. Bellows, Edward E. Hale, and Lant Carpenter; and a hopeful review of the labors of the Association was presented by the executive committee. First of all its efforts had been directed to securing religious liberty. Then came its philanthropic enterprises, and finally its missionary labors. During the quarter of a century one hundred churches that were weak and struggling, owing to their situation in towns of decreasing population or in cities not congenial to their teachings, had been aided. More than fifty vigorous churches had been planted in the west and south, nearly all of them helped in some way by the Association. There was a renewed call for strong men to enter the missionary field, and it was uttered more urgently at this time than ever before. Special pride was expressed in the high quality of the religious writings produced by Unitarians, and in the nobleness the men and women who had been connected with denominational activities.[18]

[1] An eighteenth–century term for the Congregational churches, which
    were the legally established churches throughout New England, an
    supported by the towns.

[2] Boston Unitarianism, 67.

[3] Memoir of Dr. Channing, one-volume edition, 215.

[4] Ibid., 432.

[5] Ibid., 427.

[6] Memoir of Ezra Stiles Gannett, by W.C. Gannett, 103.

[7] The records give the following names: Drs. Freeman, Channing, Lowell, Tuckerman, Bancroft, Pierce, and Allyn; Rev. Messrs. Henry Ware, Francis Parkman, J.G. Palfrey, Jared Sparks, Samuel Ripley, A. Bigelow, A. Abbot, C. Francis, L. Capen, J. Pierpont, James Walker, Mr. Harding, and Mr. Edes; and the following laymen,—Richard Sullivan, Stephen Higginson, B. Gould, H.J. Oliver, S. Dorr, Colonel Joseph May, C.G. Loring, George Bond, Samuel A. Eliot, G.B. Emerson, C.P. Phelps, Lewis Tappan, David Reed, Mr. Storer, J. Rucker, N. Mitchell, Robert Rantoul, Alden Bradford, Mr. Dwight, Mr. Mackintosh, General Walker, Mr. Strong, Dr. John Ware, and Professor Andrews Norton.

[8] John Brazer, The Christian Examiner, xx. 240; Alonzo Hill, American Unitarian Biography, i. 171.

[9] The Liberal Christian, March 3, 1875.

[10] Although Lewis Tappan took a zealous interest in the formation of the Unitarian Association, as he did in all Unitarian activities of the time, in the autumn of 1827 he withdrew from the Unitarian fellowship, and joined the orthodox Congregationalist. In a letter addressed to a Unitarian minister he explained his reasons for so doing. This letter circulated for some time in manuscript, and in 1828 was printed in a pamphlet with the title, Letter from a Gentleman in Boston to a Unitarian Clergyman of that City. Want of Piety among Unitarians, failure to sustain missionary enterprises,

and the absence of a rigid business integrity he assigned as reasons for his withdrawal. This pamphlet excited much discussion, pro and con; and it was answered in a caustic review by J.P. Blanchard.

[11] Moses George Thomas was a graduate of Brown and of the Harvard Divinity School, was settled in Dover, N.H., from 1829 to 1845, Broadway Church in South Boston from 1845 to 1848, New Bedford 1848 to 1854, and was subsequently minister at large in the same city.

[12] In writing to Charles Briggs from Newport, under date of July 30 1836, Dr. Channing wrote, "In the pressure of subjects, when I saw you, I forgot to say to you, that I cannot accept the office with which the Unitarian Association honored me." That is the whole of what he wrote on the subject. No one else was elected to the office for year. It is evident, therefore, that his name should occupy the place of president.

[13] The depositaries in Massachusetts were at Salem, Concord, Hingham, Plymouth, Yarmouth, Cambridge, Worcester, Northampton, Springfield, and Greenfield; in New Hampshire, at Concord, Portsmouth, Keene, and Amherst; in Maine, at Hallowell, Brunswick, and Eastport; and, in Connecticut, at Brooklyn. In 1828 the number had increased to twenty–five in Massachusetts, six in Maine, seven in New Hampshire, one in Rhode Island, four in New York, two in Pennsylvania, and two in Maryland. At the first annual meeting of the Unitarian Association a system of auxiliaries was recommended, which was inaugurated the next year. It was proposed to organize an auxiliary to the Association in every parish, and also in each county. These societies came rapidly into existence, were of much help to the Association in raising money and in distributing its tracts, and energetic efforts were made on the part of the officers of the Association to extend their number and influence. They continued in existence for about twenty years, and gradually disappeared. They numbered about one hundred and fifty when most prosperous.

[14] During the first twenty–five years of the Association, 272 tracts of the first series were issued, and also 29 miscellaneous tracts and 37 reports. The number of copies published was estimated as 1,764,000, making an average of 70,000 each year. Of these tracts, 103 were practical, and 93 doctrinal; and, of the doctrinal, one–half were on the Divine Unity, one–sixth on the Atonement, ten on Regeneration, five on the Ordinances, four on Human Nature, three on Retribution, and two on the Holy Spirit. In the Monthly Journal, May, 1860, Vol. I. pp. 230–240, were given the titles and authors.

[15] From a letter of Samuel K. Lothrop, afterward minister of the Brattle Street Church.

[16] The following letter is of interest, not only because of the name of the writer, but because it gives a very good idea of the work done by the first missionaries of the Association. It is dated at Northampton, Mass., October 9, 1827. "My dear Sir,—I designed when I left you to send some earlier notice of my doings than this; but as it has not been in my power to say much, I have said nothing. Mr. Hall is preparing an account of his own missions, but thinks it not worth while to send it to you till it is completed. The first Sabbath after my arrival I preached here. The second, for the convenience of the Greenfield people, an exchange was made, and I went to Deerfield, and Dr. Willard went to Colrain. There were some unfavorable circumstances which operated to diminish the audience, but they were glad to see and hear him. The fourth Sabbath (which followed the meeting of the Franklin Association) I preached at Greenfield, and Mr. Bailey went to Colrain. I enclose his journal. The fifth Sabbath at Deerfield, and Dr. Willard at Adams in Berkshire. I have not seen him since his return. I have told the Franklin Association I would remain here till November, and in consequence have been thus put to and fro, but expect to preach the three coming Sundays in Northampton. I have offered my services to preach lectures in the week, but circumstances have made it inexpedient in towns where it was proposed. The clergymen are very glad to see me, having feared that the mission was indefinitely postponed. They find the better

sort of people in most of the towns inquisitive and favorably disposed to views of liberal Christianity. It is a singular fact, of which I hear frequent mention made, that in elections Unitarians are almost universally preferred when the suffrage is by ballot, and rejected when given by hand ballot. In Franklin county it is thought there is a majority of Unitarians. I have been much disappointed in being obliged to lead a vagrant life, as you know I came hither with different expectations, and hoped for leisure and retirement for study, which I needed much. But it would not do for a missionary to be stiff necked, and so I have been a shuttle. I have promised to go to New Bedford the first three Sundays of November. With great regard, your servant, R. Waldo Emerson." From this letter it will be seen that Emerson supplied the pulpits at Northampton and Greenfield in order that the ministers in those towns might preach elsewhere.

[17] Fourteenth Annual Report, 14. "They were the following: Rev. George Ripley, Boston; Rev. A.B. Muzzey, Cambridgeport; Rev. Samuel Barrett, Boston; Rev. Mr. Green, East Cambridge; Rev. Calvin Lincoln, Fitchburg; Rev. E.B. Willson, Westford; Dr. James Kendall, Plymouth; Rev. George W. Hosmer, Buffalo; Rev. Warren Burton, Dr. Thompson, Salem; Rev. J.P.B. Storer, Syracuse; Rev. Charles Babbidge, Pepperell; Rev. John M. Myrick, Walpole; Rev. J.D. Swett, Boston; Rev. A.D. Jones, Brighton; Rev. Henry Emmons, Meadville; Rev. J.F. Clarke, Louisville; Rev. F.D. Huntington, Rev. B.F. Barrett, Rev. G.F. Simmons, Rev. C. Nightingale, Mr. Wilson, of the Divinity School; and Mr. C.P. Cranch. Among the places where they preached are Houlton Me.; Syracuse, Lockport, Lewiston, Pekin, and Vernon, N.Y.; Philadelphia and Erie, Pa.; Marietta, Zanesville, Cleveland, and Toledo, Ohio; Detroit, Mich.; Owensburg, Ky.; Chicago, Peoria, Tremont, Jacksonville, Hillsboro, and several other places in Illinois."

[18] For a most interesting account of the growth of the denomination, see The Christian Examiner for May, 1854, lvi. 397, article by John Parkman.

VII. THE PERIOD OF RADICALISM.

Before the controversy with the Orthodox had come to its end, a somewhat similar conflict of opinions arose within the Unitarian ranks. The same influences that had led the Unitarians away from the Orthodox were now causing the more radical Unitarians to advance beyond their more conservative neighbors. English philosophy had given direction to the Unitarian movement in America; and now German philosophy was helping to develop what has been designated as transcendentalism, which largely found expression within the Unitarian body. Beginning with 1835, the more liberal Unitarians were increasingly active. Hedge's[1] Club held its meetings, The Dial was published, Brook Farm lived its brief day of a reformed humanity, Parker began his preaching in Boston, Emerson was lecturing and publishing, and the more radical younger Unitarian preachers were bravely speaking for a religion natural to man and authenticated by the inner witness of the truth.

The agitation thus started went on its way with many varying manifestations, and with a growing incisiveness of statement and earnestness of feeling. The new teachings gained the interest and the faith of the young in increasing numbers. In pulpits and on the platform, in newspapers and magazines, in essays and addresses, this new teaching was uttered for the world's hearing. The breeze thus created seems to have grown into a gale, but The Christian Register and The Christian Examiner gave almost no indication that it had blown their way. In the official actions and in the publications of the Unitarian Association there was no word indicating that the discussion had come to its knowledge. All at once, however, in 1853, it came into the greatest prominence, as the result of action taken by the Unitarian Association; and, thenceforth, for a quarter of a century it was never absent as a disturbing element in the intellectual and religious life of the Unitarian body.

The early Unitarians were believers in the supernatural and in the miracles of the New Testament. They accepted without question the ideas on this subject that had been entertained by all Protestants from the days of Luther and Calvin. When Theodore Parker and the transcendentalists began to question the miraculous foundations of Christianity, many Unitarians were quite unprepared to accept their theories. They believed that the miracles of the New Testament afford the only evidence for the truthfulness of Christianity. This issue was distinctly stated in the twenty–eighth annual report of the

Unitarian Association for 1853, wherein an attempt was made to defend the Unitarian body against the charge of infidelity and rationalism made by the Orthodox. The teachings of the transcendentalists and radicals had been attributed to all Unitarians, and the leaders of the Association felt that it was time to define explicitly the position they occupied. Therefore they said, in the report of that year:—"We desire, in a denominational capacity, to assert our profound belief in the Divine origin, the Divine authority, the Divine sanctions, of the religion of Jesus Christ. This is the basis of our associated action. We desire openly to declare our belief as a denomination, so far as it can be officially represented by the American Unitarian Association, that God, moved by his own love, did raise up Jesus to aid in our redemption from sin, did by him pour a fresh flood of purifying life through the withered veins of humanity and along the corrupted channels of the world, and is, by his religion, forever sweeping the nations with regenerating gales from heaven, and visiting the hearts of men with celestial solicitations. We receive the teachings of Christ, separated from all foreign admixtures and later accretions, as infallible truth from God."[2] At the same meeting a resolution was adopted, "without a dissenting voice," which declared that "the Divine authority of the Gospel, as founded on a special and miraculous interposition of God, is the basis of the action of the Association."[3]

As these statements indicate, the majority of Unitarians were very conservative at this time in their theological position and methods. They were nearly as hesitating and reticent in their beliefs as Unitarians as they had been while connected with the older Congregational body. The reason for this was the same in the later as in the earlier period, that a predominant social conservatism held them aloof from all that was intellectually aggressive and theologically rationalistic. They had outgrown Tritheism, as it had been taught for generations in New England; they had refused to accept the fatalism that had been taught in the name of Calvin, and they had rejected the ecclesiastical tyrannies that had been imposed on men by the New England theology. But they had advanced only a little way in accepting modern thought as a basis of faith, and in seeking a rational interpretation of the relations of God and man. Their belief in a superhuman Christ was theoretically weaker, but practically stronger, than that of the churches from which they had withdrawn; while the grounds of that belief were in the one instance the same as in the other.

[Sidenote: Depression in Denominational Activities.]

114

The activities of the Unitarian Association were largely interfered with by these differences of opinion. The more conservative churches were unwilling to contribute to its treasury because it did not exclude the radicals from all connection with it. The radicals, on, the other hand, withheld their gifts because, while they were not excommunicated, they were regarded with suspicion by many of the churches, and did not have the fullest recognition from the Association.

This controversy was emphasized by that arising from the reform movements of the day, especially the agitation against slavery. Almost without exception the radicals belonged to the anti–slavery party, while the conservative churches were generally opposed to this agitation. As a result, anti–slavery efforts became a serious cause of discord in the Unitarian churches, and helped to cripple the resources of the Association. When, as the climax of all, the civil war came on, the Association was brought to a condition of almost desperate poverty. Not more than twoscore churches contributed to its treasury, and it was obliged, to curtail its expenses in every direction.[4]

Up to the year 1865 the Unitarians had not been efficiently organized; and they had developed very imperfectly what has been called denominational consciousness, or the capacity for co–operative efforts. The Unitarian Association was not a representative body, and it depended wholly upon individuals for its membership. Not more than one–fourth or, at the largest, one–third of the Unitarian churches were represented in its support and in its activities. There were: Unitarian churches, and there was a Unitarian movement; but such a thing as a Unitarian denomination, in any clearly defined meaning of the words, did not exist. This fact was explained by James Freeman Clarke in 1863, when he said that "the traditions of the Unitarian body are conservative and timid."[5] How this attitude affected the Unitarian Association was pointedly stated by Mr. Clarke, after several years of experience as its secretary. "The Unitarian churches in Boston," he wrote, "see no reason for diffusing their faith. They treat it as a luxury to be kept for themselves, as they keep Boston Common. The Boston churches, with the exception of a few noble and generous examples, have not done a great deal for Unitarian missions. I have heard, it said that they do not wish to make Unitarianism too common. The church in Brattle street contains wealthy and generous persons who have given largely to humane objects and to all public purposes; but we believe that, even while their pastor was president of the Unitarian Association, they never gave a dollar to that Association for its missionary objects. The society in King's Chapel was the first in the United States which professed Unitarianism. It is so wealthy that it might give ten or twenty thousand dollars a year to missionary objects without feeling it. It has always been very liberal to its ministers, to all philanthropic and benevolent objects, and its members have probably given away millions of dollars for public and social uses; but it never gives anything to diffuse Unitarianism."[6]

Dr. Samuel K. Lothrop continued as the president of the Unitarian Association until the annual meeting of 1858, when Dr. Edward Brooks Hall was elected to that position for one year. After short pastorates in Northampton and Cincinnati, Dr. Hall had been settled over the First Church in Providence in 1832, which position he held until his death in 1866. At the annual meeting of 1859 Dr. Frederic H. Hedge was elected president, and he was twice re-elected. His interest in the Association was active, and he often spoke at the public meetings. One of the ablest thinkers and theologians that has appeared among Unitarians in this country, he always rightly estimated the practical activities of organized religious movements. He was succeeded in 1862 by Dr. Rufus P. Stebbins, who held the office for three years. After a settlement in Leominster, Dr. Stebbins was the first president of the Meadville Theological School from 1844 to 1856. Then followed a pastorate in Woburn, after which he went to Ithaca and opened a mission for the students of Cornell University, which grew into the Unitarian church in that town. From 1877 he was pastor at Newton Centre until his death in 1885.

The secretary of the Association from 1850 to 1853 was Rev. Calvin Lincoln, who had been settled in Fitchburg for thirty-one years, and who was the minister of the First Church in Hingham from 1855 until his death in 1881. He was succeeded in 1853 by Rev. Henry A. Miles, who continued in office until 1859. Dr. Miles was settled in Hallowell and Lowell before serving the Association, and in Longwood and Hingham (Third Parish) afterward. His little book on The Birth of Jesus has gained him recognition as a theologian of ability and a critic of independent judgment. For three years Rev. James Freeman Clarke was the secretary; and in 1861 he was succeeded by George W. Fox, who served in that capacity until the annual meeting of 1865. Mr. Fox wrote the annual reports from 1862 to 1864, and efficiently performed all the duties of the secretary which could devolve upon a layman, with the exception of editing The Monthly Journal, a task which was continued by James Freeman Clarke.[7]

[Sidenote: Publications.]

116

In spite of its restricted income during this troubled period, the Association was able, owing to its invested funds,[8] to increase its publishing operations to a considerable extent. The number of tracts published, however, was much smaller; and their monthly issue was discontinued in order to publish The Quarterly Journal of the American Unitarian Association, the first number of which appeared in October, 1853. During the first year each number contained ninety–six pages, which were increased to one hundred and ninety–two in 1854, but reduced to one hundred and thirty the following year. In 1860 this publication became The Monthly Journal; and it was continued until December, 1869, each number containing forty–eight pages. The Journal was sent to all subscribers to the funds of the Association, to life members, to all churches contributing to its funds, as well as to regular subscribers. Its circulation in 1855 was 7,000, and it increased to 15,000 before it was discontinued. It was used largely, however, for free distribution as a missionary document.

The Journal served an important purpose during the seventeen years of its publication, as a means of bringing the Association into touch with its constituency and of making the people acquainted with its work. It published the records of the meetings of the executive committee as well as of the annual meeting, it gave numerous extracts from the correspondence of the secretary, it contained the news of the churches, and all the denominational activities were kept constantly before its readers. In its pages were frequently published biographies of prominent Unitarians, notable addresses were printed, sermons appeared frequently, and able theological articles. During the editorship of James Freeman Clarke it contained the successive chapters of his Orthodoxy: Its Truths and Errors. It also printed one or more chapters of Alger's History of the Doctrine of the Future Life. The secretary of the Association was its editor, and he made it at once a theological tract and a denominational newspaper.

The increase in demand for Unitarian tracts and books had been so large that early in 1854 the executive committee of the Association decided that a special effort should be made to meet it. They called a meeting in Freeman Place Chapel on the afternoon of February 1, which was largely attended. An address was given by Dr. Lothrop, the president, who said that Channing's works had reached a sale of 100,000 copies, and Ware's Formation of Christian Character 12,000, that there was an urgent call for liberal works that would meet the spiritual needs of the age. A large number of prominent ministers and laymen addressed the meeting, and expressed themselves as thoroughly sympathy with its objects. A committee was appointed to consider the proposition made by Dr. George E. Ellis, that a fund of $50,000 be raised for the publication of books. This committee reported a month later through its chairman, George B. Emerson, in favor of the project; and it was voted that the money should be raised. It was easier to pass this vote, however, than to secure the money from the churches; for in 1859, after five years of effort, the sum collected was only $28,163.33.

The money secured, however, was immediately utilized in the publication of a number of books. Three series of works were undertaken, the first of these being The Theological Library, in which were published Selections from the Works of Dr. Channing; Wilson's Unitarian Principles Confirmed by Trinitarian Testimonies; a one–volume edition of Norton's Statement of Reasons for not Believing the Doctrines of Trinitarians concerning the Nature of God and the Person of Christ, with a memoir of the author by Dr. William Newell; a volume of Theological Essays selected from the writings of Jowett, Tholuck, Guizot, Roland Williams, and others, and edited by George R. Noyes; and Martineau's Studies of Christianity, a series of miscellaneous papers, edited by William R. Alger. The Devotional Library, the second of the three series, included The Altar at Home, a series of prayers, collects, and litanies for family devotions, written by a large number of the leading Unitarian ministers, and edited by Dr. Miles, the secretary of the Association; Clarke's Christian Doctrine of Prayer; Thomas T. Stone's The Rod and the Staff, a transcendentalist presentation of Christianity as a spiritual life; The Harp and the Cross, a selection of religious poetry, edited by Stephen G. Bulfinch; Sears's Athanasia, or Foregleams of Immortality; and Seven Stormy Sundays, a volume of original sermons by well–known ministers, with devotional services, edited by Miss Lucretia P. Hale. A Biblical Library was also planned, to include a popular commentary on the New Testament, a Bible Dictionary, and other works of a like character; but John H. Morison's Disquisitions and Notes on the Gospel of Matthew was the only volume published.

[Sidenote: A Firm of Publishers.]

In May, 1859, a young business man of Boston, James P. Walker, established the firm of Walker, Wise &Co., for the publication of Unitarian books. In 1863 Horace B. Fuller joined the firm, and it became Walker, Fuller &Co. This firm took charge of all the publishing interests of the Association, and the head of the house was ambitious of bringing out all the liberal books issued in this country. Among the works published were: The New Discussion of the Trinity, a series of articles and sermons by Hedge, Clarke, Sears, Dewey, and Starr King; Lamson's Church of the First Three Centuries;

Farley's Unitarianism Defined; Recent Inquiries in Theology, essays by Jowett, Mark Pattison, Baden Powell, and other English Broad Churchmen, edited by Dr. F.H. Hedge; Alien's Hebrew Men and Times; Dall's Woman's Right to Labor; Muzzey's Christ in the Will, the Heart, and the Life; Ichabod Nichols's Sermons; Martineau's Common Prayer for Christian Worship; Cobbe's Religious Demands of the Age; Ware's Silent Pastor; Frothingham's Stories from the Patriarchs; Clarke's Hour which Cometh and Now Is; Parker's Prayers; a second series The Altar at Home; Hedge's Reason in Religion; Life of Horace Mann by his wife, as well as certain novels, historical works, and books for the young. The demand for liberal books was not large enough, however, even with the aid of the Association, to make such a business successful; and in the autumn of 1866 the publishing firm of Walker, Fuller &Co. failed. In part the business was carried on for a time by Horace B. Fuller.

[Sidenote: The Brooks Fund.]

An important work in the distribution of books was inaugurated in 1859 in connection with the Meadville Theological School, by means of the Fund for Liberal Christianity established at that time by Joshua Brooks of New York. He appointed as trustee of the fund Professor Frederick Huidekoper, who gave his services gratuitously to its care, and to the direction of the distribution of books for which it provided. The sum given to this purpose was $20,000, which was increased by favorable investments to $23,000. The original purpose was to aid in any way that seemed desirable the cause of liberal Christianity, and a part of the income was devoted to helping struggling societies. In time the whole income, with the approval of the donor, was centred upon the distribution of books to settled ministers, irrespective of denomination. In 1877 the whole number of books that had been distributed was 40,000. At the present time about $1,000 yearly are devoted to this work, the recipients being graduates of the Meadville Theological School, and the ministers of any denomination who may ask for them, provided they are settled west of the Hudson River. The demands upon the funds have increased so rapidly that it has become necessary to reduce the amount of each gift.

[Sidenote: Missionary Efforts.]

The missionary activities of the Association did not actually cease even in these dark days. In May, 1855, Rev. Ephraim Nute was sent to Kansas, which was then the battle—ground between the pro—slavery and the anti—slavery forces of the nation. He established himself at Lawrence, and was the first settled pastor in the state. With the aid of the Association a church was built at Lawrence in 1859, which was the first in the state to receive dedication and to be used as a permanent house of worship. Mr. Nute went through all the trying scenes preceding the opening of the civil war, and did his part in maintaining the cause of liberty. He was succeeded by Rev. John S. Brown in 1859, who labored in this difficult field for several years.

A church was organized in San Francisco in 1849, without the aid of a minister; and there was gathered a large and prosperous congregation. In 1850 Rev. Charles A. Farley took up the work; and he was succeeded by Rev. Joseph Harrington, Rev. Frederick T. Gray, and Rev. Rufus P. Cutler. Thomas Starr King preached his first sermon in the church April 28, 1860; and he spoke to crowded congregations until his death, March 4, 1864. On January 10, 1864, a new church was dedicated, in the morning to the worship of God, and in the afternoon to the service of man.

Among those who carried forward the Unitarian cause in the middle west was Rev. Nahor A. Staples, a brilliant preacher and a zealous worker, who was settled in Milwaukee at the end of 1856, and who made his influence widely felt around him. In 1859 Rev. Robert Collyer began his work in Chicago as a city Missionary; and the next year Unity Church was organized, with him as the pastor. In 1859 Rev. Charles G. Ames began his connection with the Unitarians at Minneapolis, and he subsequently labored at Bloomington. After a short pastorate in Albany he began general missionary labors on the Pacific coast. A characteristic type of the western Unitarian was Rev. Ichabod Codding, who preached at Bloomington, Keokuk, and Baraboo, but who had no formal settlement. He was a breezy, radical, and ardent preacher, bold in statement and picturesque in style, a zealous advocate of freedom for the slave, and warmly devoted to other reforms. He was fitted admirably for the pioneer preaching to which he largely devoted himself; and his strong, vigorous, and aggressive ideas were acceptable to those who heard him.

[Sidenote: The Western Unitarian Conference.]

There was organized in the church at Cincinnati, May 7, 1852, the Annual Conference of Western Unitarian Churches. At this meeting delegates were present from the churches in Buffalo, Meadville, Pittsburg, Wheeling, Cincinnati, Louisville, St. Louis, Cannelton, Quincy, Geneva, Chicago, and Detroit. Much enthusiasm was expressed in anticipation of this meeting, many letters were written, approving of the proposed organization, and large expectations were manifested as to its promised work. In harmony with these large and generous anticipations of the influence of the conference was its statement of purposes, as presented in its constitution. It was organized for "the promotion of the Christian spirit in the several churches which compose it, and the increase of vital, practical religion; the diffusion of Gospel truth and the accomplishment of such works of Christian benevolence as may be agreed upon; the support of domestic or home missionaries, the publication of tracts, the distribution of religious books, the promotion of theological education, and extending aid to such societies as may need it."

When the conference organized, Rev. William G. Eliot was elected the president, Mr. Charles Harlow and Rev. A.A. Livermore the recording and corresponding secretaries. During the year $994.22 were raised for missionary purposes, and three missionaries—Boyer, Conant, and Bradley—were kept in the field, mainly in Illinois and Michigan. The reports of these men, given at the second meeting of the conference, held in St. Louis, were full of enthusiasm and courage. At this meeting the constituency numbered nineteen churches, located in eleven states. Several struggling societies had been aided, assistance given to young men preparing for the ministry, and many tracts and books had been distributed. A book depositary was opened in Cincinnati, and it was proposed to establish one in every large city in the west. The call was for a much larger number of preachers, it being rightly maintained that only the living man can reach the people in such a region. "The Unitarian minister is *per se* a bookseller and colporter also, and he can thus preach to multitudes who never hear his voice."

The early anticipations of a rapid advance of Unitarianism in the west were not realized, partly owing to the want of ministers of energy and the necessary staying qualities, and partly to the fact that tradition is always far more powerful with the masses of men and women than reason. Before the organization of the conference new churches appeared at infrequent intervals, though, if those that have ceased to exist were counted, they would not be so remote from each other in time.[9] From the first there was in the west a distinctive attitude of freedom, which was the result in large, measure of its fluctuating conditions, and the absence of fixed habits and traditions. In 1853 the missionaries of the conference were instructed that "in spirit and in aim the Conference would be Christian, not sectarian, and it does not, therefore, require of them subscription to any human creed, the wearing of any distinctive name, or the doing of any merely sectarian work. All that it requires is, that they should be Christians and do Christian work, that they should believe on the Lord Jesus Christ as one who spake with authority and whose religion is the divinely appointed means for the regeneration of man individually and collectively, and that they should labor earnestly, intelligently, affectionately, and perseveringly to enthrone this religion in the hearts and make it, effective over the lives of men." Such a statement as this, indeed, was quite as conservative as anything put forth by Unitarians in New England; but behind it was an attitude of free inquiry that gave to western Unitarianism distinctive characteristics.

In 1854 a committee reported on the doctrinal basis of the conference, in the form of a little book of sixty–five pages, bearing the title of Unitarian Views of Christ.[10] It was widely circulated, and served an excellent missionary purpose. When the conference accepted the report, in which it was declared that Jesus is the Son of God and the miracles of the New Testament facts on which the gospel is based, a resolution was unanimously passed, asserting that "we have no right to adopt any statement of belief as authoritative or as a declaration of the Unitarian faith, other than the New Testament." In 1858 it was the opinion of the conference that "all who wish to take upon themselves the Christian name should be so recognized." The next year the conservatives and radicals came face to face, the one party asking for the old faith according to Channing, while one or more of the other party asserted their disbelief in the miracles and in the resurrection of Christ. In 1860 the conference declared itself willing to "welcome as fellow laborers all who are seeking to learn and to do the will of the Father and work righteousness, and recommend that in all places, with or without preaching, they organize for religious worship and culture—the work of faith and the labor of love."

The meeting at Quincy in 1860 was one of great interest and enthusiasm. The missionary spirit rose high; and it was proposed to put into the field an aggressive worker, and to give him the necessary financial support. To this end a missionary association was organized, with Rev. Robert Collyer as the president, and Artemas Carter, a successful business man of Chicago, as the treasurer. Before the result desired could be realized, the war gave a very different direction to all the interests of the western churches. Of the twenty–nine ministers in the west at this time, sixteen went into the army,—twelve as chaplains, two as officers, and two as privates,—while several others devoted themselves to hospital work for longer or shorter periods. Rev. Augustus H. Conant, Rev. Leonard Whitney, Rev. Frederick R. Newell, and Rev. L.B. Mason answered with their lives to their country's call.

The period immediately following the close of the civil war was one of generous giving and of great activity on the part of the western churches. From 1864 to 1866 the field was occupied by twenty–one new laborers, several new societies were organized, four old ones were resuscitated, seven new churches were built, and fifteen missionary stations were opened. The churches during these two years contributed $5,000 to missionary purposes and $13,000 to Antioch College. The degree of success met with in the efforts of the Western Conference depended in large degree upon the interest and activity of the western churches themselves. When they devoted themselves earnestly to missionary work, they contributed to it with a fair degree of liberality, and that work prospered. When the conference was asked to withdraw from the direction of that work by Rev. Charles Lowe, in order to secure greater unity of missionary effort by bringing all work of this kind under the direction of the Association, the contributions of the churches diminished, and the missionary activities in the west languished. However valuable the aid of the Unitarian Association,—and there can be no question that it was of the greatest importance,—local interest and co–operation were also essential to permanent success. Local activity and general oversight were alike necessary.

[Sidenote: The Autumnal Conventions.]

For more than twenty years Autumnal Conventions, as they were called, were held in the larger cities, beginning at Worcester in 1842. These meetings originated in the Worcester Association of Ministers at a meeting held July 11, 1842, when the association considered the "desirableness of a meeting of Unitarians in the autumn for the purpose of awakening mutual sympathy and considering the wants of the Unitarian body."[11]

At the invitation thereafter issued by the Worcester Association of ministers a convention was held in the church of the Second Congregational Parish in Worcester, October 18–20, 1842. On the first evening a sermon was preached by Dr. Ezra S. Gannett, and a committee of business was subsequently chosen. The next morning the convention organized, with Dr. Francis Parkman as president and Rev. Cazneau Palfrey as secretary. A series of resolutions were discussed,[12] and on the second evening a sermon was preached by Dr. A.P. Peabody. No essays were read, and nothing but the sermons were prepared beforehand. The Christian Register closed its report by saying that it could "give but a faint impression of the feeling which pervaded the meeting. The discussions were characterized by great earnestness and seriousness, and were conducted, at the same time, with entire freedom and with candor and liberality toward the differences of opinion which, amidst a general unanimity upon great principles, were occasionally elicited respecting details and methods. The expectations of those who called the convention were abundantly realized."

The second of the Autumnal Conventions was held in Providence, October 2–4, 1843. On the first evening the theme of the sermon preached by Dr. Dewey was the spiritual ministry of Dr. Channing, and it produced a great and deep impression. The resolutions discussed related to the duty, on the part of Unitarians, of making an explicit statement of their convictions, and an earnest application of them to life, and the need on the part of the denomination for a more united and vigorous action as a religious body. At the third meeting held in Albany, a statement was made by Dr. Dewey that exactly defined these gatherings, in their methods and purposes, when he said: "This and other conventions like it that are held in our body, I am inclined to think, have never been held before in the world. There is nothing like them to be found in the records of ecclesiastical history. We meet as distinct churches, on the pure democratic basis, which we believe to be the true basis of the church of Christ. We meet, without any formalities—to institute, or correct no canons—without the slightest system whatever. We come to meditate, to assist each other in experience, by unfolding our own experience, by declaring our convictions."

The subjects introduced at these meetings were practical, such as commanded the interest of both ministers and laymen of the churches. The method adopted allowed a free interchange of opinions, and the participation of all in the discussions. So great was the interest awakened that these meetings were largely attended, and they were to a considerable degree helpful in bringing the churches into vital relations with each other.[13]

At the session held in Brooklyn in 1862, great interest was manifested in the vespers, then a novelty, that were arranged by Samuel Longfellow. This meeting was marked by its glowing patriotism, that rose to a white heat. A sermon of great power was preached by Dr. Bellows, interpreting the duty of the hour and the destiny of America. The resolutions and the discussions were almost wholly along the lines of patriotic duty and devotion suggested by the sermon. At the last of the Autumnal Conventions, held in Springfield, Mass., October 13–15, 1863, the sermons were preached by Rev. Edward Everett Hale and Rev. Octavius B. Frothingham, while the essays were by Professor Charles Eliot Norton and Rev. James Freeman Clarke.

The Autumnal Conventions came to an end, probably in part because the civil war was more and more absorbing the energies of the people both in and out of the churches, and partly because the desire for a more efficient organization had begun to make itself felt. In the spring of 1865 was held the meeting in New York that resulted in the organization of the National Conference, the legitimate successor to the Autumnal Conventions.

[Sidenote: Influence of the Civil War.]

During the period of the civil war, Unitarian activities were largely turned in new directions. Unitarians bore their full share in the councils of the nation, in the halls of legislation, on the fields of battle, in the care of the sick and wounded, and in the final efforts that brought about emancipation and peace. At least fifty Unitarian ministers entered the army as chaplains, privates, officers, and members of the Sanitary Commission.[14]

The Unitarian Association also directed its attention to such work as it could accomplish in behalf of the soldiers in the field and in hospitals. Books were distributed, tracts published, and hymn−books prepared to meet their needs. Rev. John F.W. Ware developed a special gift for writing army tracts, of which he wrote about a dozen, which were published by the Association. As the war went on, the Association largely increased its activities in the army; and, when the end came, it had as many as seventy workers in the field, distributing its publications, aiding the Sanitary Commission, or acting as nurses and voluntary chaplains in the hospitals. The end of the war served rather to increase than to contract its labors, aid being largely needed for several months in returning the soldiers to their homes and in caring for those who were left in hospitals.

Early in the summer of 1863 Rev. William G. Scandlin was sent to the Army of the Potomac as the agent of the Association. Taken prisoner in July, he spent several months in Libby prison, where he was kindly treated and exercised a beneficent influence. He was followed in this work by Rev. William M. Mellen, who established a library of 3,000 volumes at the convalescent camp, Alexandria, and also distributed a large amount of reading matter in the army. Rev. Charles Lowe served for several months as chaplain in the camp of drafted men on Long Island, his salary being paid by the Association. In November, 1864, he made a tour of inspection, as the agent of the Association, to the hospitals of Philadelphia, Baltimore Annapolis, Washington, Alexandria, Fortress Monroe, City Point, and the Army of the Potomac, in order to arrange for the proper distribution of reading matter and for such other hospital service as could be rendered. More than 3,000 volumes of the publications of the Association were distributed to the soldiers and in the hospitals, largely by Rev. J.G. Forman, of St. Louis, and Rev. John H. Heywood, of Louisville. Among those who acted as agents of the Association in furnishing reading to the army and hospitals were Rev. Calvin Stebbins, Rev. Frederick W. Holland, Rev. Benjamin H. Bailey, Rev. Artemas B. Muzzey, Rev. Newton M. Mann, and Mr. Henry G. Denny. Rev. Samuel Abbot Smith worked zealously at Norfolk at the hospitals and in preaching to the soldiers, until disease and death brought his labors to a close. What this kind of work was, and what it accomplished, was described by Louisa Alcott in her Hospital Sketches, and by William Howell Reed in his Hospital Life in the Army of the Potomac.

[Sidenote: The Sanitary Commission.]

The Sanitary Commission has been described by its historian as "one of the most shining monuments of our civilization," and as an expression of organized sympathy that "must always and everywhere call forth the homage and admiration of mankind." The organizer and leader of this great philanthropic movement for relieving human suffering was Dr. Henry W. Bellows, the minister of All Souls' Church in New York, the first Unitarian church organized in that city. The Commission was first suggested by Dr. Bellows, and he was its efficient leader from the first to the last. He was unanimously selected as its president, when the government had been persuaded, largely through his influence, to establish it as an addition to its medical and hospital service. The historian of the Commission has justly said that he "possessed many remarkable qualifications for so responsible, a position. Perhaps no man in the country exerted a wider or more powerful influence over those who were earnestly seeking the best means of defending our threatened nationality, and certainly never was a moral power of this kind founded upon juster and truer grounds. This influence was not confined to his home, the city of New York, although there it was incontestably very great, but it extended over many other portions of the country, and particularly throughout New England, where circumstances had made his name and his reputation for zeal and ability familiar to those most likely to aid in the furtherance of the new scheme. This power was due, partly of course to the very eminent position which he occupied as a clergyman, partly to the persistent efforts and enlightened zeal with which he advocated all wise measures of social reform, perhaps to his widely extended reputation as an orator, but primarily, and above all, to the rare combination of wide comprehensive views of great questions of public policy with extraordinary practical sagacity, which enabled him so to organize popular intelligence and sympathy that the best practical results were attained while the life–giving principle was preserved. He had the credit of not being what so many of his profession are, an ideologue; he had the clearest perception of what could and what could not be done, and he never hesitated to regard actual experience as the best practical test of the value of his plans and theories. These qualities, so precious and so exceptional in their nature, appeared conspicuously in the efforts made by him to secure the appointment of the Commission by the Government, and it will be found that every page of its history bears the strong impress of his peculiar and characteristic views."[15]

These words of Charles J. Stille, a member of the Sanitary Commission and its authorized historian, afterward the provost of the University of Pennsylvania, indicate the remarkable qualities of leadership possessed by Dr. Bellows. These were undoubtedly added to and made more impressive by his oratorical genius, that was of a very high order. Dr. Hedge spoke of the miraculous power of speech possessed by Dr. Bellows, when he was at his best, as being "incomparably better than anything he could have possibly compassed by careful preparation or conscious effort," and of "those exalted moments when he was fully possessed by his demon."[16] He was inexhaustible in his efforts for the success of the Commission, in directing the work of committees and branches, in appealing to the indifferent, and in giving enthusiasm to all the forces under his direction.

Of the nine original members of the Sanitary Commission, four were Unitarians,—Dr. Bellows, Dr. Samuel G. Howe, Dr. Jeffries Wyman, and Professor Wolcott Gibbs. In the number of those added later was Rev. John H. Heywood, for many years the minister of the Unitarian church in Louisville, who rendered efficient service in the western department. In the convalescents' camp at Alexandria "a wonderful woman," Miss Amy Bradley, had charge of the efficient labors of the Commission, "where for two and a half years she and her assistants rendered incalculable service, in distributing clothing among the needy, procuring dainties for the sick, accompanying discharged soldiers to Washington and assisting them in procuring their papers and pay, furnishing paper and postage, and writing letters for the sick, forwarding money home by drafts that cost nothing to the soldier, answering letters of inquiry to hospital directors, securing certificates of arrears of pay and getting erroneous charges of desertion removed (the Commission saved several innocent soldiers from being shot as condemned deserters), distributing reading matter, telegraphing the friends of very ill soldiers, furnishing meals for feeble soldiers in barracks who could not eat the regulation food. Miss Bradley assisted 2,000 men to secure arrears of pay amounting to $200,000. Prisoners of war, while in prison and when released by general exchange, were largely and promptly relieved and comforted by this department."[17] Another effective worker was Frederick N. Knapp, who had been for several years a Unitarian minister, and who was the leading spirit in the special relief service of the Commission, "and organized and controlled it with masterly zeal, humanity, and success."[18] The work of Mr. Knapp was of great importance; for he was the confidential secretary of Dr. Bellows, and gave his whole time to the service of the Commission. He was a methodical worker, an efficient organizer, and supplied those qualities of persistent industry and grasp of details in which Dr. Bellows was deficient. Without his untiring energy and skilful directing power the Commission would have been less effective than it was in fact. Dr. Bellows also described William G. Scandlin as "one of the most earnest and effective of the Sanitary Commission agents."

In the autumn of 1862 the Commission was greatly crippled in its work because it could not obtain the money with which to carry on its extensive operations, and it was saved from failure by the generosity of California, and the other Pacific states and territories. The remoteness of these states at that time made it impossible for them to contribute their proportion of men, "and they indulged their patriotism and gave relief to their pent–up sympathies with the national cause by pouring out their money like water."[19] The first contribution was received by the Sanitary Commission on September 19, 1862, and was $100,000: a fortnight later the same sum was again sent; and similar contributions followed at short intervals. These sums enabled the Commission to accomplish its splendid work, and to meet the urgent needs of those trying days. How the Pacific coast was able to contribute so largely to this work may be explained in the words of Dr. Bellows, who fully understood the situation, and the vast importance of the help afforded: "The most gifted and inspiring of the patriots who rallied California and the Pacific coast to the flag of the Union was undoubtedly Thomas Starr King, minister of the first Unitarian church in San Francisco. Born in New York, but reared in Massachusetts, he had earned an almost national reputation for eloquence and wit, humanity and nobleness of soul, in the lecture–rooms and pulpits of the north and west, when at the age of thirty–five, he yielded to the religious claims of the Pacific coast and transferred himself to California. There in four years he had built up as public speaker from the pulpit and platform a prodigious popularity. His temperament sympathetic, mercurial, and electric; his disposition hearty, genial, and sweet; his mind versatile, quick, and sparkling; his tact

128

exquisite, and infallible; with a voice as clear as a bell and loud and cheering as a trumpet, his nature and accomplishments perfectly adapted to the people, and place, and the time. His religious profession disarmed many of his political enemies, his political orthodoxy quieted many of his religious opponents. Generous, charitable, disinterested, his full heart and open hand captivated the California people, while his sparkling wit, melodious cadences, and rhetorical abundance perfectly satisfied their taste for intensity and novelty and a touch of extravagance. It has been said by high authority that Mr. King saved California to the Union. California was too loyal at heart to make the boast reasonable; but it is not too much to say that Mr. King did more than any man, by his prompt, outspoken, uncalculating loyalty, to make California know what her own feelings really were. He did all that any man could have done to lead public sentiment that was unconsciously ready to follow where earnest loyalty and patriotism should guide the way."[20]

Not less important in its own degree was the work done in St. Louis by Dr. William G. Eliot, minister since 1834 of the Unitarian church in that city. He became the leader in all efforts for aiding the soldiers, and was most active in forming and directing the Western Sanitary Commission, that worked harmoniously with the national organization, but independently. A large hospital was established and maintained, a home for refugees was secured, and a large camp for "contraband" negroes was established, chiefly under the direction of Dr. Eliot, and largely maintained by his church. He was a potent force in keeping St. Louis and the northern portions of Missouri loyal to the Union. The secretary of the Western Sanitary Commission, J.G. Forman, a Unitarian minister for many years, was most faithful and efficient in this work; and he subsequently became its historian. In the Freedman's Hospital at St. Louis labored with zeal and success Rev. Frederick R. Newall; and he was also superintendent of the Freedman's Bureau in that city, his life being sacrificed to these devoted labors.

[Sidenote: Results of Fifteen Years.]

The work done by the Unitarian Association during the civil war and under the conditions it produced was not a large one, but it absorbed a considerable part of its energies for about five years. In all it printed over 3,000 copies of three books for the soldiers,[21] distributed 750,000 tracts which it had prepared for them,[22] sent to the soldiers 5,000 copies weekly of The Christian Register and The Christian Inquirer, 1,500 copies of the Monthly Journal, 1,000 of The Monthly Religious Magazine, and 1,000 of the

Sunday–school Gazette. During the last year or two of the war its tracts went out at the rate of 50,000 monthly. The tracts and the periodicals therefore numbered a monthly distribution of about 75,000 copies. The seventy volunteer agents who brought these publications to the hands of the soldiers, together with the army chaplains, agents of the Sanitary Commission, and the many nurses in the hospitals, made a considerable force of Unitarian missionaries developed by the exigencies of the war, and the attempts to meliorate its hard conditions.

The period of fifteen years, from 1850 to 1865, which has been under consideration in this chapter, was one of the greatest trial and discouragement to the Association. Its funds reached their lowest ebb, a missionary secretary could not be maintained, a layman performed the necessary office duties, and no considerable aggressive work along missionary lines was undertaken. Writing in a most hopeful spirit of the situation, in November, 1863, the editor of The Christian Register showed that in 1848 the number of Unitarian churches was 201, while in 1863 it was 205, an increase of four only in fifteen years. During this period fifty parishes had gained pastors, but fifty had lost them. Several strong parishes, he said, had come into existence, and two in large places had died. Most of those that had been closed were in small country towns. Nevertheless, with truth it could be said of these fifteen years of discouragement and failure that every one of them was a seed–time for the harvest that was soon to be reaped.

[1] Usually known as the Transcendental Club, sometimes as The Symposium.
It was started in 1836 by Emerson, Ripley, and Hedge, and met at the
houses of the members to discuss philosophical and literary subjects.
It was called Hedge's Club because it met when Rev. F.H. Hedge came
to Boston from Bangor, where he was settled in 1835. It also included
Clarke, Francis, Alcott, Dwight, W.H. Channing, Bartol, Very,
Margaret Fuller, and Elizabeth P. Peabody.

[2] Twenty–eighth Report of the American Unitarian Association, 22.

[3] Ibid., 30. For other statements made at this time see pp. 22 and 26
of this report; Quarterly Journal, L 44, 228, 243, 275, 333; and O.B.
Frothingham's Transcendentalism in New England, 123. John Gorham
Palfrey said (Twenty–eighth Report, 31) that "the evidence of
Christianity is identical with the evidence of the miraculous

character of Jesus," and that "his miraculous powers were the highest evidence that he came from God." Parker replied to this report of the Association in his Friendly Letter to the Executive Committee. Of this report John W. Chadwick has said that it is "the most curious, not to say amusing, document in our denominational archives." See The Organization of our Liberty, Christian Register, July 19, 1900.

[4] In 1854 the receipts from all sources for the year preceding, except from sales of books and interest on investments, was $4,267.32. For the next two years there was a rapid gain, the sum reported in 1856 being $11,615.90; but there was a slight decrease the next year, and the financial panic of 1857 brought the donations down to $4,602.38, the amount reported at the annual meeting of 1858. Then there was a steady gain until the civil war began, after which the contributions were small, the general donations being only $3,056.03 in 1863, which sum was brought up to $5,547.73 by contributions for special purposes, more than one–third of the whole being for the Army Fund.

[5] The Christian Register, October 17, 1863.

[6] The Monthly Journal, I. 350.

[7] Mr. Fox entered the employ of the Association in 1855 as a clerk, and then he became the assistant of the secretary by the appointment of the directors. From 1864 to the present time he has served as the assistant secretary. His services have been invaluable to the Association in many ways, because of his diligence, fidelity, unfailing devotion to its interests, and loyalty to the Unitarian cause.

[8] The beginning of a general fund seems to have been made in 1835, and was secured by special subscriptions for the purpose of paying the salary of a general secretary or missionary agent. The treasurer reported in 1836 that during the previous year $2,408.37 had been collected for this purpose.

[9] Of the churches now in existence the first in Chicago was organized in 1836, that at Quincy in 1840, Milwaukee and Geneva in 1842, Detroit in 1850. After the conference began its work, they appear more frequently, Keokuk coming into existence in 1853, Marietta in 1855, Lawrence in 1856, Unity of Chicago, Kalamazoo, and Buda in 1858, Bloomington in 1859. Then comes a blank during the war period, and a more rapid growth after it, especially when the National Conference had given impetus to missionary activities. Janesville was organized in 1864; Ann Arbor, Kenosha, and Baraboo, in 1865; Tremont, in 1866; Cleveland and Mattoon, in 1867; Unity of St. Louis, Kansas City, St. Joseph, Shelbyville, Davenport, Geneseo, Third of Chicago, and Sheffield, in 1868; Omaha, in 1869.

[10] Written by William G. Eliot, of St. Louis.

[11] Joseph Allen, The Worcester Association and its Antecedents, 268.

[12] Through the business committee the following resolutions were submitted for the consideration of the convention, and they were taken up in order:—

Resolved, That we acknowledge with profound gratitude the success which has attended our labors in the cause of religious freedom, virtue, and piety, and are encouraged to persevere with renewed zeal and energy.

Resolved, That in the character and life of Rev. William E. Channing, just removed from us, we acknowledge one of the richest gifts of God, in intellectual endowments, pure aspiration, moral courage, and disinterested devotion to the cause of truth, freedom, and humanity, and that in view of this, we feel out increased obligation to Christian fidelity and heavenward progress.

Resolved, That viewing with anxiety prevailing fanaticism and growing disregard of public trusts and private relations, we should earnestly labor for a higher religious principle, and especially urge the paramount claims of moral duty.

[13] The places and dates of the Autumnal Conventions were as follows:
Worcester, 1842; Provence, 1843; Albany, 1844; New York, 1845;
Philadelphia, 1846; Salem, 1847; New Bedford, 1848; Portland, 1849;
Springfield, 1850; Portsmouth, 1851; Baltimore, 1852; Worcester,
1853; Montreal, 1854; Providence, 1855; Bangor, 1856; Syracuse, 1857;
Salem, 1858; Lowell, 1859; New Bedford, 1860; Boston, 1861; Brooklyn,
1862; Springfield, 1863.

[14] The first regiments from Massachusetts, Rhode Island, and Kansas, had
as their chaplains Warren H. Cudworth, Augustus Woodbury, and Ephraim
Nute. Charles Babbidge was the chaplain of the sixth Massachusetts
regiment, that which was fired upon in Baltimore. The first artillery
company from Massachusetts had as its chaplain Stephen Barker. Others
who served as army chaplains were John Pierpont, Edmund B. Willson,
Francis C. Williams, Arthur B. Fuller, Sylvan S. Hunting, Charles T.
Canfield, Edward H. Hall, George H. Hepworth, Joseph F. Lovering,
Edwin M. Wheelock, George W. Bartlett, John C. Kimball, Augustus M.
Haskell, Charles A. Humphreys, Milton J. Miller, George A. Ball,
William G. Scandlin, E.B. Fairchild, Samuel W. McDaniel, Frederick R.
Newell, George W. Woodward, Stephen H. Camp, William D. Haley,
Leonard Whitney, Gilbert Cummings, Nahor A. Staples, Carlton A.
Staples, Martin M. Willis, John F. Moors, L.B. Mason, Robert Hassall,
Liberty Billings, Daniel Foster, J.G. Forman, and Augustus H. Conant.
Robert Collyer was chaplain–at–large in the Army of the Potomac.
Charles J. Bowen, William J. Potter, Charles Noyes, James Richardson,
and William H. Channing served as hospital chaplains.

Among the ministers who served as officers were: Hasbrouck Davis, who
became a general; William B. Greene, colonel; Gerald Fitzgerald, who
enlisted as a private, rose to the rank of first lieutenant, and was
elected chaplain of his regiment; Edward I. Galvin, lieutenant, also
elected chaplain; James K. Hosmer, who served through the war, at
first as a private and then as a corporal, writing his experiences
into The Color Guard and The Thinking Bayonet; George W. Shaw and

Alvin Allen, privates. Thomas D. Howard and James H. Fowler were
chaplains in colored regiments. After service as a chaplain of a Hew
Hampshire regiment, Edwin M. Wheelock became a lieutenant in a
colored regiment, as did Charles B. Webster. Thomas W. Higginson was
colonel of a colored regiment, and in another Henry Stone was
lieutenant colonel. It is doubtful if this list is complete, though
an effort has been made to have it as nearly so as possible. Those
who served in the army, and became ministers after leaving it, have
not been included. So far as known, only ordained ministers are
named.

[15] History of the United States Sanitary Commission, being the General
Report of its Work during the War of the Rebellion.

[16] J.H. Allen, Our Liberal Movement in Theology, 210.

[17] Henry W. Bellows, article on the Sanitary Commission, in Johnson's
Cyclopedia, revised edition.

[18] Ibid.

[19] Henry W. Bellows, article on the Sanitary Commission, in Johnson's
Cyclopedia, revised edition.

[20] History of the Sanitary Commission.

[21] Thoughts selected from Channing's Works, Ware's The Silent Pastor,
and Eliot's Discipline of Sorrow. The Association also issued one
number of the Monthly Journal as an Army Companion, which contained
fifty hymns of a patriotic and religions character, with appropriate
tunes, selections from the Bible, directions for preserving health in
the army, and selections from addresses on the injustice of the
rebellion and the spirit in which it should be put down.

[22] Twenty tracts were published. The first was written by Dr. George
Putnam; and was on The Man and the Soldier. The second was The

Soldier of the Good Cause, by Prof. C.E. Norton. Others were A Letter to a Sick Soldier, by Rev. Robert Collyer; An Enemy within the Lines, by Rev. S.H. Winkley. Rev. John F.W. Ware wrote fourteen of these tracts, the following being some of the subjects: The Home to the Camp, The Home to the Hospital, Wounded and in the Hands of the Enemy, Traitors in Camp, A Change of Base, On Picket, The Rebel, The Recruit, A Few Words with the Convalescent, Mustered Out, A Few Words with the Rank and File at Parting.

VIII. THE DENOMINATIONAL AWAKENING.

The war had an inspiring influence upon Unitarians, awakening them to a consciousness of their strength, and drawing them together to work for common purposes as nothing else had ever done. From the beginning they saw in the effort to save the Union, and in the spirit of liberty that animated the nation, an expression of their own principles. Whatever its effect upon other religious bodies, the war gave to Unitarians new faith, courage, and enthusiasm. For the first time they became conscious of their opportunity, and united in a determined purpose to meet its demands with fidelity to their convictions and loyalty to the call of humanity.[1]

No Autumnal Convention having been held in 1864, owing to the failure of the committee appointed for that purpose to make the necessary arrangements, a special meeting of the Unitarian Association was held in the Hollis Street Church, Boston, December 6–7, at the call of the executive committee, "to awaken interest in the work of the Association by laying before the churches the condition of our funds and the demand for our labor." The attendance was large, and the tone of the meeting was hopeful and enthusiastic. After Dr. Stebbins, the president, had stated the purpose of the meeting, Dr. Bellows urged the importance of a more effective organization of the Unitarian body. His success with the Sanitary Commission had evidently prepared his mind for a like work on the part of Unitarians, and for a strong faith in the value of organized effort in behalf of liberal religion. His capacity as leader during the war had prepared men to accept it in other fields of effort, and Unitarians were ready to use it in their behalf. The hopefulness that existed, in view of the success of the Union cause, and the enthusiastic interest in the methods of moral and spiritual reform that was manifested because of the triumph of the spirit of freedom in the nation, led many to think that like efforts in behalf of liberal

Christianity would result in like successes.

On the afternoon of the second day (a meeting in the evening of the first day only having been held) James P. Walker, the publisher, gave a resume of the activities of the Association during the forty years of its existence, and said that its receipts had been on the average only $8,038.88 yearly. He showed that much had been done with this small sum, and that the results were much larger than the amount of money invested would indicate. He pointed out the fact that the demands upon the Association were rapidly increasing, and far more rapidly than the contributions. There was an urgent need for larger giving, he said, and for a more loyal support of the missionary arm of the denomination. He offered a series of resolutions calling for the raising of $25,000 during the year. Rev. Edward Everett Hale said that $100,000 ought to be given to the proposed object, and urged that more missionaries should be sent into the field. Thereupon Mr. Henry P. Kidder arose, and said: "It is often easier to do a great thing than a small one. I move that this meeting undertake to raise $100,000 for the service of the next year." Dr. Bellows then called the attention of the conference to the importance of considering the manner of securing this large sum and of devising methods to insure success. He proposed "that a committee of ten persons, three ministers and seven laymen, should be appointed to call a convention, to consist of the pastor and two delegates from each church or parish in the Unitarian denomination, to meet in the city of New York, to consider the interests of our cause and to institute measures for its good." The two resolutions were unanimously adopted, pledging the denomination to raise $100,000, and to the holding of a delegate convention in New York. The president appointed, as members of the committee of arrangements for the convention, Rev. Henry W. Bellows, Messrs. A.A. Low, U.A. Murdock, Henry P. Kidder, Atherton Blight, Enoch Pratt, and Artemas Carter, Rev. Edward E. Hale, and Rev. Charles H. Brigham.

The convention in New York was not waited for in order to make an effort to secure the $100,000 it was proposed to raise; and early in January the president of the Association, Dr. Rufus P. Stebbins, was authorized to devote his whole time to securing that sum. A circular was sent to the churches saying that such a sum "was needed, and should and could be raised." "The hour has come," said the executive committee in their appeal to the churches, "which the fathers longed to see, but were denied the sight,—of taking our true position among other branches of the church of our Lord Jesus Christ in the spread and establishment of the Gospel."

The response to this call was prompt and enthusiastic beyond any precedent. The war had made money plentiful, and it came easily to those who were successful. Great fortunes had been rapidly gathered; and the country had never known an equal prosperity, even though the burden of the war had not yet been removed. In February the president of the Association was able to announce that $28,871.47 had been subscribed by twelve churches. By the end of March the pledges had reached $63,862.63; and when the convention met in New York, April 5, 1865, the contributions then pledged were only a few thousand dollars short of the sum desired. By the end of May the sum reported was $111,676.74, which was increased by several hundred dollars more.

[Sidenote: The New York Convention of 1865.]

It was when this success was certain that the convention met in New York. The victory of the Union cause was then assured, and the utmost enthusiasm prevailed. Some of the final and most important scenes of the great national struggle were enacted while the convention was in session. Courage and hope ran high under these circumstances; and the convention was not only enthusiastically loyal to the nation, but equally so to its own denominational interests. For the first time in the history of the Unitarian body in this country the churches were directly represented at a general gathering. The number of churches represented was two hundred and two, and they sent three hundred and eighty-five delegates. Many other persons attended, however; and throughout all the sittings of the convention the audience was a large one. Many women were present, though not as delegates, the men only having official recognition in this gathering. It is evident from the records, the newspaper reports, and the memories of those present, that the interest in this meeting was very large, and that the attendance was quite beyond what was anticipated by any one concerned in planning it. The call to all the churches, and the giving them an equality of representation in the convention, was doubtless one of the causes of its success. As a result, an able body of laymen appeared in the convention, who were accustomed to business methods and familiar with legislative procedure, and who carried through the work of the convention with deliberation and skill.

On the first evening of the convention a sermon was preached by Dr. James Freeman Clarke that was a noble and generous introduction to its deliberations. He called for the exercise of the spirit of inclusiveness, a broad and tolerant catholicity, and union on the basis of the work to be done. On the morning of April 5, 1865, at eleven o'clock, the convention met for the transaction of business in All Souls' Church, of which Henry

Whitney Bellows was the minister. Hon. John A. Andrew, then the governor of Massachusetts, was elected to preside over the convention; and among the vice–presidents were William Cullen Bryant, Rev. John Gorham Palfrey, Hon. Ebenezer Rockwood Hoar, Rev. Orville Dewey, and Rev. Ezra Stiles Gannett, while Rev. Edward Everett Hale was made the secretary. In Governor Andrew the convention had as its presiding officer a man of a broad and generous spirit, who was insistent that the main purpose of the meeting should be kept always steadily in view, and yet that all the members and all the varying opinions should have just recognition. In a large degree the success of the convention was due to his catholicity and to his skill in reconciling opposing interests.

The time of the convention was devoted almost wholly to legislating for the denomination and to planning for its future work. On the morning of the second day the subject of organization came up for consideration, and the committee selected for that purpose presented a constitution providing for a National Conference that should meet annually, and that should be constituted of the minister and two lay delegates from each church, together with three delegates each from the American Unitarian Association, the Western Conference, and such other bodies as might be invited to participate in its deliberations. This Conference was to be only recommendatory in its character, adopting "the existing organizations of the Unitarian body as the instruments of its power." The name of the new organization was the subject of some discussion, James Freeman Clarke wishing to make the Conference one of Independent and Unitarian churches, while another delegate desired to substitute "free Christian" for Unitarian. The desire strongly manifested by a considerable number to make the Conference include in its membership all liberal churches of whatever name not acceptable to the majority of the delegates, voted with a decided emphasis to organize strictly on the Unitarian basis.

As soon as the convention was organized, expression was given to the demand for a doctrinal basis for its deliberations. Though several attempts were made to bring about the acceptance of a creed, these met with complete failure. In the preamble to the constitution, however, it was asserted that the delegates were "disciples of the Lord Jesus Christ," while the first article declared that the conference was organized to promote "the cause of Christian faith and work." It was quite evident that a large majority of the delegates regarded the convention as Christian in its purposes and distinctly Unitarian in its denominational mission. A minority desired a platform that should have no theological implications, and that should permit the co–operation of every kind of liberal church. The use of the phrase Lord Jesus Christ was strongly opposed by the more radical section of the convention, but the members of it were not organized or ready to give utterance to their protest in an effective manner.

The convention gave its approval to the efforts of the Unitarian Association to secure the sum of $100,000, and urged the churches, that had not already done so, to contribute. It also advised the securing of a like sum as an endowment for Antioch College, and commended to men of wealth the needs of the Harvard and Meadville Theological Schools. The council of the Conference was asked to give its attention to the necessity and duty of creating an organ for the denomination, to be called The Liberal Christian. A resolution looking to union with the Universalist body was presented, and one was passed declaring "that there should be recognition, fellowship, and co-operation between all those various elements in our population that are prepared to meet on the basis of Christianity." James Freeman Clarke, Samuel J. May, and Robert Collyer were constituted a committee of correspondence, to promote acquaintance, fraternity, and unity between Unitarians and all of like liberal faith.[2]

A resolution offered by William Cullen Bryant expressive of thanksgiving because of the near approach of peace, and for the opening made by the extinction of slavery for the diffusion of Christianity in its true spirit as a religion of love, mercy, and universal liberty, was unanimously adopted by a rising vote.

The convention was a remarkable success in the number who attended its sessions, the character of the men who participated in its deliberations, and the skill with which the unsectarian sect had been organized for effective co-operation and work. Its influence was immediately felt throughout the denomination and upon all its activities. The change in attitude was very great, and the depressed and discouraged tone of many Unitarian utterances for a number of years preceding and following 1860 gave way to one of enthusiasm and courage.[3]

[Sidenote: New Life in the Unitarian Association.]

The annual meeting of the Unitarian Association, that soon followed, felt the new stir of life, and the awakening to a larger consciousness of power. The chief attention was directed to meeting the new opportunities that had been presented, and to preparing for the larger work required. Dr. Rufus P. Stebbins, who had been for three years the president, and who had been actively instrumental in securing the large accession to the contributions of the year, was elected secretary, with the intent that he should devote himself to pushing forward the missionary enterprises of the Association. He refused to serve, and accepted the position only until his successor could be secured. In a few weeks, the executive committee elected Rev. Charles Lowe to this office, and he immediately entered upon its duties. He proved to be eminently fitted for the place by his enthusiastic interest in the work to be accomplished, and by his skill as an organizer. His catholicity of mind enabled him to conciliate, as far as this was possible, the conservative and radical elements in the denomination, and to unite them into an effective working body. Educated at Harvard College and Divinity School, Lowe spent two years as a tutor in the college, and then was settled successively over parishes in New Bedford, Salem, and Somerville. His experience and skill as an army agent of the Association suggested his fitness for the larger sphere of labor into which he was now inducted. For six most difficult and trying years he successfully conducted the affairs of the Association.

For the first time in the history of the Association its income was such as to enable it to plan its work on a large scale, and in some degree commensurate with its opportunities. During the year and a half preceding the first of June, 1866, there was contributed to the Association about $175,000, to Antioch College $103,000, to the Boston Fraternity of Churches $22,920, to the Children's Mission $42,000, to the Freedman's Aid Societies $30,000, to the Sunday School Society $2,500, to The Christian Register $15,000, and to the Western Conference $6,000, making a total of about $400,000 given by the denomination to these religious, educational, and philanthropic purposes; and this financial success was truly indicative of the new interest in its work that had come to the Unitarian body.

[Sidenote: The New Theological Position.]

Although the New York convention voted that $100,000 ought to be raised in 1866, because the needs of the denomination demanded it, yet only $60,000 were secured. The reaction that followed the close of the war had set in, the financial prosperity of the country had begun to lessen, and the enthusiasm that had made the first great effort of the denomination so eminently successful did not continue. A chief cause for the waning interest in the denomination itself was the agitation, in regard to the theological position of the Unitarian body that began almost immediately after the New York convention.

Unitarianism in America

The older Unitarians held to the Bible and the teachings of Jesus as the great sources of spiritual truth as strongly as did the orthodox, and they differed from them only as to the purport of the message conveyed. This may be seen in a creed offered to the New York convention, by a prominent layman,[4] almost immediately after it was opened on the first morning. In this proposed creed it was asserted that Unitarians believe "in one Lord, Jesus Christ; the Son of God and his specially appointed messenger, and representative to our race; gifted with supernatural power, approved of God by miracles and signs and wonders which God did by him, and thus by divine authority commanding the devout and reverential faith of all who claim the Christian name." Although this creed was not adopted by the convention, it expressed the belief of a majority of Unitarians. To the same purport was the word spoken by Dr. Bellows, when he said: "Unitarians of the school to which I belong accept Jesus Christ with all their hearts as the Sent of God, the divinely inspired Son of the Father, who by his miraculously proven office and his sinless life and character was fitted to be, and was made revealer of the universal and permanent religion of the human race."[5] These quotations indicate that the more conservative Unitarians had not changed their position since 1853, when they made official statement of their acceptance of Christianity as authenticated by miracles and the supernatural. In fact, they held essentially to the attitude taken when they left the older Congregational body.

On the other hand, the transcendentalists and the radical Unitarians proposed a new theory of the nature of religious truth, and insisted that the spiritual message of Christianity is inward, and not outward, directly to the soul of man, and not through the mediation of a person or a book. Almost from the first Channing had been moving towards this newer conception of the nature and method of religion. He did not wholly abandon the miraculous, but it grew to have less significance for him with each year. The Unitarian conception of religion as natural to man, which was maintained strenuously from the time of Jonathan Mayhew, made it probable, if not certain, that a merely external system of religion would be ultimately outgrown. In his lecture on self–denial Channing stated this position in the clearest terms. "If," he said, "after a deliberate and impartial use of our best faculties, a professed revelation seems to us plainly to disagree with itself or to clash with great principles which we cannot question, we ought not to hesitate to withhold from it our belief. I am surer that my rational nature is from God, than that any book is an expression of his will. This light in my own breast is his primary revelation, and all subsequent ones must accord with it, and are in fact intended to blend with and brighten it."[6]

Channing was not alone in accepting Christianity as a spiritual principle that is natural and universal. As early as 1826 Alvan Lamson had defended the proposition that miracles are merely local in their nature, and that attention should be chiefly given to the tendency, spirit, and object of Christianity. He claimed that it bore on the face of it the marks of its heavenly origin, and that, when these are fully accepted, no other form of evidence is required.[7] In 1834 James Walker, in writing on The Philosophy of Man's Spiritual Nature in regard to the Foundations of Faith, had taken what was essentially the transcendentalist view of the origin and nature of religion. He contended for the "religion in the soul" that is authenticated "by the revelations of consciousness."[8] In 1836 Convers Francis, in, describing the religion of Christ as a purely internal principle, maintained the "quiet, spirit-searching character of Christianity," as "a kingdom wholly within the soul of man."[9]

When Convers Francis became a professor in the Harvard Divinity School, in 1842, the spiritual philosophy had recognition there; and he had a considerable influence upon the young men who came under his guidance. Though of the older way of thinking, George R. Noyes, who became a professor in the school in 1840, was always on the side of liberty of interpretation and expression. For the next two decades the Divinity School sent out a succession of such men as John Weiss, Octavius B. Frothingham, Samuel Longfellow, William J. Potter, and Francis E. Abbot, who were joined by William Henry Channing, Samuel Johnson, David A. Wasson, and others, who did not study there. These men gave a new meaning to Unitarianism, took it away from miracles to nature, discarded its evidences to rely on intuition, rejected its supernatural deity for an immanent God who speaks through all life his divine word.

During the interval between the New York convention and the first session of the National Conference, which was held in Syracuse, October 10–11, 1866, the questions which separated the conservatives and radicals were freely debated in the periodicals of the denomination, and also in sermons and pamphlets. The radicals organized for securing a revision of the constitution; and on the morning of the first day Francis E. Abbot, then the minister at Dover, N.H., offered a new preamble and first article as substitutes for those adopted in New York, in which he stated that "the object of Christianity is the universal diffusion of love, righteousness, and truth," that "perfect freedom of thought, which is at once the right and duty of every human being, always leads to diversity of opinion, and is therefore hindered by common creeds or statements of faith," and that therefore the churches assembled in the conference, "disregarding all sectarian or theological differences, and offering a cordial fellowship to all who will join them in Christian work, unite themselves in a common body, to be known as The National Conference of Unitarian and Independent Churches."

At the afternoon session Mr. Abbot's amendment was rejected; but on the motion of James Freeman Clarke the name was changed to The National Conference of Unitarian and Other Christian Churches. A resolution stating that the expression "Other Christian Churches was not meant to exclude religious societies which have no distinctive church organization, and are not nominally Christian, if they desire to co-operate with the Conference in what it regards as Christian work," was laid on the table.

[Sidenote: Organization of the Free Religious Association.]

The result of the refusal at Syracuse to revise the constitution of the National Conference was that the radical men on the railroad train returning to Boston held a consultation, and resolved to organize an association that would secure them the liberty they desired. After correspondence and much planning a meeting was held in Boston, at the house of Rev. Cyrus A. Bartol, on February 5, 1867, to consider what should be done. After a thorough discussion of the subject the Free Religious Association was planned; and the organization was perfected at a meeting held in Horticultural Hall, Boston, May 30, 1867. Some of those who took part in this movement thought that all religion had been outgrown, but the majority believed that it is essential and eternal. What they sought was to remove its local and national elements, and to get rid of its merely sectarian and traditional features.

At the first meeting the speakers were O.B. Frothingham, Henry Blanchard, Lucretia Mott, Robert Dale Owen, John Weiss, Oliver Johnson, Francis E. Abbot, David A. Wasson, T.W. Higginson, and R.W. Emerson; and discussion was participated in by A.B. Alcott, E.C. Towne, Frank B. Sanborn, Hannah E. Stevenson, Ednah D. Cheney, Charles C. Burleigh, and Caroline H. Dall. Of these persons, one-half had been Unitarian ministers, and about one-third of them were still settled over Unitarian parishes. Mr. Frothingham was elected president of the new organization, and Rev. William J. Potter secretary. The purposes of the Association were "to promote the interests of pure religion, to encourage the scientific study of theology and to increase fellowship in the spirit." In 1872 the constitution was revised by changing the subject of study from theology to man's religious nature and history, and by the addition of the statement that "nothing in the name or constitution of the Association shall ever be construed as limiting membership by any test of speculative opinion or belief,—or as defining the position of the Association, collectively considered, with reference to any such opinion or belief,—or as interfering in any other way with that absolute freedom of thought and expression which is the natural right of every rational being."

The original purpose of the Free Religious Association, as defined in its constitution and in the addresses delivered before it, was the recognition of the universality of religion, and the representation of all phases of religious opinion in its membership and on its platform. The circumstances of its organization, however, in some measure took it away from this broader position, and made it the organ of the radical Unitarian opinion. Those Unitarians who did not find in the American Unitarian Association and the National Conference such fellowship as they desired became active in the Free Religious organization.

The cause of Free Religion was ably presented in the pages of The Radical, a monthly journal edited by Sidney H. Morse, and published in Boston, and The Index, edited by Francis E. Abbot, at first in Toledo and then in Boston. It also found expression at the Sunday afternoon meetings held in Horticultural Hall, Boston, for several winters, beginning in 1868–69; in the conventions held in several of the leading cities of the northern states; at the gatherings of the Chestnut Street Club; and in the annual meetings of the Free Religious Association held in Boston during anniversary week. Little effort was made to organize churches, and only two or three came into existence distinctly on the basis of Free Religion. In connection with The Index, Francis E. Abbot organized the Liberal League to promote the interests of Free Religion, with about four hundred local branches; but this organization proved ineffective, and soon ceased its existence.

The withdrawal of the radicals into the Free Religious Association did not quiet the agitation in the Unitarian ranks, partly because some of the most active workers in that Association continued to occupy Unitarian pulpits, and partly because a considerable radical element did not withdraw in any manner. The conferences had an unfailing subject for exciting discussion, and the Unitarian body was at this time in a chronic condition of agitation. As in the days of the controversy about the Trinity, the more conservative ministers would not exchange pulpits with the more radical.

[Sidenote: Unsuccessful Attempts at Reconciliation.]

At the second session of the National Conference, held in New York City, October 7–9, 1868, another attempt was made to bring about a reconciliation between the two wings of the denomination. In an attitude of generous good will and with a noble desire for inclusiveness and peace, James Freeman Clarke proposed an addition to the constitution of the Conference, in which it was declared "that we heartily welcome to that fellowship all who desire to work with us in advancing the kingdom of God." Such a broad invitation was not acceptable to the majority; and, after an extended debate, this amendment was withdrawn, and the following, offered by Edward Everett Hale, and essentially the same as that presented by Mr. Clarke, with the exception of the phrase just quoted, was adopted:—

To secure the largest unity of the spirit and the widest practical co–operation, it is hereby understood that all the declarations of this conference, including the preamble and constitution, are expressions only of its majority, and dependent wholly for their effect upon the consent they command on their own merits from the churches here represented or belonging within the circle of our fellowship.

The annual meeting of the Unitarian Association in 1870 was largely occupied with the vexing problem of the basis of fellowship; and the secretary, Charles Lowe, read a conciliatory and explanatory address. He said that the wide differences of theological opinion existing in the denomination were "an inevitable consequence of the great principle on which Unitarianism rests. That principle is that Christian faith and Christian union can coexist with individual liberty."[10] Rev. George H. Hepworth, then the minister of the Church of the Messiah in New York, asked for an authoritative statement of the Unitarian position, urging this demand with great insistence; and he presented a resolution calling for a committee of five to prepare "a statement of faith, which shall, as nearly as may be, represent the religious opinions of the Unitarian denomination."

While Dr. Bellows had been the leader in securing the adoption of the Christian basis for the National Conference, and the insertion into the preamble of its constitution of the expression of faith in the Lordship of Jesus Christ, he was strongly opposed to any attempt to impose a creed upon the denomination, however attenuated it might be. He has been often charged with inconsistency, and it is difficult to reconcile his position in 1870 with that held in 1865. What he attempted to secure, however, was the utmost of liberty possible within the limits of Christianity; and, when he had committed the Unitarian body to the Christian position, he desired nothing more, believing that a creed would be inconsistent with the liberty enjoyed by all Unitarians. Without doubt his address at this meeting, in opposition to Mr. Hepworth's proposal, made it impossible to secure a vote in favor of a creed. "We want to represent a body," he said, "that presents itself to the forming hand of the Almighty Spirit of God in a fluid, plastic form. We cannot keep our denomination in that state, and yet give it the character of being cast into a positive mould. You must either abandon that great work you have done, as the only body in Christendom that occupies the position of absolute and perfect liberty, with some measure of Christian faith, or you must continue to occupy that position and thank God for it without hankering after some immediate victories that are so strong a temptation to many in our denomination." When the resolution in favor of a creed was brought to a vote, it was "defeated by a very large majority." By this act the Unitarian body again asserted its Christian position, but refused to define or to limit its Christianity.

Notwithstanding the refusal of the Unitarian Association to adopt a creed, the attempt to secure one was renewed in the National Conference with as much energy as if this were not already a lost cause. At the session held in New York, October, 1870, the subject came up for extended consideration, several amendments to the constitution were proposed, and, after a prolonged discussion, that offered by George H. Hepworth was adopted:—

Reaffirming our allegiance to the Gospel of Jesus Christ, and desiring
to secure the largest unity of the spirit and the widest practical
co–operation, we invite to our fellowship all who wish to be followers
of Christ.

[Sidenote: The Year Book Controversy.]

One result of this controversy was that in 1873 it having come to the attention of Rev. O.B. Frothingham, the president of the Free Religious Association, that his name was in the list of Unitarian ministers published in the Year Book of the Unitarian Association, he expressed surprise that it should have been continued there, and asked for its removal. The same action was taken by Francis E. Abbot, the editor of The Index, and others of the radicals. This action was in part the result of the attitude taken by Rev. Thomas J. Mumford, editor of The Christian Register, who in 1872 insisted that the word "Religious" had no proper place in the name of the Free Religious Association, and who invited those Unitarians "who have ceased to accept Jesus as pre–eminently their spiritual leader and teacher" to withdraw from the Unitarian body.

In November, 1873, Mr. George W. Fox, the assistant secretary of the Unitarian Association and the editor of its Year Book, wrote to several of the radicals, calling their attention to the action of Mr. Frothingham in requesting the removal of his name, and asked if their names remained in that publication "with their knowledge and consent." In a subsequent letter to William J. Potter, the minister of the Unitarian church in New Bedford and the secretary of the Free Religious Association, he explained that "the Year Book lists of societies and ministers are simply a directory, prepared by the Association for the accommodation of the denomination, and that the Association does not undertake to decide the question as to what are or are not Unitarian societies or ministers, but merely puts into print facts, in the making of which it assumes no responsibility and has no agency."

Mr. Potter expressed his purpose not to ask for the removal of his name, but wrote that he did not call himself a Unitarian Christian or by any denominational name. The officers of the Association thereupon instructed the editor of the Year Book to remove Mr. Potter's name from the list of Unitarian ministers published therein. The reason for this action was stated in a letter from the editor to Mr. Potter, announcing that his name had been removed. The letter said, "While there might be no desire to define Christianity in the case of those who claim that they are in any sense of the term entitled to be called Christians, for those persons who, like yourself, disavow the name, there seems to be no need of raising any question as to how broad a range of opinion the name may properly be stretched to cover."[11]

There followed a vigorous discussion of the action of the Association in dropping Mr. Potter's name, it being recognized that no more thoroughly religious man was to be found in the denomination, and that none more truly exemplified the Christian spirit, whatever might be his wish as to the use of the Christian name. At the sixth session of the National Conference, held at Saratoga in September, 1874, the Essex Conference protested against the erasure of the name of a church in long and regular fellowship with the Unitarian Association from its Year Book; and a resolution offered by Dr. Bellows, indorsing the action of the officers of the National Conference in inviting the New Bedford church to send delegates, was passed without dissent. At the session of the Western Conference held in Chicago during 1875, resolutions were passed protesting against the removing of the name of any person from the accredited list of Unitarian ministers until he requested it, had left the denomination, joined some other sect, or been adjudged guilty of immorality. As a result of this discussion and of the broad sympathies and inclusive spirit of the conference, the following platform, in the shape of a resolution, was adopted:—

That the Western Unitarian Conference conditions its fellowship on no dogmatic tests, but welcomes all thereto who desire to work with it in advancing the kingdom of God.

The attitude of the Unitarian Association and the National Conference—that is, of a large majority of Unitarians at this time—may be accurately defined in the words of Charles Lowe, who said: "I admit that we make a belief in Christianity a test of fellowship. No stretch of liberality will make me wish to deny that a belief in Jesus Christ is the absolutely essential qualification. But I will oppose, as a test, any definition of Christianity, any words about Christ, for Christ himself, as the principles of our fellowship and union."[12] These words exactly define what was sought for, which was liberty within the limits of Christianity. The primary insistence was upon discipleship to Jesus Christ, but it was maintained that loyalty to Christ is compatible with the largest degree of personal liberty.

Fundamentally, this controversy was a continuation of that which had agitated New England from the beginning, that had divided those opposed to "the great awakening" of the middle of the eighteenth century from those who favored it, that led the Unitarians away from the Orthodox, and that now divided radical and conservative Unitarians. The advance was always towards a more pronounced assertion of individualism, and a more positive rejection of tradition, organization, and external authority. Indeed, it was towards this end that Unitarianism had directed its energies from the beginning; and the force of this tendency could not be overcome because some called for a creed, and more had come to see the need of an efficient organization for practical purposes.

What the radicals desired was freedom, and the broadest assertion of individuality. It was maintained by Francis E. Abbot that "the spiritual ideal of Free Religion is to develop the individuality of the soul in the highest, fullest, and most independent manner possible."[13] The other distinctive principle of the radicals was that religion is universal, that all religions are essentially, the same, and that Christianity is simply one of the phases of universal religion. David A. Wasson defined religion as "the consciousness of universal relation,"[14] and as "the sense of unity with the infinite whole," adding that "morals, reason, freedom, are bound up with it."[15] This means, in simple statement, that religion is natural to man, and that it needs no authentication by miracle or supernatural manifestation. It means that all religions are essentially the same in their origin, and that none can claim the special favor of God in their manner of presentation to the world. According to this conception of religion, as was stated by. William J. Potter, Christianity is "provisional, preparatory, educational, containing, alongside of the most valuable truth, much that is only human error and bigotry and superstitious imagination."[16] "The spiritual ideal of Christianity," said Francis E. Abbot, "is the suppression of self and perfect imitation of Jesus the Christ. The spiritual ideal of Free Religion is the development of self, and the harmonious education of all its powers to the highest possible degree."[17]

Through all this controversy what was sought for was a method of reconciling fellowship with individuality of opinion, of establishing a church in which freedom of faith for the individual shall have full recognition. In a word, the Unitarian body had a conviction that tradition is compatible with intuition, institutions with personal freedom, and co−operation with individual initiative. The problems involved were too large for an immediate solution; and what Unitarians accepted was an ideal, and not a fact fully realized in their denominational life. The doctrinal phases of the controversy have always been subsidiary to this larger search, this desire to give to the individual all the liberty that is compatible with his co−operation with others. The result of it has been to teach the Unitarian body, in the words of Francis E. Abbot at Syracuse, in 1866, that "the only reconciliation of the duties of collective Christian activity and individual freedom of thought lies in an efficient organization for practical Christian work, based rather on unity of spirit than on uniformity of belief."[18]

[Sidenote: Missionary Activities.]

During this period of controversy, from 1865 to 1880, the Unitarian Association had at its head several able men, who were actively interested in its work. The president for 1865−66 was Rev. John G. Palfrey; and he was succeeded, in 1867, by Hon. Thomas D. Eliot, of New Bedford, who was in both houses of the Massachusetts legislature, and then for a number of years in the lower house of Congress. From 1870 to 1872 the president was Mr. Henry Chapin, of Worcester, an able lawyer and judge, loyally devoted to the Sunday−school work of his city and county. He was succeeded by Hon. John Wells, chief justice of the Supreme Court of Massachusetts, who was deeply interested in the church with which he was connected. In 1876 Mr. Henry P. Kidder was elected to this office,—a position he held for ten years. He was prominent in the banking interests of Boston, gave much attention to the charities of the city, and was an efficient worker in the South Congregational Church.

Rev. Charles Lowe, the secretary from 1865 to 1871, wisely directed the activities of the Association through the early period of the great awakening of the denomination, and kept it from going to pieces on the Scylla and Charybdis of creed and radicalism. He was followed at a most critical and difficult time by Rev. Rush R. Shippen, who continued to hold the office until 1881. The reaction succeeding the great prosperity that followed the close of the civil war brought great burdens of debt to many individuals, and to cities, states, and the nation. These troubles distracted attention from spiritual interests, and joined with various other calamities in making this a trying time for churches and religious organizations.

The discussions as to the theological position of the denomination naturally resulted in more or less of disorganization, and made it impossible to secure the unity of effort which is essential to any positive missionary growth. In spite of these drawbacks, however, denominational interests slowly advanced. During this period the Unitarian Association began to receive a considerable increase of its funds from legacies,—a result of its enlarged activities, and of the new interest awakened by the formation of the National Conference.

A few facts may be mentioned to illustrate the never–failing generosity of Unitarian givers when specific needs are presented. In October, 1871, occurred the great fire in Chicago and the burning of Unity Church in that city, which was aided with $60,000 in rebuilding; while the Third Church and All Souls' were helped liberally in passing through this crisis. The following year the Boston fire crippled sadly the resources of the Association, and instead of the $150,000 asked for only $42,000 were received. Yet in 1876 the church in Washington was built, and $30,000 were contributed to that purpose by the denomination. In 1879; the denomination gave $56,000 to free the Church of the Messiah in New York from debt. During this period $100,000 were contributed to the Young Men's Christian Union in Boston, $90,000 to the Harvard Divinity School, $20,000 to the Prospect Hill School at Greenfield, and $30,000 towards the Channing Memorial Church in Newport.

During these trying times the administration of Unitarian affairs in the west was in judicious hands, In 1865 Rev. Charles G. Ames began those missionary efforts on the Pacific coast that have led on to the establishment of a considerable number of churches in that section of the country. In central Illinois the devoted labors of Jasper L. Douthit from 1868 to the present time have produced wide–reaching results in behalf of a genuine religion, temperance, good government, and education. In 1868 Rev. Carlton A. Staples was made the missionary agent of the Association in the west, with headquarters in Chicago, where a book–room was established. He was succeeded in 1872 by Rev. Sylvan S. Hunting, who was a tireless worker in the western field for many years. In 1874 Rev. Jenkin Lloyd Jones became the missionary of the Wisconsin Conference, and the next year of the Western Conference. For ten years Mr. Jones labored in this position with enthusiasm for the Unitarian cause in the west.

[Sidenote: College Town Missions.]

In the spring of 1865 the attention of the Unitarian Association was directed to the growing University of Michigan; and Rev. Charles H. Brigham, then the minister of the church in Taunton, was invited to proceed to Ann Arbor, and see what might be accomplished there. Meetings were held in the court–house, but in 1866 an old Methodist church was purchased by the Association and adapted to the uses of the new society. The congregation numbered at first about eighty persons, but gradually increased, especially from the attendance of university students. Mr. Brigham was asked by the students who listened to him to form a Bible class for their instruction, and this increased in numbers until it included from two hundred to three hundred persons. On Sunday evenings he delivered lectures wherein his wide and varied learning was made subservient to high ideals and to a noble interpretation of Christianity. He led many young men and women into the liberal faith, and he exercised through them a wide influence throughout the west. His gifts as a lecturer were also made available at the Meadville Theological School, with which institution he was connected for ten years.[19]

The success of Mr. Brigham led to the founding of other college town churches, that at Ithaca, the seat of Cornell University, being established in 1866. In 1878 such a mission was begun at Madison for the students of the University of Wisconsin, and another at Iowa City for the University of Iowa. In more recent years college missions have been started at Lawrence, Kan.; Lincoln, Neb.; Minneapolis, Minn.; Berkeley, Cal.; Colorado Springs; and Amherst, Mass. This has proved to be one of the most effective ways of extending Unitarianism as a modern interpretation of Christianity.

[Sidenote: Theatre Preaching.]

Another interest developed by the awakening of 1865 was the popularization of Unitarianism by the use of theatres. In January, 1866, was begun in the Cooper Institute, New York, a Sunday evening course of lectures by Clarke, Bellows, Osgood, Frothingham, Putnam, Chadwick, and Joseph May, which was largely attended. Some of the most important doctrinal subjects were discussed. A few weeks later a similar course was undertaken in Washington with like success. In March, 1867, the Suffolk Conference undertook such a series of lectures in the Boston Theatre, which was crowded to its utmost capacity. Then followed courses of sermons or lectures in Lawrence, New Bedford, Salem, Springfield, Providence, Chicago, and San Francisco, as well as in other places. The council of the National Conference, in 1868, commended this as an important work that should be encouraged. Rev. Adams Ayer was made an agent of the Association to organize such meetings, and their success was remarkable for several years. In 1869 Rev. Charles Lowe spoke of "that wonderful feature of our recent experience," and urged that these meetings should be so organized as to lead to definite results.

An earnest effort was made to organize the theatre congregations into unsectarian societies. It was proposed to form Christian unions that should work for Christian improvement and usefulness. The first result of this effort was the reorganization of the Boston Young Men's Christian Union in the spring of 1868. A similar institution was formed in Providence, to promote worship, education, hospitality and benevolence. Unions were also formed in, Salem, Lowell, Cambridge, New Bedford, New York, and elsewhere.

[Sidenote: Organization of Local Conferences.]

In the autumn of 1865, in order to facilitate the collection of money for the Unitarian Association, a number of local conferences were held in Massachusetts. The first of these met at Somerville, November 14, and was primarily a meeting of the Cambridge Association of Ministers, including all the lay delegates to the New York convention from the churches which that association represented. The result of this meeting was an increase of contributions to the Unitarian Association, and the determination to organize permanently to facilitate that work. Dr. E.E. Hale has stated that the initial suggestion of these meetings came from a conversation between Dr. Bellows and Dr. E.H. Sears, in which the latter said "that a very important element in any effort which should reveal the Unitarian church to itself would be some plan by which neighboring churches would be brought together more familiarly."[20]

The local conferences had distinct antecedents, however, by which their character was doubtless in some degree determined. The early county and other local auxiliaries to the Unitarian Association begun in 1826 and continued for at least twenty years, which were general throughout New England, afforded a precedent; but a more immediate initiative had been taken in New Hampshire, where the New Hampshire Unitarian Association had been organized at Manchester, February 25, 1863. It does not appear that this organization was in any way a revival of the former society of the same name in that state, which was organized at Concord in 1832, and which was very active for a brief period. A Unitarian Church Association of Maine was organized at Portland, September 21, 1852, largely under the influence of Rev. Sylvester Judd, of Augusta; but it had only a brief existence. The Maine Conference of Unitarian Churches was organized at Farmington, July 8, 1863.[21] These organizations antedated the movement for the formation of local conferences on the part of the National Conference; and they doubtless gave motive and impetus to that effort.

On November 30, 1865, a meeting similar to that at Somerville was held by the Franklin Evangelical Association[22] at Springfield, and with similar results. Other meetings were held at Lowell, Dedham, Quincy, Salem, Taunton, Worcester, and Boston. The attendance at all these meetings was large, they developed an enthusiastic interest, and pledges were promptly made looking to larger contributions to the Unitarian Association.

At the Syracuse meeting of the National Conference, in 1866, Dr. Bellows reported for the council in favor of local organizations, auxiliary to the national body. "No great national convention of any kind succeeds," it was declared, "which is not the concurrence of many local conventions, each of which has duties of detail and special spheres of influence upon whose co-operation the final and grand success of the whole depends." A series of resolutions, calling for the formation of local conferences, "to meet at fixed periods, at convenient points, for the organization of missionary work," was presented by Dr. E.E. Hale. In order to carry into effect the intent of these resolutions, Charles Lowe devised a plan of organization, which declared that the object of the local conference "shall be to promote the religious life and mutual sympathy of the churches which unite in it, and to enable them to co-operate in missionary work, and in raising funds for various Christian purposes." The work of organizing such local missionary bodies was taken up at once, and proceeded rapidly. The first one was organized at Sheboygan, Wis., October 24, 1866; and nearly all the churches were brought within the limits of such conferences during the next two years.[23]

In the local conferences, as in the National Conference, two purposes contended for expression that were not compatible with each other as practical incentives to action. The one looked to the uniting of all liberal individuals and denominations in a general organization, and the other aimed at the promotion of distinctly Unitarian interests. In the National Conference the denominational purpose controlled in shaping its permanent policy; but the other intent found expression in the addition of "Other Christian Churches" to the name, though in only the most limited way did such churches connect themselves with the Conference.[24] The local conferences made like provision for those not wishing to call themselves distinctly Unitarian. Such desire for co-operation, however, was in a large degree ineffective because of the fact that the primary aim in the calling into existence of such conferences was an increase in the funds of the Unitarian Association.

[Sidenote: Fellowship and Fraternity.]

Under the leadership of the National Conference the Unitarian body underwent material changes in its internal organization and in its relations to other denominations. Not only did it bring the churches to act together in the local conferences and in its own sessions, but it taught then to co-operate for the protection of their pulpits against adventurers and immoral men. Before it was organized, the excessive spirit of independency in the churches would permit of no exercise of control as to their selection of ministers to fill their pulpits. At the fourth session of the National Conference, held in New York in October, 1870, the council, through Dr. Bellows, suggested that the local conferences refuse to acknowledge as ministers men of proven vices and immoralities. To carry out the spirit of this suggestion, Dr. Hale presented a resolution, which was adopted, asking the local conferences to appoint committees of fellowship to examine and to act upon candidates for the ministry. In October, 1870, the New York and Hudson River Conference created such a committee "to examine the testimonials of such as desire to become members of the conference and enter the Unitarian ministry."

Unitarianism in America

The seventh session of the National Conference, held at Saratoga in 1876, provided for the appointment of a committee of fellowship, and the list of names of those appointed to its membership appears in the printed report; but there is no record that the committee ever organized. In 1878 the council reported at considerable length on the desirableness of establishing such a committee; and, again, a committee of fellowship was appointed "to take into immediate consideration the subject of the introduction into the Unitarian ministry of those persons who seek an entrance into that ministry from other churches." This committee consisted of twelve persons, three each for the eastern, middle, western, and Pacific states.

At the session of 1880 the council of the Conference stated that it had created a substitute for the old ecclesiastical council, that was called together from the neighboring ministers and churches whenever a minister was to be inducted into office. That method was costly and had dropped into desuetude; but the new method of a committee of fellowship saved true Congregational methods and freed the churches from unworthy men. At this session the committee reported that it had adopted a uniform plan of action; but a resolution was passed recommending that each local conference establish its own committee of fellowship. Having once been instituted, however, the committee of the National Conference came slowly to be recognized as the fit means of introducing ministers into the Unitarian fellowship. Its authority has proven beneficent, and in no sense autocratic. It has shown that churches may co–operate in this way without intruding upon each others' rights, and that such a safeguarding of the pulpits of the denomination is essential to their dignity and morality. In 1896 the Minnesota Conference went one step further, and provided for a committee of fellowship with power to exclude for "conduct unbecoming a minister."

[Sidenote: Results of the Denominational Awakening.]

The most marked feature in the history of Unitarianism in this country during the period from 1865 to 1880 was the organization of the National Conference as the legislative body of the denomination, and the adjustment to it of the American Unitarian Association as its executive instrument. Attendant upon this organizing movement was the termination of the theological discussion that had begun twenty years earlier between the conservatives and radicals, the supernaturalists and the idealists, or transcendentalists. In 1865 the large majority of Unitarians were conservatives and supernaturalists, but in 1880 a marked change in belief had come about, that had apparently given the victory to the more moderate of the radicals. The majority of Unitarians would no longer assert that miracles are necessary to faith in Christ and the acceptance of his teachings as worthy of credence.

The change that came about during these years was largely due to the leadership of Henry W. Bellows. What he did was to keep actively alive in the Unitarian body its recognition of its Christian heritage, while at the same time he boldly refused assent to its being committed to any definite creed. He insisted upon the right of Unitarians to the Christian name, and to all that Christianity means as a vital spiritual force; but at the same time he refused to accept any limits for the Christian tradition and heritage, and left them free for growth. Sometimes apparently reactionary and conservative, he was at other times boldly radical and progressive. The cause of this seeming inconsistency was to be found in those gifts of imagination and emotion that made him a great preacher; but the inconsistency was more apparent than real, for in his leadership he manifested a wisdom and a capacity for directing the efforts of others that has never been surpassed in the history of religion and philanthropy in this country. He was both conservative and radical, supernaturalist and transcendentalist, a believer in miracles with a confident trust in the functions of reason. He saw both before and after, knew the worth of the past, and recognized that all the roots of our religious life are found therein, and yet courageously faced the future and its power to transform our faith by the aid of philosophy and science. Consequently, his sympathies were large, generous, and inclusive. Sometimes autocratic in word and action, his motives were catholic, and his intentions broad and appreciative. He gave direction to the newer Unitarianism in its efforts to organize and perpetuate itself. Had it been more flexible to his organizing skill, it would have grown more rapidly; but, with all its individualism and dislike of proselyting, it has more than doubled in strength since 1865. He showed the Unitarian body that freedom is consistent with organized effort, and that personal liberty is no more essential than co-ordinated action. He may be justly described as the real organizer of the Unitarian body in this country.

[1] Henry W. Bellows, in Monthly Journal, iv. 336: "These two years of war have witnessed a more rapid progress in liberal opinions than the whole previous century. The public mind has opened itself as it has never been open before." In vi. 3, he said: "There are great and striking changes going on. Men are breaking away from old opinions, and there is a great work for us to do." This was said in December, 1864. William G. Eliot, Monthly Journal, iv. 349: "The war has proved

that our Unitarian faith works well in time of trial. No other church has been so uniformly and thoroughly loyal, and no other church has done more for the sick and dying." Many other similar words could be quoted.

[2] James Freeman Clarke reported for this committee at the Syracuse session of 1866, and stated that its members had conferred with Christians, Universalists, Methodists, Congregationalists, and others. The committee made several suggestions as to what could be done to promote general fellowship, and recommended that the title of the National Conference be so changed as to permit persons of other religions bodies to find a place within it, if they so desired. The committee was reappointed; and at the third session of the Conference it reported that it had visited the annual gatherings of the Universalists, Methodists, and Free Religionists, and had been cordially welcomed. They were received into the pulpits of different denominations, they found everywhere a cordial spirit of fellowship and a breaking down of sectarian barriers. At this session the Conference expressed its desire "to cultivate the most friendly relations with, and to encourage fraternal intercourse between, the various liberal Christian bodies in this country." A committee of three was appointed "to represent our fraternal sentiments and to consider all questions which relate to mutual intercourse and co—operation."

This committee reported through Edward E. Hale that it had been well received at two Methodist conferences and at several state conventions of the Universalists. Especially had it been welcomed by the African Methodist Church, which was the beginning of cordial relations between the two bodies for several years. The committee reported, however, that "there are but few regularly organized bodies in this country which, in their formal action, express much desire for intercourse or co—operation with us as an organized branch of the church." A resolution offered by the committee, expressing the desire of the National Conference "to cultivate the most friendly relations with all Christian churches and to encourage fraternal intercourse between them," was adopted. The members of the committee appointed in 1870 attended the session of the American Board of Foreign Missions in 1871; and they were received with courtesy, Athanase Coquerel addressing the board as their representative. The committee reported that "in every direction, from clergymen and laymen of different Protestant churches, we have received informal expressions of what we believe to be a very general desire that there might be a more formal and public expression of the fellowship which undoubtedly really exists between the different Protestant communions."

At the session of the National Conference held in 1874 the council suggested the propriety of preparing a register of the free or liberal churches of the world, and it enumerated the various bodies that might be properly included; but no action was taken on this recommendation. At this session an amendment to the by–laws, offered by Dr. Hale, was adopted, providing for a fellowship committee with other churches. This committee was not appointed, and the amendment was not printed in its proper place in the report. Apparently, the interest in efforts of this kind had exhausted itself, partly because any active co–operation with the more conservative churches was impossible, and partly because the growth of denominational feeling directed the energies of the National Conference into other channels.

[3] The sessions of the National Conference have been held as follows: 1, New York, April 5–6, 1865; 2, Syracuse, October 10–11, 1866; 3, New York, October 7–9, 1868; 4, New York, October 19–21, 1870; 5. Boston, October 22–25, 1872; 6, Saratoga, September 15–18, 1874; 7, Saratoga, September 12–15, 1876; 8, Saratoga, September 17–20, 1878; 9, Saratoga, September 21–24, 1880; 10, Saratoga, September 18–22, 1882; 11, Saratoga, September 22–26, 1884; 12, Saratoga, September 20–24, 1886; 13, Philadelphia, October 28–31, 1889; 14, Saratoga, September 21–25, 1891; 15, Saratoga, September 24–27, 1894; 16, Washington, October 21–24, 1895; 17, Saratoga, September 20–23, 1897; 18, Washington, October 16–19 1899; 19, Saratoga, September 23, 1901. A meeting was held in Chicago, in 1893, in connection with the Parliament of Religions. The presidents of the National Conference

have been Hon. John A. Andrew, who served in 1866; Hon. Thomas D. Eliot, whose term of service lasted to 1869; Judge Ebenezer R. Hoar, from 1869 to 1878, and again from 1882 to 1884; Hon. John D. Long, from 1878 to 1882; Judge Samuel F. Miller, 1884 to 1891; Mr. George William Curtis, 1891 to 1894; and Hon. George F. Hoar, 1894 to 1901. Hon. Carroll D. Wright was elected to the office in 1901. The secretaries have been Rev. Edward Everett Hale, Rev. George Batchelor, Rev. Russell N. Bellows, Rev. William H. Lyon, and Rev. Daniel W. Morehouse. The first chairman of the council was Rev. Henry W. Bellows, D.D., who served to 1872, and again from 1876 to 1878; Professor Charles Carroll Everett, D.D., from 1874 to 1876; Rev. Edward Everett Hale, D.D., from 1880 to 1882, and from 1891 to 1894; Rev. James De Normandie, D.D., from 1884 to 1889; Rev. Brooke Herford, D.D., from 1889 to 1891; Rev. George Batchelor, from 1894 to 1895; Rev. Minot J. Savage, D.D., from 1895 to 1899; and Rev. Howard N. Brown, from the later year to 1901, when Rev. Thomas R. Slicer was elected.

[4] A.A. Low, a member of the first Unitarian congregation in Brooklyn, N.Y.

[5] Lecture delivered in Cooper Institute, New York, on Unitarian Views of Christ, published in The Christian Examiner, November, 1866, xxxi, 310.

[6] Works, iv. 110.

[7] The Christian Examiner, March–April, 1826, iii. 136.

[8] First Series of Tracts of A.U.A. No. 87.

[9] First Series of A.U.A. Tracts, No. 105, April, 1836.

[10] Forty–fifth Annual Report of the American Unitarian Association, 11, 14.

[11] This correspondence was published in full in The Christian Register for December 13 and 20, 1873, Mr. Potter's letter protesting against the action of the Association being printed on the later date.

[12] Memoir of Charles Lowe, 454, 458.

[13] Freedom and Fellowship in Religion, 261.

[14] Freedom and Fellowship in Religion, 24.

[15] Ibid., 42.

[16] Ibid., 216.

[17] Fifty Affirmations, 47.

[18] Report of the Second Meeting of the National Conference, 20.

[19] Memoir of Charles H. Brigham, with Sermons and Lectures.

[20] Christian Register. March 15, 1900, lxxxix. 300; Twenty–fifth Anniversary of the Worcester Conference, 7, address by Dr. Hale. See Memoir of Charles Lowe, 372.

[21] Church Exchange, May, 1899, vi. 59.

[22] This association of ministers was organized August 17, 1819, and was orthodox, but found itself Unitarian when the denominational change took place.

[23] See Appendix for a complete list of the local conferences and the dates of their organization.

[24] In a small number of instances such churches did join the Conference, but the number was too small to be in any degree significant.

IX. GROWTH OF DENOMINATIONAL CONSCIOUSNESS.

The period from 1880 to the present time is marked by a growing denominational unity. Gradually Unitarians have come to the acceptance of their fellowship as a religious body, and to a recognition of their distinct mission. The controversy between the conservatives and the radicals was transferred to the west in 1886, and continued to have at its basis the problem of the relation of the individual to religious institutions and traditions. The conservative party maintained that Unitarians are Christians, and gave recognition to that continuity of human development by which every generation is connected with and draws its life from those which precede it, and is consciously dependent upon them. On the other hand, the radical party was not willing to accept traditions and institutions as having a binding authority over individuals. Some of them were reluctant to call themselves Christians, not because they rejected the more important of the Christian beliefs, but because they were not willing to bind any individual by the action of his fellows. It was their claim that religion best serves its own ends when it is free to act upon the individual without compulsion of any kind from others, and that its attractions should be without any bias of external authority.

[Sidenote: "The Western Issue."]

At the meeting of the Western Conference held in Cleveland in 1882, arrangements were made looking to its incorporation, and its object was defined to be "the transaction of business pertaining to the general interests of the societies connected with the Conference, and the promotion of rational religion." It was voted that the motto on the conference seal should be "Freedom, Fellowship, and Character in Religion," which was the same as that of the Free Religious Association, with the addition of the word "character." These results were reached after much discussion, and by the way of compromise. The issues thus raised were brought forward again at St. Louis, in 1885, when Rev. J.T. Sunderland, the secretary and missionary of the conference, deplored the growing spirit of agnosticism and scepticism in the Unitarian churches of the west. His report caused a division of opinion in the conference; and in the controversy that ensued the conservatives were represented by The Unitarian, edited by Rev. Brooke Herford and Rev. J.T. Sunderland, and the radicals by Unity, edited by Rev. J.Ll. Jones and Rev. W.C. Gannett.

Unitarianism in America

At the Western Conference meeting of 1886, held in Cincinnati, the controversy found full expression. The session was preceded a few days before by the publication of a pamphlet on The Western Issue from the pen of Mr. Sunderland, in which he contended for the theistic and Christian character of the conference. A resolution offered by Rev. Oscar Clute, "that the primary object of this Conference is to diffuse the knowledge and promote the interests of pure Christianity," was rejected by a considerable majority. Another, offered by Mr. Sunderland—"that, while rejecting all creeds and creed limitations, the Conference hereby expresses its purpose as a body to be the promotion of a religion of love to God and love to man"—was also rejected. That presented by William C. Gannett was carried by a majority of thirty–four to ten, and declared that

> the Western Unitarian Conference conditions its fellowship on no
> dogmatic tests, but welcomes all who wish to join it to establish
> truth, righteousness, and love in the world.

The result was a pronounced division between the two parties within the conference; and a considerable number of churches, including some of the oldest and strongest, withdrew from co–operation in the work of the Conference. At the session of 1887, held in All Souls' Church, Chicago, an effort was made to bring about a reconciliation; but this was not completely secured.[1] A resolution was carried, however, by a majority of fifty–nine to three, reaffirming Mr. Gannett's, declaration adopted at Cincinnati, but also accepting a statement in regard to fellowship and doctrines, which was called The Things Most Commonly Believed To–day among Us, and read as follows:—

> In all matters of church government we are strict Congregationalists.
> We have no creed in the usual sense; that is, articles of doctrinal
> belief which bind our churches and fix the conditions of our
> fellowship. Character has always been to us the supreme matter. We have
> doctrinal beliefs, and for the most part hold such beliefs in common;
> but above all doctrines we emphasize the principles of freedom,
> fellowship, and character in religion. These principles make our
> all–sufficient test of fellowship. All names that divide religion are
> to us of little consequence compared with religion itself. Whoever
> loves truth and loves the good is, in a broad sense, of our religious
> fellowship; whoever loves the one or lives the other better than
> ourselves is our teacher, whatever church or age he may belong to. So

our church is wide, our teachers many, and our holy writings large.

With a few exceptions we may be called Christian Theists: Theists as worshipping the One–in–All, and naming that One, God our Father; Christian, because revering Jesus as the highest of the historic prophets of religion; these names, as names, receiving more stress in our older than in our younger churches. The general faith is hinted well in words which several of our churches have adopted for their covenant: "In the freedom of the truth, and in the spirit of Jesus Christ, we unite for the worship of God and the service of man." It is hinted in such words as these: "Unitarianism is a religion of love to God and love to man." "It is that free and progressive development of historic Christianity which aspires to be synonymous with universal ethics and universal religion." But because we have no creed which we impose as test of fellowship, specific statements of belief abound among us, always somewhat differing, always largely agreeing. One such we offer here:—

We believe that to love the Good and live the Good is the supreme thing in religion. We hold reason and conscience to be final authorities in matters of religious belief. We honor the Bible and all inspiring scriptures, old and new. We revere Jesus and all holy souls that have taught men truth and righteousness and love, as prophets of religion. We believe in the growing nobility of man. We trust the unfolding universe as beautiful, beneficent, unchanging Order; to know this order is truth; to obey it is right and liberty and stronger life. We believe that good and evil inevitably carry their own recompense, no good things being failure, and no evil things success; that heaven and hell are states of being; that no evil can befall the good man in either life or death; that all things work together for the victory of Good. We believe that we ought to join hands and work to make the good things better and the worst good, counting nothing good for self that is not good for all. We believe that this self–forgetting, loyal life awakes in man the sense of union, here and now, with things eternal—the sense of deathlessness; and this is to us an earnest of the life to come. We

worship One–in–All,—that Life whence suns and stars derive their
orbits and the soul of man its Ought,—that Light which lighteth
every man that cometh into the world, giving us power to become the
sons of God,—that Love with whom our souls commune. This One we
name the Eternal God, our Father.

This action not satisfying the remonstrants, the controversy went on with considerable vigor for three or four years. Both parties to it were characteristically Unitarian in their attitude and in their demands. Both sought the truth with an attempt at unbiassed judgment; and neither wished to disfellowship the other, or to put any restrictions upon its expression of its opinions. Much heat was engendered by the controversy, but light was desire by both parties with sincere purpose. The conflict was finally brought to an end by the action of the National Conference at its session of 1894, held at Saratoga, though this result had been practically reached in 1892. A committee on the revision of the constitution had been appointed by the council of the session of 1891; and this committee reported the following preamble, which was unanimously adopted as a substitute for the preamble of 1865 and 1868:—

The Conference of Unitarian and other Christian Churches was formed in
the year 1865, with the purpose of strengthening the churches and
societies which should unite in it for more and better work for the
kingdom of God. These churches accept the religion of Jesus, holding,
in accordance with his teaching, that practical religion is summed up
in love to God and love to man. The Conference recognizes the fact that
its constituency is Congregational in tradition and polity. Therefore,
it declares that nothing in this constitution is to be construed as an
authoritative test; and we cordially invite to our working fellowship
any who, while differing from us in belief, are in general sympathy
with our spirit and our practical aims.

This preamble to the new constitution proved to be so far acceptable to both parties in the Western Conference, as well as to their sympathizers elsewhere, that harmony was restored throughout the denomination. While the Unitarian body thus retained its use of the Christian name and its insistence upon loyalty to the teachings of Jesus, yet it put aside every form of dogmatic test and of creedal statement. Its fellowship was made very broad in its character, and all were invited to join it who so desired.

[Sidenote: Fellowship with Universalists.]

At the annual meeting of the Unitarian Association in 1899 resolutions were passed looking to joint action between Unitarians and Universalists with reference to furthering their common interests. A committee was appointed to confer with a similar committee of the Universalist General Convention for the purpose of considering "plans of closer co–operation, devise ways and means for more efficient usefulness." In October this proposal was accepted by the General Convention, and a committee appointed. At the annual meeting of the Unitarian Association in 1900 the report of the joint committee was presented, in which it was declared that "closer co–operation is desirable and practicable"; but the committee expressed the wish to go on record "as not desiring nor expecting to disturb in any way the separate organic autonomy of the two denominations. We seek co–operation, not consolidation, unity, non union." The committee recommended that it be given authority to consider the cases in which the two denominations are jointly interested, such as opportunities of instituting churches or missions in new fields, the circulation of tracts and books, the holding of joint meetings of ministers and churches, or other efforts to promote intellectual agreements and deep faiths of the heart, and to recommend the appropriate action to the proper organizations. At the next sessions of the Unitarian Association and of the Universalist General Convention these recommendations were accepted, and permanent members of the joint committee were appointed. This committee has entered upon its duties, and important results may be anticipated in the promotion of harmony and co–operation.

[Sidenote: Officers of the American Unitarian Association.]

Mr. Henry P. Kidder continued as the president of the Unitarian Association until the annual meeting of 1886. He was then succeeded by Hon. George D. Robinson, who held the office for only one year. He had been in both houses of the Massachusetts legislature, in the national House from 1877 to 1883, and was governor of Massachusetts from 1884 to 1886. His successor was Hon. George S. Hale, from 1887 to 1895, who was a distinguished lawyer, and was greatly interested in charities and reforms. Hon. John D. Long was the president from 1895 to 1897. He had been in the lower house of the Massachusetts legislature, was lieutenant governor in 1879, governor in 1880–82, in the national House from 1883 to 1889, and from 1897 to 1902 was Secretary of the Navy. Hon. Carroll D. Wright held the office from 1897 to 1900. He was in the Massachusetts Senate in 1871 and 1872, was chief of the Massachusetts bureau of statistics from 1873 to

1888, superintendent of the United States census in 1880, has been commissioner of the national Bureau of Labor since 1885, and in 1902 became president of Clark College at Worcester. At the annual meeting of 1900 it was thought best to make a change in the nature of the presidency, in order that the head of the Association might become its chief executive officer. In that way it was sought to add dignity and efficiency to the position of the executive officer, as well as to meet the greatly increased work of the Association by this addition to its salaried force. The secretary, Rev. Samuel A. Eliot, was elected to the presidency.

In 1881 Rev. Grindall Reynolds became the secretary of the Association. He had previously held pastorates in Jamaica Plain and Concord. He had rare executive abilities, was gifted with sound common sense and a judicial temper; and he had a most efficient business capacity. Under his leadership the growth of the Unitarian denomination was more rapid than it had been at any earlier period; and this was largely due to his zeal, energy, and wisdom.

In December, 1894, Rev. George Batchelor became the secretary, and he continued in office until November, 1897, when he became the editor of The Christian Register. He had previously held pastorates in Salem, Chicago, and Lowell. He was succeeded, January 1, 1898, by Rev. Samuel A. Eliot, who had been settled over churches in Denver and Brooklyn, and who became the president of the Association in 1900. Rev. Charles E. St. John, who had been settled in Northampton and Pittsburg, became the secretary at the annual meeting of 1900.

[Sidenote: The American Unitarian Association as a Representative Body.]

In the report of the council of the National Conference at the session of 1880, Dr. Bellows pointed out the fact that the American Unitarian Association was "not a union of churches, but an association of individuals belonging to Unitarian churches, who became members of it and entitled to vote by signing its constitution and the annual payment of one dollar. This Association never had, and has not now, any explicit relation to our churches as churches, but only to such individuals as choose to become voluntary subscribers to its funds, and members by signing its constitution, and to such churches as choose to employ its services."

This statement led to the appointment of a committee "to consider how the National Conference and the American Unitarian Association can more effectually co–operate without sacrifice of the advantages belonging to either." The committee reported in 1882 in favor of so changing the charter of the Association that a church might become a member. At the annual meeting of the Association in 1884, after a prolonged discussion, its by–laws were so amended that, while the life membership was retained, the sum creating it was raised from $30 to $50; and churches were given representation on the condition of regular yearly contributions to its treasury, two of such contributions being necessary to establish a church in this right. Since that time the delegates from churches have considerably outnumbered the life members voting at the annual meetings. This has practically given the churches the controlling voice in the activities of the Association.

The giving a representative character to the Association had the effect of increasing the contributions made to its support by the churches. Under the leadership of Dr. Bellows, at the National Conference in 1884, there began a movement looking to the establishment of a conference in every state and the employment of a missionary by every such conference. This plan has not yet been fully carried out; but in 1885 and the following years missionary superintendents were appointed by the Association for five general sections of the country, and, with some variations, this, system has continued in operation to the present time.[2]

[Sidenote: The Church Building Loan Fund.]

The work of building churches was greatly facilitated by the establishment, in 1884, of a Church Building Loan Fund. The proposition to create such a fund was first brought forward by the finance committee at a meeting of the directors of the Unitarian Association on February 11, 1884. At the March meeting a committee was appointed to mature plans; and at the meeting of the National Conference in September, held at Saratoga, a resolution was passed asking the Association to set apart $25,000 for this purpose, and pledging the Conference to add $20,000 to this sum. At the November meeting of the directors of the Association the organization of the fund was completed, a board of trustees was created, and the sum of $43,000 was reported as secured. The fund was steadily increased by contributions from the churches and by gifts and legacies until in 1900 it amounted to $142,820.92. Up to May, 1900, an aggregate sum of $294,310 had been disbursed, in one hundred loans to ninety societies, chiefly to aid in the erection of new church edifices.[3]

[Sidenote: The Unitarian Building in Boston.]

For several years after the organization of the American Unitarian Association the records give no indication of the place of meeting of the directors. During the latter part of 1825, and in 1826, David Reed was the general agent of the Association; and his place of business was at 81 Washington Street. It is probable that the directors met at the study of the secretary or at the place of business of the agent. In December, 1826, the firm of Bowles &Dearborn, booksellers, became the agents, their store being first at 72 and then at 50 Washington Street. Here all Unitarian publications were kept on sale, the name of "general repositary" being given to their stock of books, tracts, periodicals, and other publications of a liberal character. In 1829 the agent was Leonard C. Bowles, evidently a continuation of Bowles &Dearborn.

In 1830 the depositary was removed to 135 Washington Street, and was under the management of the firm of Gray &Bowen, who were paid $144.44 for their services. In 1831 the place of business of this firm was 141 Washington Street; and the sum it received from the Association was $200, which was the next year increased to $300. Leonard C. Bowles, located at 147 Washington Street, again became the agent in 1836. In 1837 James Munroe & Co. appear as the publishers of the annual report, but they are not mentioned as agents or as having charge of the repositary. The sum of $150 was paid in that year for the rent of a room for the general secretary, Rev. Charles Briggs; and the location of the room is probably indicated by the record that in 1838 Munroe &Co. were paid $133.34 for rent of room and clerk hire, their store being at 134 Washington Street. Here the headquarters of the Association were at last established, for they continued in this place until 1846. In 1839 the rental paid was $300, and for the six succeeding years it was $200. Surely, these were the days of small things; but here the Association carried on such activities as it had in hand, and the Unitarian ministers met for conversation and consultation.

In 1846 Crosby, Nichols &Co. became the agents of the Association, first at 118 and then at 111 Washington Street. This firm brought out several Unitarian books, and issued The Christian Examiner and other Unitarian periodicals. For a number of years they were intimately associated with Unitarian interests, and the theological and literary traditions of the time connect them with many of the leading men and movements of Boston. In the rear of their store the Association had its office, its meeting–place for the directors and other officers, as well as for the Monday gatherings of ministers.

After these many wanderings from the rear of one bookstore to another the Association at last secured an abode of its own. On March 9, 1854, rooms for the use of the Association were opened at 21 Bromfield Street. On this occasion a small company came together, and listened to an address by Dr. Samuel K. Lothrop, the president of the Association. Another change was made in October, 1859, when Walker, Wise &Co. undertook the book–selling, and publishing work of the Association at 21 Bromfield Street.

In the year 1865 there came to the Association an opportunity for securing a building of its own. The sum of $16,000 was paid for a house at 26 Chauncy Street, which was occupied in the spring of 1866. The enlarged activities of the Association at this time here found the housing they needed. Affiliated organizations also found a home in this building, especially the Sunday School Society, the Christian Register Association, and The Monthly Religious Magazine.

The theatre meetings, begun in Boston in 1866, having suggested the need of a larger denominational building, The Monthly Journal of November, 1867, proposed the erection of a building with a spacious hall for these great popular meetings, smaller rooms for social gatherings, offices for the Association and other affiliated societies, and an attractive bookstore. "In short, we would have it comprise all that might properly belong to a denominational headquarters or home. We would have it in a convenient and conspicuous situation, and every way worthy of our position." This dream of Mr. Lowe's he brought forward again in his annual report of 1870, when he said: "The building now occupied by the Association has become wholly inadequate to its uses; and steps were taken more than a year ago by its friends in Boston towards providing more suitable accommodations, and at the same time providing in connection with it for such other uses as might make the building to be erected worthy to be the headquarters of the denomination in the city which gave it birth." Mr. Shippen called attention to the needs of the Association in his report of 1872, saying that the project of a large hall had been abandoned, but that there was urgent demand for a building suited to the business and social needs of the denomination in Boston.

The great fire of November, 1872, brought this project to a sudden termination. The Chauncy Street building was for many hours in danger of being burned, out it was finally saved. Its market value was much increased by the fire, however; and in February, 1873, it was sold for $37,000. Purchase was soon made, at a cost of $30,000, of the estate at 7 Tremont Place, belonging to Hon. Albert Fearing, who had been active in the work of the

Association and prominent in the Unitarian circles of Boston. This building, entered by the Association in May, 1873, was somewhat larger than its predecessor and in some respects better suited to the needs of the Association; yet the secretary, at the annual meeting held in the same month, called for the more convenient building, which should serve "as a worthy centre in this city for the various charitable and missionary activities of our faith."[4]

In his report of 1880 Mr. Shippen again presented his demand for a suitable home for the Association and its kindred organizations. This appeal was renewed in the following year by Mr. Reynolds, who urged "the need of a denominational house in Boston, which should be commodious, accessible, easily found, and where all our charities and all our works should find a home." "Very fitting it is," he added, "that such a house should be named after him who, by his personal influence in life and by the power of his written word after his death, has been the mightiest single force for the diffusion of rational Christianity."

In January, 1882, the Unitarian Club of Boston was organized; and it soon after took up the task of erecting the desired building. The initiative was taken at a meeting of the club held December 13, 1882, when Mr. Henry P. Kidder offered to head a subscription for this purpose with the sum of $10,000. The proposal was received with much enthusiasm, and a committee was appointed, consisting of Henry P. Kidder, Charles Faulkner, Charles W. Eliot, William Endicott, Jr., Francis H. Brown, M.D., Dr. John Cordner, Arthur T. Lyman, Henry Grew, Thomas Gaffield, and Rev. Grindall Reynolds, to whom authority was given to raise funds, purchase a lot, and erect a building. It was arranged by this committee that the Association should contribute $50,000 from the sale of its Tremont Place building, and that the club should raise $150,000. Subscriptions were opened February 9, 1883; and in November over $154,000 had been secured. A suitable lot was purchased at the corner of Beacon and Bowdoin Streets, and the erection of the building was begun in 1884. A prolonged labor strike delayed the completion of the building, so that the service of its dedication, which had been arranged for the evening of May 25, 1886, was held in Tremont Temple. The presiding officer on that occasion was George William Curtis; and addresses were made by Drs. Frederic H. Hedge, Andrew P. Peabody, and Horatio Stebbins. In July the building was occupied by the Association. "The denominational house is but brick and stone," said Mr. Reynolds in his report of 1886; "but it is brick and stone which testify to the new hope, vigor, life, which have been coming in these later years into our body, and without which it could not have been reared. It is brick and stone which are the pledges of a noble future, which stimulate to good work, and furnish the means of doing it."[5]

[Sidenote: Growth of the Devotional Spirit.]

The last twenty years of the nineteenth century saw an increased use of the simpler Christian rites in Unitarian churches. In that time a distinct advance was made in the acceptableness of the communion service, and probably in the number of those willing to join in its observance. The abandonment of its mystical features and its interpretation as a simple memorial service, that would help to cherish loved ones gone hence, and the saintly and heroic of all ages, as well as the one great leader of the Christian body, has given it for Unitarians a new spiritual effectiveness. The same causes have led to the adoption of the rite of confirmation in a considerable number of churches. Gradually the idea has grown that what Rev. Sylvester Judd called "the birthright church" is the true one, and that it is desirable that all children should be religiously trained, and admitted to the church at the age of adolescence. Mr. Judd gave noble utterance to this conception of a church in a series of sermons published after his death,[6] as well as in a sermon prepared for the Thursday lecture in Boston.[7] The same idea was elaborated by Rev. Cyrus A. Bartol in his Church and Congregation: A Plea for their Unity,[8] wherein he contended for the union of church and parish, the opening of the communion to all as a rite accepted by the whole congregation, and not by a few church members, and the education of children as constituent members of the church from birth.

It was not until much later, however, that the rite of confirmation came into use,[9] largely because of the interpretations of the purposes and methods of Christian nurture presented by Bushnell, Bartol, and Judd. This rite could have meaning only as the expression of social responsibility on the part of parents and church alike, that true religion is not merely a question of individual opinion, but that there is high worth in those spiritual forces that are carried forward from generation to generation, and must descend from parent to child if they have effective power. In a word, the use of the confirmation rite is an abandonment of extreme individualism, and is an acceptance of the socialistic conception of spiritual development.[10] This is distinctly a return to the conception of a church maintained by Solomon Stoddard at the beginning of the eighteenth century, and to that broader Congregationalism he desired to see established throughout New England. It was also theoretically that of the Puritan founders of New England, who maintained that all children Of church members were also members of the church, but who inconsistently insisted upon a supernatural conversion in order to full membership. It is even more positively an acceptance of the theory of Christian nurture held by the Catholic and the Episcopal churches. That theory is based on the social conception of the church, that it is an organic body, and that every child is born into it and is to be trained as a member by nature and by right.

There has also been a marked change in the forms of Sunday worship, especially in the general adoption of responsive readings or more elaborate rituals. The tendency has been away from the bare and unattractive service of the Puritan churches, which was the acme of individualism in worship, towards the more social conception that brings the whole congregation to join in the act and in the spirit of devotion. This social conception of worship had its first distinct expression in a Unitarian church when James Freeman Clarke organized the Church of the Disciples, in 1843.[11] His example was a potent force in introducing into many churches a richer and more expressive form of worship. Another influence was that of Samuel Longfellow, who became the minister of the Second Unitarian Church in Brooklyn, in 1853. He soon after introduced vesper services in place of the second sermon in the afternoon, making them largely devotional in their character. "His own taste and deep feeling were largely a condition of the full success of the vespers," says his biographer, "which were seldom elsewhere so impressive or seemed so genuine as a devotional act. They needed, for their perfect effect, the influence of a leader with whom worship was an habitual mental attitude, and who, combined with the instinct of religion the art of a poet and of a musician."[12] The form of service thus initiated was adopted in many other churches, and slowly had its influence in giving greater beauty and spiritual expressiveness to worship in Unitarian churches.

About 1885 the tendency to adopt a more social and a more aesthetic form of worship came to assert itself more distinctly. To its furtherance Rev. Howard N. Brown gave, perhaps, greater emphasis than any other person; but there were others who took an active part in the movement. The old Congregational demand for simplicity, however, was very great; and there was strong feeling against anything like ritualism. The use of some kind of liturgy became quite general in the face of this objection, and a considerable number of books of a semi–ritual character were published. The most elaborate work of this nature was compiled by a committee appointed by the Unitarian Association, and published by it in 1891. What is to be recognized in this tendency is not the more general use of liturgies, however simple or however elaborate, but the growth in Unitarian churches of the worshipping spirit. With the development of a rational theology there has

172

been a corresponding evolution of a simple but earnest attitude of devotion.

The devotional spirit of Unitarians, however, has found its most emphatic and beautiful expression in religious hymns and poems. The older Unitarian piety found voice in the hymns of the younger Henry Ware, Norton, Pierpont, Frothingham, Peabody, Lunt, Bryant, and many others. It was rational and yet Christian, simple in sentiment and yet it found in the New Testament traditions its themes and its symbolisms. Then followed the older transcendentalists, who sought in the inward life and the soul's oneness with God the chief motives to spiritual expression. The hymns and the religious poems of Furness, Hedge, Longfellow, Johnson, Clarke, Very, Brooks, and Miss Scudder,[13] have an interior and spiritual quality seldom found in devotional poetry. They are not the mere utterances of conventional sentiments or the repetition of ecclesiastical symbolisms, but the voicing of deep inward experiences that reveal and interpret the true life of the soul. Of the same character are the hymns and religious poems of Gannett, Hosmer, and Chadwick, who have but accentuated the tendencies of their predecessors. It is the more radical theology that has voiced itself in the religious songs of these men, but with a mystical or spiritual insight that fits them to the needs of all devout, worshippers. It is these genuinely poetical interpretations of the spiritual life that most often claim utterance in song on the part of Unitarian congregations. A body of worshippers that can produce such a hymnology must possess a large measure of genuine piety and devotion.

[Sidenote: The Seventy–fifth Anniversary.]

Many of the tendencies of the Unitarian movement found utterance on the occasion of the seventy–fifth anniversary of the American Unitarian Association. The meetings were held in Tremont Temple, May 22, 1900; and the attendance was large and enthusiastic, many persons coming from distant parts of the country. This meeting brought into full expression the denominational consciousness, and showed the harmony that had been secured as the result of the controversies of many years. As never before, it was realized that the Unitarian body has a distinct mission, that it has organic and vital power, and that its individual members are united by a common faith for the promotion of the interests of a rational and humanitarian religion.

This was also a notable occasion because it brought together representatives from nearly all the countries in which Unitarianism exists in an organized form, thus clearly indicating that it is a cosmopolitan movement, and not one of merely local significance.

173

At the morning session addresses were made by the representatives from Hungary, Great Britain, Germany, Belgium, India, and Japan. In the afternoon addresses were delivered by the missionaries of the Association. Other meetings of much interest were held during the week, that were of value as interpretations of the past of Unitarianism in this country.

During this anniversary week, on May 26, 1900, upon the suggestion of Rev. S.A. Eliot, there was organized The International Council of Unitarian and Other Liberal Religious Thinkers and Workers, its object being "to open communication with those in all lands who are striving to unite pure religion and perfect liberty, and to increase fellowship and co-operation among them." Professor J. Estlin Carpenter, of Oxford, England, was selected as the president, and Rev. Charles W. Wendte, who shortly after became the minister of the Parker Memorial in Boston, was made the secretary. The executive committee included representatives from the United States, Great Britain, Japan, Hungary, Germany, France, Italy, Belgium, and Switzerland. The first annual meeting was held in London, May 30 and 31, 1901, with delegates present from the above-named countries, as well as from Holland, Norway, India, Denmark, Australia, and Canada.[14]

The anniversary exercises, as well as the organization of the International Council, gave concrete emphasis to the growing interest in Unitarian ideas and principles in many parts of the world. They gave the sense of a large fellowship, and kindled new enthusiasm. As interpreted by these meetings, the Unitarian name has largely ceased to be one of merely theological signification, and has come to mean "an endeavor to unite for common and unselfish endeavors all believers in pure religion and perfect liberty."[15]

[1] The Unitarian, June, 1887, II. 156. For historical accounts of this
    controversy see Mrs. S.C.Ll. Jones's Western Unitarian Conference:
    Its Work and its Mission, Unity Mission Tract, No. 38; W.C. Gannett's
    The Flowering of Christianity, Lesson XII., Part IV.; and The
    Unitarian, II. and III. A Western Unitarian Association was organized
    in Chicago, June 21, 1886. Some of the older and leading churches
    were connected with it, including those at Meadville, Ann Arbor,
    Louisville, Shelbyville, Church of the Messiah and Unity in Chicago,
    Church of the Messiah in St. Louis, Keokuk, and others. Hon. George
    W. McCrary was elected the president, and Mrs. Jonathan Slade the
    recording secretary. In October, 1887, Rev. George Batchelor became
    the Western agent of the American Unitarian Association. He was

succeeded the next year by Rev. George W. Cutter. In September, 1890, Rev. T.B. Forbush was made the Western superintendent of the American Unitarian Association, with headquarters in Chicago; and he held this position until 1896. During the period covered by these dates Rev. J.R. Effinger was the general missionary of the Western Unitarian Conference, and he was succeeded by Rev. F.L. Hosmer and Rev. A.W. Gould. In 1896 the Western churches were reunited in the Western Conference, and its secretary has been the superintendent of the American Unitarian Association. As defining the position of the American Unitarian Association during this period of controversy, it may be recalled that in June, 1886, the directors adopted a resolution, in which they said they "would regard it as a subversion of the purpose for which its funds have been contributed, as well as of the principles cherished by its officers, to give assistance to any church or organization which does not rest emphatically on the Christian basis."

[2] New England, Middle States and Canada, Western States, Southern States, and Pacific Coast.

[3] These loans are made without interest under established conditions, one of which is that they must be repaid in ten annual instalments.

[4] Annual Report of 1873, 7.

[5] The building seemed to be ample, when it was first occupied, for any growth that was likely to be made for many years to come. At the present time, only sixteen years later, it is crowded; and an extension is urgently demanded. It does not now afford room for the work required, and much of that work is done at a considerable disadvantage because of the want of room. The promise for the immediate future is that much more room will be required in order to facilitate the growing work of the Association.

[6] The Church: in a Series of Sermons, Boston, 1857.

[7] The Birthright Church: A Discourse, printed for the Association of the Unitarian Church of Maine, Augusta, 1854. Mr. Judd's conception of the church as a social organism was shown in the name given to the organization formed under his leadership in 1852, called The Association of the Unitarian Church in Maine. In the preamble to the constitution he wrote: "We, the Unitarian Christians of Maine, ourselves, and our posterity are a Church.... We are a church, not of creeds, but of the Bible; not of sect, but of humanity; seeking not uniformity of dogma, but communion in the religious life. We embrace in our fellowship all who will be in fellowship with us." In defining a local church, he says: "These Christians, with their families, uniting for religious worship, instruction, growth, and culture, having the ordinances and a pastor, constitute a parochial church."

[8] Boston, 1858.

[9] Probably Dr. William G. Eliot, of St. Louis, was the first Unitarian minister to make a systematic use of this rite. He prepared a brief manual for use in his church, the preface to which bears date of December 6, 1868. Seth C. Beach, while minister in Dedham, printed a paper on the subject in the Unitarian Review, January, 1886. He held a confirmation service in the Dedham church, April 25, 1886. At a meeting of the Western Sunday School Society, held in Cincinnati, May 12, 1889, Rev. John C. Learned, read a paper on The Sacrament of Confirmation.

[10] The views of Bartol and Judd are appropriate to a state church, wherein they first found expression; and their motive is always distinctly social.

[11] Life of J.F. Clarke, by E.E. Hale, 145

[12] Memoir of Samuel Longfellow, by Joseph May, 193.

[13] Miss Scudder's best hymns were all written while she was a Unitarian. Unitarian hymnology has been nobly treated by Dr. Alfred P. Putnam,

in his Singers and Songs of the Liberal Faith, Boston, 1875. It is
understood that he is preparing a second volume. The tendency to a
deeper recognition of the spirit of worship has found fitting
expression in The Spiritual Life: Studies of Devotion and Worship,
George H. Ellis, 1898.

[14] The addresses and papers of this meeting were published under the
title of Liberal Religious Thought at the Beginning of the Twentieth
Century, London, 1901. They give the most complete account yet
published of the various liberal movements in many parts of the
world, and the book is one of great interest and value.

[15] From the first circular of the International Council.

X. THE MINISTRY AT LARGE.

One of the most important of the philanthropies undertaken by the early Unitarians was
the ministry to the poor and unchurched in Boston, usually known as the ministry at
large. It began in 1822, came under the direction of the American Unitarian Association
and the shaping hand of Dr. Joseph Tuckerman in 1826, and was taken in charge by the
Benevolent Fraternity of Churches in 1834. It was not begun by Tuckerman, though its
origin is usually attributed to him. Even before 1822 attempts had been made to establish
missions amongst the poor by the evangelical denominations; but their work was not
thoroughly organized, and it had reached no efficient results when Tuckerman entered
upon his labors. The work of Tuckerman was to take up what had been tentatively begun
by others, give it a definite purpose and method, and so to inform it with his own genius
for charity that it became a great philanthropy in its intent and in its methods.

[Sidenote: Association of Young Men.]

When the Hancock Grammar School–house in the north end of Boston was being
erected, a young man, in passing it on a September evening, said to a companion, "Why
cannot we have a Sunday–school here?" The proposition was received with favor, and
the two discussed plans while they continued their walk. They met frequently to mature
their methods of procedure, and they invited others to join them in the undertaking. On

the evening of October 2, 1822, these two young men—Frederick T. Gray and Benjamin H. Greene—met with Moses Grant, William P. Rice, and others, to give more careful consideration to their purpose of forming a society for mutual religious improvement.[1]

These young men met with little encouragement, and for some time there was small prospect of their succeeding in their undertaking. They continued to meet weekly, however; and on November 27 they formed The Association of Young Men for their own Mutual Improvement and for the Religious Instruction of the Poor. In 1824 the name was changed to The Association for Religious Improvement. The members met at each other's houses weekly, for the purpose of considering topics which related to their own personal improvement or to the wants of the community, always keeping in view the fact that their own religious growth must lie at the foundation of any great good which could be done by them for society. By degrees their number increased; and during the six years following, as appears from the records, the subjects to which their meetings were successively devoted were the desirableness of employing a missionary and building a mission–house, the condition and wants of vagrant children, the diffusion of Christianity in India, the importance of issuing tracts and other religions publications, the means and best method of improving our state prisons, the utility of forming a Unitarian Association, the best means to be adopted to abolish intemperance, the character of theatrical entertainments, the want of infant schools, and the best methods which could be taken to aid in the promotion of peace. All of these subjects were then comparatively new, and they were but just beginning to attract attention. Their importance was by no means generally understood, and least of all was the place which they were soon to occupy in public estimation anticipated.[2] The Association was discontinued in December, 1835.

[Sidenote: Preaching to the Poor.]

One of the first enterprises entered upon by this society was the securing of preaching for the poor and those connected with no religious organization. In this effort they had the co–operation of the younger Henry Ware, then the minister of the Second Church, and of John G. Palfrey, then the minister of the Brattle Street Church. In November, 1822, Henry Ware began these meetings; and four series of them were held throughout the winter, in Charter Street, in Hatters' or Creek Square, in Pitts Court, and in Spring Street. The Charter Street meetings were at first held in a room of a primary school, and then in a small chapel that had been built by a benevolent man for teaching and preaching purposes. In this place Mr. Ware was assisted by Dr. Jenks of the Christian denomination, and the chapel was afterwards occupied by the latter as a minister at large. The meetings in Pitts Court were also held in a school–room. Those in Hatters' Square occupied a room in a large tenement house and "here the accommodations, and probably the audience, were of a humbler character than elsewhere."[3]

[Sidenote: Tuckerman as Minister to the Poor.]

Early in the year 1826 Dr. Joseph Tuckerman expressed his willingness to devote himself to this ministry; and the American Unitarian Association was appealed to, that the necessary financial support might be secured. Dr. Tuckerman had been for twenty–five years the parish minister in Chelsea, but his health was such that he had been obliged to relinquish that position. On September 4 the sum of $600 was appropriated to the support of Dr. Tuckerman for one year as a missionary among the poor in Boston; and Ware, Barrett, and Gannett were made a committee to ascertain what amount of money could be raised for this purpose. It was thought wise not to use the regular funds of the Association for so special and local an object. The women of the Boston churches were therefore appealed to in behalf of this cause; and during the first year contributions were received from those connected with the congregations of the Brattle Street, Federal Street, West, New South, New North, Twelfth, and Chauncey Place Churches, amounting to $712. These contributions by the women of the churches were continued until the Benevolent Fraternity was organized.

Tuckerman entered upon his work November 5, 1826. On the evening of that day he met with the Association for, Religious Improvement, and discussed with its members the work to be undertaken. He began at once the visiting of the poor and the study of their condition in the several parts of the city, though confining himself largely to the north end. In making his first quarterly report to the Unitarian Association, February 5, 1827, he said that he had taken fifty families into his pastoral charge. He had given special attention to the children, had arranged that those should be sent to school who had not previously attended, and provided them with shoes and clothes where these were necessary. He had also aided the sick, provided necessaries for those who were helpless and deserving, secured work for those out of employment, and given religious consolation and correction where these were required.

After Dr. Tuckerman had entered upon his work of visiting the poor, the Young Men's Association arranged to have him resume the discontinued evening meetings. They accordingly secured the use of a room up two flights of stairs, in what was known as the "Circular Building," at the corner of Merrimac and Portland Streets. In this rude place, that had been used as a paint–shop, services were begun on Sunday evening, December 3, 1826. Tuckerman recorded in his diary that he had "a large and very attentive audience";[4] and on the same evening he met at the house of Dr. Channing "a large circle of ladies and gentlemen, who formed a society to help him visit."[5] As soon as services were begun in the Circular Building, it was proposed to form a Sunday–school; and on a very cold December day seven teachers and three children met to inaugurate it. They hovered about the little stove, by means of which the room was warmed, and began their work. The school grew rapidly, soon filled the room, and was given the name of the Howard School. Very soon, also, this room became too small to accommodate the attendants at the preaching services. In recognition of this need the Friend Street Free Chapel was erected, and opened for use on November 1, 1828.

[Sidenote: Tuckerman's Methods.]

During the first year of his ministry Dr. Tuckerman reported quarterly to the American Unitarian Association, and then semi–annually. In all there were printed four of the quarterly reports and fifteen of the others. It was not his custom in these reports to confine himself to an account of his work, which usually received only a brief statement at the end; but he discussed important topics relating to the condition of the poor and their needs. His third quarterly report was devoted to a consideration of the remedies to be used for confirmed intemperance. Others of the topics upon which he reported were the condition of the poor in cities, the duties of a minister at large (a title invented by him, which he preferred to that of city or domestic missionary), the effects of poverty on the moral life of the poor, the means of relieving pauperism, the causes of poverty and the social remedies, the several classes amongst the poor and the best means of reaching each of them, the means to be employed for the recovery of those sunk in pauperism, poor laws and outdoor relief. Among the subjects he discussed incidentally, and sometimes at considerable length, were the duty of providing seats for the poor in the churches at a small rental, the employment of children, education as a means of saving children from growing up to a life of vagrancy and pauperism, the wages of the poor and how they can be increased.[6] He was especially interested in the rescuing of children from ignorance and vice, and he strongly advocated the establishment of schools for the instruction of dull children and those whose education had been neglected. Through his efforts the Broad Street Infant School was established, in order to reach the younger children of the poor. In 1829 he made a careful study of the religious condition of the poor; and he found that out of a population of 55,000, which the city then contained, there were 4,200 families, or about 18,000 persons, who were not connected with any of the churches or who did not attend them with any degree of regularity. This gave him an opportunity to urge upon the public more strongly than before the importance of procuring free chapels, and a sufficient number of ministers to care for this large unchurched population. One or two ministers had labored amongst the poor before he began his work, and three or four had entered upon the same line of effort since he had done so; but these workers were too few in number to meet the large demands made upon them.

In carrying on his work, Dr. Tuckerman sought out all who were in need of his services, without distinction of nationality, color, creed, social position, or moral condition. If he gave the preference to any, it was those who were the most wretched and debased. "It is the first object of the ministry at large, never to be lost sight of," he wrote, "and to which no other is to be preferred, as far as shall be possible to extend its offices to the poor and the poorest, to the low and the lowest, to the most friendless and most uncared for, the most miserable."[7] He recognized the individuality of the poorest and the most vicious: he sought to foster it, and to make it the basis of moral reform and social recovery.

[Sidenote: Organization of Charities.]

The influence of Tuckerman's work was soon felt outside the city in which it was carried on. The people of the state came to take an interest in it, and to feel that its principles should be applied throughout the commonwealth. Therefore, a commission was appointed by the lower house of the state legislature, February 29, 1832, to inquire into the condition of the poor in all parts of the state, and to make such report as might be the basis of needed legislation. Dr. Tuckerman was made a member of this commission. The work of investigation largely fell upon him, as well as the writing of the report. His suggestions were accepted, and the results were beneficent. In the mean time the work of visiting the poor was carried on by a young man, Charles F. Barnard, then a student in the Divinity School, who entered upon his duties in April. In October he was joined by Frederick T. Gray, the founder of the Association for Religious Improvement and of the first Sunday–schools for the poor. These workers were ordained in the Federal Street Church on the evening of November 5, 1834, after having thoroughly tested their capacities for the task they had assumed.

Dr. Tuckerman set forth all the principles which have since been described under the name of "scientific charity," and he put them all into practice. In the spring of 1832 he organized a company of visitors to the poor, the members of which were to act as friends and advisers of those who were needy. In October, 1833, he brought about a union of the ministers at large of all denominations for purposes of consultation and mutual helpfulness. This union resulted in a meeting held in February, 1834, at which those interested in the proper care of the poor took counsel together as to the best methods to be followed. At a later meeting in March, it was decided to secure the aid of all the charitable societies in the city with a view to their co-operation and the prevention of the duplication of relief. There was accordingly organized the Association of Delegates from the Benevolent Societies of Boston, the objects of which were "to adopt measures for the most effectual prevention of fraud and deception in the applicants for charity; to obtain accurate and thorough information with regard to the situation, character, and wants of the poor; and generally to interchange knowledge, experience, and advice upon all the important subjects connected with the duties and responsibilities of Benevolent Societies." The principle upon which this organization acted was that "the public good requires that the character and circumstances of the poor should be thoroughly investigated and known by those who administer our public charities, in order that all the relief which a pure and enlarged benevolence dictates may be freely bestowed, and that almsgiving may not encourage extravagance or vice, nor injuriously affect the claims of society at large upon the personal exertions and moral character of its members." The first annual report of this Association, which appeared in October, 1835, was written by Dr. Tuckerman, and was one of the best he produced. He laid down certain rules he had accepted as the results of his experience: that beggary was to be broken up; that all misapplications of charity should be reported to the board of visitors; that those asking for alms should be relieved only at their homes and after investigation; that industry, forethought, economy, and self-denial were to be fostered in order to prevent pauperism, and that no help should be given where it led to dependence and reliance upon charity. Registration, investigation, prevention of duplication of alms, and the fostering of self-help were the methods brought to bear by Dr. Tuckerman in the organization of this Association.[8]

[Sidenote: Benevolent Fraternity of Churches.]

182

In the spring of 1834 the part of the ministry at large in Boston supported by Unitarians consisted of Dr. Tuckerman's work in visiting and ministering to the poor in their own homes, two chapels, in which Barnard and Gray preached and conducted their Sunday–schools, and the office of the Visitors to the Poor. In order more effectually to organize the support of this work, the Benevolent Fraternity of Churches was then suggested. The Second, Brattle Street, New South, New North, King's Chapel, Federal Street, Hollis Street, Twelfth, and Purchase Street Churches entered upon the work; and there was organized in each a society for the purpose of aiding the ministry at large. Each of these societies was privileged to send five delegates to a central body that should undertake the support and direction of that ministry. At a meeting held April 27, 1834, an organization of such delegates was effected. It was distinctly stated that "it was not the wish to add another to the eleemosynary institutions of the city to which the poor might resort either for the supply of the comforts or for the relief of necessities which belong to their bodily condition"; but the object of the Fraternity was described as being "the improvement of the moral state of the poor and irreligious of this city by the support of the ministry at large, and by other means."[9]

[Sidenote: Other Ministers at Large.]

Dr. Tuckerman continued his work of visiting the poor, so far as his health permitted, until his death, which occurred April 20, 1840. His assistants and successors continued the work of visitation outside of their own congregations. In August, 1844, Rev. Warren Burton was assigned to this special form of ministry, and to that of a systematic investigation of the condition of the poor. He gave much attention to the needs of children, and made inquiry as to intemperance, licentiousness, and other forms of social degeneration. He was a diligent and successful worker until his ministry came to an end in October, 1848. For about a year, in 1847, Rev. William Ware also devoted himself to the house–to–house ministry; but failing health compelled his withdrawal. In April, 1845, Rev. Andrew Bigelow took charge of the Pitts Street Chapel for a few months; and then for thirty–two years, until his death, in April, 1877, he continued to visit the poor. With the assistance of his wife, he went about to the homes of the people, administering to their physical needs, acting as their friend and adviser, and giving them such moral instruction and spiritual consolation as was possible.

For about one year, beginning in March, 1856, Rev. A. Rumpff visited German families in behalf of the Fraternity. He was succeeded in 1857 by Rev. A. Uebelacker, who continued the work for two or three years. From 1860 to 1864 Professor J.B. Torricelli carried on a ministry amongst the Italians, Spaniards, Greeks, and other natives of southern Europe resident in Boston. After the death of Dr. Bigelow this personal ministry was discontinued, owing to the increase in the number of other agencies for doing this kind of work.

[Sidenote: Ministry at Large in Other Cities.]

The work of the ministry at large was not confined to Boston. The original vote of the Unitarian Association establishing it was that it should be aided in New York as well. In December, 1836, Rev. William Henry Channing entered on such a ministry in New York; and it was continued there for some years. It was also established in Charlestown, Roxbury, Cambridge, Salem, Portsmouth, Portland, Lowell, New Bedford, Providence, Worcester, and elsewhere in New England. With the aid of the Unitarian Association it was undertaken in Baltimore, Cincinnati, Louisville, and St. Louis. In 1845 Rev. Lemuel Capen was carrying on the ministry in Baltimore, Rev. W.H. Farmer in Louisville, and Rev. Mordecai de Lange in St. Louis. The ministry at large was begun in Cincinnati in 1830, and was in charge for a short time of Christopher P. Cranch, who was succeeded by Rev. James H. Perkins, a most efficient worker, who soon became the popular minister of the Unitarian church in that city. It was established in St. Louis in 1840, and a day school for colored children was opened in 1841. A mission–house was built, and Rev. Charles H.A. Dall was put in charge. In 1841 the Mission Free School was founded, and now has a matron, nursery, kindergarten, Sunday–school, with lectures and entertainments. Dall was succeeded by Mordecai de Lange, Corlis B. Ward, Carlton A. Staples, and Thomas L. Eliot. The City Mission, as it was called, grew so large that in 1860 no one denomination could carry it on; and it became the St. Louis Provident Association, which has done an extensive and important work.[10]

In July, 1850, was formed the Association of Ministers at Large in New England, of which Rev. Charles F. Barnard was for many years the president, and Rev. Horatio Wood, of Lowell, the secretary. It met quarterly, or oftener, essays were read on subjects connected with the work of ministering to the poor, and the special phases of that work were discussed. In the spring of 1841 Rev. Charles F. Barnard began the publication of the Journal of the Ministry at Large as a sixteen–page octavo monthly, which was continued until 1860, part of the time as The Record; but during the later years it was issued irregularly.

In 1838 Dr. Tuckerman published The Principles and Results of the Ministry at Large in Boston, which embodied an account of his work for twelve years, and the conclusions at which he had arrived. It did much to give direction and purpose to the ministry, and to extend its influence. It can be read with interest and profit at the present time; for it contains all the principles since put into practice in many forms of charitable activity. Dr. Andrew P. Peabody truly said of Tuckerman's enterprise in behalf of the poor that it "was the earliest organized effort in that direction. Its success and its permanent establishment as an institution were due to its founder's strenuous perseverance, his self–sacrifice, his apostolic fervor of spirit, and the power of his influence."[11] Joseph Story spoke of the ministry at large as being one of "extraordinary success." "I deem it," he wrote, "one of the most glorious triumphs of Christian charity over the cold and reluctant doubts of popular opinion." The labors of Dr. Tuckerman "initiated a new sphere of Protestant charity," as his nephew well said.[12] "This has been the most characteristic, the best organized, and by far the most successful co–operative work that the Unitarian body has ever attempted by way of church action," was the testimony of Dr. Joseph Henry Allen.[13]

[1] The record of the first meeting states the objects for which the
young men met, as follows: "Feeling impressed with the importance of
giving religious instruction to the youths of that class of our poor
who are destitute of any regard for their future well–being, and who,
from being under the care of vicious parents, have no attention paid
to their moral conduct; and also wishing to become acquainted with
those persons of the different religious societies who profess to be
followers of the same Master, they agreed to associate themselves.
Having great reason to believe that God will bless their humble
efforts for the spread of pure religion and virtue, and looking to
Him for guidance, the meeting was organized."

[2] Ephraim Peabody, Christian Examiner, January, 1853, LIV. 93.

[3] John Ware, Life of Henry Ware, Jr., 132–135.

[4] The secretary of the Association for Religious Improvement made this
record of the meeting: "December 3, 1826. The Lectures under the
conduct of the Association commenced this evening at 6–1/2 o'clock at

Smith's circular building, corner of Merrimack and Portland Streets, which was very fully attended by those for whom it was intended. The services were of the first order. Rev. Dr. Tuckerman officiated."

[5] Eber R. Butler, Lend a Hand, V. 693, October, 1890.

[6] The substance of these reports has been reproduced in a book edited by E.E. Hale in 1874, Joseph Tuckerman on the Elevation of the Poor.

[7] The Principles and Results of the Ministry at Large in Boston, 61.

[8] Ministry at Large in Boston, 124.

[9] The following is a list of the churches now maintained by the Benevolent Fraternity of Churches, with the date when each was formed, or when it came under Unitarian management: Bulfinch Place Church, successor to Wend Street Chapel (1828); Pitts Street Chapel (1836), 1870. North End Union (begun in 1837); Hanover Street Chapel (1854); Parmenter Street Chapel (1884), 1892. Morgan Chapel, 1884. Channing Church, Dorchester, successor to Washington Village Chapel, 1854. The Suffolk Street Chapel (1837), succeeded by the New South Free Church (1867), continues its life in the Parker Memorial, 1889. The Warren Street Chapel (1832), now known as the Barnard Memorial Church, continues its work, but is not under the direction of the Benevolent Fraternity. In 1901 the churches constituting the Benevolent Fraternity were the First Church, Second Church, Arlington Street Church, South Congregational Church, King's Chapel, Church of the Disciples; First Parish, Dorchester; First Parish, Brighton; Hawes Church South Boston; First Parish, West Roxbury; First Congregational Society, Jamaica Plain.

[10] In 1830 the British and Foreign Unitarian Association began to consider the value of this ministry, and in 1832 the first mission was opened in London. In 1835 was formed the London Domestic Mission Society for the purpose of carrying on the work in that city. In 1833 a similar movement was made in Manchester, and in 1835 was organized

the Liverpool Domestic Mission Society. The visit of Dr. Tuckerman to
England in 1834 gave large interest to this movement. He then met
Mary Carpenter, and she was led by him to begin her great work of
charity. It was during the next year that she entered upon the work
in Bristol that made her name widely known. In 1847 there were two
ministers at large in London, two in Birmingham, and one each in
Liverpool, Bristol, Leeds, Manchester, Halifax, and Leicester. The
writings of Dr. Tuckerman were translated into French by the Baron de
Gerando, a leading philanthropist and statesman of that day, who
praised them highly, and introduced their methods into Paris and
elsewhere. Of Tuckerman's book on the ministry at large M. de Gerando
said that it throws "invaluable light upon the condition and wants of
the indigent and the influence which an enlightened charity can
exert." He also said of Tuckerman that "he knew the difference
between pauperism and poverty," thus recognizing one of those
cardinal distinctions made by the philanthropist in his efforts to
aid the poor to self–help and independence.

[11] Memorial History of Boston, III. 477.

[12] Sprague's Annals of the Unitarian Pulpit, 345, the words quoted being
from the pen of Henry T. Tuckerman, the well–known essayist.

[13] Our Liberal Movement in Theology, 59.

XI. ORGANIZED SUNDAY–SCHOOL WORK.

The first Sunday–schools organized in this country distinctly for purposes of religious
training were by persons connected with Unitarian churches. Several schools had been
opened previously, but they were not continued or were organized in the interests of
secular instruction. In the summer of 1809 Miss Hannah Hill, then twenty–five years of
age, and Miss Joanna B. Prince, then twenty, both teachers of private schools for small
children, and connected with the First Parish in Beverly, Mass., of which Dr. Abiel Abbot
was the pastor, opened a school in one room of a dwelling–house for the religious
training of the children who did not receive such teaching at home. In the spring of 1810

the same young women reopened their school in a larger room, using the Bible as their only book of instruction. Sessions were held in the morning before church, and in the afternoon following the close of the services.[1]

The first season about thirty children attended, but the interest grew; and in 1813 the school occupied the Dane Street chapel, and became a union or town school. Jealousies resulted, and a school was soon established by each church in the town. In 1822 the First Parish received the original school under its sole care, and it was removed to the meeting-house.

A Sunday-school was begun in Concord in the summer of 1810, under the leadership of Miss Sarah Ripley, daughter of Dr. Ezra Ripley, the minister of the town. On Sunday afternoons she taught a number of children in her father's house, since known as the "Old Manse." About five years later a school was opened at the centre of the town, near the church, by three young women. In 1818 a Sunday-school was begun in connection with the church itself, which absorbed the others, or of which they formed the nucleus.[2]

A teacher of a charity school supported by the West Church in Boston was the first person to open a Sunday-school in that city. In October, 1812, the teacher of this school, Miss Lydia K. Adams, then a member of the West Parish, according to the statement of Dr. Charles Lowell, minister of the church at the time, "having learned on a visit to Beverly that some young ladies of the town were in the practice of giving religious instruction to poor children on the Sabbath, consulted her minister as to the expediency of giving like instruction to the children of her school, and to those who had been members of it, on the same day. The project was decidedly approved, and immediately carried into effect." In December of the same year, Miss Adams was compelled by ill-health to leave her school; and ladies of the West Church took charge of it, and in turn instructed the children, both on the week-days and the Sabbath, till a suitable permanent teacher could be obtained. On this event they relinquished the immediate care of the week-day school, but continued the instruction of the Sunday-school, till it was transferred to the church, and was enlarged by the addition of "children of a different description," in 1822.[3] Sunday-schools were also begun in Cambridgeport, in 1814; Wilton, N.H., in 1816; and Portsmouth, in 1818. The latter school had the enthusiastic support of Nathaniel A. Haven, a young lawyer and rising politician, who devoted himself with great zeal and success to such instruction of the young.[4]

The Association of Young Men for Mutual Improvement and for the Religious Instruction of the Poor began the work of forming Sunday–schools for the children of the poor in Boston during the year 1823. A school was begun in the Hancock School–house, then recently built for grammar–school purposes.[5] Soon after they opened a school in Merrimac Street, called the Howard Sunday–school, in connection with the work of Dr. Tuckerman; and in 1826 the Franklin Sunday–school was begun by the same persons and for the same purposes. In connection with these schools was formed the Sunday School Benevolent Society, composed of charitable women, who provided such children as were needy with suitable clothing.

In 1825 a parish Sunday–school was organized in connection with the Twelfth Congregational Church, of which Rev. Samuel Barrett was the minister. It was reorganized in 1827, with the object of giving "a religious education apart from all sectarian views, as systematically as it is given to the same children in other branches of learning."[6] In July, 1828, The Christian Register spoke of "the rapid and extensive establishment of Sunday–schools by individuals attached to Unitarian societies," and said that in the course of two or three years "large and respectable Sunday–schools have been established by Unitarians in various parts of the city. Several of these are parish schools, under the immediate guidance of the pastors. Others are more general in their plan, receiving children from all quarters."

[Sidenote: Boston Sunday School Society.]

At a meeting of the teachers of the Franklin Sunday–school held December 16, 1826, it was proposed that there be organized an association of all the teachers connected with Unitarian parishes in Boston and the vicinity. On February 27, 1827, a meeting was held in the Berry Street vestry for this purpose; and on April 18 a constitution was adopted for the Boston Sunday School Society. The schools joining in this organization were the Hancock, Franklin, and Howard, and those connected with the West, Federal Street, Hollis Street, and Twelfth Congregational Churches. Dr. Joseph Tuckerman was elected president; Moses Grant, vice–president; Dr. J.F. Flagg, corresponding secretary; and Rev. Frederick T. Gray, recording secretary. The first annual meeting was held November 28, 1827; and the above–named officers were re–elected. On December 12 a public meeting was held in the Federal Street Church, which was well filled. Reports of the work of the schools, including that at Cambridgeport, were read; and addresses were made.

The objects of the Sunday School Society were the helping of teachers, the extending of the interests of the schools, and the publishing of books. It was difficult to procure suitable books for use in Sunday–schools and for their libraries, and the prices were very high. In the autumn of 1828 arrangements were made for the publishing of books, the American Unitarian Association co–operating therein by providing a capital of $300 for this purpose, the profits going to the Sunday School Society, and the money borrowed being returned without interest. This connection was abandoned in 1831 because it was found that the Unitarian name on the title–page of the books hindered their sale. In April, 1828, was issued the first number of the Christian Teacher's Manual, a small monthly, of which Mrs. Eliza Lee Follen was the editor, intended for the use of families and Sunday–schools. According to the preface the subjects chiefly considered were the best methods of addressing the minds of children, suggestions to teachers, explanations of Scripture, religious instruction from natural objects, histories taken from real life, stories and hymns adapted to children, and accounts of Sunday–schools.

The Manual was continued for two years; and it was followed by The Scriptural Interpreter, edited by Rev. Ezra S. Gannett. The editor of the Interpreter preferred to publish it under his own name, because he did "not wish it to be considered the organ or the representative of a denomination of Christians." "It will have one object," he said, "to furnish the means of acquaintance with the true sense and value of Scripture, and particularly of the New Testament; but whatever will promote this object will come within the scope the publication." It was issued bi–monthly, and was continued for five years. It was wholly devoted to the exposition of the Bible, a systematic series of translations and interpretations of the Gospels forming a distinct feature of its pages. A considerable part of it was prepared by the editor, who drew freely upon expository works. Among the contributors were William H. Furness, Orville Dewey, Alexander Young, Edward B. Hall, James Walker, Henry Ware, Jr., and J.P. Dabney. In 1836, Dr. Gannett's health having failed, the magazine was edited by Theodore Parker, George E. Ellis, and William Silsbee, then students in the Harvard Divinity School.

One important feature of the work of the Sunday School Society was the extension of the cause it represented. In December, 1829, reports were presented at the annual meeting from nearly fifty schools; and it was thought desirable that they should be brought into closer relations with the society. Accordingly, Frederick T. Gray, the secretary, visited many of these schools. The next year, as a result, a considerable number of those outside the city connected themselves with the society; and the lists of vice–presidents and directors were enlarged to include them in its operations. Afterwards this work was carried on by a committee of the society, the members of which visited the schools, giving addresses, and in other ways helping to give strength and purpose to the work in which they were engaged. Schools were visited in Maine, New Hampshire, Massachusetts, Rhode Island, New York, Pennsylvania, Kentucky, and other states. To give better opportunity for the attendance of delegates from schools outside the city, the yearly meeting was changed from December to anniversary week in May.

The society published a considerable number of tracts, which were distributed gratuitously by the agents and in other ways. It also issued lesson–books, as well as books for the juvenile libraries which were forming at this time in all the churches. To meet this demand, the younger Henry Ware began editing, in 1833, the Sunday–school Library for Young Persons, in which were included his own Life of the Saviour, Mrs. John Farrar's Life of Howard, Rev. Stephen G. Bulfinch's Holy Land, and Rev. Thomas B. Fox's Sketch of the Reformation. The next year Mr. Ware began a series of books which he called Scenes and Characters illustrating Christian Truth. Another method used by the society was the giving of expository lectures.

The society at first held quarterly meetings; but the interest grew, and the meetings became monthly. Great enthusiasm was felt at this time in regard to the work of these schools, and many persons of prominence praised them and took part in their management. "The institution of Sunday–schools constitutes one of the most remarkable features of the present age," wrote Dr. Joseph Allen, in 1830. "It has already done much to supply the deficiencies of domestic education, and, if wisely conducted, is destined, we trust, to become at no distant day one of the most efficient instruments in forming the characters of the young."[7] Writing in 1838, the younger Henry Ware said that "the Sunday–school has become one of the established institutions of religion in connection with the church, and the character of religion is henceforth to depend, in no small degree, on the wisdom with which it shall be administered."[8]

In 1834 was organized the Worcester Sunday School Society. It had its origin as far back as November 17, 1817, when a committee of the Worcester Association of Ministers was appointed to report on the subject of Sunday–schools. A meeting was held in Lancaster, October 9, 1834, when an organization was perfected. The succeeding meetings were largely attended, and much interest was awakened.[9] In 1842 a similar society was organized in Middlesex County; and at about the same time one came into existence in

Cheshire County, New Hampshire. Soon after societies were organized in the counties of Norfolk, Plymouth (North), Middlesex (West), Worcester, and in Portland and its neighborhood.

In April, 1831, the directors of the Boston Sunday School Society discussed the feasibility of starting a weekly paper for the use of the schools. In July, 1836, Rev. Bernard Whitman began the publication of The Sunday School Teacher and Children's Friend. In January, 1837, The Young Christian was begun, and was published weekly at the office of The Christian Register, by David Reed. These papers were continued only for a few years. From 1845 to 1857 Mrs. Eliza Lee Follen edited a monthly magazine for children, called The Children's Friend. The first number of the Sunday School Gazette was published in Worcester, August 7, 1849, under the direction of the Worcester Sunday School Society. It was established at the suggestion of Rev. Edward Everett Hale, then a minister in that city, in connection with Rev. Edmund B. Willson, then settled in Grafton. The editor was Rev. Francis Le Baron, the minister at large in Worcester, though Mr. Hale was a frequent contributor. When the National Sunday School Society was organized, the Sunday School Gazette was transferred to, its charge; but the publication of this paper was continued in Worcester until 1860.[10]

[Sidenote: Unitarian Sunday School Society.]

As time went on, and the work of the Sunday–schools enlarged, it was felt that it was necessary there should be one general organization which should bring together all Unitarian schools into a compact working force. To meet this growing need, a convention of the county societies and of local schools was held in Worcester, October 4, 1854, at which time the Sunday School Society was organized as a general denominational body. Hon. Albert Fearing, of Boston, was made the president, and Rev. Frederick T. Gray the secretary. The society provided itself with a desk in the rooms of the Unitarian Association, and provision was made for the collection and sale of all the helps demanded by the schools.

From 1855 until 1865 the society was sadly crippled by the lack of funds. The hard times preceding the Civil War, and the absorption of public interest in that great national event, made it difficult for the society to continue its work with any degree of success. For some years little was done but to hold the annual meeting in the autumn and that in anniversary week, and to continue the publication of the Sunday School Gazette. For a number of years, however, Teachers' Institutes were held; and these were continued at irregular intervals until about 1875. The Sunday School Teachers' Institute was organized in 1852, and continued in existence for ten years.

After the death of Rev. Frederick T. Gray in 1855, he was succeeded in the position of secretary of the Sunday School Society by Rev. Stephen G. Bulfinch. In 1856 Rev. Warren H. Cudworth became the secretary, and the editor of the Gazette; and he held these positions until May, 1861, when he became the chaplain of the first Massachusetts regiment taking part in the Civil War. In the October following, Mr. Joseph H. Allen, a Boston merchant, afterwards the editor of The Schoolmate, became the secretary and editor. He continued to edit the Gazette until November, 1865; but Mr. M.T. Rice was made secretary in 1863. At the end of 1865, when the society was in a condition of almost complete collapse, Rev. Thomas J. Mumford became the secretary, and the editor of the Gazette for one year. He restored confidence in the society, and made the paper a success. During the war the paper was published monthly for the sake of economy; but with the first of January, 1866, it was restored to its former semi-monthly issue.

The new life that came to the denomination in 1865 had its influence upon the Sunday School Society. In the autumn of 1866, when the Unitarian Association had secured a large increase of funds, it was proposed that the Sunday School Society should unite with it, and that the larger organization should have the direction of all denominational activities, especially those of publishing. The more zealous friends of the society did not approve of such consolidation, and succeeded in reanimating its work by appointing as its secretary Mr. James P. Walker, who had been the head of the publishing firm of Walker, Wise &Co., a young man of earnest purpose, a successful Sunday-school teacher and superintendent, and an enthusiastic believer in the mission of Unitarianism. Mr. Walker devoted his whole time to the interests of the society, and an energetic effort was made to revive and extend its work. He proved to be the man for the position, largely increasing the bookselling and publishing activities, visiting schools and conferences, and awakening much enthusiasm in regard to the interests of Sunday-schools. He wore himself out in this work, however, and died in March, 1868, greatly lamented throughout the denomination.[11]

After the death of Mr. Walker, consolidation with the Association was again urged; but Rev. Leonard J. Livermore was in June elected the secretary. At the annual meeting it was resolved to raise $5,000 for the work of the society, and the next year it was proposed to make the annual contribution $10,000. The name was changed to the Unitarian Sunday School Society at the annual meeting of 1868, held in Worcester. In 1871 Mr. John Kneeland became the secretary; and with the beginning of 1872 the Gazette was changed to The Dayspring, which was issued monthly. In the autumn of that year the society began the publication of monthly lessons, and there was issued with them a Teachers' Guide for the lessons of the year. With the beginning of 1877 the Guide was discontinued, and the lesson papers enlarged. In November, 1875, Rev. George F. Piper became the secretary,—a position he held until May 1, 1883. During his administration about three hundred lessons were prepared by him, and these had a circulation of about nine thousand copies. The transition condition of the denomination made it difficult to carry on the work of the society at this time, for it was impossible to please both conservatives and radicals with any lessons that might be prepared. One superintendent warned his school against the heretical tendencies of lessons which, from the other point of view, a minister condemned as being fit for orthodox schools, but not for Unitarians. In the same mail came a letter from a minister saying the lessons were too elementary, and from another saying they were much too advanced. In the latter part of Mr. Piper's term service was begun an important work of preparing manuals thoroughly modern in their spirit and methods.[12]

In May, 1883, Rev. Henry G. Spaulding became the secretary; and the work of publishing modern manuals was largely extended.[13] At the suggestion and with the co-operation of the secretary there was organized, November 12, 1883, the Unitarian Sunday School Union of Boston, having for its object "to develop the best methods of Sunday-school work." At about the same time a lending library of reference books was established in connection with the work of the society. In the autumn of 1883 the society began to hold in Channing Hall weekly lectures for teachers. In 1885 The Dayspring was enlarged and became Every Other Sunday, being much improved in its literary contents as well as in its illustrations. The same year the society was incorporated, and the number of directors was increased to include representatives from all sections of the country; while all Sunday-schools contributing to the society's treasury were given a delegate representation in its membership. Mr. Spaulding continued his connection with the society until January 1, 1892.

Rev. Edward A. Horton, who had for several years taken an active part in the work of the society, assumed charge February 1, 1892. Mr. Horton was made the president, it being deemed wise to have the head of the society its executive officer. During his administration there has been a steady growth in Sunday–school interest, which has demanded a rapid increase in the number and variety of publications. The book department has been taxed to the utmost to meet the demand. A new book of Song and Service, compiled by Mr. Horton, has reached a sale of nearly 25,000 copies. A simple statement of "Our Faith" has had a circulation of 40,000 copies, and in a form suitable for the walls of Sunday–school rooms it has been in considerable demand.[14] A series of lessons, covering a period of seven years, upon the three–grade, one–topic plan, has been largely used in the schools. Besides the twenty manuals published in this course of lessons, forty other text–books have been published, making a total of sixty in all, from 1892 to 1902.[15] There have also been many additions to Sunday–school helps by way of special services for festival days, free tracts, and statements of belief. The Channing Hall talks to Sunday–school teachers have been made to bear upon these courses of lessons. Every Other Sunday has been improved, and its circulation extended. The number of donating churches and schools has been steadily increased, the number in 1901 being 255, the largest by far yet reached. At the annual meeting of the society and at local conferences representative speakers have presented the newest methods of Sunday–school work. Sunday–school unions have been formed in various parts of the country, and churches are awakened to a new interest in the work of religious instruction. "Home and School Conferences" have been held with a view to bringing parents and teachers into closer sympathy and co–operation.

[Sidenote: Western Unitarian Sunday School Society.]

In the west the first movement towards Sunday–school activities began in 1871 with the publication of a four–page lesson–sheet at Janesville, Wis., by Rev. Jenkin Lloyd Jones. This was continued for two or three years. Through the interest of Mr. Jones in Sunday–school work a meeting for organization was called in the fourth church, Chicago, October 14, 1873, when the Western Unitarian Sunday School Society was organized, with Rev. Milton J. Miller as president and Mr. Jones as secretary. At the meeting the next year in St. Louis a committee was appointed to prepare a song–book for the schools, which resulted in the production of The Sunny Side, edited by Rev. Charles W. Wendte. The next step was to establish headquarters in Chicago, where all kinds of material could be furnished to the schools, with the necessary advice and encouragement. Through successive years the effort of the society was to systematize the work of Unitarian Sunday–schools, to put into them the best literature, the best song and service books, the best lesson papers, and other tools,—in short, to secure better and more definite teaching, such as is in accord with the best scholarship and thought of the age.[16]

In 1882 the society became incorporated, and its work from this time enlarged in all directions. To develop these results more fully, an Institute was held in the Third Church, Chicago, in November, 1887, at which five sessions were given to Sunday–school work, and two to Unity Club interests. In the course of several years of encouraging success, the Institute developed into a Summer Assembly of two or more weeks' continuance at Hillside, Helena Valley, Wis., which still continues its yearly sessions. In May, 1902, The Western Sunday School Society was consolidated with the national organization; and the plates and stock which it possessed were handed over to the Unitarian Sunday School Society. A western headquarters is maintained in Chicago, where all the publications of the two societies are kept on sale.

[Sidenote: Unity Clubs.]

As adjuncts to the Sunday–school, and to continue its work for adults and in other spheres of ethical training, the Unity Club came into existence about the year 1873, beginning with the work of Rev. Jenkin Ll. Jones at Janesville. In the course of the next ten years nearly every Unitarian church in the west organized such a club, and the movement to some degree extended to other parts of the country. In 1887 there was organized in Boston the National Bureau of Unity Clubs. These clubs devoted themselves to literary, sociological, and religious courses of study; and they furnished centres for the social activities of the churches. About the year 1878 began a movement to organize societies of young people for the cultivation of the spirit of worship and religious development. This resulted in 1889 in the organization of the National Guild Alliance; and in 1890 this organization joined with the Bureau of Unity Clubs and the Unitarian Temperance Society in supporting an agency in the Unitarian Building, Boston, with the aid of the Unitarian Association. The Young People's Religious Union was organized in Boston, May 28, 1896; and in large degree, it took the place of the Bureau and the Alliance, uniting the two in a more efficient effort to interest the young people of the churches.[17]

[Sidenote: The Ladies' Commission on Sunday–school Books.]

In the autumn of 1865, Rev. Charles Lowe, then the secretary of the Unitarian Association, invited a number of women to meet him for the purpose of conference on the subject of Sunday–school libraries. At his suggestion they organized themselves on October 12 as The Ladies' Commission on Sunday–school Books, with the object of preparing a catalogue of books read and approved by competent persons. At the first meeting ten persons were present, but the number was soon enlarged to thirty; and it was still farther increased by the addition of corresponding members in cities too remote for personal attendance. Among those taking part in the work of the commission at first were Miss Lucretia P. Hale, Miss Anna C. Lowell, Mrs. Edwin P. Whipple, Mrs. Ednah D. Cheney, Mrs. A.D.T. Whitney, Mrs. S. Bennett, Mrs. Caroline H. Dall, Mrs. E.E. Hale, Mrs. E.P. Tileston, and Miss Hannah E. Stevenson.

The commission not only aimed to select books for Sunday–school libraries, but also those for the home reading of young persons and for the use of teachers. It undertook also the procuring of the publication of suitable juvenile books. The first catalogue was issued in October, 1866, and contained a list of two hundred books, selected from twelve hundred examined. In the spring of 1867 a catalogue of five hundred and seventy–three books was printed, as the result of the reading of nineteen hundred volumes.

In the beginning of its work the commission did not confine its activities to the selecting of juvenile books; for the Sunday School Hymn and Tune Book, published in 1869, was largely due to its efforts. Under the administration of Mr. James P. Walker the Sunday School Society undertook to procure the publication of a number of books of fiction suitable for Sunday–school libraries, and offered prizes to this end. The commission gave its encouragement to this effort, read the manuscripts, and aided in determining to whom the prizes should be given. The result was the publication of a half–dozen volumes by the Sunday School Society and the Unitarian Association. The society also aided to some extent in meeting the expenses of the commission, though these were usually met by the Association.

For many years the books approved by the commission were grouped under three heads: books especially recommended for Unitarian Sunday–school libraries; those highly recommended for their religious tone, but somewhat impaired for this purpose by the use of phrases and the adoption of a spirit not in accord with the Unitarian faith; and those profitable and valuable, but not adapted to the purposes of a Sunday–school library. Every book recommended was read and approved by at least five persons, discussed in committee of the whole, and accepted by a two–thirds vote of all the members. Books about which there was much diversity of opinion were read by a larger number of persons. This classification proved rather cumbersome, and it was often found difficult to decide into which list a book should be placed; and the result was that about 1890 the simpler plan was adopted of putting all titles in their alphabetical order, with explanatory notes for each book. In 1882 the list of books for teachers was discontinued as being no longer necessary.

Annual lists of books have been published by the commission since 1866; and, in addition, several catalogues have been issued, containing all the books approved during a period of five years. In the early days of the commission, supplementary lists for children and young persons were issued, containing books of a more secular character than were thought suitable for Sunday–school libraries. Gradually, it has extended its work to include the needs of all juvenile libraries; and these books are now incorporated into the one annual catalogue. In thirty–four years the commission has examined 10,957 books, and has approved 3,076, or about one–third.[18]

[1] Sunday School Times, September 15, 1860.

[2] Asa Bullard, Fifty Years with the Sabbath Schools, 37.

[3] C.A. Bartol, The West Church and its Ministers, Appendix.

[4] See the Remains of Nathaniel Appleton Haven, with a Memoir of his
    life, by George Ticknor.

[5] The Hancock Sunday–school assembled at eight in the morning and at
    one in the afternoon, Moses Grant being the first superintendent.

[6] At the school of the Twelfth Congregational Society, Carpenter's
    Catechism was used for the small children. This was followed by the
    Worcester Catechism, compiled in 1822 by the ministers of the
    Worcester Association of Ministers, Dr. Joseph Allen being the real
    author. The Geneva Catechism in its three successive parts, followed
    in order. In the Bible class, use was made of Hannah Adams's Letters
    on the Gospels, under the immediate charge of the Pastor. A hymn–book

issued by the Publishing Fund Society was in use by the whole school.

[7] Christian Examiner, March, 1830, VIII. 49.

[8] Ibid., May, 1838, XXIV. 182.

[9] Joseph Allen, History of the Worcester Association, 261–264.

[10] In 1852 was published a graded series of eight manuals of Christian instruction for Sunday–schools and families,—a result of the activities of the Sunday School Society. The titles and authors of these books were Early Religious Lessons; Palestine and the Hebrew People, Stephen G. Bulfinch; Lessons on the Old Testament, Rev. Ephraim Peabody; The Life of Christ, Rev. John H. Morison; The Books and Characters of the New Testament, Rev. Rufus Ellis; Lessons upon Religious Duties and Christian Morals, Rev. George W. Briggs; Doctrines of Scripture, Rev. Frederic D. Huntington; Scenes from Christian History, Rev. Edward E. Hale. Two other books connected with the early history of Unitarian Sunday–schools properly demand notice here. In 1847 was published The History of Sunday Schools and of Religious Education from the Earliest Times, by Lewis G. Pray, who was treasurer of the Boston Sunday School Society from 1834 to 1853, and chairman of its board of agents from 1841 to 1848. He was one of the first workers in the establishing of Sunday–schools in Boston, and he zealously interested himself in this cause so long as he lived. He compiled the first book of hymns used in Unitarian schools, and also the first book of devotional exercises. For twenty years he was superintendent of the school connected with the Twelfth Congregational Society, holding that place from its organization in 1827. In one of the concluding chapters of his book Mr. Pray gave an account of the early history of Unitarian Sunday–schools in Boston and its neighborhood. In 1852 was published a series of addresses which had been given by Rev. Frederick T. Gray at Sunday–school anniversaries and on other similar occasions. The volume contains most interesting information in regard to the origin of Sunday–schools in Boston, and the beginnings of the Sunday School

Society, as well as the work of Dr. Tuckerman and his assistants in the ministry, at large.

[11] Memoir of James P. Walker, with Selections from his Writings, by Thomas B. Fox. American Unitarian Association, 1869.

[12] The first of these was Rev. Edward H. Hall's First Lessons on the Bible, which appeared in 1882; and it was soon followed by Professor C.H. Toy's History of the Religion of Israel.

[13] Among these were Religions before Christianity, by Professor Charles Carroll Everett, D.D., 1883; Manual of Unitarian Belief, by Rev. James Freeman Clarke, D.D., 1884; Lessons on the Life of St. Paul, by Rev. Edward H. Hall, 1885; Early Hebrew Stories, by Rev. Charles F. Dole, 1886; Hebrew Prophets and Kings, by Rev. Henry G. Spaulding, 1887; The Later Heroes of Israel, by Mr. Spaulding, 1888; Lessons on the Gospel of Luke, by Mr. Spaulding and Rev. W.W. Fenn, 1889; A Story of the Sects, by Rev. William H. Lyon, in 1891. In 1890 appeared the Unitarian Catechism of Rev. Minot J. Savage, though not published by the Sunday School Society. These books attracted wide attention, were largely used in Unitarian schools, and were adopted into those of other sects to some extent. In 1886 the president of the American Social Science Association publicly urged the use of the ethical manuals of the society by all Sunday–schools. Several of these books were republished in London, and Dr. Toy's manual was translated into Dutch. The society also published a new Service Book and Hymnal, which went into immediate use in a large number of schools, and did much for the enrichment of the devotional exercises and the promotion of an advanced standard of both words and music in the hymns.

[14] The Fatherhood of God, the Brotherhood of Man, the leadership of Jesus, salvation by character, the progress of mankind onward and upward forever.

[15] Among the publications under Mr. Horton's administration, which may justly be called significant, are: Beacon Lights of Christian History, in three grades; Noble Lives and Noble Deeds, Dole's Catechism of Liberal Faith, Mott's History of Unitarianism, Pulsford's various manuals on the Bible, Mrs. Jaynes's Illustrated Primary Leaflets, Miss Mulliken's Kindergarten Lessons, Story of Israel and Great Thoughts of Israel, in three grades, Fenn's Acts of the Apostles, Chadwick's Questions on the Old Testament Books in their Right Order, Mrs. Kate Gannett Wells's forty Illustrated Primary Lessons, and Walkley's Helps for Teachers. Mr. Horton, during this ten years, has written fourteen manuals on various subjects. Co-extensive with the large increase of text-books has been the enrichment of lessons by pictorial aids. Excellent half-tone pictures have been prepared from the best subjects.

[16] Among the publications of the Western Unitarian Sunday School Society have been Unity Services and Songs, edited by Rev. James Vila Blake, and published in 1878; a service book called The Way of Life, by Rev. Frederick L. Hosmer, issued in 1877; and Unity Festivals, services for special holidays, 1884. Of the lesson-books published by the society, those that have been most successful have been Corner-stones of Character, by Mrs. Kate Gannett Wells; A Chosen Nation, or the Growth of the Hebrew Religion, by Rev. William C. Gannett; and The More Wonderful Genesis, by Rev. Henry M. Simmons. In 1890 the society entered upon the publication of a six-year course of studies, which included Beginnings according to Legend and according to the Truer Story, by Rev. Allen W. Gould; The Flowering of the Hebrew Religion, by Rev. W.W. Fenn; In the Home, by Rev. W.C. Gannett; Mother Nature's Children, by Rev. A.W. Gould; and The Flowering of Christianity, the Liberal Christian Movement toward Universal Religion, by Rev. W.C. Gannett.

[17] The objects of The Young People's Religious Union are: (a) to foster the religious life; (b) to bring the young into closer relations with one another; and (c) to spread rational views of religion, and to put into practice such principles of life and duty as tend to uplift

mankind. The cardinal principles of the Union are truth, worship, and service. Any young people's society may become a member of the Union by affirming in writing its sympathy with the general objects of the Union, adopting its cardinal principles, making a contribution to its treasury, and sending the secretary a list of its officers. The annual meeting is held in May at such day and place as the executive board may appoint. Special union meetings are held as often as several societies may arrange. The Union has its headquarters at Room 11, in the Unitarian Building, Boston, in charge of the secretary, whose office hours are from 9 A.M. to 1 P.M. daily. Organization hints, hymnals, leaflets, helps for the national topics, and other suggestive materials are supplied. The national officers furnish speakers for initial meetings, visit unions, and help in other ways. The Union maintains a department in The Christian Register, under the charge of the secretary, for notes, notices, helps on the topics, and all matters of interest to the unions, and also publishes a monthly bulletin in connection with the National Alliance of Unitarian Women.

[18] In the thirty–five years which comprise the life of the commission a gradual but marked change has been in operation. Sunday–school libraries are being used less and less, and town libraries have become much more numerous and better patronized by both old and young. In the spring of 1896 the question arose in the commission whether, with the decline of the Sunday–school library, the need which called it into being had not ceased to exist; and, in order to secure information as to the advisability of continuing its work, cards were sent to 305 ministers of the denomination and to 507 public libraries, mostly in New England, asking if the lists of the commission were found useful, and whether it was desired that the sending of them should be continued. From Unitarian ministers 209 replies were received, one–half using the lists frequently and the other half occasionally or for the selection of special books. From the town libraries cordial replies were received in 220 instances, most of them warmly approving of the lists, which had been found very useful. The result of this investigation was to bring the commission more directly into touch with the various libraries, and to give it a

better understanding of their needs.

XII. THE WOMEN'S ALLIANCE AND ITS PREDECESSORS.

The Unitarian body has been remarkable for the women of intellectual power and philanthropic achievement who have adorned its fellowship. In proportion to their numbers, they have done much for the improvement and uplifting of society. In the early Unitarian period, however, the special work of women was for the most part confined to the Sunday–school and the sewing circle. Whatever the name by which it was known, whether as the Dorcas Society, the Benevolent Society, or the Ladies' Aid, the sewing circle did a work that was in harmony with the needs of the time, and did it well. It helped the church with which it was connected in many quiet ways, and gave much aid to the poor and suffering members of the community. Nor did it limit its activities to purely local interests; for many a church was helped by it and the early missionary societies received its contributions gladly.

Before the organization of the Benevolent Fraternity of Churches, the women of Boston raised the money necessary for the support of the ministry at large in that city. One of the earliest societies organized for general service, was the Tuckerman Sewing Circle, formed in 1827. Its purpose was to assist Dr. Tuckerman in his work for the poor of the city by providing clothing and otherwise aiding the needy. The work of this circle is still going on in connection, with the Bulfinch Place Church; and every year it raises a large sum of money for the charitable work of the ministry at large.

The civil war helped women to recognize the need of organization and co–operation, on their part. In working for the soldiers, not only in their homes and churches, but in connection with the Sanitary Commission, and later in seeking to aid the freedmen, they learned their own power and the value of combination with others. In Massachusetts the work of the Sanitary Commission was largely carried on by Unitarians. In describing this work, Mrs. Ednah D. Cheney has indicated what was done by Unitarian women. "During the late war," she wrote, "a woman's branch of the Sanitary Commission was organized in New England. Mary Dwight (Parkman) was its first president; but Abby Williams May soon took her place, which she held till the close of the war. With unwearied zeal Miss May presided over its councils, organized its action, and encouraged others to work. She went down to the hospitals and camps, to judge of their needs with her own eyes, and travelled from town to town in New England, arousing the women to new effort. These might be seen, young and old, rich and poor, bearing bundles of blue flannel through the streets, and unaccustomed fingers knitting the coarse yarn, while the heart throbbed with anxiety for the dear ones gone to the war. A noble band of nurses volunteered their services, and the strife was as to which should go soonest and do the hardest work. Hannah E. Stevenson, Helen Stetson, and many another name became as dear to the soldiers as that of mother or sister. A committee was formed to supply the colored soldiers with such help as other soldiers received from their relations; and, when one of the noblest of Boston's sons passed through her streets at their head, his mother 'thanked God for the privilege of seeing that day.' The same spirit went into the work of educating the freedmen. Young men and women, the noblest and best, went forth together to that work of danger and toil."[1]

[Sidenote: Women's Western Unitarian Conference.]

It was such experiences as these that encouraged Unitarian women to enter upon other philanthropic and educational labors when the civil war had come to an end. Leaders had been trained during this period who were capable of guiding such movements to a successful issue. The example of the women of the evangelical churches in organizing their home and foreign missionary associations also undoubtedly influenced, to a greater or lesser degree, the women of the liberal churches. After the organization of the National Conference, Unitarian women began to realize, as never before, the need of co−operation in behalf of the cause they had at heart.[2] It was in the central west, however, that the first effort was made to organize women in the interest of denominational activities. In 1877, at the meeting of the Western Unitarian Conference held in Toledo, it was voted that the women connected with that body be requested to organize immediately for the purpose of co−operating in the general work of the conference. At this meeting two women, Mrs. E.P. Allis of Milwaukee and Mrs. Mary P. Wells Smith of Cincinnati, were placed on the board of directors.

At the next annual meeting of the Western Conference, held in Chicago, the committee on organization, consisting of thirteen women, reported the readiness of the women to give their aid to the conference work, saying in their report "that we signify not only our willingness, but our earnest desire to share henceforth with our brothers in the labors and responsibilities of this Association, and that we pledge ourselves to an active and hearty support of those cherished convictions which constitute our liberal faith." In response to their request, the conference selected an assistant secretary to have charge of everything relating to the work of women. They also recommended that the women of the several churches connected with the conference should organize for "the study and dissemination of the principles of free thought and liberal religious culture, and the practical assistance of all worthy schemes and enterprises intended for the spread and upholding of these principles." In 1881, at St. Louis, there was organized the Women's Western Unitarian Conference, with Mrs. Eliza Sunderland as president and Miss F.L. Roberts as secretary. During the seventeen years of its existence this conference raised much money for denominational work, developed many earnest workers, and accomplished much in behalf of the principles for which it stood. It aided in the support of several missionaries, organized the Post–office Mission and made it effective, and encouraged a number of women to enter the ministry.

[Sidenote: Women's Auxiliary Conference.]

At the National Conference session of 1878, held at Saratoga, where much enthusiasm had been awakened, it was suggested that the women, who had been hitherto listeners only, should take an active part in, denominational work. At a gathering in the parlor of the United States Hotel, called by Mrs. Charles G. Ames, Mrs. Fielder Israel, Mrs. J.P. Lesley, and one or two others, a plan of action was adopted that led, in 1880, to the formation of the Women's Auxiliary Conference. The aim of this organization was to quicken the religious life of the churches, to stimulate local charitable and missionary undertakings, and to raise money for missionary enterprises; but its work was to be done in connection with the National Conference, and not as an independent organization. The purpose was stated in a circular sent to the churches immediately after the organization was effected. "Hitherto," it was said, "women have not been specially represented upon the board of the National Conference, and have not fully recognized how helpful they might be in its various undertakings or how much they themselves might gain from a closer relation with it. But the time has now come when our service is called for in the broad field, and also when we feel the need of being at work there; for our faith in the great truths of religion is no less vital than that of our brethren; and since the service we can render, being different from theirs, is needed to supplement it, and because it is peculiarly women's service, we must do it, or it will be left undone. It is one of the glories of such a work as ours that there is need and room in it for the best effort of every individual; indeed, without the faithful service of all it must be incomplete."

In 1890, after ten years of active existence, the conference had about eighty branches, with a membership of between 3,000 and 4,000 women. Much of the success of the conference was due to its president, Abby W. May. Miss May was well known as a philanthropist and educator, and had occupied many prominent positions before she assumed the presidency of the auxiliary; but this was her first active work in connection with the denomination.

[Sidenote: The National Alliance.]

Admirable as were the aims, and excellent as was the work of this organization, it was auxiliary to the National Conference, and had no independent life. After the first enthusiasm was past, it failed to gain ground rapidly, the membership remaining nearly stationary during the last few years of its existence. As time went on, therefore, it became evident that a more complete organization was needed in order to arouse enthusiasm and to secure the loyalty of the women of all parts of the country. The New York League of Unitarian Women, including those of New York, Brooklyn, and New Jersey, organized in 1887, showed the advantages of a closer union and a more definite purpose; and the desire to bring into one body all the various local organizations hastened the change. It was seen that, in the multiplication of organizations, there was danger of wasting the energies used, and that one efficient body was greatly to be desired.

In May, 1888, a committee was formed for the purpose of drafting a constitution for a new association, "to which all existing organizations might subscribe." The constitution provided by this committee was adopted October 24, 1890, and the new organization took the name of the National Alliance of Unitarian and Other Liberal Christian Women. The object proposed was "to quicken the life of our Unitarian churches, and to bring the women of the denomination into closer acquaintance, co–operation, and fellowship." In 1891 there were ninety branches, with about 5,000 members. While the membership, doubled under the impulse of the new organization, the increase in the amount of money raised was fivefold.

The admirable results secured by the Women's Alliance, which has finally drawn all the sectional organizations into co–operation with itself, are in no small measure due to the energy and the organizing skill of the women who have been at the head of its activities. Mrs. Judith W. Andrews, of Boston, was the president during the first year of its existence. From 1891 to 1901 the president was Mrs. B. Ward Dix, of Brooklyn, who was succeeded by Miss Emma C. Low, of the same city. Mrs. Emily A. Fifield, of Boston, has been the recording secretary; Mrs. Mary B. Davis, of New York, the corresponding secretary; and Miss Flora L. Close, of Boston, the treasurer from the first.

[Sidenote: Cheerful Letter and Post–office Missions.]

In 1891 the executive board appointed a committee to organize a Cheerful Letter Exchange, of which Miss Lilian Freeman Clarke was made the chairman. One of its chief purposes is to cheer the lonely and discouraged, invalids and others, by interchange of letters and by gifts of books and periodicals. To young persons in remote places it affords facilities for securing a better education, with the aid of correspondence classes. By means of a little monthly magazine, The Cheerful Letter, religious teaching is brought to many persons, who in this find a substitute for church attendance where that is not possible. Through the same channel, as well as by correspondence, these workers help young mothers in the right training of their children. Libraries have been started in communities destitute of books, and struggling libraries have been aided with gifts. Forty travelling libraries are kept in circulation.

Although much had been done to circulate Unitarian tracts and the other publications of the American Unitarian Association, by means of colporteurs, by the aid of the post–office, as well as by direct gift of friend to friend, it remained for Miss Sallie Ellis, of Cincinnati, in 1881, to systematize this kind of missionary effort, and to make it one of the most valuable of all agents for the dissemination of liberal religious ideas. Miss Ellis was aided by the Cincinnati branch of the Women's Auxiliary, but she was from the first the heart and soul of this mission. "If there had been no Miss Ellis," says one who knew her work intimately, "there would have been no Post–office Mission. Many helped about it in various ways, but she was the mission."

Miss Ellis was a frail little woman, hopelessly deaf and suffering from an incurable disease. Notwithstanding her physical limitations, she longed to be of service to the faith she cherished; and the missionary spirit burned strong within her. "I want," she said often, "to do something for Unitarianism before I die"; but the usual avenues of opportunity seemed firmly closed to her. At last, in the winter of 1877–78, Rev. Charles W. Wendte, then her pastor, anxious to find something for her to do, proposed that she should send the Association's tracts and copies of the Pamphlet Mission to persons in the west who were interested in the liberal faith. She took up this work gladly, and during that winter distributed 1,846 tracts and 211 copies of the Pamphlet Mission in twenty–six States.

A tract table in the vestibule of the church was started by Miss Ellis; and she not only distributed sermons freely in this way, but she also sold Unitarian books. It was in 1881 that she was made the secretary of the newly organized Women's Auxiliary in Cincinnati, and that her work really began systematically. At the suggestion of Mrs. Mary P. Wells Smith, advertisements were inserted in the daily papers, and offers made to send Unitarian publications, when requested. Many doubted the advisability of such an enterprise, but the letters received soon indicated that an important method of mission work had been discovered. Rev. William C. Gannett christened this work the Post–office Mission, and that name it has since retained.

Only four and one–half years were permitted to Miss Ellis in which to accomplish her work,—a work dear to her heart, and one for which her many losses and sufferings had prepared her. During this period she wrote 2,500 letters, sent out 22,000 tracts and papers, sold 286 books, and loaned 258. The real value of such work cannot be rightly estimated in figures. Through her influence, several young men entered the ministry who are to–day doing effective work. She saved several persons from doubt and despair, gave strength to the weak, and comfort to those who mourned. At her death, in 1885, the letters received from many of her correspondents showed how strong and deep had been her influence.[3]

The movement initiated by Miss Ellis grew rapidly, and has become one of the most valuable of all agents for the dissemination of liberal religious ideas. In the year 1900 the number of correspondents was about 5,000, and the number of tracts, sermons, periodicals, and books distributed was about 200,000. The extent of this mission is also seen in the fact that in that year about 8,000 letters were written by the workers, and about 6,000 were received.

By means of the Post–office Mission the literature of the denomination, the tracts of the Unitarian Association, copies of The Christian Register, and other periodicals have been scattered all over the world. Thousands of sermons are distributed also from tables in church vestibules. Several branches publish and exchange sermons, and a loan library has been established to supplement this work.[4]

Unitarianism in America

From the distribution of tracts and sermons has grown the formation of "Sunday Circles" and "Groups" of Unitarians, carefully planned circuit preaching, the employment of missionaries, and the building of chapels or small churches. Two of these are already built; and the Alliance has insured the support of their ministers for five years, and two others are in the process of erection.

[Sidenote: Associate Alliances.]

The women on the Pacific coast have been compelled in a large measure to organize their own work and to adopt their own methods, the distance being too great for immediate co–operation with the other organizations. In this work they have not only displayed energy and perseverance, but, says one who knows intimately of their efforts, "they have shown executive ability and power as organizers that have furnished an example to many non–sectarian organizations of women, and have made the Unitarian women conspicuous in all charitable and social activities."

The oldest society of Unitarian women on the Pacific coast was connected with the First Church in San Francisco. In 1873 it was reorganized as the Society for Christian Work. Its work has been mainly social and philanthropic, contributing reading matter to penal institutions, money for the care of the poor of the city, and aiding every new Unitarian church in the State. The Channing Auxiliary combines the activities of the churches in the vicinity of San Francisco with those in the city. Its objects are "moral and religious culture, practical literary work, and co–operation with the denominational and missionary agencies of the Unitarian faith." From 1890 to 1899 this society spent over $6,000 in aid of denominational enterprises, and it appropriates annually a large sum for Post–office Mission work. While these two organizations represent San Francisco and its neighborhood, the women up and down the coast have also been earnest workers. In 1890 they felt the need of a closer bond of union, and organized the Women's Unitarian Conference of the Pacific Coast. In 1894 this conference became a branch of the National Alliance, and has co–operated cordially with it since that time.

The New York League of Unitarian Women has been active in forming Alliance branches and new churches, as well as in affording aid to Meadville students. The Chicago Associate Alliance, the Southern Associate Alliance, and the Connecticut Valley Associate Alliance were organized in 1890. The Worcester League of Unitarian Women began its existence in 1889, and was reorganized in connection with the National

Alliance in 1892.

[Sidenote: Alliance Methods.]

In thus coming into closer relations with each other and forming a national organization, each local branch continues free in its own action, chooses its own methods of carrying on its work, but keeps close knowledge of what the Alliance as a whole is doing, that all interference with others and overlapping of assistance may be avoided, and the greatest mutual benefit may be secured. This method gives the utmost independence to the branches, while preserving the element of personal interest in all financial disbursements, and creates a strong bond of sympathy between those who give and those who receive.

The first duty of each branch is to strengthen the church to which its members belong; and the value of such an organized group of women, meeting to exchange ideas and experiences on the most vital topics of human interest, has been everywhere recognized. Each branch is expected to engage in some form of religious study, not only for the improvement of the members themselves, but to enable them to gain, and to give others, a comprehensive knowledge of Unitarian beliefs. A study class committee provides programmes for the use of the branches, arranges for the lending and exchange of papers, and assists those who do not have access to books of reference or are remote from the centres of Unitarian thought and activity.

With this preparation the Alliance undertakes the higher service of joining in the missionary activities of the denomination, supplementing as far as possible the work of the American Unitarian Association. This includes sending missionaries into new fields, aiding small and struggling churches, helping to found new ones, supporting ministers at important points, and and distributing religious literature among those who need light on religious problems.

[1] Memorial History of Boston, IV. 353.

[2] See later chapters for account of admission of women to National
    Conference, Unitarian Association, the ministry, Boston school board,
    and various other lines of activity.

[3] Mary P.W. Smith, Miss Ellis's Mission.

[4] This library is in the Unitarian Building, 25 Beacon Street, Boston.

XIII. MISSIONS TO INDIA AND JAPAN.

Foreign missions have never commanded a general interest on the part of Unitarians. Their dislike of the proselyting spirit, their intense love of liberty for others as well as for themselves, and the absence of sectarian feeling have combined to make them, as a body, indifferent to the propagation of their faith in other countries. They have done something, however, to express their sympathy with those of kindred faith in foreign lands.

In 1829 the younger Henry Ware visited England and Ireland as the foreign secretary of the Unitarian Association; and at the annual meeting of 1831 he reported the results of his inquiries.[1] This was the beginning of many interchanges of good fellowship with the Unitarians of Great Britain, and also with those of Hungary, Transylvania, France, Germany, and other European countries. During the first decade or two of the existence of the Unitarian Association much interest was taken in the liberal movements in Geneva; and the third annual report gave account of what was being done in that city and in Calcutta, as well as in Transylvania and Great Britain. Some years later, aid was promised to the Unitarians of Hungary in a time of persecution; but they were dispossessed of their schools before help reached them. In 1868 the Association founded Channing and Priestley professorships in the theological school at Kolozsvar, and Mrs. Anna Richmond furnished money for a permanent professorship in the same institution. Soon after the renewed activity of 1865 an unsuccessful attempt was made to establish an American Unitarian church in Paris; and aid was given to the founding of an English liberal church in that city. These are indications of the many interchanges of fellowship and helpfulness between the Unitarians of this country and those of Europe.

[Sidenote: Society respecting the State of Religion in India.]

As early as 1824 began a movement to aid the native Unitarians of India, partly the result of a lively interest in Rammohun Roy and the republication in this country of his writings. On June 7, 1822, The Christian Register gave an account of the adoption of Unitarianism by that remarkable Hindoo leader; and it often recurred to the subject in later years. In February of the next year it described the formation of a Unitarian society in Calcutta, and the conversion to Unitarianism of a Baptist missionary, Rev. William

Adam, as a result of his attempt to convert Rammohun Roy. There followed frequent reports of this movement, and after a few months a letter from Mr. Adam was published. Even before this there had appeared accounts of William Roberts, of Madras, a native Tamil, who had been educated in England, and had there become a Unitarian. On his return to his own country he had established small congregations in the suburbs of Madras.

In 1823 a letter from Rev. William Adam was received in Boston, addressed to Dr. Channing. It was put into the hands of the younger Henry Ware, who wrote to Mr. Adam and Rammohun Roy, propounding to them a number of questions in regard to the religious situation in India. In 1824 were published in a volume the letter of Ware and the series of questions sent by him to India, together with the replies of Rammohun Roy and William Adam.[2] This book was one of much interest, and furnished the first systematic account that had been given to the public of the reformatory religious interest awakened at that time in India. In February, 1825, was organized the Society for obtaining Information respecting the State of Religion in India, "with a view to obtain and diffuse information and to devise and recommend means for the promotion of Christianity in that part of the world." The younger Henry Ware was made the president, and Dr. Tuckerman the secretary. Already a fund had been collected to aid the British Indian Unitarian Association of Calcutta in its missionary efforts, especially in building a church and maintaining a minister.

During the year 1825 there was published at the office of The Christian Register a pamphlet of sixty–three pages, written by a member of the Information Society, being An Appeal to Liberal Christians for the Cause of Christianity in India. In 1826 Dr. Tuckerman addressed A Letter on the Principles of the Missionary Enterprise to the executive committee of the Unitarian Association, in which he gave a noble exposition of the work of foreign missions, especially with reference to the Indian field. This letter and other writings of Tuckerman served to arouse much interest. The Appeal urged what many Unitarians had large faith in,—the promulgation of "just and rational views of our religion" "upon enlarged and liberal principles, from which we may hope for the speedy establishment and the wider extension there of the uncorrupted truth as it is in Jesus."

In 1826 the sum of $7,000 was secured for this work; and in the spring of 1827 a pledge was made to send yearly to Calcutta the sum of $600 for ten years. These pledges were in connection with like efforts made by the British and Foreign Unitarian Association. In

1839 Mr. Adam visited the United States, and spoke at the annual meeting of the Unitarian Association. Following this, he was for a few years professor of Oriental literature in Harvard University.

[Sidenote: Dall's Work in India.]

In 1853 Rev. Charles T. Brooks, who was for many years the minister of the church in Newport, visited India in search of health; and he was commissioned by the Unitarian Association to make inquiries as to the prospects for missionary labors in that country. In Madras he met William Roberts, the younger son of the former Unitarian preacher there and visited the several missions carried on by him. In Calcutta he found Unitarians, but the work of Mr. Adam had left almost no results. The report of Mr. Brooks was such that an effort was at once made to secure a missionary for India.[3] In 1855 Rev. Charles H.A. Dall undertook this mission. He had been a minister at large in St. Louis, Baltimore, and Portsmouth, and settled over parishes in Needham and Toronto. Mr. Ball was given the widest liberty of action in conducting his mission, as his instructions indicate: "There you are to enter upon the work of a missionary; and whether by preaching, in English or through an interpreter, or by school–teaching or by writing for the press, or by visiting from house to house, or by translating tracts, or by circulation of books, you are instructed, what we know your heart will prompt you to do, to give yourself to a life of usefulness as a servant of the Lord Jesus Christ."

On his arrival at Calcutta, Mr. Ball was in a prostrate condition, and had to be carried ashore. After a time he rallied and began his work. He gathered a small congregation about him, then began teaching; and his work grew until he had four large and flourishing schools under his charge. In these he gave special attention, to moral and religious training, and to the industrial arts. In his school work he had the efficient aid of Miss Chamberlain, and after her death of Mrs. Helen Tompkins. One of the native teachers, Dwarkanath Singha, was of great service in securing the interest of the natives, being at the head, for many years, of all the schools under Mr. Dall's control. Mr. Dall founded the Calcutta School of Industrial Art, the Useful Arts' School, Hindoo Girls' School, as well as a school for the waifs of the streets. In these schools were 8,000 pupils, mostly Hindoos, who were taught a practical religion,—the simple principles of the gospel. In education Mr. Dall accomplished large results, not only by his schools, but by talking and lecturing on the subject. His influence was especially felt in the education of girls and in industrial training, in both of which directions he was a pioneer. Only one of his schools is now in existence, simply because the government took up the work he began, and gave it a larger support than was possible on the part of any individual or any society.

Mr. Dall wrote extensively for the leading journals of India, and in that way he reached a larger number of persons throughout the country. This brought him a large correspondence, and he frequently journeyed far to visit individuals and congregations thus brought to his knowledge. For many years he was one of the leading men of Calcutta. Few great public meetings of any reformatory or educational kind were held without his having a prominent part in them. He published great numbers of tracts and lectures,[4] and translated the works of the leading Unitarians of America and Great Britain into Hindostanee, Bengali, Tamil, Sanscrit, and other native languages. His zeal in circulating liberal writings was great, and met with a large reward. He distributed hundreds of copies of the complete Works of Dr. Channing, and these brought many persons to the acceptance of Unitarianism. When Rev. Jabez T. Sunderland was in India, in 1895–96, he found many traces of these volumes, even in remote parts of the country. When he was in Madras, a very intelligent Hindoo walked one hundred and fifty miles to procure of him a copy of Channing's biography to replace a copy received from Mr. Dall, which, had been reread and loaned until it was almost worn out.

A considerable part of Mr. Ball's influence was in connection with the Brahmo–Somaj, in directing its religious, educational, and reformatory work. He did not make many nominal Unitarians; but he had a very large influence in shaping the life of India by his personal influence and by the weight of his religious character. Everywhere he was greatly beloved. He earned considerable sums as a reporter and author in aid of his mission, and he lived in a most abstemious manner in order to devote as much money as possible to his work.[5] In this devoted service he continued until his death, which took place July 18, 1886.

[Sidenote: Recent Work in India.]

Since the death of Mr. Dall the aid given to India by American Unitarians has been through the natives themselves. The work of Pundita, Ramabai has received considerable assistance, as has also that of Mozoomdar. Early in the year 1888, Rev. Brooke Herford, then minister of the Arlington Street Church in Boston, received from India a letter addressed "To the chief pastor of the Unitarian congregation at Boston." It proved to be from a young lawyer or pleader in Banda, North–west Provinces, named Akbar Masih.

His father was an educated Mohammedan, who in early life had been converted to Calvinistic Christianity, and had become a missionary. At the Calcutta University the son had outgrown the faith he had been taught; and a volume of Channing's Works, put in circulation by Mr. Dall, had given him the mental and spiritual teaching he desired. Tracts and books were sent him, and a correspondence followed. He read with great delight what he received, and in a year or two he desired to become a missionary. Mr. Herford sent him money, and he was employed to spend one–third of his time in the missionary service of Unitarianism. When Mr. Herford removed to London, the support of Akbar Masih was arranged for in England; and he has done a large work in preaching, lecturing, holding conferences, and publishing tracts and books.

Nearly in the same week in which Mr. Herford received his first letter from Akbar Masih, Mr. Sunderland, in Ann Arbor, received one from Hajam Kissor Singh, Jowai, Khasi Hills, Assam. He was a young man employed by the government as a surveyor, was well educated, but belonged to one of the primitive tribes that retain their aboriginal religion and customs to a large extent. He had been taught orthodox Christianity, however; but it was not satisfactory to him. A Brahmo friend loaned him a copy of Channing, and furnished him with Mr. Dall's address. In the bundle of tracts sent him by Mr. Dall was a copy of The Unitarian, which led him to write to its editor, Mr. Sunderland. A correspondence followed, and the sending of many tracts and books. Mr. Singh began to talk of his new views to others, who gathered in his room on Sunday afternoons for religious inquiry and worship. Soon there was a call for similar meetings in another village, and Mr. Singh began to serve as a lay–preacher. A church was organized in Jowai, and then a day school was opened. Tracts and books being necessary in order to carry on the work successfully, Mr. Sunderland raised the necessary money, printed them in Khasi at Ann Arbor, and forwarded them to Assam, thus greatly facilitating the labors of Mr. Singh and his assistants. Also, through the help of American Unitarians, Mr. Singh was able to secure the aid of two paid helpers. When Mr. Sunderland visited the Khasi Hills, in 1895, as the agent of the British and Foreign Unitarian Association, he helped to ordain a regular pastor; and he found church buildings in five villages, day–schools in four, and religious circles meeting in eight or nine others. This mission is now being supported by the English Unitarians.

[Sidenote: The Beginnings in Japan.]

After the death of Mr. Dall it was not found desirable to continue his educational work, and the missionary activities in India naturally came under the jurisdiction of the British Unitarian Association. At the same time, Japan offered an inviting field for missionary effort, and one not hitherto occupied by Unitarians. In 1884 a movement began in that country, looking to the introduction of a rational Christianity, the leader being Yukichi Fukuzawa, a prominent statesman, head of the Keiogijiku University and editor of the leading newspaper. In 1886 Fumio Yano, after a visit to England, took up the same mission, and urged the adoption of Christianity as a moral force in the life of the nation. The latter interpreted Unitarianism as being the form of Christianity needed in Japan, and strongly urged its acceptance. Other prominent men joined with these two in commending a rational Christianity to their countrymen. Not long afterwards the American Unitarian Association was asked to establish a mission in that country. In 1887 Rev. Arthur M. Knapp was sent to Japan to investigate the situation, and in the spring of 1889 he returned to report the results of his inquiries. He had; been welcomed; by the leading men, such as the Marquis Tokujawa and Kentaro Kaneko, who opened to him many avenues of influence. He had written for the most important newspapers, had come into personal contact with the leading men of all parties, had lectured; on many occasions to highly educated audiences, and had opened a wide–reaching correspondence.

On his return to Japan, in 1889, Mr. Knapp was prepared to begin systematic work in behalf of rational Christianity. It was not his purpose, however, to seek to establish Unitarianism there as the basis of a new Japanese sect, but to diffuse it as a leaven for the moral and spiritual elevation of the people of Japan. "The errand of Unitarianism in Japan," said Mr. Knapp to the Japanese, "is based upon the familiar idea of the sympathy of religions. With the conviction that we are the messengers of distinctive and valuable truths which have not yet been emphasized, and that, in return, there is much in your faith and life which to our harm we have not emphasized, receive us not as theological propagandists, but as messengers of the new gospel of human brotherhood in the religion of man."

With Mr. Knapp were associated Rev. Clay MacCauley as colleague, and also Garrett Droppers, John H. Wigmore, and William Shields Liscomb, who were to become, professors in the Keiogijiku, a leading university, situated in Tokio, and to give such aid as they could to the Unitarian mission. With these men was soon associated Rev. H.W. Hawkes, a young English minister, who gave his services to this important work. There also accompanied the American party Mr. Saichiro Kanda, who had become a Unitarian

216

while residing in San Francisco, and had attended the Meadville Theological School. In the winter of 1890–91, Mr. Knapp returned to the United States, and a little later Mr. Hawkes went back to England. In 1891 Rev. William I. Lawrance joined the mission force; and he continued with it until 1894, when a severe illness compelled his resignation. Professor Wigmore returned to America in 1892 to accept a chair in the North–western University; Professor Liscomb came home in 1893, dying soon after his return; while Professor Droppers remained until the winter of 1898, when he became the president of the University of South Dakota. In the beginning of 1900, Mr. MacCauley, after having had direction of the mission for nine years, returned to America; and it was left in control of the Japanese Unitarian Association, the American Association continuing to give it generous financial aid and counsel.

As already indicated, the purpose of the mission has not been Unitarian propagandism as such. It has been that of religious enlightenment, the bringing to the Japanese, in a catholic and humanitarian spirit, of the body of religious truths and convictions known as Unitarianism, and then permitting them to organize themselves after the manner of their own national life. No churches were organized by the representatives of the American Unitarian Association. Those that have come into existence have been wholly at the initiative of the natives. Early in 1894 was erected, in Tokio, Yuiitsukwan, or Unity Hall, with money furnished largely from the United States. This building serves as the headquarters for Unitarian work, including lectures and social and religious meetings. In 1896 was organized the Japanese Unitarian Association for the work of diffusing Unitarian principles throughout the country. The mission is organized into the three departments of church extension, publication, and education. Of this Association, Jitsunen Saji, formerly a prominent Buddhist lecturer and a member at present of the city council of Tokyo, is the superintendent. The secretary has been Saichiro Kanda, who has faithfully given his time to this work since he returned to Japan with the mission party, in 1889. The broad purposes of the Japanese Unitarian Association have been clearly defined in its constitution: "We desire to act in accordance with God's will, which we perceive by our inborn reason. We strive to follow the guidance of noble religion, exact science and philosophy, and to discover their truth. We believe it to be a natural law of the human mind to investigate freely all phenomena of the universe. We aim to maintain the peace of the world, and to promote the happiness of mankind. We endeavor to assert our rights, and to fulfil our duties as Japanese citizens; and to increase the prosperity of the country by all honorable means."

Early in 1891 was begun the publication in Japanese of a magazine called at first The Unitarian, but afterwards Religion. The paid circulation was about 1,000 copies, but it was largely used as a tract for free distribution. In 1897 this magazine was merged into a popular religious monthly called Rikugo–Zasshi or Cosmos, which has a large circulation. It is published at the headquarters of the Japanese Unitarian Association, and is the organ of the liberalizing work carried on by that institution. The Association has translated thirty or forty American and English tracts,—some have been added by native writers; and these were distributed to the number of 100,000 in 1900. A number of important liberal books, including Bixby's Crisis in Morals, Clarke's Steps in Belief, and Fiske's Idea of God, have been translated into Japanese, and obtain a ready sale. An extensive work of education, is carried on through the press, nearly all the leading journals having been freely open to the Unitarians since the beginning of the mission.

The direct work of education has been the most important of all the phases of the mission's activities. A library of several thousand volumes, representing all phases of modern thought, has been collected in Unity Hall; and it is of great value to the teaching carried on there. Lectures are given every Sunday in Unity Hall, and listened to by large audiences. Much has been done in various parts of Tokyo, as well as elsewhere, to reach the student class, and educated persons in all classes of society; and many persons have thus been brought to an acceptance of Unitarianism. In 1890 were begun systematic courses of lectures, with a view to giving educated Japanese inquirers a thorough knowledge of modern religious ideas; and these grew into the Senshin Gakuin, or School of Advanced Learning, a theological school with seven professors, and an annual attendance of thirty or forty students, nearly all of whom have been graduates of colleges and universities. Unhappily, the failure of financial support compelled the abandonment of this school in 1898. The chief educational work, however, has been done in the colleges and universities, through the general diffusion of liberal religious principles, and by the free spirit of inquiry characteristic of all educated Japanese.

The success of the Japanese mission is chiefly due to Rev. Clay MacCauley, who gave it the wise direction and the organizing skill necessary to its permanent growth. It is a noble monument to his devotion, and to his untiring efforts for its advancement. His little book on Christianity in History is very popular, both in its English and Japanese versions; and thousands of copies are annually distributed.

Unitarianism in America

The results of the Japanese mission are especially evident in a general liberalizing of religious thought throughout the country in both the Buddhist and Christian communions, and in the wide–spread approval shown towards its methods and principles among the upper and student classes. Its chief gain, however, consists of the scholarly and influential men who have accepted the Unitarian faith, and given it their zealous support. Among these men are the late Hajime Onishi, president of the College of Literature in the new Imperial University at Kyoto; Nobuta Kishimoto, professor of ethics in the Imperial Normal School; Tomoyoshi Murai, professor of English in the Foreign Languages School of Japan; Iso Abe, professor in the Doshisha University; Kinza Hirai, professor in the Imperial Normal School; Yoshiwo Ogasawara, who is leading an extensive work of social and moral reform in Wakayama; Saburo Shimada, proprietor of the Mainichi, one of the largest daily newspapers of the empire; and Zennosuki Toyosaki, professor in the Kokumin Eigakukwai, and associate editor of the Rikugo Zasshi.[6] These men are educating the Japanese people to know Christianity in its rational forms; and their influence is being rapidly extended throughout the country. In their hands the future of liberal religion in Japan is safe; and what they do for their own people is more certain of permanent results than anything that can be accomplished by foreigners. The real significance of the Japanese Unitarian mission is that it has inaugurated a new era in religious propagandism; that it has been for the followers of the religions traditional to Japan, as well as for those of the Christian missions, eminently a means for presenting them with the world's most advanced thought in religion, and that it has been a stimulus to a purer faith and a larger fellowship.

[1] First Report of the Executive Committee of the American Unitarian
    Association, 16. "The thoughts of the committee have been turned to
    their brethren in other lands. A correspondence has been opened with
    Unitarians in England, and the coincidence is worthy of notice, that
    the British and Foreign Unitarian Association, and the American
    Unitarian Association were organized on the same day, for the same
    objects, and without the least previous concert. Our good wishes have
    been reciprocated by the directors of the British Society. Letters
    received from gentlemen who have recently visited England speak of
    the interest which our brethren in that country feel for us, and of
    their desire to strengthen the bonds of union. A constant
    communication will be preserved between the two Associations and your
    committee believe it will have a beneficial effect, by making us

better acquainted with one another, by introducing the publications
of each country into the other, by the influence which we shall
mutually exert, and by the strength which will be given to our
separate, or it may be, to our united efforts for the spread of the
glorious gospel of our Lord and Saviour."

[2] Correspondence relative to the Prospects of Christianity and the
  Means of Promoting its Reception in India. Cambridge: Billiard   Metcalfe. 1824. 138
pp.

[3] Christian Examiner, LXIII 36, India's Appeal to Christian Unitarians,
  by Rev. C.T. Brooks.

[4] Some Gospel Principles, in Ten Lectures, by C.H.A. Dall, Calcutta,
  1856. Also see The Mission to India instituted by the American
  Unitarian Association. Boston: Office of the Quarterly Journal.
  1857.

[5] See Out Indian Mission and Our First Missionary, by Rev. John H.
  Heywood, Boston, 1887.

[6] The Unitarian Movement in Japan: Sketches of the Lives and Religious
  Work of Ten Representative Japanese. Tokyo, 1900.

XIV. THE MEADVILLE THEOLOGICAL SCHOOL.

In a few years after the movement began for the organization of churches west of the
Hudson River, the needs of theological instruction for residents of that region were being
discussed. In 1827 the younger Henry Ware was interested in a plan of uniting Unitarians
and "the Christian connection" in the establishment of a theological school, to be located
in the eastern part of the state of New York. In July of that year he wrote to a friend: "We
have had; no little talk here within a few days respecting a new theological school. Many
of us think favorably of the plan, and are disposed to patronize it, if feasible, but are a
little fearful that it is not. Others start strong objections to it *in toto*. Something must be
done to gain us an increase of ministers."[1] This proposition came from the Christians,

and their plan was to locate the school on the Hudson.

Although this project came to nothing for the time being, it was revived a decade later. When the Unitarian Association had entered upon its active missionary efforts west of the Alleghanies, the new impulse to denominational life manifested itself in a wide–spread desire for an increase in the number of workers available for the western field. The establishment of a liberal theological school in that region was felt to be almost a necessity, if the opportunities everywhere opening there for the dissemination of a purer faith were not to be neglected. Plans were therefore formed about 1836 for the founding of a theological school at Buffalo under the direction of Rev. George W. Hosmer, then the minister in that city; but, business becoming greatly depressed the following year, the project was abandoned. In 1840 the importance of such a school was again causing the western workers to plan for its establishment, this time in Cincinnati or Louisville; but this expectation also failed of realization. Then Rev. William G. Eliot, of St. Louis, undertook to provide a theological education for such young men as might apply to him. But the response to his offer was so slight as to indicate that there was little demand for such instruction.

[Sidenote: The Beginnings in Meadville.]

The demand for a school had steadily grown since the year 1827, and the fit occasion only was awaited for its establishment. It was found at Meadville, Penn., in the autumn of 1844. In order to understand why it should have been founded in this country village instead of one of the growing and prosperous cities of the west, it is necessary to give a brief account of the origin and growth of the Meadville church. The first Unitarian church organized west of the Alleghanies was that in Meadville, and it had its origin in the religious experiences of one man. The founder of this church, Harm Jan Huidekoper, was born in the district of Drenthe, Holland, at the village of Hogeveen, in 1776. At the age of twenty he came to the United States; and in 1804 he became the agent of the Holland Land Company in the north–western counties of Pennsylvania, and established himself at Meadville, then a small village. He was successful in his land operations, and was largely influential in the development of that part of the state. When his children were of an age to need religious instruction, he began to study the Bible with a view to deciding what he could conscientiously teach them. He had become a member of the Reformed Church in his native land, and he had attended the Presbyterian church in Meadville; but he now desired to form convictions based on his own inquiries. "When I had become a father," he wrote, "and saw the time approaching when I should have to give religious instruction to my children, I felt it to be my duty to give this subject a thorough examination. I accordingly commenced studying the Scriptures, as being the only safe rule of the Christian's faith; and the result was, that I soon acquired clear, and definite views as to the leading doctrines of the Christian religion. But the good I derived from these studies has not been confined to giving me clear ideas as to the Christian doctrines. They created in me a strong and constantly increasing interest in religion itself, not as mere theory, but as a practical rule of life."[2] As the result of this study, he arrived at the conclusion that the Bible does not teach the doctrines of the Trinity, the total depravity of man, and the vicarious atonement of Christ. Solely from the careful reading of the Bible with reference to each of the leading doctrines he had been taught, he became a Unitarian.

With the zeal of a new convert Mr. Huidekoper began to talk about his new faith, and he brought it to the attention of others with the enthusiasm of a propagandist. In conversation, by means of the distribution of tracts, and with the aid of the press he extended the liberal faith. He could not send his children to the church he had attended, and he therefore secured tutors for them from Harvard College who were preparing for the ministry; and in October, 1825, one of these tutors began holding Unitarian services in Meadville.[3] In May, 1829, a church was organized, and a goodly number of thoughtful men and women connected themselves with it. But this movement met with persistent opposition, and a vigorous controversy was carried on in the local papers and by means of pamphlets. This was increased when, in 1830, Ephraim Peabody, afterwards settled in Cincinnati, New Bedford, and at King's Chapel in Boston, became the minister, and entered upon an active effort for the extension of Unitarianism. With the first of January, 1831, he began the publication of the Unitarian Essayist, a small monthly pamphlet, in which the leading theological questions were discussed. In a few months Mr. Peabody went to Cincinnati; and the Essayist was continued by Mr. Huidekoper, who wrote with vigor and directness on the subjects he had carefully studied.

In 1831 the church for the first time secured an ordained minister, and three years later one who gave his whole time to its service.[4] A church building was erected in 1836, and the prosperity of the congregation was thereby much increased. In 1843 a minister of the Christian connection, Rev. E.G. Holland, became the pastor for a brief period. At this time Frederic Huidekoper, a son of the founder of the Unitarian church in Meadville, had returned from his studies in the Harvard Divinity School and in Europe, and was ordained in Meadville, October 12, 1843. It was his purpose to become a Unitarian evangelist in the region about Meadville, but his attention was soon directed by Rev. George W. Hosmer to the importance of furnishing theological instruction to young men preparing for the Unitarian ministry. He was encouraged in this undertaking by Mr. Holland, who pointed out to him the large patronage that might be expected from the Christian body. It was at first intended that Mr. Huidekoper should give the principal instruction, and that he should be assisted by the pastor of the Independent Congregational Church (Unitarian) and by Mr. Hosmer, who was to come from Buffalo for a few weeks each year, exchanging pulpits with the Meadville minister. When the opening of the school was fixed for the autumn of 1844, the prospective number of applicants was so large as to necessitate a modification of the proposed plan; and it was deemed wise to secure a competent person to preside over the school and to become the minister of the church. Through the active co–operation of the American Unitarian Association, Rev. Rufus P. Stebbins, then settled at Leominster, Mass., was secured for this double service.

The students present at the opening of the school on the first day of October, 1844, were but five; but this number was increased to nine during the year. The next year the number was twenty–three, nine of them from New England. For several years the Christian connection furnished a considerable proportion of the students, and took a lively interest in the establishment and growth of the school, although contributing little or nothing to its pecuniary support. It was also represented on the board of instruction by a non–resident lecturer. At this time the Christian body had no theological school of its own, and many of its members even looked with disfavor upon all ministerial education. What brought them into some degree of sympathy with Unitarians of that day was their rejection of binding creeds and their acceptance of Christian character as the only test of Christian fellowship, together with their recognition of the Bible, interpreted by every man for himself, as the authoritative standard of religious truth. The churches of this denomination in the northern states were also pronounced in their rejection of the doctrines of the Trinity and predestination. Unitarians themselves have not been more strenuous in the defence of the principle of religious liberty than were the leaders among the Christians of the last generation. The two bodies also joined in the management of Antioch College, in southern Ohio; and when Horace Mann became its president in 1852, he was made a minister of the Christian connection, in order that he might work more effectually in the promotion of its interests.

The Meadville school began its work in a simple way, with few instructors and a limited course of study. Mr. Stebbins taught the Old Testament, Hebrew, Biblical antiquities, natural and revealed religion, mental and moral philosophy, systematic theology, and pulpit eloquence. Mr. Huidekoper gave instruction in the New Testament, hermeneutics, ecclesiastical history, Latin, Greek, and German. Mr. Hosmer lectured on pastoral care for a brief period during each year. A building for the school was provided by the generosity of the elder Huidekoper; and the expenses of board, instruction, rent, fuel, etc., were reduced to $30 per annum. Many of the students had received little education, and they needed a preliminary training in the most primary studies. Nevertheless, the school at once justified its establishment, and sent out many capable men, even from among those who came to it with the least preparation.

Dr. Stebbins was president of the school for ten years. During his term of service the school was incorporated by the legislature of Pennsylvania in the spring of 1846. The charter was carefully drawn with a view to securing freedom in its administration. No denominational name appeared in the act of incorporation, and the original board of trustees included Christians as well as Unitarians. Dr. Stebbins was an admirable man to whom to intrust the organization of the school, for he was a born teacher and a masterful administrator. He was prompt, decisive, a great worker, a powerful preacher, an inspirer of others, and his students warmly admired and praised him.

[Sidenote: The Growth of the School.]

The next president of the school was Oliver Stearns, who held the office from 1856 to 1863. He was a student, a true and just thinker, of great moral earnestness, fine discrimination, and with a gift for academic organization. He was a man of a strong and deep personality, and his spiritual influence was profound. He had been settled at Northampton and over the third parish in Hingham before entering upon his work at Meadville. In 1863 he went to the Harvard Divinity School as the professor of pulpit eloquence and pastoral care until 1869, when he became the professor of theology; and from 1870 to 1878 he was the dean of the school. He was a preacher who "held and deserved a reputation among the foremost," for his preaching was "pre–eminently spiritual." "In his relations to the divinity schools that enjoyed his services, it is impossible to over–estimate the extent, accuracy, and thoroughness of his scholarship, and his unwearying devotion to his work."[5]

During Dr. Stearns' administration the small building originally occupied by the school was outgrown; and Divinity Hall was built on land east of the town, donated by Professor

Frederic Huidekoper, and first occupied in 1861. In 1857 began a movement to elevate, the standard of admission to the school, in order that its work might be of a more advanced character. To meet the needs of those not able to accept this higher standard, a preparatory department was established in 1858, which was continued until 1867.

Rev. Abiel A. Livermore became the president of the school in 1863, and he remained in that position until 1890. He had been settled in Keene, Cincinnati, and Yonkers before going to Meadville. He was a Christian of the finest type, a true gentleman, and a noble friend. Under his direction the school grew in all directions, the course of study being largely enriched by the addition of new departments. In 1863 church polity and administration, including a study of the sects of Christendom, was made a special department. In 1868 the school opened its doors to women, and it has received about thirty women for a longer or shorter term of study. In 1872 the academic degree of Bachelor of Divinity was offered for the first time to those completing the full course. In 1879 the philosophy of religion, and also the comparative study of religions, received the recognition they deserve. The same year ecclesiastical jurisprudence became a special department. In 1882 Rev. E.E. Hale lectured on charities, and from that time this subject has been systematically treated in connection with philanthropies. A movement was begun in 1889 to endow a professorship in memory of Dr. James Freeman Clarke, which was successful. These successive steps indicate the progress made under the faithful administration of Dr. Livermore. He became widely known to Unitarians by his commentaries on the books of the New Testament, as well as by his other writings, including volumes of sermons and lectures.

In 1890 George L. Cary, who had been for many years the professor of New Testament literature, became the president of the school, a position he held for ten years. Under his leadership the school has largely advanced its standard of scholarship, outgrown studies have been discarded, while new ones have been added. New professorships and lectureships have been established, and the endowment of the school has been greatly increased. Huidekoper Hall, for the use of the library, was erected in 1890, and other important improvements have been added to the equipment of the school. In 1892 the Adin Ballou lectureship of practical Christian sociology was established, and in 1895 the Hackley professorship of sociology and ethics.

From the time of its establishment the Huidekoper family have been devoted friends and benefactors of the Theological School.[6] Frederic Huidekoper occupied the chair of New

Testament literature from 1844 to 1855, and from 1863 to 1877 that of ecclesiastical history. His services were given wholly without remuneration, and his benefactions to the school were numerous. He also added largely to the Brookes Fund for the distribution of Unitarian books. His historical writings made him widely known to scholars, and added to the reputation of the school. His Belief of the First Three Centuries concerning Christ's Mission to the Underworld appeared in 1853; Judaism at Rome, 1876; and Indirect Testimony of History to the Genuineness of the Gospels, 1879. He also republished at his own expense many valuable works that were out of print.

Among the other professors have been Rev. Nathanial S. Folsom, who was in charge of the department of Biblical literature from 1848 to 1861. Of the regular lecturers have been Rev. Charles H. Brigham, Rev. Amory D. Mayo, and Dr. Thomas Hill. There has been an intimate relation between the Meadville church and the Theological School, and several of the pastors have been instructors and lecturers in the Theological School, including Rev. J.C. Zachos, Rev. James T. Bixby, and Rev. James M. Whiton. The Christian denomination has been represented among the lecturers by Rev. David Millard and Rev. Austin Craig.

The whole number of graduates of the Meadville Theological School up to April, 1902, has been 267; and eighty other students have entered the ministry. At the present time 156 of its students are on the roll of Unitarian ministers. Thirty–two of its students served in the civil war, twenty per cent of its graduates previous to the close of the war being engaged in it as privates, chaplains, or in some other capacity. The endowment of the school has steadily increased until it now is somewhat more than $600,000.

[1] Memoir of Henry Ware, Jr. 202.

[2] J.F. Clarke, Christian Examiner, September, 1854, LVII. 310. "Mr.
      Huidekoper had the satisfaction, in the later years of his life, of
      seeing a respectable society worshipping in the tasteful building
      which he loved and of witnessing the prosperity of the theological
      school in which he was so much interested. We have never known any
      one who seemed to live so habitually in the presence of God. The form
      which his piety mostly took was that of gratitude and reliance. His
      trust in the Divine goodness was like that of a child in its mother.
      His cheerful views, of this life and of the other, his simple tastes,

his enjoyment of nature, his happiness in society, his love for children, his pleasure in doing good, his tender affection for those nearest to him,—these threw a warm light around his last days and gave his home the aspect of a perpetual Sabbath. A well–balanced activity of faculties contributed still more to his usefulness and happiness. He was always a student, occupying every vacant hour with a book, and so had attained a surprising knowledge of biography and history." Mr. Huidekoper died in Meadville, May 22, 1854.

[3] John M. Merrick, afterwards settled in Hardwick and Walpole, Mass., who was in Mr. Huidekoper's family from October, 1825, to October, 1827. He was succeeded by Andrew P. Peabody, who did not preach. In 1828–30 Washington Gilbert, who had settlements in Harvard, Lincoln, and West Newton, was the tutor and preacher.

[4] Rev. George Nichols, July, 1831, to July, 1832; Rev. Alanson Brigham, who died in Meadville, August 24, 1833; Rev. John Quincy Day, October, 1834, to September, 1837.

[5] A.P. Peabody, Harvard Reminiscences, 165, 166

[6] The first treasurer of the school was Edgar Huidekoper, who was succeeded by Professor F. Huidekoper, and he in turn by Edgar Huidekoper, the son of the first treasurer. Among the other generous friends and benefactors of the school have been Alfred Huidekoper, Miss Elizabeth Huidekoper, and Mrs. Henry P. Kidder.

XV. UNITARIAN PHILANTHROPIES.

The liberal movement in religion was characterized in its early period by its humanitarianism. As theology grew less important for it, there was an increase in its philanthropy. With the waning of the sectarian spirit there was a growth in desire for practical reforms. The awakened interest in man and enlarged faith in his spiritual capacities showed itself in efforts to improve his social condition. No one expressed this tendency more perfectly than Dr. Channing, though he was a spiritual teacher rather than a reformer or philanthropist.

Any statement concerning the charities in connection with which Channing was active will give the most inadequate idea of his actual influence in this direction. He was greatly interested in promoting the circulation of the Bible, in aiding the cause of temperance, and in bringing freedom to the slave. His biographer says that his thoughts were continually becoming concentrated more and more upon the terrible problem of pauperism, "and he saw more clearly each year that what the times demanded was that the axe should be laid at the very root of ignorance, temptation and strife by substituting for the present unjust and unequal distribution of the privileges of life some system of cordial, respectful brotherly co-operation."[1] His interest in education was most comprehensive, and he sought its advancement in all directions with the confident faith that it would help to uplift all classes and make them more truly human.[2]

[Sidenote: Unitarian Charities.]

The liberals of New England, in the early years of the nineteenth century, were not mere theorizers in regard to human helpfulness and the application of Christianity to life; for they endeavored to realize the spirit of charity and service. Largely under their leadership the Massachusetts Bible Society was organized in 1809. A more distinctly charitable undertaking was the Fragment Society, organized in 1812 to help the poor by the distribution of garments, the lending of bedding to the sick and clothes to children in charity schools, as well as the providing of such children with shoes. This society also undertook to provide Bibles for the poor who had none. Under the leadership of Rev. Joseph Tuckerman, then settled in Chelsea, there was organized, May 11, 1812, the Boston Society for the Religious and Moral Improvement of Seamen, "to distribute tracts of a religious and moral kind for the use of seamen, and to establish a regular divine service on board of our merchant vessels." In 1813 the Massachusetts Society for the Suppression of Intemperance, in 1815 the Massachusetts Peace Society, and at about the same time the Society for the Employment of the Poor came into existence.

Of the early Unitarians Rev. Octavius B. Frothingham justly said: "They all had a genuine desire to render the earthly lot of mankind tolerable. It is not too much to say that they started every one of our best secular charities. The town of Boston had a poor-house, and nothing more until the Unitarians initiated humane institutions for the helpless, the blind, the insane. The Massachusetts General Hospital (1811), the McLean

228

Asylum for the Insane (1818), the Perkins Blind Asylum (1832), the Female Orphan Asylum (1800), were of their devising."[3] What this work meant was well stated by Dr. Andrew P. Peabody, when he said there was "probably no city in the world where there had been more ample provision for the poor than in Boston, whether by private alms–giving, benevolent organizations, or public institutions."[4] Nor was this altruistic spirit manifested alone in Boston, for Mr. Frothingham quotes the saying of a lady to Dr. E.E. Hale: "A Unitarian church to you merely means one more name on your calendar. To the people in this town it means better books, better music, better sewerage, better health, better life, less drunkenness, more purity, and better government."[5] The Unitarian conception of the relations of altruism and religion was pertinently stated by Dr. J.T. Kirkland, president of Harvard College during the early years of the nineteenth century, when he said that "we have as much piety as charity, and no more."[6] One who knew intimately of the work of the ministry at large has truly said of the labors of Dr. Tuckerman: "From the beginning he had the moral and pecuniary support of the leaders of life in Boston; her first merchants and her statesmen were watching these experiments with a curious interest, and although he was often so radical as to startle the most conservative notions of men engaged in trade, or learned in the old–fashioned science of government, there was that in the persistence of his life and the accuracy of his method which engaged their support."[7]

Another instance of Unitarian philanthropy is to be found in the support given to Rev. Edward T. Taylor, usually known as "Father Taylor," in his work for sailors. When he went to Boston in 1829 to begin his mission, the first person he visited was Dr. Channing, and the second Ralph Waldo Emerson, then a settled pastor in the city. Both of these men made generous contributions to his mission, and aided him in securing the attention of wealthy contributors.[8] In fact, his Bethel was almost wholly supported by Unitarians. For thirty years Mr. Albert Fearing was the president of the Boston Port Society, organized for the support of Taylor's Seamen's Bethel. The corresponding secretary was Mr. Henry Parker. Among other Unitarian supporters of this work was Hon. John A. Andrew.[9]

We have no right to assume that the Unitarians alone were philanthropic, but they had the wealth and the social position to make their efforts in this direction thoroughly effective.[10] That the results were beneficent may be understood from the testimony of Mrs. Horace Mann. "The liberal sects of Boston," she wrote to a friend, "quite carried the day at that time in works of benevolence and Christian charity. They took care of the needy without regard to sectarianism. Such women as Helen Loring and Elizabeth Howard, (Mrs. Cyrus A. Bartol), Dorothea Dix, Mary Pritchard (Mrs. Henry Ware), and many others less known to the world, but equally devoted to the work, with many youthful coadjutors, took care of the poor wonderfully."[11] After spending several weeks in Boston in 1842, and giving careful attention to the charities and philanthropies of the city, Charles Dickens wrote: "I sincerely believe that the public institutions and charities of this capital of Massachusetts are as nearly perfect as the most considerate wisdom, benevolence, humanity, can make them. I never in my life was more affected by the contemplation of happiness, under circumstances of privation and bereavement, than in my visits to these establishments."[12]

[Sidenote: Education of the Blind.]

The pioneer in the work of educating the blind and the deaf was Dr. Samuel G. Howe, who had been one of those who in 1824 went to Greece to aid in the establishment of Greek independence. On his return, in 1832, he became acquainted with European methods of teaching the blind; and in that year he opened the Massachusetts School and Asylum for the Blind, "the pioneer of such establishments in America, and the most illustrious of its class in the world."[13] In his father's house in Pleasant Street, Dr. Howe began his school with a few pupils, prepared books for them, and then set about raising money to secure larger facilities. Colonel Thomas H. Perkins, of Boston, gave his house in Pearl Street, valued at $50,000, on condition that a like sum should be contributed for the maintenance of the school. In six weeks the desired sum was secured, and the school was, afterwards known as the Perkins Institution for the Blind. Dr. Howe addressed seventeen state legislatures on the education of the blind, with the result of establishing schools similar to his own. His arduous task, however, was that of providing the blind with books; and he used his great inventive skill in perfecting the necessary methods. He succeeded in making it comparatively easy to print books for the blind, and therefore made it possible to have a library of such works.

In the autumn of 1837 Dr. Howe discovered Laura Bridgman, who had only the one sense of touch remaining in a normal condition; and his remarkable success, in her education made him famous. In connection with her and other pupils he began the process of teaching the deaf to use articulate speech, and all who have followed him in this work have but extended and perfected his methods. While teaching the blind and deaf, Dr. Howe found those who were idiotic; and he began to study this class of persons about 1840, and to devise methods for their education. As a member of the Massachusetts legislature in 1846, he secured the appointment of a commission to investigate the condition of the idiotic; and for this commission he wrote the report. In 1847, the state having made an appropriation for the teaching of idiotic, children, ten of them were taught at the Blind Asylum, under the care of Dr. Howe. In 1851 a separate school was provided for such children.

Dr. Howe was called "the Massachusetts philanthropist," but his philanthropy was universal in its humanitarian aims. He gave large and faithful attention, in 1845 and later, to prisons and prisoners; he was a zealous friend of the slave and the freedman; and in 1864 he devoted arduous service to the reform of the state charities of Massachusetts. His biographer justly says of his spirit of universal philanthropy: "He joined in the movement in Boston which abolished imprisonment for debt; he was an early and active member of the Boston Prison Discipline Society, which once did much service; and for years, when interest in prison reform was at a low ebb in Massachusetts, the one forlorn relict of that once powerful organization, a Prisoner's Aid Society, used to hold its meetings in Dr. Howe's spacious chamber in Bromfield Street. He took an early interest in the care of the insane, with which his friends Horace Mann, Dr. Edward Jarvis, and Dorothea Dix were greatly occupied; and in later years he introduced some most useful methods of caring for the insane in Massachusetts. He favored the temperance reform, and wrote much as a physician on the harm done to individuals and to the human stock by the use of alcoholic liquors. He stood with Father Taylor of the Seamen's Bethel in Boston for the salvation of the sailors and their protection from cruel punishments, and he was one of those who almost abolished the flogging of children in schools. During his whole career as a reformer of public schools in New England, Horace Mann had no friend more intimate or helpful than Dr. Howe, nor one whose support was more indispensable to Mann himself."[14]

Dr. Howe was an attendant upon the preaching of Theodore Parker, and was his intimate friend. In after years he was a member of the congregation of James Freeman Clarke at the Church of the Disciples. "After our return to America," says Mrs. Howe of the year 1844, "my husband went often to the Melodeon, where Parker preached until he took possession of the Music Hall. The interest which my husband showed in these services led me in time to attend them, and I remember as among the great opportunities of my life the years in which I listened to Theodore Parker."[15]

[Sidenote: Care of the Insane.]

Another among the many persons who came under the influence of Dr. Channing was Dorothea Dix, who, as a teacher of his children, lived for many months in his family and enjoyed his intimate friendship. Her biographer says: "She had drunk in with passionate faith Dr. Channing's fervid insistence on the presence in human nature, even under its most degraded types, of germs, at least, of endless spiritual development. But it was the characteristic of her own mind that it tended not to protracted speculation, but to immediate, embodied action."[16] Her work for the insane was the expression of the deep faith in humanity she had been taught by Channing.

When she entered upon her humanitarian efforts, but few hospitals for the insane existed in the country. A notable exception was the McLean Asylum at Somerville, which had been built as the result of that same philanthropic spirit that had led the Unitarians to establish the many charities already mentioned in these pages. In March, 1841, Miss Dix visited the House of Correction in East Cambridge; and for the wretched condition of the inmates, she at once set to work to provide remedies. Then she visited the jails and alms–houses in many parts of the state, and presented a memorial to the legislature recounting what she had found and asking for reforms. She was met by bitter opposition; but such persons as Samuel G. Howe, Dr. Channing, Horace Mann, and John G. Palfrey came to her aid. The bill providing for relief to the insane came into the hands of a committee of which Dr. Howe was the chairman, and he energetically pushed it forward to enactment. Thus Miss Dix began her crusade against an enormous evil.

In 1845 Miss Dix reported that in three years she had travelled ten thousand miles, visited eighteen state penitentiaries, three hundred jails and houses of correction, and five hundred almshouses and other institutions, secured the establishment or enlargement of six hospitals for the insane, several county poorhouses, and several jails on a reformed plan. She visited every state east of the Rocky Mountains, and also the British Provinces, to secure legislation in behalf of the insane. She secured the erection of hospitals or other reformatory action in Rhode Island, New Jersey, Pennsylvania, Indiana, Illinois, Kentucky, Tennessee, Missouri, Mississippi, Louisiana, Alabama, South Carolina, Nova Scotia, and Newfoundland. Her labors also secured the establishment of a hospital for the insane of the army and navy, near Washington. All this was the work of nine years.

In 1853 Miss Dix gave her attention to providing an adequate life–saving equipment for Sable Island, one of we most dangerous places to seamen on the Atlantic coast; and this became the means of saving many lives. In 1854 she went to England for needed rest; but almost at once she took up her humanitarian work, this time in Scotland, where she secured a commission of inquiry, which in 1857 resulted in reformatory legislation on the part of Parliament. In 1855 she visited the island of Jersey, and secured great improvements in the care of the insane. Later in that year she visited Switzerland for rest, but in a few weeks was studying the charities of Paris and then those of Italy. In Rome she had two interviews with the pope, and the erection of a new hospital for the insane on modern principles resulted. Speaking only English, and without letters of introduction, she visited the insane hospitals and the prisons of Greece, Turkey, Austria, Sclavonia, Russia, Germany, Sweden, Norway, Denmark, Holland, and Belgium. "Day by day she patiently explored the asylums, prisons, and poor–houses of every place in which she set her foot, glad to her heart's core when she found anything to commend and learn a lesson from, and patiently striving, where she struck the traces of ignorance, neglect, or wrong, to right the evil by direct appeal to the highest authorities."

On her return home, in September, 1856, she was met by many urgent appeals for help in enlarging hospitals and erecting new ones; and she devoted her time until the outbreak of the civil war in work for the insane in the southern and middle north–western states. As soon as the troops were ordered to Washington, she went there and offered her services as a nurse, and was at once appointed superintendent of women nurses for the whole army. She carried through the tasks of this office with energy and devotion. In 1866 she secured the erection of a monument to the fallen soldiers in the National Cemetery, at Hampton.

Then she returned at once to her work in asylums, poorhouses, and prisons, continuing this task until past her seventy–fifth year. "Her frequent visits to our institutions of the insane now, and her searching criticisms," wrote a leading alienist, "constitute of themselves a better lunacy commission than would be likely to be appointed in many of our states."[17] The last five years of her life were spent as a guest in the New Jersey State Asylum at Trenton, it being fit that one of the thirty–two hospitals she had been the means of erecting should afford her a home for her declining years.

Miss Dix was called by many "our Lady," "our Patron Saint"; and well she deserved these expressions of reverence. President Fillmore said in a letter to her, "Wealth and power never reared such monuments to selfish pride as you have reared to the love of mankind." She had the unreserved consecration to the needs of the poor and suffering that caused her to write: "If I am cold, they are cold; if I am weary, they are distressed; if I am alone, they are abandoned."[18] Her biographer justly compares her with the greatest of the saints, and says, "Precisely the same characteristics marked her, the same absolute religious consecration, the same heroic readiness to trample under foot the pains of illness, loneliness, and opposition, the same intellectual grasp of what a great reformatory work demanded."[19] Truly was it said of her that she was "the most useful and distinguished woman America has produced."[20]

[Sidenote: Child–saving Missions.]

As was justly said by Professor Francis G. Peabody, "the Boston Children's Mission was the direct fruit of the ministry of Dr. Tuckerman, and antedates all other conspicuous undertakings of the same nature. The first president of the Children's Mission, John E. Williams, a Unitarian layman, moved later to New York, and became the first treasurer of the newly created Children's Aid Society of that city, formed in 1853. Thus the work of the Children's Mission and the kindred service of the Warren Street Chapel, under the leadership of Charles Barnard, must be reckoned as the most immediate, if not the only American antecedent, of the great modern works of child–saving charity."[21]

The Children's Mission to the Children of the Destitute grew out of the work of the Howard Sunday–school, then connected with the Pitts Street Chapel. When several men connected with that school were discussing the fact that a great number of vagrant children were dealt with by the police, Fanny S. Merrill said to her father, Mr. George Merrill, "Father, can't we children do something to help those poor little ones?" This question suggested a new field of work; and a meeting was held on April 27, 1849, under the auspices of Rev. Robert C. Waterston, to consider this proposition. On May 9 the society was organized "to create a special mission to the poor, ignorant, neglected children of this city; to gather them into day and Sunday schools; to procure places and employment for them; and generally to adopt and pursue such measures as would be most likely to save or rescue them from vice, ignorance and degradation." In the beginning this mission was supported by the Unitarian Sunday–schools in Boston, but gradually the number of schools contributing to its maintenance was enlarged until it included nearly all of those connected with Unitarian churches in New England.

As soon as the mission was organized, Rev. Joseph E. Barry was made the missionary; and he opened a Sunday-school in Utica Street. Beginning in 1853, one or more women were employed to aid him in his work. In May, 1857, Rev. Edmund Squire began work as a missionary in Washington Village; but this mission was soon given into the hands of the Benevolent Fraternity. In June, 1858, Mr. B.H. Greene was engaged to visit the jail and lockup in aid of the young persons found there. In 1859 work was undertaken in East Boston, and also in South Boston. From this time onward from three to five persons were constantly employed as missionaries, in visiting throughout the city, persuading children to attend day-schools, sewing-schools, and Sunday-schools, securing employment for those old enough to labor, and in placing children in country homes. In April, 1857, Mr. Barry took a party of forty-eight children to Illinois; and five other parties followed to that state and to Michigan and Ohio. Since 1860 homes have been found in New England for all children sent outside the city.

In November, 1858, a hall in Eliot Street was secured for the religious services of the mission, which included boys' classes, Sunday-school, and various organizations of a moral and intellectual character. In 1859 a house was rented in Camden Street especially for the care of the boys who came under the charge of the mission. In March, 1867, was completed the house on Tremont Street in which the work of the mission has, since been carried on. An additional building for very young children was provided in October, 1890. For years Mr. Barry continued his work as the missionary of this noble ministry to the children of the poor. Since 1877 Mr. William Crosby has been the efficient superintendent, having served for eighteen years previously as the treasurer. The mission has cared for more than five thousand children.

[Sidenote: Care of the Poor.]

It has been indicated already that much attention was given to the care of the poor and to the prevention of pauperism. It is safe to assume that every Unitarian minister was a worker in this direction. It is well to notice the efforts of one man, because his work led to the scientific methods of charitable relief which are employed in Boston at the present time. When Rev. Ephraim Peabody became the minister of King's Chapel, in 1846, he turned his attention to the education of the poor and to the prevention of pauperism. In connection with Rev. Frederick T. Gray he opened a school for those adults whose education had been neglected. Especial attention was given to the elementary instruction of emigrant women. Many children and adults accepted the opportunity thus afforded, and a large school was maintained for several years.

With the aid of Mr. Francis E. Parker another important work was undertaken by Mr. Peabody. Although Dr. Tuckerman had labored to prevent duplication of charitable gifts and to organize the philanthropies of Boston in an effective manner, with the increase of population the evils he strove to prevent had grown into large proportions. In order to prevent overlapping, imposition, and failure to provide for many who were really needy, but not eager to push their own claims, Mr. Peabody organized the Boston Provident Association in 1851. This society divided the city into small districts, and put each under the supervision of a person who was to examine every case that came before the society within the territory assigned him. The first president of this society was Hon. Samuel A. Eliot, who was a mayor of the city, a representative in the lower house of Congress, and an organizer of many philanthropies. This society was eminently successful in its operations, and did a great amount of good. Its friendly visits to the poor and its judicious methods of procuring the co-operation of many charity workers prepared the way for the introduction, in 1879, of the Associated Charities of Boston, which extended and effectively organized the work begun by Mr. Peabody.[22] Numerous other organizations might be mentioned that have been initiated by Unitarians or largely supported by them.[23]

[Sidenote: Humane Treatment of Animals.]

The work for the humane treatment of animals was begun, and has been largely carried on, by Unitarians. The founder of the American Society for the Prevention of Cruelty to Animals was Henry Bergh, who was a member of All Souls' Church in New York, under the ministry of Dr. Bellows. In 1865 he began his work in behalf of kindness to animals in New York City, and the society he organized was incorporated April 10, 1866. It was soon engaged in an extensive work. In 1873 Mr. Bergh proceeded to organize branch humane societies; and, as the result of his work, most of the states have legislated for the humane care of animals.

A similar work of a Unitarian is that of Mr. George T. Angell in Boston, who in 1868 founded, and has since been the president of, the Massachusetts Society for the Prevention of Cruelty to Animals. In 1889 he became the president of the American Humane Education Society, a position he continues to hold. He is the editor of Our Dumb Animals, and has in many ways been active in the work of the great charity with which he has been connected.

[Sidenote: Young Men's Christian Unions.]

The initiative in the establishment of Christian unions for young men in cities, on a wholly unsectarian basis, was taken by a Unitarian. Mr. Caleb Davis Bradlee, a Harvard undergraduate, who was afterward a Boston pastor for many years, gathered together in the parlor of his father's house a company of young men, and proposed to them the formation of a society for mutual improvement. This was on September 17, 1851; and the organization then formed was called the Biblical Literature Society. Those who belonged to the society during the winter of 1851–52 were so much benefited by it that they decided to enlarge their plans and to extend their influence to a greater number. At the suggestion of Rev. Charles Brooks, minister of the Unitarian church in South Hingham, the name was changed to the Boston Young Men's Christian Union, the first meeting under the new form of organization being held March 15, 1852. On October 11 of the same year the society was incorporated, many of the leading men of the city having already given it their encouragement and support.[24]

[Sidenote: Educational Work in the South.]

After the close of the civil war there was a large demand for help in the South, especially amongst the negroes. Most of the aid given by Unitarians was through other than denominational channels; but something was done by the Unitarian Association as well as by other Unitarian organizations. Miss Amy Bradley, who had been a very successful worker for the Sanitary Commission, opened a school for the whites in Wilmington, N.C. Her work extended to all the schools of the city, and was eminently successful. She became the city and then the county superintendent of schools. She was supported by the Unitarian Association and the Soldiers' Memorial Society. Among the Unitarians who at that time engaged in the work of educating the negroes were Rev. Henry F. Edes in Georgia, Rev. James Thurston in North Carolina, Miss M. Louisa Shaw in Florida, Miss Bottume on Ladies' Island, and Miss Sally Holley and Miss Caroline F. Putnam in Virginia.

In 1868 the Unitarian Association entered upon a systematic effort to aid the negroes through co–operation with the African Methodist Episcopal Church. The sum of $4,000 was in that year devoted to this work; and it was largely spent in educational efforts, especially in aid of college and theological students. Wilberforce University had the benefit of lectures from Dr. George W. Hosmer, president of Antioch College, and of Edward Orton, James K. Hosmer, and other professors in that institution. Libraries of about fifty volumes of carefully selected books, including elementary works of science, history, biography, and a few theological works, were given to ministers of that church who applied for them. This connection continued for several years, and was of much importance in the advancement of the South.

With the first of January, 1886, the Unitarian Association established a bureau of information in regard to southern education, of which General J.B.F. Marshall, who had been for many years the treasurer of the Hampton Institute, was made the superintendent. This bureau, during its existence of three years, investigated the claims of various schools, and recommended those most deserving of aid.

In 1891 Miss Mabel W. Dillingham and Miss Charlotte R. Thorn, who had been teachers for several years in the Hampton Institute, opened a school for negroes in Calhoun, Ala. Miss Dillingham died in 1894; and she was succeeded by her brother, Rev. Pitt Dillingham, as the principal of the school. The Calhoun School has been supported mostly by Unitarians, and it has been successful in doing a practical and important work.

During the first eight years of the Tuskegee Institute it received $5,000 annually from Unitarians, and in more recent years $10,000 annually. This has been given by individuals, churches, and other organizations, but in no sense as a denominational work. Concerning the aid given to the Hampton Institute this statement has been made by the principal: "The Unitarian denomination has had a very important part in the work of Hampton. Our first treasurer was General J.F.B. Marshall, a Unitarian who made it possible for General Armstrong first to gain access to Boston and secure friends there, many of whom have been lifelong contributors to this work. General Marshall came to Hampton in 1872, and for some twelve years took a most important part in building up this institution. He trained young men for the treasurer's office, who still hold important positions in the school, and others who have been sent to various institutions. The home of General and Mrs. Marshall here was of incalculable help in many ways, brightening and cheering the lives of our teachers and students. Unitarians have always had a prominent part in the support of Hampton. Mrs. Mary Hemenway was the largest donor to the Institute during her lifetime. She gave $10,000 for the purchase of our Hemenway Farm, and helped General Armstrong in many ways."[25]

At three different periods the Unitarian Association has undertaken educational work amongst the Indians. The first of these proved abortive, but is of much interest. James Tanner,[26] a half–breed Chippeway or Ojibway from Minnesota, appeared before the board of the Association, February 12, 1855, in behalf of his people. He had been a Baptist missionary to the Ojibways, but had found that he could accomplish little while the Indians continued their roving life and their wars with the Sioux. He therefore wished to have his people adopt a settled agricultural life. The Baptist Home Missionary Society, with which he was laboring, would not accede to his plans in this respect, and desired that he should confine himself to the preaching of the gospel. Unable to do this on account of his liberal views, he went to Boston with the hope that he might secure aid from the Baptists there. He was soon told that he was a Unitarian, and he sought a knowledge of those of that faith. He was thus led to apply to the Unitarian Association for help, which was granted. He secured an outfit of agricultural and other implements, and returned to his people in the spring of 1855. In December of that year Mr. Tanner attended a meeting of the board of the Association, accompanied by six Ojibway chiefs. On this unique occasion the calumet was smoked by all present, and addresses were made by the Indians. In April, 1856, the board reluctantly abandoned this enterprise, because the money for the yearly expenditure of $4,000, which it required, could not be secured.[27]

In 1871 President Grant inaugurated the policy of educating the Indians under the direction of the several religious denominations of the country. To the Unitarians were assigned the Utes of Colorado. The reservation at White River was placed in charge of Mr. J.S. Littlefield, and that at Los Pinos of Rev. J. Nelson Trask. Several other persons took up this work, including Rev. Henry F. Bond and his wife. In 1885 the Utes were removed to a reservation in Utah. In the spring of 1886 Mr. Bond returned to them for the purpose of establishing a boarding–school amongst them; but, not getting sufficient encouragement, he went to Montana, where in the autumn he opened the Montana Industrial School, with eighteen pupils from the Crows in attendance. Buildings were erected, farm work begun, carpenter and blacksmith shops put in operation, all at a cost of $20,000. The school was located on the Big Horn River, thirty miles from Fort Custer.

It was the object of the Montana Industrial School to remove the Indian children from their nomadic conditions and to give them a practical education, with so much of instruction in books as would be of real help to them. The boys were taught farm work and the use of tools, while the girls were trained in sewing, cooking, and other useful employments. At the same time there was constant training in cleanliness, good manners, and right living. The school was fairly successful; and the results would doubtless have been important, could the experiment have gone on for a longer period. In 1891 Mr. Bond withdrew from the school on account of his age, and it was placed in charge of Rev. A.A. Spencer. With the 1st of July, 1895, however, the care of the school was assumed by the national government.

Extended as this chapter has become, it has failed to give anything like an exhaustive statement of the philanthropies of Unitarians. Their charitable activities have been constant and in many directions. This may be seen in the wide–reaching philanthropic interests of Dr. Edward Everett Hale, whose Lend–a–hand Clubs, King's Daughters societies, and kindred movements admirably illustrate the practical side of Unitarianism, its broad humanitarian spirit, its philanthropic and reformatory purpose, and its high ideal of Christian fidelity and service.

[1] Memoir, III. 17; one–volume edition, 465.

[2] Memoir, III. 61, 62; one–volume edition, 487, 488.

[3] Boston Unitarianism, 127.

[4] Harvard Graduates, 155.

[5] Boston Unitarianism, 253.

[6] Elizabeth P. Peabody, Reminiscences of Dr. W.E. Channing, 290.

[7] Eber R. Butler, Lend a Hand, October, 1890, V. 681.

[8] Elizabeth P. Peabody, Reminiscences of W.E. Channing, 273.

[9] Gilbert Haven, Anecdotes of Rev. Edward T. Taylor, 114.

[10] Ibid., 119.

[11] Gilbert Haven, Anecdotes of Rev. Edward T. Taylor, 330.

[12] American Notes, chap. iii.

[13] Frank B. Sanborn, Biography of Dr. S.G. Howe, Philanthropist, 110.

[14] Frank B. Sanborn, Biography of Dr. S.G. Howe, Philanthropist, 170.

[15] Reminiscences, 161.

[16] Francis Tiffany, Life of Dorothea Lynde Dix, 58.

[17] Francis Tiffany, Life of Dorothea Lynde Dix, 355.

[18] Ibid., 327.

[19] Ibid., 290.

[20] Ibid., 375.

[21] Report of the National Conference, 1895, 205.

[22] Sermons of Ephraim Peabody, introductory Memoir, xxv; Memorial History of Boston, IV. 662, George S. Hale on the Charities of Boston; A.P. Peabody, Harvard Graduates, 155.

[23] Besides the Fragment Society, the Children's Mission, and the Boston Provident Society, already mentioned and still vigorously at work, several other societies are wholly supported by Unitarians. Of these may be named the Howard Benevolent Society in the City of Boston, organized in 1812, incorporated in 1818; Young Men's Benevolent Society, organized in 1827, incorporated in 1852; Industrial Aid Society for the Prevention of Pauperism, organized in 1835, incorporated in 1884.

[24] Alfred Manchester, Life of Caleb Davis Bradlee, 8; First Anniversary, address before the Boston Young Men's Christian Union by Rev. F.D. Huntington, Appendix.

[25] Personal letter from Mr. H.B. Frissell.

[26] Edwin James, A Narrative of the Captivity and Adventures of John Tanner during Thirty Tears' Residence among the Indians of North America. (John Tanner was the father of James.)

[27] Quarterly Journal, II. 326, 344; III. 64, 257, 449, 625.

XVI. UNITARIANS AND REFORMS.

The belief of Unitarians in the innate goodness of man and in his progress towards a higher moral life, together with their desire to make religion practical in its character and to have it deal with the actual facts of human life, has made it obligatory that they should give the encouragement of their support to whatever promised to further the cause of justice, liberty, and purity. Their attitude towards reforms, however, has been qualified by their love of individual freedom. They have had a dread of ecclesiastical restriction and of any attempt to coerce opinions or to establish a despotism over individual convictions. And yet, with all this insistence upon personal liberty, no body of men and women has ever been more devoted to the furthering of practical reforms than those connected with Unitarian churches. No one, for instance, was ever more zealous for individual freedom than Theodore Parker; but he was essentially a reformer. He was a persistent advocate of peace, temperance, education, the rights of women, the rights of the slave, the abolition of capital punishment, reform in prison discipline, and the application of humanitarian principles to the conduct of life.

[Sidenote: Peace Movement.]

"It may be doubted whether any man who ever lived contributed more to spread just sentiments on the subject of war and to hasten the era of universal peace," said Dr. Channing of Noah Worcester, who has been often called "the Apostle of Peace." It was the second contest with Great Britain that led Dr. Worcester to consider the nature and effects of war. In August, 1812, on the day appointed for a national fast, he preached a sermon in which he maintained that the war then beginning was without sufficient justification, and that war is always an evil. In 1814 he further studied the subject, with the result that he wrote a little book which he called A Solemn Review of the Custom of War.[1]

The Solemn Review was widely circulated, it was translated into many languages, it made a deep and lasting impression, and it had a world–wide influence in preparing the minds of men for the acceptance of peace principles. The remedy for war it proposed was an international court of arbitration.[2] Through the efforts of Dr. Worcester the Massachusetts Peace Society was organized December 28, 1815, one of the first societies of the kind in the world.[3] William Phillips was made the president, and Dr. Noah Worcester the corresponding secretary, with Dr. Henry Ware, Dr. Channing, and Rev. Francis Parkman among his councillors. On the executive committee with Dr. Worcester in 1819 were Rev. Ezra Ripley and Rev. John Pierce. Other Unitarian members and workers were James Freeman, Nathaniel L. Frothingham, Charles Lowell, Samuel C. Thacher, J.T. Kirkland, and Joseph Tuckerman; and, of laymen, Moses Grant, Josiah Quincy, and Colonel Joseph May. In 1819 Dr. Worcester began the publication of The Friends of Peace, a small quarterly magazine, a large part of the contents of which he wrote himself. After the first number, having obtained the assistance of several wealthy Friends, he relinquished the copyright; and the numbers were republished in several parts of the country, thus obtaining a wide circulation. He devoted himself almost wholly to this publication and the advocacy of the cause of peace until 1829, when he relinquished its editorship. "This must be looked upon as a very remarkable work," wrote Henry Ware, the younger. "To his wakeful mind everything that occurred and everything that he read offered him materials; he appeared to see nothing which had not a bearing on this one topic; and his book becomes a boundless repository of curious, entertaining, striking extracts from writers of all sorts and the history of all times, displaying the criminality and folly of war, and the beauty and efficacy of the principles of peace."[4]

In his efforts hi behalf of peace, Dr. Worcester had the support of Dr. Channing's "respectful sympathy and active co–operation."[5] According to Dr. John Pierce, Channing was the life and soul of the Massachusetts Peace Society. "For years," says his biographer, "he devoted himself to the work of extending its influence with unwavering zeal, as many of his papers of that period attest."[6] From his pulpit Dr. Channing frequently expressed his faith in the principles of peace, and he strongly advocated those

Christian convictions and that spirit of good will which would make war impossible if they were applied to the conduct of nations.

Not less devoted to the cause of peace was Dr. Ezra S. Gannett, of whom his son says: "He thought that reason, religion, the whole spirit as well as the letter of the gospel, united in forbidding war. Probably, he was non–resistant up to, rather than in, the absolutely last extremity; although he writes that an English book which Dr. Channing lent him as the best he knew upon the subject, 'has made me a thorough peace man!'"[7] "Let the fact of brotherhood be fairly grasped," wrote Dr. Frederic H. Hedge, "and war becomes impossible."[8] "The tremendous extent and pertinacity of the habit of human slaughter in battle," wrote Dr. William R. Alger, "its shocking criminality, and its incredible foolishness, when regarded from an advanced religious position, are three facts calculated to appall every thoughtful man and startle him into amazement." "It is vain," he said, "to undertake to impart a competent conception of the crimes and miseries belonging to war. Their appalling character and magnitude stun the imagination and pass off like the burden of a frightful dream."[9]

Worcester's Solemn Review convinced Rev. Samuel J. May "that the precepts, spirit, and example of Jesus gave no warrant to the violent, bloody resistance of evil; that wrong could be effectually overcome by right, hatred by love, violence by gentleness, evil of any kind by its opposite good. I preached this," he said, "as one of the cardinal doctrines of the gospel, and endeavored especially to show the wickedness and folly of the custom of war."[10] In 1826 he organized a county peace society, the first in the country; and his first publication was in advocacy of this reform.[11]

Of the men connected with political life, Charles Sumner was the most devoted and influential friend of the peace cause. As early as March, 1839, he wrote to a friend, "I hold all wars, as unjust and, unchristian." His address on The True Grandeur of Nations, given before the mayor and other officials of Boston, July 4, 1845, was one of the noblest and most effective utterances on the subject. Though a considerable part of the audience was in military array, Sumner showed the evils of war in uncompromising terms, denouncing it as cruel and unnecessary, while with true eloquence, great learning, and deep conviction he made his plea for peace. "The effect was immediate and striking," wrote George W. Curtis. "There were great indignation and warm protest on the one hand, and upon the other sincere congratulation and high compliment. Sumner's view of the absolute wrong and iniquity of war was somewhat modified subsequently; but the great purpose of a peaceful solution of international disputes he never relinquished."[12] He said in this oration that "in our age there can be no peace that is not honorable; there can be no war that is not dishonorable." This statement was severely criticised, but it indicates his uncompromising acceptance of peace principles.[13] He added these pertinent sentences: "The true honor of a nation is to be found only in deeds of justice and in the happiness of its people, all of which are inconsistent with war. In the clear eye of Christian judgment vain are its victories, infamous are its spoils."[14] He further declared that "war is utterly and irreconcilably inconsistent with true greatness."[15] These views he continued to hold throughout his life, though in a more conciliatory spirit; and on several occasions he presented them before the Peace Society and elsewhere. When in the Senate he was a leader of the cause of arbitration, and exerted his large influence in securing its adoption by the United States as a means of preventing war with foreign countries. As late as July, 1873, he wrote to one of his friends: "I long to witness the harmony of nations, which I am sure is near. When an evil so great is recognized and discussed, the remedy must be near at hand."[16]

The work done by Julia Ward Howe for the cause of peace is eminently worthy of recognition. One chapter of her Reminiscences is devoted to her "Peace Crusade" of 1870. The cruel and unnecessary character of the Franco–Prussian war led her to write an appeal to mothers to use their influence in behalf of peace. "The august dignity of motherhood and its terrible responsibilities now appeared to me in a new aspect," she writes, "and I could think of no better way of expressing my sense of these than of sending forth an appeal to womanhood throughout the world, which I then and there composed."[17] She printed and distributed her appeal, had it translated into French, Spanish, Italian, German, and Swedish, and then spent many months in corresponding with leading women in various countries. She invited these women to a Women's Peace Congress to be held in London. After holding two successful meetings in New York, she began her crusade in England, holding meetings in many places, and also attending a Peace Congress in Paris. She hired a hall in London, and held Sunday meetings to promote the reform she had deeply at heart. The Women's Congress was a success, and after two years of earnest effort Mrs. Howe had the satisfaction of knowing that she had done something to promote peace on earth and good will among men.

[Sidenote: Temperance Reform.]

Unitarians have been active in the cause of temperance, but again as individuals rather than as a denomination. The emphasis they have put on the importance of individual opinion and personal liberty has made them often reluctant to join societies that sought to promote this reform by restrictive and coercive measures. As a body, therefore, they have shown a greater inclination to the use of moral suasion than legislative power.

From Dr. Channing this reform had the most earnest approval. "The temperance reform which is going on among us," he wrote, "deserves all praise, and I see not what is to hinder its complete success. I believe the movements now made will succeed, because they are in harmony with and are seconded by the general spirit and progress of the age. Every advance in knowledge, in refined manners, in domestic enjoyments, in habits of foresight and economy, in regular industry, in the comforts of life, in civilization, good morals and religion, is an aid to the cause of temperance; and believing as we do that these are making progress, may we not hope that drunkenness will be driven from society?"[18] He regarded the subject from a broader point of view than many, and urged that a sound physical education for all youth, as well as larger opportunities for intellectual improvement on the part of workingmen, would do much to prevent intemperance.[19] He maintained that to give men "strength within to withstand the temptations of intemperance" is incalculably more important than to remove merely outward temptations. Better education, innocent amusements, a wider spirit of sympathy and brotherhood, discouragement of the use and sale of ardent spirits, were among the means he recommended for suppressing this evil.[20]

The Massachusetts Society for the Suppression of Intemperance was organized at the State House in Boston on February 5, 1813, "to discountenance and suppress the too free use of ardent spirits, and to encourage and promote temperance and general morality." This was one of the first temperance societies organized in the country, and its chief promoters were Unitarians. Dr. John C. Collins, who published the records of the society, said of the year 1827, when he became a member, that "Channing, Gannett, and others were the most active men at that time in the temperance cause."[21] Dr. Abiel Abbot was the first corresponding secretary of the society, and on the council were Drs. Kirkland, Lothrop, Worcester, and Pierce. Among the other Unitarian ministers who were active in the society were Charles Lowell, the younger Henry Ware, John Pierpont, and John G. Palfrey. Among the laymen were Moses Grant, Nathan Dane, Dr. John Ware, Stephen Fairbanks, Dr. J.F. Flagg, William Sullivan, Amos Lawrence, Samuel Dexter, and Isaac Parker.[22] Auxiliary societies were organized in Salem, Beverly, and other towns; and these gave to the temperance cause the activities of such Unitarians as Theophilus Parsons, Robert Rantoul, and Samuel Hoar.[23]

Of the more recent interest of Unitarians in questions of temperance reform there may be mentioned the thorough study made by the United States Commissioner of Labor, and printed in 1898 under the title of Economic Aspects of the Liquor Problem.[24] This investigation was ordered by Congress as the result of a petition sent to that body by the Unitarian Temperance Society. Probably few petitions have ever been sent to Congress that contained so many prominent names of leading statesmen, presidents of colleges and universities, bishops, clergymen, well–known literary men, and other persons of influence. The Unitarian Temperance Society was organized September 23, 1886, in connection with the meeting of the National Conference at Saratoga. Its purpose is "to work for the cause of temperance in whatever ways may seem to it wise and right; to study the social problems of poverty, crime, and disease, in their relation to the use of intoxicating drinks, and to diffuse whatever knowledge may be gained; to discuss methods of temperance reform; to devise and, so far as possible, to execute plans for practical reform; to exert by its meetings and by its membership such influence for good as by the grace of God it may possess." It has held annual meetings in Boston, and other meetings in connection with the National Conference; it has published a number of important tracts, temperance text–books, and temperance services for Sunday–schools; and it has exerted a considerable influence on the denomination in shaping public opinion in regard to this reform. The presidents of the society have been Rev. Christopher R. Eliot, Rev. George H. Hosmer, and Rev. Charles F. Dole.

The subject of temperance reform has been before the National Conference on several occasions and in various forms. At the session of 1882 a resolution offered by Miss Mary Grew was adopted:—

That the unutterable evils continually wrought by intemperance, the easy descent from moderate to immoderate drinking, and the moral wrecks strewn along that downward path, call upon Christians and patriots to practise and advocate abstinence from the use of all intoxicating liquors as a beverage.

In 1891 a series of resolutions recommended by the Unitarian Temperance Society were adopted as expressing the convictions of the Conference:—

First, that the liquor saloon, as it exists to–day in the United States, is the nation's chief school of crime, chief college of corruption in politics, chief source of poverty and ruined homes, chief menace to our country's future, is the standing enemy of society, and, as such, deserves the condemnation of all good men.

Second, that, whatever be the best mode of dealing with the saloon by law, law can avail little until those who condemn the saloon consent to totally abstain themselves from the use of alcoholic drink for pleasure.

Third, that we affectionately and urgently call on every minister and all laymen and women in our denomination—our old, our young, our rich, our poor, our leaders, and our humblest—to take this stand of total abstinence, remembering those that are in bonds as bound with them, and throw the solid influence of our church against the influence of the saloon.

[Sidenote: Anti–slavery.]

In proportion to its numbers no religious body in the country did so much to promote the anti–slavery reform as the Unitarian. No Unitarian defended slavery from the pulpit or by means of the press, and no one was its apologist.[25] Many, however, did not approve of the methods of the abolitionists, and some strongly opposed the extreme measures of a part of that body of reformers. The desire of Unitarians to be just, rational, and open–minded, exposed many of them to the criticism of being neither for nor against slavery. But it is certain that they were not indifferent to its evils nor recreant to their humanitarian principles.

The period of the anti–slavery agitation was truly one that tried the souls of men; and those who were equally conscientious, desirous of serving the cause of justice and humanity, and solicitous for the welfare of the slave, widely differed from one another as to what was the wise method of action. Among those severely condemned by the anti–slavery party were several Unitarian ministers of great force of character and of a genuinely humanitarian spirit. Three of them may be selected as representative.

Dr. Orville Dewey had seen something of slavery, and was strongly opposed to it. He thought the system hateful in itself and productive of nearly unmingled evil, and yet he was not in favor of immediate emancipation. His frequent indictments of slavery in his sermons and lectures were severe in the extreme; but his demand for wise and patient counsel, and for a rational method of gradual emancipation, subjected him to severe condemnation. "And nothing else brings out the nobleness of Dr. Dewey into such bold relief as the fact," says Rev. John W. Chadwick, "that the immeasurable torrent of abuse that greeted his expressed opinion did not in any least degree avail to make him one of the pro-slavery faction. He differed from the most earnest of the anti-slavery men only as to the best method of getting rid of the curse of human bondage."[26]

As early as 1830 Dr. E.S. Gannett said that "the greatest evil under which our nation labors is the existence of slavery. It is the only vicious part of our body politic, but this is a deep and disgusting sore. It must be treated with the utmost judgment and skill." The violence of the abolitionists he did not approve, however; for his respect for law and constituted authority was so great that he was not ready for radical measures. He abhorred slavery, but he was not willing to condemn the slaveholder. He was therefore regarded by the abolitionists as more hostile to them than any other Unitarian minister. His attitude as a peace man, his strong regard for justice and fair dealing, as well as his earnest faith in the gentle influence of the gospel, forbade his accepting the strenuous methods of the abolitionists. He would not, however, permit anti-slavery ministers to be silenced in Unitarian meetings. When he saw something of slavery, in 1833, he expressed his convictions in regard to it in these forcible words: "It is the attempt to degrade a human being into something less than a man,—not the confinement, unjust as this is, nor the blows, cruel as these are,—but the denial of his equal share in the rights, prerogatives, and responsibilities of a human being, which brands the institution of slavery with its peculiar and ineffaceable odiousness."[27]

Another minister who came under the condemnation of the abolitionists was Rev. John H. Morison, and yet he preached sermons against slavery that met with the vigorous disapproval of his congregation. "We all agree," he wrote in 1844, "in the sad conviction that slavery in its political influence, more than all other subjects, threatens to upturn the foundation of our government; that in its moral and religious bearings it is a grievous wrong to master and slave; and that, as it is in violation of the fundamental principles of Christian duty, it must, if continued beyond the absolute necessity of the case, be attended with consequences the most disastrous." Again, when Daniel Webster made his

7th of March speech in 1850, Dr. Morison, then the editor of The Christian Register, took the earliest possible opportunity to express himself as strongly as he could against it. "We at the North," he wrote, "believe that slavery is morally wrong." He said that the government, in its attempt to defend slavery as against the moral convictions of a large number of the people, was doing the country a great harm.[28]

The position of these men and of others who thought and acted with them can best be understood by recognizing the fact that they were opposed to sectarian methods in promoting reforms as in advancing the interests of religion. It is probable that in these heated times neither party did full justice to the spirit and purposes of the other. Even so gentle and charitable a man as Rev. Samuel J. May speaks of the "discreditable pro–slavery conduct of the Unitarian denomination." "The Unitarians as a body," he says again, "dealt with the question of slavery in anything but an impartial, courageous, and Christian way. Continually in their public meetings the question was staved off and driven out because of technical, formal, verbal difficulties which were of no real importance, and ought not to have caused a moment's hesitation. Avowing among their distinctive doctrines the fatherly character of God and the brotherhood of man, we had a right to expect from the Unitarians a steadfast and unqualified protest against so unjust, tyrannical, and cruel a system as that of American slavery. And considering their position as a body, not entangled with any pro–slavery alliances, not hampered with any ecclesiastical organization, it does seem to me that they were pre–eminently guilty in reference to the enslavement of the millions in our land with its attendant wrongs, cruelties, horrors. They refused to speak as a body, and censured, condemned, execrated their members who did speak faithfully for the down–trodden, and who co–operated with him whom a merciful Providence sent as the prophet of the reform."[29]

The testimony of Rev. O.B. Frothingham is fully as condemnatory of Unitarian timidity and conservatism, even of the moral cowardice betrayed by many of the leaders. He says the Unitarians, as such, "were indifferent or lukewarm; the leading classes were opposed to the agitation. Dr. Channing was almost alone in lending countenance to the reform, though his hesitation between the dictates of natural feeling and Christian charity towards the masters hampered his action, and rendered him obnoxious to both parties,—the radicals finding fault with him for not going further, the conservatives blaming him because he went so far."[30] Mr. Frothingham finds, however, that the transcendentalists were quite "universally abolitionists, their faith in the natural powers of man making them zealous promoters of the cause of the slave." He insists that as a class "the

Unitarians were not ardent disciples of any moral cause, and took pride in being reasoners, believers in education and in general social influence, in the progress of knowledge and the uplifting of humanity by means of ideas," but that they permitted these qualities to cool their ardor for reform and to mitigate their love of humanity.[31]

The biographers of William Lloyd Garrison are never tired of condemning Dr. Channing for what they call his timidity, his shunning any personal contact with the great abolitionist, his failure to grapple boldly with the evils of slavery, and his half–hearted espousal of the cause of abolition. The Unitarians generally are by these writers regarded in the same manner.[32]

Most of the accounts mentioned were written by those who took part in the agitation against slavery, in condemnation of those who had not kept step with their abolition pace or in apology for those whose words and conduct were thought to need defence. The time has come, perhaps, when it is possible to consider, the attitude of individuals and the denomination without a partisan wish to condemn or to defend. In this spirit the statement of Samuel J. May is to be accepted as true and just, when he says: "We Unitarians have given to the anti–slavery cause more preachers, writers, lecturers, agents, poets, than any other denomination in proportion to our numbers, if not without any comparison."[33]

Among those who listened to William Lloyd Garrison when in October, 1830, he first presented in Boston his views in favor of immediate emancipation, were Samuel J. May, Samuel E. Sewall, and A.B. Alcott; and these men at once became his disciples and friends.[34] When Garrison organized the New England Anti–slavery Society in December, 1832, he was actively supported by Samuel E. Sewall, David Lee Child, and Ellis Gray Loring. It was to the financial support of Sewall and Loring, though they did not at first accept his doctrine of immediate emancipation, that Garrison owed his ability to begin The Liberator, and to sustain it in its earliest years.[35] For many years, Edmund Quincy was connected with The Liberator, serving as its editor when Garrison was ill, absent on lecturing tours, or journeying in Europe. The Massachusetts Anti–slavery Society, which in 1835 succeeded the New England Society, had during many years Francis Jackson as its president, Edmund Quincy as its corresponding secretary, and Robert F. Walcutt as its recording secretary, all Unitarians.

In 1834 was formed the Cambridge Anti–slavery Society, under the leadership of the younger Henry Ware; and the membership was largely Unitarian, including the names of

Dr. Henry Ware, Sidney Willard, Charles Follen, William H. Charming, Artemus B. Muzzey, Barzillai Frost, Charles T. Brooks, and Frederic H. Hedge. The purposes of the society were stated in its constitution:—

> We believe that the emancipation of all who are in bondage is the
> requisition, not less of sound policy, than of justice and humanity;
> and that it is the duty of those with whom the power lies at once to
> remove the sanction of the law from the principle that man can be the
> property of man,—a principle inconsistent with our free institutions,
> subversive of the purposes for which man was made, and utterly at
> variance with the plainest dictates of reason and Christianity.

In 1843 Samuel May visited England, and at Unitarian meetings described the obstacles in the way of the abolition of slavery, and spoke of the apathy of American Unitarians. He advised the sending a letter of fraternal counsel to the Unitarian ministers of the United States "in behalf of the unhappy slave." Such a letter was prepared, and signed by eighty–five ministers. It was published in the Unitarian papers in this country, a meeting was held to consider it, and a reply sent to England signed by one hundred and thirty ministers. Mr. May was severely condemned for his part in causing such a letter to be sent, and the reply was rather in the nature of a protest than a friendly acceptance of the advice given.

A year later, however, this letter was again the subject of earnest discussion. In anniversary week, 1845, a meeting of Unitarian ministers was held to "discuss their duties in relation to American slavery." The call for this meeting was signed by James Thompson, Joseph Allen, Caleb Stetson, Samuel Ripley, Converse Francis, William Ware, Samuel J. May, Artemus B. Muzzey, Oliver Stearns, James W. Thompson, Alonzo Hill, Andrew P. Peabody, Henry A. Miles, Frederic H. Hedge, James F. Clarke, George W. Briggs, Samuel May, Barzillai Frost, Nathaniel Hall, David Fosdick, and John Weiss. At the third session, by a vote of forty–seven to seven, it was declared "that we consider slavery to be utterly opposed to the principles and spirit of Christianity, and that, as ministers of the gospel, we feel it our duty to protest against it, in the name of Christ, and to do all we may to create a public opinion to secure the overthrow of the institution." It was also decided to appoint a committee to draw up, secure signatures to, and publish "a protest against the institution of American slavery, as unchristian and inhuman." Though some of those who spoke at these meetings condemned the abolitionists, yet all of them expressed in the strongest terms their opposition to slavery.

The committee selected to prepare this protest consisted of Caleb Stetson, James F. Clarke, John Parkman, Stephen G. Bulfinch, A.P. Peabody, John Pierpont, Samuel J. May, Oliver Stearns, George W. Briggs, William P. Tilden, and William H. Channing. The protest was written by James Freeman Clarke and was accepted essentially as it came from his hands. It was signed by one hundred and seventy–three ministers,[36] the whole number of Unitarian ministers at that time being two hundred and sixty–seven. Some of the most prominent ministers were conspicuous by the absence of their names from this protest. It must be understood, however, that those who did not sign it were as much opposed to slavery as those who did. "This protest," said the editor of The Christian Register, in presenting it to the public,[37] "is written with great clearness of expression and moderation of spirit. It exhibits unequivocally and distinctly the sentiments of the numerous and most enlightened body of clergy whose names are attached to it, as well as many other ministers of the denomination who may be disinclined to act conjointly, or do not feel called upon to act at all in any prescribed way, on the subject." It was not a desire to defend slavery that kept these ministers from signing the protest, but their excessive individualism, and their unwillingness to commit the denomination to opinions all might not accept. A few paragraphs from the protest will indicate its spirit and purpose:—

"Especially do we feel that the denomination which takes for its motto Liberty, Holiness and Love should be foremost in opposing this system. More than others we have contended for three great principles,—individual liberty, perfect righteousness, and human brotherhood. All of these are grossly violated by the system of slavery. We contend for mental freedom; shall we not denounce the system which fetters both mind and body? We have declared righteousness to be the essence of Christianity; shall we not oppose the system which is the sum of all wrong? We claim for all men the right of brotherhood before a universal Father; ought we not to testify against that which tramples so many of our brethren under foot?"

"We, therefore, ministers of the gospel of truth and love, in the name of God the universal Father, in the name of Christ the Redeemer, in the name of humanity and human brotherhood, do solemnly protest against the system of slavery as unchristian, and inhuman," "because it is a violation of right, being the sum of all unrighteousness which man can do to man," "violates the law of love," "degrades man, the image of God, into a thing," "necessarily tends to pollute the soul of the slave," "to defile the soul of the master," "restricts education, keeps the Bible from the slave, makes life insecure, deprives female innocence of protection, sanctions adultery, tears children from parents and husbands from wives, violates the divine institutions of families, and by hard and hopeless toil makes existence a burden," "eats out the heart of nations and tends every year more and more to sear the popular conscience and impair the virtue of the people."

"We implore all Christians and Christian preachers to unite in unceasing prayer to God for aid against this system, to leave no opportunity of speaking the truth and spreading the light on this subject, in faith that the truth is strong enough to break every yoke." "And we do hereby pledge ourselves, before God and our brethren, never to be weary of laboring in the cause of human rights and freedom until slavery be abolished and every slave made free."

Although many ministers and laymen took the position that the question of slavery was not one that should receive attention in the meetings of the Unitarian Association or other religious organizations, that these should be kept strictly to their own special purposes, it was not possible to exclude the one great exciting topic of the age. How persistently it intruded itself is clearly indicated in words used by Dr. Bellows at the annual meeting of the Association, in 1856. "Year after year this horrid image of slavery come in here," he said, "and obtruded itself upon our concerns. It has prevented our giving attention to any other subject; we could not keep it out of our minds; and why is that awful crime against humanity still known in the world, still supported and active in this age of Christendom, but because it is in alliance with certain views of theology with which we are at war?"[38] At the same meeting strong resolutions of sympathy with the free settlers of Kansas, and with Charles Sumner because "the barbarity of the slave power had attempted to silence him by brutal outrage," were unanimously adopted.[39]

In 1857 the subject of slavery came before the Western Conference in its session at Alton. The most uncompromising anti-slavery resolutions were presented at the opening of the meeting, and everything else was put aside for their consideration, a day and a half being devoted to them. The opinion of the majority was, in the words of one of the speakers, that slavery is a crime that "denies millions marital and parental rights, requires ignorance as a condition, encourages licentiousness and cruelty, scars a country all over with incidents that appall and outrage the human world." Dr. W.G. Eliot, of St. Louis, and others, thought it not expedient to press the subject to an issue, though he regarded slavery in much the same way as did the other members of the conference. When the conference finally took issue with slavery, he and his delegates withdrew from its membership. His assistant, Rev. Carlton A. Staples, and Rev. John H. Heywood, of Louisville, went with the majority. A committee appointed to formulate a statement the conference could accept said that it had no right to interfere with the freedom of action of individual churches; but it recommended them to do all they could in opposition to slavery, and said that the conference was of one mind in the conviction "that slavery is an evil doomed by God to pass away." This report was accepted by the conference with only one opposing vote.[40] When the year 1860 had arrived, Unitarians were practically unanimous in their condemnation of slavery.

When the names of individual Unitarians who took an active part in the anti−slavery movement are given, it is at once seen how important was the influence of the denomination. Early in the century Rev. Noah Worcester uttered his word of protest against slavery. Rev. Charles Follen joined the Massachusetts Anti−slavery Society in the second year of its existence, and no nobler champion of liberty ever lived. If Dr. Channing was slow in applying his Christian ideal of liberty to slavery, there can be no question that his influence was powerful on the right side, and all the more so because of his gentle and ethical interpretation of individual and national duty. His various publications on the subject, his identification of himself with the abolitionists by joining their ranks in the Massachusetts State House in 1836, his speech in Faneuil Hall in protest against the killing of Lovejoy in Alton during the same year, exerted a great influence in behalf of abolition throughout the North. It is only necessary to mention John Pierpont, Theodore Parker, William H. Furness, William H. Channing, William Goodell, Theodore D. Weld, Ichabod Codding, Caleb Stetson, and M.D. Conway in order to recognize their uncompromising fidelity to the cause of freedom. Only less devoted were such men as Charles Lowell, Nahor A. Staples, Sylvester Judd, Nathaniel Hall, Thomas T. Stone, O.B. Frothingham, Abiel A. Livermore, Samuel Johnson, Samuel Longfellow, Thomas J. Mumford, and many others.

Samuel J. May and his cousin, Samuel May, were both employed by the Massachusetts Anti−slavery Society. From 1847 until 1865 the latter was the general agent of that organization; and his assistant was another Unitarian minister, Robert F. Walcutt. James Freeman Clarke, though settled at Louisville from 1833 to 1840, was opposed to slavery; and in the pages of The Western Messenger, of which he was publisher and editor, he took every occasion to press home the claims of emancipation. John G. Palfrey emancipated the slaves that came into his possession from his father's estate, insisting on receiving them for that purpose, though the opportunity was given him to accept other property in their stead. In accordance with this action was his attitude toward slavery in the pulpit and on the platform, as well as when he was a member of the lower house of Congress.

Of Unitarian laymen who were loyal to the ideal of freedom, the list may properly open with the name of Josiah Quincy, afterwards mayor of Boston and president of Harvard College, who began as early as 1804 his opposition to slavery, and carried it faithfully into his work as a member of the national House of Representatives soon after. The fidelity of John Quincy Adams to freedom during many years is known to every one, and his service in the national House has given him a foremost place in the company of the anti–slavery leaders. Not less loyal was the service of Charles Sumner, Horace Mann, John P. Hale, George W. Julian, John A. Andrew, Samuel G. Howe, Henry I. Bowditch, William I. Bowditch, Thomas W. Higginson, George F. Hoar, Ebenezer R. Hoar, George S. Boutwell, and Henry B. Anthony. Of the poets the anti–slavery reform had the support of Longfellow, Lowell, Bryant, and Emerson. The Unitarian women were also zealous for freedom. The loyalty of Lydia Maria Child is well known, as are the sacrifices she made in publishing her early anti–slavery books. Lucretia Mott, of the Unitarian branch of the Friends, was a devoted supporter of the anti–slavery cause. Mrs. Maria W. Chapman was one of the most faithful supporters of Garrison, doing more than any one else to give financial aid to the anti–slavery reform movement in its earlier years. With these women deserve to be mentioned Eliza Lee Follen, Angelina Grimke Weld, Lucy Stone, and many more.

A considerable group of persons who had been trained in evangelical churches became essentially Unitarians as a result of the anti–slavery agitation. Of these may be mentioned William Lloyd Garrison, Gerrit Smith, Beriah Green, Joshua R. Giddings, Myron Holley, Theodore D. Weld, and Francis W. Bird. Of the first four of these men, George W. Julian has said: "They were theologically reconstructed through their unselfish devotion to humanity and the recreancy of the churches to which they had been attached. They were less orthodox, but more Christian. Their faith in the fatherhood of God and the brotherhood of man became a living principle, and compelled to reject all dogmas which stood in its way."[41]

[Sidenote: The Enfranchisement of Women.]

Unitarianism in America

It is not surprising that the first great advocate of "the rights of women" in this country should have been the Unitarian, Margaret Fuller. She did no more than apply what she had been taught in religion to problems of personal duty, professional activity, and political obligations. With her freedom of faith and liberty of thought meant also freedom to devote her life to such tasks as she could best perform for the good of others. It was inevitable that other Unitarian women should follow her example, and that many women, trained in other faiths, having come to accept the doctrine of universal political rights, should seek in Unitarianism the religion consonant with their individuality of purpose and their sense of human freedom.

Among the leaders of the movement for the enfranchisement of women have been such Unitarians as Elizabeth Cady Stanton, Susan B. Anthony, Lucy Stone, Julia Ward Howe, Mary A. Livermore, Maria Weston Chapman, Caroline H. Dall, and Louisa M. Alcott. The first pronounced woman suffrage paper in the country was The Una, begun at Providence in 1853, with Mrs. Caroline H. Dall as the assistant editor. Among other Unitarian contributors were William H. Charming, Elizabeth P. Peabody, Thomas W. Higginson, Ednah D. Cheney, Amory D. Mayo, Elizabeth Oakes Smith, Lucy Stone, and Mrs. E.C. Stanton. The next important paper was The Revolution, begun at New York in 1868, with Susan B. Anthony as publisher and Elizabeth Cady Stanton and Parker Pillsbury as editors. Then came The Woman's Journal, begun at Boston in 1870, with Mary A. Livermore, Lucy Stone, Julia Ward Howe, T.W. Higginson, and Henry B. Blackwell, all Unitarians, as the editors.

The first national woman's suffrage meeting was held in Worcester, October 28 and 24, 1850; and among those who took part in it by letter or personal presence were Emerson, Alcott, Higginson, Pillsbury, Samuel J. May, William H. Channing, William H. Burleigh, Elizabeth C. Stanton, Catherine M. Sedgwick, Caroline Kirkland, and Lucy Stone. In April, 1853, when the Constitution of Massachusetts was to receive revision, a petition was presented, asking that suffrage should be granted to women. Of twenty–seven persons signing it, more than half were Unitarians, including Abby May Alcott, Lucy Stone, T.W. Higginson, Anna Q.T. Parsons, Theodore Parker, William I. Bowditch, Samuel E. Sewall, Ellis Gray Loring, Charles K. Whipple, and Thomas T. Stone. Among other Unitarians who have taken an active part in promoting this cause have been Lucretia Mott, Mary Grew, Caroline M. Severance, Celia C. Burleigh, Angelina Grimke Weld, and Maria Giddings Julian. Of men there have been Dr. William F. Channing, James F. Clarke, George F. Hoar, George W. Curtis, John S. Dwight, John T. Sargent,

Samuel Johnson, Samuel Longfellow, Octavius B. Frothingham, Adin Ballou, George W. Julian, Frank B. Sanborn, and James T. Fields.

Unitarians have been amongst the first to recognize women in education, literature, the professions, and in the management of church and denominational interests. At the convention held in New York in 1865, which organized the National Conference, no women appeared as delegates; and the same was true at the second session, held at Syracuse in 1866. At that session Rev. Thomas J. Mumford moved "that our churches shall be left to their own wishes and discretion with reference to the sex of the delegates chosen to represent them in the conference"; and this resolution was adopted. At the third meeting, held at New York in 1868, thirty-seven women appeared as delegates, including Julia Ward Howe and Caroline H. Dall. The lay delegates to the session held at Washington in 1899 numbered four hundred and two; and, of these, two hundred and twenty seven were women.

At the annual meeting of the Unitarian Association in 1870, Rev. John T. Sargent brought forward the subject of the representation of women on its board of directors. Dr. James F. Clarke made a motion looking to that result, which was largely discussed, much opposition being manifested. It was urged by many that women were unfit to serve in a position demanding so much business capacity, that they would displace capable men, and that it was improper for them to assume so public a duty. Charles Lowe, James F. Clarke, John T. Sargent, and others strongly championed the proposition, with the result that Miss Lucretia Crocker was elected a member of the board.[42]

The first woman ordained to the Unitarian ministry was Mrs. Celia C. Burleigh, who was settled over the parish in Brooklyn, Conn., October 5, 1871. The sermon was preached by Rev. John W. Chadwick, and the address to the people was given by Mrs. Julia Ward Howe. A letter was read from Henry Ward Beecher, in which he said to Mrs. Burleigh: "I do cordially believe that you ought to preach. I think you had a *call* in your very nature." Mrs. Burleigh continued at Brooklyn for less than three years, ill-health compelling her to resign.

The second woman to enter the Unitarian ministry was Miss Mary H. Graves, who was ordained at Mansfield, Mass., December 14, 1871. She was subjected to a thorough examination; and the committee reported "that her words have commanded our thorough respect by their freedom and clearness, and won our full sympathy and approval by their earnest, discreet, and beautiful spirit." Mrs. Eliza Tupper Wilkes was ordained by the Universalists at Rochester, Minn., May 2, 1871, though she had preached for two or three years previously; and she subsequently identified herself with the Unitarians. Mrs. Antoinette Brown Blackwell was ordained in Central New York, in 1853, by the Orthodox Congregationalists; but somewhat later she became a Unitarian.

The first woman to receive ordination who has continued without interruption her ministerial duties was Miss Mary A. Safford, ordained in 1880. She has held every official position in connection with the Iowa Unitarian Association, and she has also been an officer of the Western Conference and a director of the American Unitarian Association.

Several women have also frequently appeared in Unitarian pulpits who have not received ordination or devoted themselves to the ministry as a profession. Among these are Mrs. Caroline H. Dall, Mrs. Julia Ward Howe, and Mrs. Mary A. Livermore. In 1875 Mrs. Howe was active in organizing the Women's Ministerial Conference, which met in the Church of the Disciples, and brought together women ministers of several denominations. Of this conference Mrs. Howe was for many years the president.

In most Unitarian churches there is no longer any question as to the right of women to take any place they are individually fitted to occupy. On denominational committees and boards, women sit with entire success, their fitness for the duties required being called in question by no one. In those conferences where women have for a number of years been actively engaged in the work of the ministry they are received on a basis of perfect equality with men, and the sex question no longer presents itself in regard to official positions or any other ministerial duty.

[Sidenote: Civil Service Reform.]

The first advocate of the reform of the civil service was Charles Sumner, who as early as December, 1847, anticipated its methods in a series of articles contributed to a newspaper.[43] He was the first to bring this reform before Congress, which he did April 30, 1864, when he introduced a bill to provide a system of competitive examinations for admission to and promotion in the civil service, which made merit and fitness the conditions of employment by the government, and provided against removal without cause. This bill was drawn by Sumner without consultation with any other person, but the time had not yet arrived when it could be successfully advocated.

The next person to advocate the reform of the civil service in Congress was Thomas A. Jenckes, of Rhode Island, who in 1867 brought the merit system forward in the form of a report from the joint committee on retrenchment, which reported on the condition of the civil service, and accompanied its report with a bill "to regulate the civil service and to promote its efficiency." The next year Mr. Jenckes made a second report, but it was not until 1871 that action on the subject was secured.[44] George W. Curtis says that at first he "pressed it upon an utterly listless Congress, and his proposition was regarded as the harmless hobby of an amiable man, from which a little knowledge of practical politics would soon dismount him."[45] Most members of Congress thought the reform a mere vagary, and that it was brought forward at a most inopportune time.[46] Mr. Jenckes was the pioneer of the reform, according to Curtis, who says that he "powerfully and vigorously and alone opened the debate in Congress."[47] He drew the amendment to the appropriation bill in 1871 that became the law, and under which the first civil service commission was appointed. "By his experience, thorough knowledge, fertility of resource and suggestion and great legal ability, he continued to serve with as much efficiency as modesty the cause to which he was devoted."[48]

One of the first persons to give attention to this subject was Dorman B. Eaton, an active member of All Souls' Church in New York, who was for several years chairman of the committee on political reform of the Union League Club of New York. In 1866, and again in 1870 and 1875, he travelled in Europe to secure information in regard to methods of civil service. The results of these investigations were presented in his work on Civil Service in Great Britain, a report made at the request of President Hayes. In 1873 he was appointed a member of the Civil Service Commission by President Grant; in 1883 he was the chairman of the committee appointed by President Arthur; and in 1885 he was reappointed by President Cleveland. The bill of January, 1883, which firmly established civil service by act of Congress, was drawn by him. He was a devoted worker for good government in all its phases; and the results of his studies of the subject may be found in his books on The Independent Movement in New York and The Government of Municipalities. He was described by George William Curtis as "one of the most conspicuous, intelligent, and earnest friends of reform."[49]

The most conspicuous advocate of the merit system was Mr. George William Curtis, another New York Unitarian, who was the chairman of the Civil Service Commission of

1871. In 1880 he became the president of the New York Civil Service Reform Association, a position he held until his death. The National Civil Service Reform League was organized at Newport in August, 1881; and he was the president from that time as long as he lived. His annual addresses before the league show his devoted interest in its aims, as well as his eloquence, intellectual power, and political integrity.[50] In an address before the Unitarian National Conference, in 1878, Mr. Curtis gave a noble exposition and vindication of the reform which he labored zealously for twelve years to advance.[51]

It has been justly said of Mr. Curtis that "far above the pleasures of life he placed its duties; and no man could have set himself more sternly to the serious work of citizenship. The national struggle over slavery, and the re–establishment of the Union on permanent foundations enlisted his whole nature. In the same spirit, he devoted his later years to the overthrow of the spoils system. He did this under no delusion as to the magnitude of the undertaking. Probably no one else comprehended it so well. He had studied the problem profoundly, and had solved every difficulty, and could answer every cavil to his own satisfaction." There can be no question that "his name imparted a strength to the movement no other would have given." Nor can there be much question that "among public men there was none who so won the confidence of sincere and earnest men and women by his own personality. The powers of such a character, with all his gifts and accomplishments, was what Mr. Curtis brought to the civil service reform."[52]

[1] American Unitarian Biography, edited by William Ware; Memoir of
    Worcester, by Henry Ware, Jr., I. 45, 46.

[2] Solemn Review, edition of 1836 by American Peace Society, 7.

[3] It had been preceded by societies in Ohio and New York, results of
    the influence of the Solemn Review.

[4] Unitarian Biography, I. 49.

[5] Memoir, II. 284; one–volume edition, 111.

[6] Ibid., III. 111; one–volume edition, 284.

[7] Memoir, 139.

[8] Christian Examiner, May, 1850, XLVIII. 378.

[9] Ibid., November, 1861, LXXI. 313.

[10] Life, 83.

[11] Ibid., 115.

[12] Cyclopedia of American Biography, V. 746.

[13] Memoir, II. 348.

[14] Memoir.

[15] Ibid., 351.

[16] Ibid., IV. 572.

[17] Reminiscences, 328.

[18] Memoir, III. 36; one–volume edition, 477.

[19] Memoir, III. 31; one–volume edition, 474, 475.

[20] Works, II. 301.

[21] When will the Day come? and other tracts of the Massachusetts
    Temperance Society, 135.

[22] Of the twenty–seven annual addresses given before this society from
    1814 to 1840, at least sixteen were by Unitarians; and among these
    were John T. Kirkland, Abiel Abbot, William E. Channing, Edward
    Everett, the younger Henry Ware, Gamaliel Bradford, Charles Sprague,
    James Walker, Alexander H. Everett, William Sullivan, and Samuel K.

Lothrop. The first four presidents of this society—Samuel Dexter, Nathan Dane, Isaac Parker, and Stephen Fairbanks—were Unitarians. Of the same faith were also a large proportion of the vice-presidents and other officers. Many of the tracts published by the society were written by Unitarians.

[23] Unitarians of every calling have been the advocates of temperance. Among those who have been loyal to it in word and action may be named John Adams, Jeremy Belknap, Jonathan Phillips, Charles Lowell, Ezra S. Gannett, John Pierpont, Samuel J. May, Amos Lawrence, Horace Mann, William H. and George S. Burleigh, Governor Pitman, William G. Eliot, Rufus P. Stebbins, and William B. Spooner. "Many of the leading men and women who were eminent as lawyers, judges, legislators, scholars, also prominent in the business walks of life, and in social position, gave this cause the force of their example, and the inspiration of their minds. By their contributions of money, by their personal efforts, by their public speeches and writings, and by their practice of total abstinence, they rendered very valuable service."

[24] Twelfth Annual Report of the Commissioner of Labor, 1897.

[25] Theodore Clapp, of New Orleans, may be an exception, though he is claimed by the Universalists. See S.J. May's Recollections of the Anti-slavery Conflict, 335.

[26] Autobiography and Letters, 117, 127, 129. The criticism of Dr. Dewey may be found in S.J. May's Recollections, 367.

[27] Memoir, 139, 284, 296. See S.J. May, Recollections, 341, 367, for an anti-slavery indictment of Dr. Gannett.

[28] Memoir, chapter on Slavery.

[29] Recollections of the Anti-slavery Conflict, chapter on the Unitarians, 335.

[30] See Lydia Maria Child's account of conversations with Channing on this subject, in her Letters from New York.

[31] Recollections and Impressions, 47, 183.

[32] The Story of his Life as Told by his Children.

[33] Recollections, 335.

[34] S.J. May, Recollections, 19; Life of A.B. Alcott, 220; Life of Garrison, I. 212.

[35] Life of Garrison, I. 223.

[36] The more prominent names are herewith given as they were printed in The Christian Register: Joseph Allen, J.H. Allen, S.G. Bulfinch, C.F. Barnard, Charles Briggs, W.G. Babcock, C.T. Brooks, Warren Burton, C.H. Brigham, Edgar Buckingham, William H. Channing, James F. Clarke, S.B. Cruft, A.H. Conant, C.H.A. Dall, R. Ellis, Converse Francis, James Flint, William H. Furness, N.S. Folsom, Frederick A. Farley, Frederick T. Gray, Henry Giles, F.D. Huntington, E.B. Hall, N. Hall, F.H. Hedge, F. Hinckley, G.W. Hosmer, F.W. Holland, Thomas Hill, Sylvester Judd, James Kendall, William H. Knapp, A.A. Livermore, S.J. May, Samuel May, M.I. Mott, A.B. Muzzey, J.F. Moors, Henry A. Miles, William Newell, J. Osgood, S. Osgood, Andrew P. Peabody, John Parkman, John Pierpont, Theodore Parker, Cyrus Pierce, J.H. Perkins, Cazneau Palfey, O.W.B. Peabody, Samuel Ripley, Chandler Robbins, Caleb Stetson, Oliver Stearns, Rufus P. Stebbins, Edmund Q. Sewall, Charles Sewall, John T. Sargent, George F. Simmons, William Silsbee, William P. Tilden, J.W. Thompson, John Weiss, Robert T. Waterston, William Ware, J.F.W. Ware, E.B. Willson, Frederick A. Whitney, Jason Whitman.

[37] Printed in The Christian Register, October 4, 1845.

[38] Quarterly Journal, III. 567.

[39] Ibid., 572.

[40] Unity, Sept. 4, 1886, Mrs. S.C.Ll. Jones, Historic Unitarianism in the West.

[41] Life of Joshua R. Giddings, 399.

[42] Memoir of Charles Lowe, 486. In 1901 four of the eighteen directors of the American Unitarian Association were women.

[43] Life, III. 149.

[44] Life of Charles Sumner, IV. 191; Works, VII. 452.

[45] G.W. Curtis, Orations and Addresses, II. 30.

[46] Ibid., 173.

[47] Ibid., 180.

[48] Ibid., 223.

[49] G.W. Curtis, Orations and Addresses, II. 458.

[50] See Curtis's Orations and Addresses, II.; also, his Reports as civil service commissioner, and various addresses before the Social Science Association.

[51] Edward Cary, Life of Curtis, American Men of Letters, 294.

[52] George William Curtis and Civil Service Reform, by Sherman S. Rogers, in Atlantic Monthly, January, 1893, LXXI. 15.

XVII. UNITARIAN MEN AND WOMEN.

Many of the most influential Americans have been in practical accord with Unitarianism, while not actually connected with Unitarian churches. They have accepted its principles of individual freedom, the rational interpretation of religion, and the necessity of bringing religious beliefs into harmony with modern science and philosophy. Among these may be properly included such men as Benjamin Franklin, John Marshall, Gerrit Smith, John G. Whittier, William Lloyd Garrison, Andrew D. White, and Abraham Lincoln. Whittier was a Friend, and White an Episcopalian; but the religion of both is acceptable to all Unitarians. Marshall was undoubtedly a Unitarian in his intellectual convictions, and he sometimes attended the Unitarian church in Washington; but his church affiliations were with the Episcopalians. John C. Calhoun was all his life a member of an Episcopal church and a communicant in it; but he frequently attended the Unitarian church in Washington, and intellectually he discarded the doctrines taught in the creeds of his church.

Lincoln belonged to no church, and had no interest in the forms and disputes that constitute so large a part of outward religion; but he was one of those men whose great deeds rest on a basis of simple but profoundest religious conviction. The most explicit statement he ever made of his faith was in these words: "I have never united myself to any church, because I have found difficulty in giving my assent, without mental reservation, to the long, complicated statements of Christian doctrine which characterize their articles of belief and confessions of faith. When any church will inscribe over its altar, as its sole qualification of membership, the Saviour's condensed statement of both law and gospel, 'Thou shalt love the Lord thy God with all thy heart and with all thy soul and with all thy mind, and thy neighbor as thyself,' that church will I join with all my heart and all my soul."[1] This declaration brings Lincoln into fullest harmony with the position of the Unitarian churches.

[Sidenote: Eminent Statesmen.]

The intellectual tendencies of the eighteenth century led many of the leading Americans to discard the Puritan habit of mind and the religious beliefs it had cherished. An intellectual revolt caused the rejection of many of the Protestant doctrines, and a political revolt in the direction of democracy led to the acceptance of religious principles not in harmony with those of the past. Many Americans shared in these protests who did not openly break with the older faiths. Washington was of this class; for, while he remained outwardly a churchman, he had little intellectual or practical sympathy with the stricter beliefs. Franklin was thoroughly of the Deistic faith of the thinkers of England and France in his time. These tendencies had their effect upon such men as John Adams, Timothy Pickering, Joseph Story, and Theophilus Parsons, as well as upon Thomas Jefferson and William Cranch. They showed themselves with especial prominence in the case of Jefferson, who always remained outwardly faithful to the state religion of Virginia, in which he had been educated, attended the Episcopal church in the neighborhood of his home, sometimes joining in its communion, but who was, nevertheless, intellectually a pronounced Unitarian.

With Jefferson his Unitarianism was a part of his democracy, for he was consistent enough to make his religion and his politics agree with each other. As he would have kings no longer rule over men, but give political power into the hands of the people, so in religion he would put aside all theologians and priests, and permit the people to worship in their own way. It was for this reason that he rejoiced in the emancipating work of Channing, of which he wrote in 1822, "I rejoice that in this blessed country of free inquiry and belief, which has surrendered its creeds and conscience neither to kings nor priests, the genuine doctrine of only one God is reviving; and I trust there is not a young man now living who will not die a Unitarian."[2] Jefferson's revolt against authority was tersely expressed in his declaration: "Had there never been a commentator, there never would have been an infidel."[3] This was in harmony with his saying, that "the doctrines of Jesus are simple and tend all to the happiness of man."[4] It also fully agrees with the claims of the early Unitarians with regard to the teachings of Jesus. "No one sees with greater pleasure than myself," he wrote, "the progress of reason in its advance toward rational Christianity. When we shall have done away with the incomprehensible jargon of the Trinitarian arithmetic, that three are one, and one are three; when we shall have knocked down the artificial scaffolding reared to mask from view the simple structure of Jesus; when, in short, we shall have unlearned everything taught since his day, and got back to the pure and simple doctrines he inculcated—we shall then be truly and worthily his disciples; and my opinion is that, if nothing had ever been added to what flowed purely from his lips, the whole world would at this day have been Christian."[5]

However mistaken Jefferson may have been in the historical opinions thus expressed, we cannot question the sincerity of his beliefs or fail to recognize that he had the keenest interest in whatever gave indication of the growth of a rational spirit in religion. These opinions he shared with many of the leading men of his time; but he was more outspoken in their utterance, as he was more consistent in holding them. That Washington, though remaining an Episcopalian, was in fullest accord with Jefferson in his principles of toleration and religious freedom, is apparent from one of his letters. "I am not less ardent in my wish," he wrote, "that you may succeed in your toleration in religious matters. Being no bigot myself to any mode of worship, I am disposed to indulge the professors of Christianity in the church with that road to heaven which to them shall seem the most direct, easiest, and least liable to exception."[6] Intellectually, Franklin was a Deist of essentially the same beliefs with Jefferson, as may be seen in his statement of faith: "I believe in one God, the creator of the universe; that he governs it by his providence; that he ought to be worshipped; that the most acceptable service we render to him is doing good to his other children; that the soul of man is immortal, and will be treated with justice in another life respecting its conduct in this. These I take to be the fundamental points in all sound religion. As to Jesus of Nazareth, I think his system of morals and his religion, as he left them to us, the best the world ever saw, or is likely to see; but I apprehend it has received various corrupting changes, and I have some doubts of his divinity; though it is a question I do not dogmatize upon, having never studied it."[7] Franklin was a member of a Unitarian church in London.

[Sidenote: Some Representative Unitarians.]

The church in Washington, not having been popular or of fine appointments, has been a test of the Unitarian faith of those frequenting the capital city. It has included in its congregation, from time to time, such men as John Adams, John Quincy Adams,[8] John Marshall, Joseph Story, Samuel F. Miller, Millard Fillmore, William Cranch, George Bancroft, Nathan K. Hall, James Moore Wayne, and Senators Daniel Webster, John C. Calhoun, William S. Archer, Henry B. Anthony, William B. Allison, Timothy O. Howe, Edward Everett, Justin S. Morrill, Charles Sumner, William E. Chandler, George F. Hoar, and John P. Hale. William Winston Seaton and Joseph Gales, once prominent in Washington as editors and publishers of The National Intelligencer, were both Unitarians.

In New York the Unitarian churches have had among their attendants and members such persons as William Cullen Bryant, Catherine M. Sedgwick, Henry D. Sedgwick, Henry Wheaton, Peter Cooper, George William Curtis, George Ticknor Curtis, Moses H. Grinnell, Dorman B. Eaton, and Joseph H. Choate. The churches in Salem have had connected with them such men as John Prince, Nathaniel Bowditch, Benjamin Peirce,

Timothy Pickering, John Pickering, Leverett Saltonstall, Joseph Story,[9] Jones Very, William H. Prescott, and Nathaniel Hawthorne.[10]

[Sidenote: Judges and Legislators.]

During the early Unitarian period "the judges on the bench" included such men as Theophilus Parsons, Isaac Parker, and Lemuel Shaw, all of whom held the office of chief justice in Massachusetts. Other lawyers, jurists, and statesmen were Fisher Ames, political orator and statesman; Nathan Dane, who drew the ordinance for the north–western territory; Samuel Dexter, senator, and secretary of the treasury under John Adams; Christopher Gore, senator, and governor of Massachusetts; and Benjamin R. Curtis, of the United States Supreme Court. Other chief justices of the Supreme Court of Massachusetts have been George T. Bigelow, John Wells, Pliny Myrick, Walbridge A. Field, Charles Allen; and of associates in that court have been Ebenezer Rockwood Hoar, Benjamin F. Thomas, Seth Ames, Samuel S. Wilde, Levi Lincoln, and John Lowell. Among the governors of Massachusetts have been Levi Lincoln, Edward Everett, John Davis, John H. Clifford, John A. Andrew, George S. Boutwell, John D. Long, Thomas Talbot, George D. Robinson, J.Q.A. Brackett, Oliver Ames, Frederic T. Greenhalge, and Roger Wolcott. The first mayors of Boston, John Phillips, Josiah Quincy,[11] and Harrison Gray Otis, were Unitarians. Then, after an interval of one year, followed Samuel A. Eliot and Jonathan Chapman.

It has often been assumed that Unitarianism attracts only intellectual persons; but it also appeals to practical business men, legislators, and the leaders of political life. In Maine have been Vice–President Hannibal Hamlin, Governor Edward Kent, and Chief Justice John Appleton. In New Hampshire it has appealed to such men as Chief Justices Cushing, Henry A. Bellows, Jeremiah Smith, and, Charles Doe, as well as to Governors Onslow Stearns, Charles H. Bell, Benjamin F. Prescott, and Ichabod Goodwin; in Rhode Island, Governors Lippitt and Seth Paddelford, Chief Justices Samuel Ames and Samuel Eddy, General Ambrose E. Burnside, and William B. Weeden, historian and economist. Alphonso Taft and George Hoadly, both governors of Ohio, were Unitarians, as were Austin Blair, John T. Bagley, Charles S. May, and Henry H. Crapo, governors of Michigan. Among the prominent Unitarians of Iowa have been Senator William B. Allison and General George W. McCrary. In California may be named Leland Stanford, Horace Davis, Chief Justice W.H. Beatty, and Oscar L. Shafter of the Supreme Court.

Unitarianism in America

[Sidenote: Boston Unitarianism.]

What Unitarianism has been in the lives of its men and women may be most conspicuously seen in Boston and the region about it, for there throughout the first half of the nineteenth century Unitarianism was the dominant form of Christianity. Of the period from 1826 to 1832, when Dr. Lyman Beecher was settled in Boston, Mrs. Stowe has given this testimony: "All the literary men of Massachusetts were Unitarians. All the trustees and professors of Harvard College were Unitarians. All the elite of wealth and fashion crowded Unitarian churches. The judges on the bench were Unitarian, giving decisions by which the peculiar features of church organization, so carefully ordained by the Pilgrim fathers, had been nullified."[12] Of the same period Dr. Beecher wrote, "All offices were in the hands of Unitarians."[13]

These statements were literally true, except in so far as they implied that Unitarians used high positions in order to overthrow the old institutions of Massachusetts and substitute those of their own devising. The calmer judgment of the present day would not accept this conclusion, and it has no historic foundation. The religious development of Boston brought its churches into the acceptance of a tolerant, rational, and practical form of Christianity, that was not dogmatic or sectarian. It took the Unitarian name, but only in the sense of rejecting the harsher interpretations of the doctrine of the Trinity and of election. The members of the Unitarian churches during this period were devout in an unostentatious manner, pious after a simple fashion, loyal Christians without excess of zeal, lovers of liberty, but in a conservative spirit. This simple form of piety enabled the men who accepted it to govern the state in a most faithful manner. They managed its affairs justly, wisely, and in the true intent of economy. Sometimes it was complained that they held a much larger number of offices than was their proportion according to population; but to this John G. Palfrey replied that the people of the state had confidence in them, and elected them because nobody else governed so well.

With the aid of the biography of James Sullivan, judge, legislator, attorney–general, and diplomatist,[14] we may study the constituency of a single church in Boston, the Brattle Street Church. We find there James Bowdoin and John Hancock, rival candidates for the position of governor of the state in 1785. The same rivalry occurred twenty years later between James Sullivan and Caleb Strong, both of the number of its communicants. On the parish committee of this church at one time were Hancock, Bowdoin, and Sullivan, who became governors of the state, and Judges Wendell and John Lowell.[15] Some years later there were included in the congregation such men as Daniel Webster, Harrison Gray Otis, Abbott Lawrence, and Amos Lawrence, who was one of the deacons for many years.

Of the distinguished business men of Boston may be named John Amory Lowell, John C. Amory, Jonathan Phillips (the confidential friend and supporter of Dr. Channing), Thomas Wigglesworth, J. Huntington Wolcott, Augustus Hemenway, Stephen C. Phillips, and Thomas Tileston. Francis Cabot Lowell was largely concerned in building up the manufacturing interests of Massachusetts, especially the cotton industry; and the city of Lowell took his name in recognition of the importance of his leadership in this direction. For similar reasons the city of Lawrence was named after Abbott Lawrence, minister of the United States to Great Britain, who was one of the leading merchants of Boston in the China trade, and was also largely concerned in the development of cotton manufacturing. With these business and manufacturing interests Amos Lawrence was also connected. Nathan Appleton[16] was associated with Francis C. Lowell in the establishment of the great manufacturing interests that have been a large source of the wealth of Massachusetts. Thomas H. Perkins, from whom was named the Perkins Institute for the Blind, was also concerned in the China trade and in the first development of railroads. Robert Gould Shaw was another leading merchant, who left a large sum of money for the benefit of the children of mariners. John Murray Forbes was a builder of railroads, notably active in the financial support of the national government during the civil war, and a generous friend of noble men and interests.[17] Nathaniel Thayer was a manager of railroads, erected Thayer Hall at Harvard College, and bore the expenses of Agassiz's expedition to South America.

A Boston man by birth and training, who knew the defects as well as the merits of the class of men and women who have been named, has given generous testimony to the high qualities of mind and heart possessed by these Unitarians. In writing of his maternal grandfather, Octavius Brooks Frothingham has said: "Peter C. Brooks was an admirable example of the Unitarian laymen of that period, industrious, honest, faithful in all relations of life, charitable, public–spirited, intelligent, sagacious, mingling the prudence of the man of affairs with the faith of the Christian.... As one recalls the leading persons in Brattle Street, Federal Street, Chauncy Place, King's Chapel, the New North, the New South,—men like Adams, Eliot, Perkins, Bumstead, Lawrence, Sullivan, Jackson, Judge Shaw, Daniel Webster, Jacob Bigelow, T.B. Wales, Dr. Bowditch,—forms of dignity and of worth rise before the mind. Better men there are not. More honorable men, according to the standard of the time, there are not likely to be.... He joined the church and was a consistent church member. He was not effusive, demonstrative, or loud–voiced. His name did not stand high on church lists or among the patrons of the faith. His was the calm, rational, sober belief of the thoughtful, educated, honorable men of his day,—men like Lemuel Shaw, Joseph Story, Daniel A. White,—intellectual, noble people, with worthy aims, a lofty sense of duty, a strong conviction of the essential truths of revealed Christianity; sincere believers in the gospel, of enduring principle, of pure, consistent, blameless life and conduct. Speculative theology he cared little or nothing about. He was no disputant, no doubter, no casuist; of the heights of mysticism, of the depths of infidelity, he knew nothing. He was conservative, of course, from temperament rather than from inquiry. He took the literal, prose view of Calvinism, and rejected doctrines which did not commend themselves to his common sense. In a word, he was a Unitarian of the old school.... The Unitarian laity in general, both men and women, had a genuine desire to render the earthly lot of mankind more tolerable. It is not too much to say that they started every one of our best secular charities. They were exceedingly liberal in their gifts to Harvard College, and to other colleges as well—for they were not at all sectarian, as their large subscriptions to the Roman Catholic cathedral proved. Whatever tended to exalt humanity, in their view, was encouraged. They were as noble a set of men and women as ever lived."[18]

This estimate of the Unitarians of Boston during the first half of the nineteenth century is eminently just and accurate. To a large extent these men and their associates in the Unitarian churches gave to the city its worth and its character; and they built up the industries, the commerce, the educational and philanthropic interests, and the progressive legislation of Massachusetts. They were men of integrity and sincerity, who were generous, faithful, and just. They accepted the religion of the spirit, and they gave it expression in daily conduct and character.

[1] F.B. Carpenter, Six Months in the White House, 190.

[2] James Parton, Life of Thomas Jefferson, 711.

[3] Charles W. Upham, Life of Timothy Pickering, IV. 327.

[4] P.L. Ford's edition Jefferson's Works, X.220.

[5] Life of Pickering, IV. 326.

[6] P.L. Ford, The True George Washington, 81.

[7] P.L. Ford, The Many–sided Franklin, 174. See Diary of Ezra Stiles, III. 387.

[8] John Quincy Adams, in reply to a question about the church in Washington, said: "I go there to church, although I am not decided in my mind as to all the controverted doctrines of religion." Years later he said to a preacher in the Unitarian church at Quincy: "I agree entirely with the ground you took in your discourse. You did not speak of any particular class of doctrines that were everlasting, but of the great, fundamental principles in which all Christians agree; and these, I think, are what will be permanent." See A.B. Muzzey, Reminiscences and Memorials of the Men of the Revolution and their Families, 53.

[9] William W. Story, Life and Letters of Joseph Story, 57, 93. Joseph Story grew away from Calvinism in early manhood, and accepted a humanitarian view of the nature of Christ. "No man was ever more free from a spirit of bigotry and proselytism," says his biographer. "He gladly allowed every one freedom of belief and claimed only that it should be a genuine conviction and not a mere theologic opinion, considering the true faith of every man to be the necessary exponent of his nature, and honoring a religious life more than a formal creed. He admitted within the pale of salvation Mohammedan and Christian, Catholic and infidel. He believed that whatever is sincere and honest is recognized by God—that as the views of any sect are but human opinion, susceptible of error on every side, it behooves all men to be on their guard against arrogance of belief—and that in the sight of God it is not the truth or falsehood of our views, but the spirit in which we believe which alone is of vital consequence. His moral sense was not satisfied with a theory of religion founded upon the depravity of man and recognizing an austere and vengeful God, nor could he give his metaphysical assent to the doctrine of the

Trinity. In the doctrines of liberal Christianity he found the resolution of his doubts, and from the moment he embraced the Unitarian faith he became a warm and unhesitating believer."

[10] For an interesting picture of New England Unitarianism see Recollections of my Mother (Mrs. Anne Jean Lyman), by Mrs. J.P. Lesley. Mrs. Lyman's home was in Northampton, Mass. The Reminiscences of Caroline C. Briggs describe life in the same town and under similar conditions. Also Memoir of Mary L. Ware, Memorial of Joseph and Lucy Clark Allen by their Children, and Life of Dr. Samuel Willard.

[11] Edmund Quincy, Life of Josiah Quincy, 532. In a speech to the overseers of Harvard University in 1845, Josiah Quincy said: "I never did and never will call myself a Unitarian; because the name has the aspect, and is loaded by the world with the imputation of sectarianism." His biographer says: "He regarded differences as of slight importance, especially as to matters beyond the grasp of the human intellect. His catholicity of spirit fraternized with all who profess to call themselves Christians, and who prove their title to the name by their lives." It was precisely this catholicity of spirit that was the most characteristic feature of early American Unitarianism, and not the rejection of the doctrine of the Trinity. However, Josiah Quincy was undoubtedly a Unitarian, both in what he rejected and in what he affirmed, as may be seen from these words recorded in his diary in 1854: "From the doctrines with which metaphysical divines have chosen to obscure the word of God,—such as predestination, election, reprobation, etc.,—I turn with loathing to the refreshing assurance which, to my mind, contains the substance of revealed religion,—in every nation he who feareth God, and worketh righteousness, is accepted of him."

[12] Autobiography, Correspondence, etc., of Lyman Beecher, II. 109.

[13] Ibid., 144.

[14] Thomas C. Amory. Life of James Sullivan.

[15] John Lowell, a son of Judge John Lowell, and a brother of Dr. Charles Lowell of the West Church, was the author of an effective controversial pamphlet entitled Are you a Christian or a Calvinist? Or do you prefer the Authority of Christ to that of the Genevan Reformer? Both the Form and Spirit of these Questions being suggested by the Late Review of American Unitarianism in The Panoplist, and by the Rev. Mr. Worcester's Letter to Mr. Channing. By a Layman. Boston, 1815.

[16] Nathan Appleton's interest in theology may be seen in his book entitled The Doctrine of Original Sin and the Trinity, discussed in a Correspondence between a Clergyman of the Episcopal Church, in England, and a Layman of Boston, United States, published in Boston in 1859. "I was brought up," he said in one of these letters, "in the strictest form of Calvinistic Congregationalism; but since arriving at an age capable of examining the subject, and after a careful study of it, I have renounced what appear to me unworthy views of the Deity, for a system which appears to me more worthy of him, and less abhorrent to human reason." "I can say," he wrote in another letter, "that the Unitarian party embraces the most intelligent and high–minded portion of the community. It is my opinion that the views of the Unitarians are the best and only security against the spirit of infidelity which is prevailing so extensively amongst the most highly educated and intelligent men in Europe." See Memoir of Nathan Appleton, by Robert C. Winthrop.

[17] John Murray Forbes: Letters and Recollections, edited by his daughter, Sarah Forbes Hughes.

[18] Boston Unitarianism, 93, 94, 101, 127.

XVIII. UNITARIANS AND EDUCATION.

The interest of Unitarians in education has always been very great, but it has not been in the direction of building and fostering sectarian institutions. As a body, Unitarians have not only been opposed to denominational colleges, but they have been leaders in promoting unsectarian education. Freedom of academic teaching and the scientific study of theology may be found where Unitarianism has no existence, and yet it is significant that in this country such mental liberty should have first found expression under Unitarian auspices. From the first, American Unitarianism has been unsectarian and liberty–loving, taking an attitude of toleration, free investigation, and loyalty to truth. That it has always been faithful to its ideal cannot be maintained, and yet its history shows that the open–mindedness and the spirit of freedom have never been wholly ignored.

[Sidenote: Pioneers of the Higher Criticism.]

The attitude of the early Unitarians towards the Bible, their trust in it as the revealed word of God and the source of divine authority in all matters of faith, and their confidence that a return to its simple principles would liberate men from superstition and bigotry, naturally made them the first to welcome the higher criticism of the Bible in this country. Such men as Noah Worcester and his successors brought to the Bible new and common–sense interpretations, and began the work of pointing out the defects in the common version. The Unitarians were not hampered by the theory of the verbal infallibility of the Bible; and they were therefore prepared to advance the critical work of the scholars, as it came to them from England and Germany, as was no other religious body in this country.

Joseph, S. Buckminster was an enthusiastic student of the Bible, securing when in Europe all the apparatus of the more advanced criticism that could then be procured; and after his return to Boston he gave his attention to bringing out the New Testament in the most scholarly form that was then possible. In 1808, in connection with William Wells, and under the patronage of Harvard College, he republished Griesbach's Greek Testament, with a selection of the most important various readings. He also formed a plan of publishing in this country all the best modern English versions of the Hebrew prophets, with introductions and notes; but he did not find the necessary support for this project. In

The Monthly Anthology and in The General Repository he "first discussed subjects of Biblical criticism in a spirit of philosophical and painstaking learning, and took the critical study of the Scriptures from the old basis on which it had rested during the Arminian discussions and placed it on the solid foundation of the text of the New Testament as settled by Wetstein and Griesbach, and elucidated by the labors of Michaelis, Marsh, Rosenmueller, and by the safe and wise learning of Grotius, Le Clerc, and Simon." "It has," wrote George Ticknor, "in our opinion, hardly been permitted to any other man to render so considerable a service as this to Christianity in the western world."[1] In 1811 Mr. Buckminster was made the first lecturer in Biblical criticism at Harvard, on, the foundation established by the gift of Samuel Dexter; and he entered with great interest and enthusiasm upon the work of preparing for the duties of this office. We are assured that "this appointment was universally thought to be an honor most justly due to his pre−eminent attainments in this science";[2] but his death the next year brought these plans to an untimely end.

To some extent the critical work of Buckminster was continued by Edward Everett, his successor in the Brattle Street Church. Mr. Everett's successor in that pulpit, Rev. John G. Palfrey, became the professor of sacred literature in the Harvard Divinity School in 1831, and was the dean of that institution. In his lectures on the Jewish Scriptures and Antiquities, published in four volumes, from 1833 to 1852, he gave the most advanced criticism of the time. A more important work was done by Professor Andrews Norton, who was as radical in his labors as a Biblical critic as he was conservative in his theology. For the time when they were published, his Statement of Reasons, the first edition of which appeared in 1819, Historical Evidences of the Genuineness of the Gospels, 1837−44, Translation of the Gospels, with Notes, 1855, Internal Evidences of the Genuineness of the Gospels, 1855, have not been surpassed by any other work done in this country. As a scholar, he was careful, thorough, honest, and uncompromising in his search for the truth. In an extended note added to the second volume of his work on the Genuineness of the Gospels he investigated the origin of the Pentateuch and the validity of its historical statements. He showed that the work could not have bee its man written by Moses, that it was a compilation from prior accounts, and that its marvels were not to be accepted as authentic history.[3] In dealing with the New Testament, Professor Norton discarded the first two chapters of Matthew, regarding them as later additions. Frothingham speaks of Norton as "an accomplished and elegant scholar," and says that his interpretations of the Bible were by Unitarians "tacitly received as final." "He was the great authority, as bold, fearless, truthful, as he was exact and careful."[4] Although these words of praise intimate that Unitarians were too ready to accept the conclusions of Professor Norton as needing no emendation, yet his work was searching in its character and thoroughly sincere in its methods. Considering the general attitude of scholarship in his day, it was bold and uncompromising, as well as accurate and just.

Another scholar was George Rapall Noyes, who was a country pastor in Brookfield and Petersham from 1827 to 1840, and devoted his leisure to Biblical studies. He became the professor of Hebrew and, lecturer on Biblical Literature in the Harvard Divinity School in 1840. His translations, with notes, of the poetical books of the Old Testament, beginning with Job in 1827, were of great importance as aids, to the interpretation of the Hebrew Scriptures. His translation of the New Testament, which appeared after his death, in 1868, gave the best results of critical studies in homely prose, and with painstaking fidelity to the original. That Noyes was in advance of the criticism of his time may be indicated by the fact that, when he published his conclusions in regard to the Messianic prophecies in 1834,[5] he was threatened with an indictment for blasphemy by the attorney-general of Massachusetts. Better judgment prevailed against this attempt to coerce opinion, but that such an indictment was seriously considered shows how little genuine criticism there was then in existence. What are now the commonplaces of scholarship were then regarded as destructive and blasphemous. Noyes said that the truth of the Christian religion does not in any sense depend upon the literal fulfilment of any predictions in the Old Testament by Jesus as a person.[6] He said that the apostles partook of the errors and prejudices of their age,[7] that the commonly received doctrine of the inspiration of the whole Bible is a millstone about the neck of Christianity,[8] and that the Bible contains much that cannot be regarded as revelation.[9] Even as early as 1835 these opinions were generally accepted by Unitarians; and they were not thought to impair the true worth of the spiritual revelation contained in the Bible, and especially not the divine nature of the teachings of Christ. It was very important, as Dr. Joseph Henry Allen has said, in speaking of Norton and Noyes, that "these decisive first steps were taken by deliberate, conscientious, conservative scholars,—the best and soberest scholars we had to show."[10]

The work of Ezra Abbot especially deserves notice here, because of "the variety and extent of his learning, the retentiveness and accuracy of his memory, the penetration and fairness of his judgment."[11] For fourteen years previous to his death, in 1884, he was the professor of New Testament criticism and interpretation in the Harvard Divinity School. He also rendered important service as a member of the American committee on the revision of the New Testament. His essay on The Authorship of the Fourth Gospel was one of the ablest statements of the conservative view of the origin of that writing. The volume of his Critical Essays, collected after his death, shows the ripe fruits of his "punctilious and vigilant scholarship." He was a zealous Unitarian, and did much to show that the New Testament is in harmony with that faith. In 1843 Rev. Theodore Parker published his translation of De Wette's Introduction to the New Testament, with learned notes. The extreme views of Baur and Zeller were interpreted by Rev. O.B. Frothingham in his The Cradle of the Christ, 1872.

Various attempts were also made by those who were not professional scholars to bring the Bible into harmony with modern religious ideas. One of the most notable of these was that of Dr. William Henry Furness, pastor of the church in Philadelphia from 1825 to 1875. His Remarks on the Four Gospels appeared in 1835, and was followed by Jesus and his Biographers, 1838, Thoughts on the Life and Character of Jesus of Nazareth, 1859, and The Veil Partly Lifted and Jesus Becoming Visible, 1864, as well as several other works. His attempt was to give a rational interpretation of the life of Jesus that should largely eliminate the miraculous and yet preserve the spiritual. These works have little critical value, and yet they have much of charm and suggestiveness as religious expositions of the Gospels. Of somewhat the same nature was Dr. Edmund H. Sears's The Fourth Gospel: The Heart of Christ, 1872, a work of deep spiritual insight.

[Sidenote: The Catholic Influence of Harvard University.]

The catholic and inclusive spirit manifested by the Unitarians in their Biblical studies is worthy of notice, however, much more than any definite results of scholarship produced by them. In the cultivation of the broader academic fields which their control of Harvard University brought within their reach this attitude is especially conspicuous. At no time since it came under their administration has it been used for sectarian purposes, to make proselytes or to compel acceptance of their theology. During the first half of the nineteenth century, Harvard was in some degree distinctly Unitarian; but since 1870 it has been wholly non-sectarian. When the Divinity School was organized, it was provided in its constitution that no denominational requirements should be exacted of professors or students; yet the school was essentially Unitarian until 1878. In that year the president, Charles W. Eliot, asked of Unitarians the sum of $130,000 as an endowment for the school; but he insisted that it should be henceforth wholly unsectarian, and this demand was received with approval and enthusiasm by Unitarians themselves.

Unitarianism in America

In 1879 President Eliot said at a meeting held in the First Church in Boston for the purpose of appealing to Unitarians in behalf of the school: "The Harvard Divinity School is not distinctly Unitarian either by its constitution or by the intention of its founders. The doctrines of the unsectarian sect, called in this century Unitarians, are indeed entitled to respectful consideration in the school so long as it exists, simply because the school was founded, and for two generations, at least, has been supported, by Unitarians. But the government of the University cannot undertake to appoint none but Unitarian teachers, or to grant any peculiar favors to Unitarian students. They cannot, because the founders of the school, themselves Unitarians, imposed upon the University the following fundamental rule for its administration: that every encouragement shall be given to the serious, impartial, and unbiassed investigation of Christian truth, and that no assent to the peculiarities of any denomination of Christians shall be required either of the instructors or students."[12] Dr. Charles Carroll Everett, dean of the school from 1878 to 1900, has said that "in some respects it differs from every other theological seminary in the country." "No pains are taken to learn the denominational relations of students even when they are applicants for aid." "No oversight is exercised over the instruction of any teacher. No teacher is responsible for any other or to any other."[13]

In 1886 compulsory attendance upon prayers was abolished at Harvard University. Religious services are regularly held every week–day morning, on Thursday afternoons, and on Sunday evenings, being conducted by the Plummer professor of Christian morals, with the co–operation of five other preachers, who, as well as the Plummer professor, are selected irrespective of denominational affiliations. In this and other ways the university has made itself thoroughly unsectarian. Its attitude is that of scientific investigation, open–mindedness towards all phases of truth, and freedom of teaching. Theology is thus placed on the same basis with other branches of knowledge, and religion is made independent of merely dogmatic considerations.

This undenominational temper at Harvard University has been developed largely under Unitarian auspices. Its presidents for nearly a century have been Unitarians, namely: John T. Kirkland, 1810–28; Josiah Quincy, 1829–45; Edward Everett, 1846–49; Jared Sparks, 1849–53; James Walker, 1853–60; Cornelius C. Felton, 1860–62; Thomas Hill, 1862–68; and Charles W. Eliot since 1869. Kirkland, Everett, Sparks, Walker, and Hill were Unitarian ministers; but under their administration the university was as little sectarian as at any other time.

280

Unitarianism in America

When the new era of university growth began in 1865, with the founding of Cornell University, the influence of Harvard was widely felt in the development of great unsectarian educational institutions. Although Ezra Cornell was educated as a Friend, he was expelled from that body, and connected himself with no other religious sect. He was essentially a Unitarian, often attending the preaching of Dr. Rufus P. Stebbins. The university which took his name was inspired with the Harvard ideal, and, while recognizing religion as one of the great essential phases of human thought and life, gave and continues to give equal opportunity to all sects.

Another instance of the same spirit is Washington University, which began under Unitarian auspices, but soon developed into an entirely undenominational institution. Members of the Unitarian church in St. Louis secured a charter for a seminary, which in 1853 was organized as the Washington Institute. In 1857 it was reorganized as Washington University, and the charter declared, "No instruction, either sectarian in religion or party in politics, shall be allowed in any department of said university, and no sectarian or party test shall be allowed in the selection of professors, teachers, or other officers of said university or in the admission of scholars thereof, or for any purpose whatever." Sectarian prejudice, however, regarded the university as essentially Unitarian; and for the first twenty years of its existence three–fourths of the gifts and endowments came from persons of that religious body.

Although Dr. William G. Eliot knew nothing of the original movement for forming a seminary under liberal auspices, he gave the institution his unstinted support and encouragement. He was the president of the board of management from the first, and in 1871 he became the chancellor. At his death, in 1887, the university included Smith Academy, Mary Institute, and a manual training school, these being large preparatory schools; the college proper, school of engineering, Henry Shaw school of botany, St. Louis school of fine arts, law school, medical school, and dental college. It then had sixteen hundred students and one hundred and sixty instructors. The endowments have since been largely increased, the number of students has increased to two thousand, and important new buildings have been added. Dr. Eliot gave the university its direction and its unsectarian methods, and it has attained its present position because of his devoted labors. The Leland Stanford Jr. University in California, and Clark University in Massachusetts, both founded by Unitarians, further illustrate the Harvard spirit in education.

[Sidenote: The Work of Horace Mann.]

Horace Mann was an earnest and devoted Unitarian, the intimate friend of Channing and Parker, to both of whom he was largely indebted for his intellectual and spiritual ideals. He was inspired by their ideas of reform and progress, and to their personal sympathy he owed much. It is now universally conceded that to him we are indebted for the diffusion of the common−school idea throughout the country, that he developed and brought to full expression the conception of universal education. In full sympathy with him in this work were such men as Dr. Channing, Edward Everett, Theodore Parker, Josiah Quincy, Samuel J. May, and the younger Robert Rantoul; but he made the common school popular, and put it forward as a national institution. When Mann became the secretary of the Massachusetts Board of Education on its creation, in 1837, the theory that all children should be educated by the state, if not otherwise provided for, was by no means generally accepted; nor was it an accepted theory that such education should be strictly unsectarian.[14] Mann fought the battle for these two ideas, and virtually established them for the whole nation. On the first board one−half the members were Unitarians,—Horace Mann, the younger Robert Rantoul, Jared Sparks, and Edmund Dwight. Some of the staunchest and most devoted and most liberal friends of Mann were of other denominations; but the work for common schools was thoroughly in harmony with Unitarian principles. Edmund Dwight was largely instrumental in securing the establishment of a Board of Education in Massachusetts, and he brought about the election of Horace Mann to fill the position of its secretary. He was a leading merchant in Boston, and his house was a centre for meetings and consultations relating to educational interests. He contributed freely for the purpose of enlarging and improving the state system of common schools, his donations amounting to not less than $35,000.[15]

The first person to clearly advocate the establishment of schools for the training of teachers was Rev. Charles Brooks, minister of the Second Unitarian Church in Hingham from 1821 to 1839, afterwards professor of natural history in the University of the City of New York, and a reformer and author of some reputation in his day. In 1834 he began to write and lecture in behalf of common schools, and especially in the interest of normal schools.[16] He spoke throughout the state in behalf of training schools, with which he had become acquainted in Prussia; he went before the legislature on this subject; and he carried his labors into other states.[17]

Horace Mann took up the idea of professional schools for teachers and made it effective. Edmund Dwight gave $10,000 to the state for this purpose, and schools were established in 1838. When the first of these normal schools opened in Lexington, July 3, 1839, its principal was Rev. Cyrus Peirce, who had been the minister of the Unitarian church in North Reading from 1819 to 1829, and then had been a teacher in North Andover and Nantucket. "Had it not been for Cyrus Peirce," wrote Henry Barnard, "I consider the cause of Normal Schools would have failed or have been postponed for an indefinite period."[18] Dr. William T. Harris has said that "all Normal School work in this country follows substantially one tradition, and this traces back to the course laid down by Cyrus Peirce."[19] In the Lexington school Peirce was succeeded by Samuel J. May, who had been settled over Unitarian churches in Brooklyn and Scituate.[20]

The work done by Horace Mann for education includes his labors as president of Antioch College from 1852 to 1859. He maintained that the chief end of education is the development of character; and he sought to make the college an altruistic community, in which teachers and students should labor together for the best good of all. He put into practice the nonsectarian principle, made the college coeducational, and developed the spirit of individual freedom as one of cardinal importance in education. "The ideas for which he stood," has written one who has carefully studied his work in all its phases, "spread abroad among the people of the Ohio valley, and showed themselves in various state institutions, normal schools, and high schools that were planted in the central west. Altogether, apart from Mr. Mann's visible work in Antioch College may be found agencies which he set at work, whose influence only eternity can measure. It was a great thing to the new west that a high standard of scholarship should be placed before her sons and daughters, and that a few hundred of them should be sent out into every corner of the state, and ultimately to the farthest boundaries of the nation, with a sound scholarship and a love for truth there and then wholly new. His reputation for scholarship and zeal gave his opinions greater weight than those of almost any other man in the country. As a result the most radical educational ideas were received from him with respect; and he carried forward the work of giving a practical embodiment to co–education, non–sectarianism, and the requirements of practical and efficient moral character, as perhaps no other educator could have done. His influence among people, and the aspirations which he kindled in thousands of minds by public addresses and personal contact, did for the people of the Ohio valley a work, the extent and value of which can never be measured."[21]

Unitarianism in America

[Sidenote: Elizabeth Peabody and the Kindergarten.]

Horace Mann was largely influenced by Dr. Channing throughout his career as an educational reformer,[22] as was his wife and her sister, Elizabeth P. Peabody. It was to Channing that Miss Peabody owed her interest in the work of education; and his teachings brought her naturally into association with Bronson Alcott, and made her the leader in introducing the kindergarten into this country. She was influenced by the kindergarten method, at an early date, and she gave years of devoted labor to its extension. In connection with her sister, Mrs. Horace Mann, she wrote Culture in Infancy, 1863, Guide to the Kindergarten, 1877, and Letters to Kindergartners, 1886. As a result of her enthusiastic efforts, kindergartens were opened in Boston in 1864; and it was in 1871 that she organized the American Froebel Union, which became the kindergarten department of the National Educational Association in 1885. The Kindergarten Messenger was begun by her in 1873, and was continued under her editorship until 1877, when it was merged in The New Education.

Miss Peabody's Kindergarten Guide has been described as one of the most important original contributions made to the literature of the subject in this country. Her name is most intimately associated with the educational progress of the country because of her enthusiasm for the right training of children and her spiritual insight as a teacher.

[Sidenote: Work of Unitarian Women for Education.]

Much has been done by Unitarian women to advance the cause of education. The conversations of Margaret Fuller, held in Boston from 1839 to 1844, were an important influence in awakening women to larger intellectual interests; and many of those who attended them were afterwards active in promoting the educational enterprises of the city. In 1873 Miss Abby Williams May, Mrs. Ann Adeline Badger, Miss Lucretia Crocker, and Miss Lucia M. Peabody were elected members of the school committee of Boston, but did not serve, as their right to act in that capacity was questioned. Thereupon the legislature took action, making women eligible to the office. The next year Misses May, Crocker, and Peabody, with Mrs. Kate Gannett Wells, Mrs. Mary Safford Blake, and Miss Lucretia Hale, were elected, and served. In 1875 Misses Crocker, Hale, May, and Peabody were re-elected; and in 1876 Miss Crocker was elected one of the supervisors of the public schools of Boston. It is significant that the first women to hold these positions were Unitarians. It is also worthy of note that Miss Sarah Freeman Clarke, sister of James Freeman Clarke, was the first landscape painter of her sex in the country; and that Mrs. Cornelia W. Walter was the first woman to edit a large daily newspaper, she having become the editor and manager of the Boston Transcript at an early date.

In 1873 was organized by Miss Anna E. Ticknor, daughter of Professor George Ticknor, the historian, the Society to encourage Studies at Home. During the twenty–four years of its existence it conducted by correspondence the reading and studies of over 7,000 women in all parts of the country, and did an important work in enlarging the sphere of women, preparing them for the work of teachers and for social and intellectual service in many directions. The society was discontinued in 1897, because, largely through its influence, many other agencies had come in to do the same work; but the large lending library, which had been an important feature of the activities of the society, was continued under the management of the Anna Ticknor Library Association until 1902. The memorial volume, published in 1897, shows how important had been the work of the Society to encourage Studies at Home, and how many women, who were otherwise deprived of intellectual opportunities, were encouraged, helped, and inspired by it. It was said of Miss Ticknor, by Samuel Eliot, the president of the society throughout the whole period of its existence: "While appreciative of the restrictions which she wished to remove, she was desirous to gratify, if possible, the aspirations of the large number of women throughout the country who would fain obtain an education, and who had little, if any, hope of obtaining it. She was very highly educated herself, and thought more and more of her responsibility to share her advantages with others not possessing them. In addition to these moral and intellectual qualifications, she possessed an executive ability brought into constant prominence by her work as secretary of the society. She was a teacher, an inspirer, a comforter, and, in the best sense, a friend of many and many a lonely and baffled life."[23]

The service of Mrs. Mary Hemenway to education also deserves recognition. Possessed of large wealth, she devoted it to advancing important educational and intellectual interests. She established the Normal School of Swedish Gymnastics in Boston, and provided for its maintenance until it was adopted by the city as a part of its educational system. With her financial support the Hemenway South–western Archaeological Expedition was carried on by Frank H. Cushing and J.W. Fewkes. It was largely because of her efforts that the Montana Industrial School was established, and maintained for about ten years. Her chief work, however, was in the promotion of the study of American history on the part of young persons. When the Old South Meeting–house was threatened with destruction, she contributed $100,000 towards its preservation; and by her energy and perseverance it was devoted to the interests of historical study. The Old South Lectures for Young People were organized in 1883, soon after was begun the publication of the Old South Leaflets, a series of historical prizes was provided for, the Old South Historical Society was organized, and historical pilgrimages were established. All this work was placed in charge of Mr. Edwin D. Mead; and the New England Magazine, of which he was the editor, gave interpretation to these various educational efforts.

Mrs. Hemenway devoted her life to such works as these. It is impossible to enumerate here all her noble undertakings; but they were many. "Mrs. Hemenway was a woman whose interests and sympathies were as broad as the world," says Edwin D. Mead, "but she was a great patriot; and she was pre-eminently that. She had a reverent pride in our position of leadership in the history and movement of modern democracy; and she had a consuming zeal to keep the nation strong and worthy of its best traditions, and to kindle this zeal among the young people of the nation. With all her great enthusiasms, she was an amazingly practical and definite woman. She wasted no time nor strength in vague generalities, either of speech or action. Others might long for the time when the kingdom of God should cover the earth as the waters cover the sea, and she longed for it; but, while others longed, she devoted herself to doing what she could to bring that corner of God's world in which she was set into conformity with the laws of God,—and this by every means in her power, by teaching poor girls how to make better clothes and cook better dinners and make better homes, by teaching people to value health and respect and train their bodies and love better music and better pictures and be interested in more important things. Others might long for the parliament of man and the federation of the world, and so did she; but while others longed, she devoted herself to doing what she could to make this nation, for which she was particularly responsible, fitter for the federation when it comes. The good state for which she worked was a good Massachusetts; and her chief interest, while others talked municipal reform, was to make a better Boston."[24]

[Sidenote: Popular Education and Public Libraries.]

The interest of Unitarians in popular education and the general diffusion of knowledge may be further indicated by a few illustrations. One of these is the Lowell Institute in Boston, founded by John Lowell, son of Francis Cabot Lowell, and cousin of James Russell Lowell. He was a Boston merchant, became an extensive traveller, and died in

Bombay, in 1836, at the age of thirty–four. In his will he left one–half his fortune for the promotion of popular education through lectures, and in other ways. John Amory Lowell became the trustee of this fund, nearly $250,000; and in December, 1839, the Lowell Institute began its work with a lecture by Edward Everett, which gave a biographical account of John Lowell, and a statement of the purposes of the Institute. Since that time the Lowell Institute has given to the people of Boston, free of charge, from fifty to one hundred lectures each winter. The topics treated have taken a wide range, and the lecturers have included many of the ablest men in this and other countries. The work of the Lowell Institute has also included free lectures for advanced students given in connection with the Massachusetts Institute of Technology, science lectures to the teachers of Boston, and a free drawing school.

In 1846 Louis Agassiz came to this country to lecture before the Lowell Institute. The result was that he became permanently connected with Harvard University, and transferred his scientific work to this country. This was accomplished by means of the gift of Abbott Lawrence, who founded the Lawrence Scientific School in 1847. Although the Lowell Institute was founded by a Unitarian, and although it has always been largely managed by Unitarians, it has been wholly unsectarian in its work. Many of its lecturers have been of that body, but only because they were men of science or of literary attainments.

In 1854 Peter Cooper founded the Cooper Union in New York for the Advancement of Science and Art, to promote "instruction in branches of knowledge by which men and women earn their daily bread; in laws of health and improvement of the sanitary conditions of families as well as individuals; in social and political science, whereby communities and nations advance in virtue, wealth, and power; and finally in matters which affect the eye, the ear, and the imagination, and furnish a basis for recreation to the working classes." He erected a large building, and established therein the Cooper Institute, with its reading–room, library, lectures, schools, and other facilities for bringing the means of education within reach of those who could not otherwise obtain them.

Peter Cooper was an earnest Unitarian in his opinions, attending the church of Dr. Bellows; but he was wholly without sectarian bias. In a letter addressed to the delegates to the Evangelical Alliance, at its session held in New York in 1873, he expressed the catholicity and the humanitarian spirit of his religion. "I look to see the day," he wrote, "when the teachers of Christianity will rise above all the cramping power and influence of conflicting creeds and systems of human device, when they will beseech mankind by all the mercies of God to be reconciled to the government of love, the only government that can ever bring the kingdom of heaven into the hearts of mankind either here or hereafter."

About 1825 there was opened in Dublin, N.H., under the auspices of Rev. Levi W. Leonard, minister of the Unitarian church in that village, the first library in the country that was free to all the inhabitants of a town or city. In the adjoining town of Peterboro, in 1833, under the leadership of Rev. Abiel Abbot, also the Unitarian minister, a library was established by vote of the town. This library was maintained by the town itself, being the first in the country supported from the tax rates of a municipality. In the work of these Unitarian ministers may be found the beginnings of the present interest in the establishment and growth of free public libraries.

In the founding and endowment of libraries, Unitarians have taken an active part. What they have done in this direction may be illustrated by the gift of Enoch Pratt of one and a quarter million dollars to the public library in Baltimore. Concerning the time when Jared Sparks was the minister of the Unitarian church in Baltimore, Professor Herbert B. Adams has said: "Some of the most generous and public-spirited people of Baltimore were connected with the first independent church. Afterwards, men who were to be most helpful in the upbuilding of Baltimore's greatest institutions—the Peabody Institute, the Pratt Library, and the Johns Hopkins University—were associated with the Unitarian society."[25]

Professor Barrett Wendell speaks of George Ticknor as "the chief founder of the chief public library in the United States."[26] Ticknor undoubtedly did more than anybody else to make the Boston Public Library the great institution it has become, not only in giving it his own collection of books, but also in its inception and in its organization. The best working library in the country, that of the Boston Athenaeum, also owes a very large debt to the early Unitarians, with whom it originated, and by whom it was largely maintained in its early days.

[Sidenote: Mayo's Southern Ministry of Education.]

One of the most important contributions to the work of education has been that of Rev. Amory D. Mayo, known as the "Ministry of Education in the South." After settlements over churches in Gloucester, Cleveland, Albany, Cincinnati, and Springfield, Mr. Mayo began his southern work in 1880. He had an extensive preparation for his southern labors, having served on the school boards of Cincinnati and Springfield for fifteen years, lectured extensively on educational subjects, and been a frequent contributor to educational periodicals. He has written a History of Common Schools, which is published by the national Bureau of Education, prepared several of the Circulars of Information of that bureau, and printed a great number of educational pamphlets and addresses.

"One of the most helpful agencies in the work of free and universal education in the South, for the last twenty years," says Dr. J.L.M. Curry in a personal letter, "has been the ministry of A.D. Mayo. His intelligent zeal, his instructive addresses, his tireless energy, have made him a potent factor in this great work; and any history of what the Unitarian denomination has done would be very imperfect which did not make proper and grateful recognition of his valuable services."

[1] Christian Examiner, XLVII. 186; Mrs. E.B. Lee, Memoirs of the
    Buckminsters, 325.

[2] Memoir of Buckminster, introductory to his Sermons, published in
    1814, xxxii.

[3] The Pentateuch and its Relation to the Jewish and Christian
    Dispensation. By Andrews Norton. Edited by John James Tayler, London,
    1863. This was the Note, with introduction.

[4] Boston Unitarianism, 244.

[5] Hengstenberg's Christology, Christian Examiner, July, 1834, XVI. 321.

[6] Ibid., 327.

[7] Ibid., 356.

[8] Ibid., 357.

[9] Ibid., 358.

[10] Our Liberal Movement in Theology, 68.

[11] The Authorship of the Fourth Gospel and Other Critical Essays selected from the published papers of Ezra Abbot, edited, with preface, by Professor J.H. Thayer.

[12] The Divinity School of Harvard University: Its History, Courses of Study, Aims, and Advantages, published by the University, 9.

[13] The Divinity School as it is, Harvard Graduates' Magazine, June, 1897.

[14] B.A. Hinsdale, Horace Mann and the Common School Revival in the United States, 127.

[15] B.A. Hinsdale, Horace Mann and the Common School Revival in the United States, 148.

[16] Henry Barnard, Normal Schools, 125.

[17] B.A. Hinsdale, Horace Mann, 147.

[18] Quoted by J.P. Gordy, Rise and Growth of the Normal School Idea in the United States, Circular of Information of the Bureau of Education, 1891, 49.

[19] Ibid., 43.

[20] S.J. May, Memoir of Cyrus Peirce, Barnard's American Journal of Education, December, 1857.

[21] G.A. Hubbell, Horace Mann in Ohio: A Study of the Application of his Public School Ideals to College Administration, No. IV. of Vol. VII., Columbia University Contributions to Philosophy, Psychology, and Education, 50.

[22] Mary Mann, Life of Horace Mann, 44; Henry Barnard, Normal Schools, 93.

[23] Memorial Volume, 2.

[24] Edwin D. Mead, The Old South Work, 1900; also Memorial Sermon, by Charles G. Ames, 17.

[25] Life and Writings of Jared Sparks, I. 141.

[26] A Literary History of America, 266.

XIX. UNITARIANISM AND LITERATURE.

The history of American literature is intimately connected with the history of Unitarianism in this country. The influences that caused the growth of Unitarianism were those, to a large extent, that produced American literature. It was not merely Harvard College that had this effect, as has been often asserted; for the other colleges did not become the centres of literary activity. It was more distinctly the freedom, the breadth of intellectual interest, and the sympathy with what was human and natural developed by the Unitarian movement that were favorable to the growth of literature. Yet from the beginning of the eighteenth century Harvard fostered the spirit of inquiry, and helped to set the mind free from the theological and classical predispositions that had checked its natural growth. A taste for literature was encouraged, theology took on a broad and humanitarian character, and there was a growing appreciation of art and poetry. Harvard College helped to bring men into contact with European thought, and thus opened to them fresh and stimulating sources of intellectual interest.

During the last quarter of the eighteenth century and the first half of the nineteenth New England was largely devoted to commercial enterprises. Every coast town of any size from Newport to Belfast was concerned with ship-building and with trade to foreign ports. Such towns as Boston and Salem traded with China, India, and many other parts of the world. Not only was wealth largely increased by this commercial activity, but the influence upon life and thought was very great. The mind was emancipated, and religion grew more liberal and humane, as the result of this contact with foreign lands. Along the whole coast, within the limits named, there was an abandonment of Puritanism and a growth into a genial and humanitarian interpretation of Christianity. In New York City somewhat the same results were produced, at least on social and intellectual life, though with less immediate effect upon religion. It was in these regions, in which commercial contact with the great outside world set the mind free and awakened the imagination, that American literature was born.

[Sidenote: Influence of Unitarian Environment.]

The influence of Unitarian culture and literary tastes is shown by the considerable number of literary men who were the sons of Unitarian ministers. Ralph Waldo Emerson was the son of William Emerson, the minister of the First Church in Boston at the beginning of the nineteenth century. George Bancroft was the son of Aaron Bancroft, the first Unitarian minister in Worcester, and the first president of the American Unitarian Association. To Charles Lowell, of the West Church in Boston, were born James Russell Lowell and Robert T.S. Lowell. The father of Francis Parkman was of the same name, and was for many years the minister of the New North Church in Boston. Richard Hildreth was the son of Hosea Hildreth, Unitarian minister in Gloucester. Octavius Brooks Frothingham was the son of Nathaniel L. Frothingham, minister of the First Church in Boston. Joseph Allen, father of Joseph Henry Allen and William Francis Allen, was the minister in Northboro for many years. Of literary workers now living William Everett is the son of Edward Everett, Charles Eliot Norton of Andrews Norton, and William Wells Newell of William Newell, minister of the First Church in Cambridge for many years.

This influence is shown in the large number of literary men who studied at the Harvard Divinity School and began their career as Unitarian ministers. It may be partly accounted for by the fact that at the beginning of the nineteenth century literature offered but a precarious opportunity to men of talent and genius. The respect then accorded to ministers, the wide influence they were able to exert, and the many intellectual opportunities offered by the profession, naturally attracted many young men. During the first part of the nineteenth century no other profession was so attractive, and enthusiasm for it was large amongst the students of Harvard College. As literary openings began to present themselves, many of these men found other occupations, partly because their tastes were intellectual rather than theological, and partly because the radical ferment made the pulpit no longer acceptable. Such a man as Edward Everett would never have entered the pulpit, had it not been socially and intellectually most attractive at the time when he began his career. In the instance of Samuel A. Eliot, who took the full course in the Divinity School, but did not preach, being afterward mayor of Boston and member of Congress the influences at work were probably much the same.

George Bancroft is another instance of a graduate of the Divinity School who did not enter the pulpit, but, beginning his career as a teacher, devoted his life to literature and diplomacy. With such men as Christopher P. Cranch, artist and poet; George P. Bradford, teacher, thinker, and friend of literary men; H.G.O. Blake, editor of Thoreau's Journals; J.L. Sibley, librarian; John Albee, poet and essayist; and William Cushing, bibliographer, the cause operating was probably the same,—the discovery that the chosen profession was not acceptable or that some other was preferable. Another group of men, including John G. Palfrey, Jared Sparks, William Ware, Horatio Alger, James K. Hosmer, Edward Rowland Sill and William Wells Newell, who occupied Unitarian pulpits for brief periods, were drawn into literary occupations as more congenial to their tastes. The same influence doubtless served to withdraw Emerson, George Ripley, John S. Dwight, Thomas W. Higginson, Moncure D. Conway, and Francis E. Abbot, from the pulpit; but with these men there was also a break with traditional Christianity.

[Sidenote: Literary Tendencies.]

The early Unitarian movement in New England was literary and religious rather than theological. The men who have been most influential in determining the course of Unitarian development, such as Charming, Dewey, Parker, and Hedge, not to include Emerson, who has been a greater affirmative leader than either of the others, were first of all preachers, and their published works were originally given to the world from the pulpit. They made no effort to produce a Unitarian system of theology; and it would have been quite in opposition to the genius of the movement, had they entered upon such a task.

With the advent of the Unitarian movement, for the first time in the history of the American pulpit did the sermon become a literary product. Channing and his coworkers, especially Buckminster and Everett, departed widely from the pulpit traditions of New England, ceased to quote texts, abandoned theological exposition, refrained from the exhortatory method, and addressed men and women in literary language about the actual interests of daily life. Their preaching was not metaphysical, and it was not declamatory.

The illustrations used were human rather than Biblical, a preference was given to what was intellectual rather than to what was emotional, and the effect was instruction rather than conversion. It resulted in faithful living, good citizenship, fidelity to duty, love of the neighbor, and an earnest helpfulness toward the poor and unfortunate.

[Sidenote: Literary Tastes of Unitarian Ministers.]

In studying any considerable list of Unitarian ministers, and taking note of their personal tastes and their avocations, it will be seen that a large number of them were lovers of literature, and ardently devoted much of their time to literary pursuits. Not only was there a decidedly literary flavor about their preaching, but they were frequent contributors to The Christian Examiner and The North American Review; and they wrote poems, novels, books of travel, essays, and histories. They were conspicuous in historical and scientific societies, in promoting scientific investigations, in advancing archaeological researches, in every kind of learned inquiry. Their intellectual interests were so catholic and so vigorous that they were not contented with parish and pulpit, and in some cases it would seem that the avocation was as important as the vocation itself.

Dr. Channing would be named as the man who has done most to give direction to the currents of Unitarian thought on theological problems, but he was also conspicuously a philanthropist and reformer. He was less a theologian, in the technical sense, than one who taught men to live in the spirit. His spiritual insight, humanitarian sympathies, and imaginative fellowship with all forms of human experience gave his writings a literary charm and power of a high order. He was a great religious teacher and inspirer, a preacher of unsurpassed gifts of spiritual interpretation, and a prophet of the truer religious life.

The Unitarian leaders who were influenced by the transcendental movement, of which the most prominent were Parker, Hedge, Clarke, and C.C. Everett, interpreted theology in the broadest spirit. Parker was essentially a preacher and reformer. It was the one conspicuous aim of his life to liberate religion from the intellectual thraldom of the past, and to bring it into the open air of the world, where it might be informed of daily experience and gain for itself a rightful opportunity. He was therefore literary, imaginative, ethical, practical. He wrote for The Dial, and established The Massachusetts Review, he was one of the most widely heard of popular lecturers, and he was a leader in the most radical of the reforms prominent in his day. Parker made all wisdom subservient to his religion, treated a wide range of subjects in his pulpit, and brought religion into immediate contact with human life.

Frederic H. Hedge did more than any other man to give Unitarianism a consistent philosophy and theology. His Reason in Religion and Ways of the Spirit have had a profound influence in shaping the thought of the denomination, and have led all American Unitarians to accept his view of the universality of incarnation and the consubstantiality of man and God. He was wise as an interpreter, and by no means wanting in originality, a brilliant essayist, a philosophical historian, and a student of high themes. His Prose Writers of Germany, Hours with the German Classics, Primeval World of Hebrew Tradition, and Atheism in Philosophy show the range of his interests and his ability as a thinker.

James Freeman Clarke may be selected as a typical Unitarian minister, who wrote poetry, was more than once an editor, often appeared on the lecture platform, was a frequent contributor to the leading periodicals, wrote several works of biography and history, gave himself zealously to the advocacy of the noblest reforms, and produced many volumes of sermons that have in an unusual degree the merit of directness, literary grace, suggestiveness, and spiritual warmth and insight. His theological writings have been widely read by Unitarians and those not of that fellowship. His Self—culture has been largely circulated as a manual of practical ethics. His Ten Great Religions and its companion volume opened the way in this country for the recognition of the comparative study of religious developments. Not content with so wide a range of studies, he wrote Thomas Didymus, an historical romance concerned with New Testament characters, How to find the Stars, and Exotics, a volume of poetical translation. He was a maker of many books, and all of them were well made. His theology was all the more humane, and his preaching was all the more effective, because he was interested in many subjects and had a real mastery of them.

Charles Carroll Everett was a philosophical thinker and theologian, and the younger generation of Unitarian ministers has been largely influenced by him. His theological work was done in the lecture—room, but it was of first—rate importance. He was a profound thinker, a vigorous writer, and an inspiring teacher. He was an able theologian, philosophical in thought, but deeply spiritual in insight. His work on The Science of Thought shows the depth and vigor of his thinking; but his volumes on The Gospel of Paul, Religions before Christianity, Poetry, Comedy, and Duty, suggest the breadth of his inquiries and the richness of his philosophical investigations. In his position as the dean of the Harvard Divinity School he accomplished his best work, and there his great ability as theologian and philosophical thinker made itself amply manifest.

Another group of men largely influenced by the transcendental movement included David A. Wasson, John Weiss, Samuel Johnson, Samuel Longfellow, Cyrus A. Bartol, Octavius K Frothingham, and William J. Potter. Here we see the literary tendency showing itself distinctly and to much advantage. The first four of these men wrote exquisite hymns and spiritual lyrics, and all of them were contributors to periodical literature or writers of books. Weiss was a literary critic of no mean merit in his lectures on Greek and Shakespearean subjects; and his volumes on American Religion and Immortal Life were purely literary in their method. However deficient were Johnson's books on the religions of India, China, and Persia, from the point, of view of the science of religion, they have not yet been surpassed as interpretations of the inner spirit of Oriental religions. Bartol was a master of an incisive literary method in the pulpit, that gives to his Radical Problems, The Rising Faith, and Principles and Portraits a scintillating power all their own, with epigram and flash of wit on every page. Frothingham published many a volume of sermons; but his biographies of Parker, Gerrit Smith, Wasson, Johnson, Ripley, Channing, and his volume on the History of Transcendentalism in New England, as well as his Boston Unitarianism, and Recollections and Impressions, indicate that his literary interests were quite as active as his theological.

The literary tastes of Unitarian ministers are indicated by the large number of them who have written poetry that passes beyond the limits of mediocrity. The names of John Pierpont, Andrews Norton, Samuel Gilman, Nathaniel L. Frothingham, the younger Henry Ware, W.B.O. Peabody, William Henry Furness, William Newell, William Parsons Lunt, Frederic H. Hedge, James F. Clarke, Theodore Parker, Chandler Robbins, Edmund H. Sears, Charles T. Brooks, Robert C. Waterston, Thomas Hill, and others, have been lovingly commemorated in Alfred P. Putnam's Singers and Songs of the Liberal Faith. Hymns of nearly all these men are in common use in many congregations, and some of their work has found a place in every hymnal.

No one can read the sermons of Thomas Starr King without feeling their literary grace and finish of style, as well as their intellectual vigor. His lectures marked his literary interest, which shows itself in his Christianity and Humanity and his Substance and

Show. Especially does it appear in his delightful book on The White Hills, their Legends, Landscape, and Poetry. In his day, Henry Giles was widely known as a lecturer; and his numerous volumes of literary interpretation and criticism, especially his Human Life in Shakespeare, were read with appreciation. In his District School as it was, and My Religious Experience at my Native Home, Warren Burton described in simple but effective prose a kind of life that has long since passed away. His educational lectures and books helped on the cause of public school education, a subject in which he was greatly interested.

Unitarian ministers have also made many contributions to local and general history. The history of King's Chapel by Francis W.P. Greenwood may be mentioned as a specimen of the former kind of work; but Greenwood also published several volumes of sermons, as well as biographical and literary volumes. A History of the Second Church in Boston, with Lives of Increase and Cotton Mather, was published by Chandler Robbins. The theological history of Unitarianism was ably discussed by George E. Ellis in A Half–century of the Unitarian Controversy. He devoted much attention to the history of New England, gave many lectures and addresses on subjects connected therewith, published biographies of Anne Hutchinson, William Penn, Count Rumford, Jared Sparks, and Charles W. Upham. His volumes on The Red Man and the White Man in North America, The Puritan Theocracy, and others, show his historical ability and his large grasp of his subjects. Joseph Henry Allen published an Historical Sketch of the Unitarian Movement since the Reformation, in the American Church History series. In Our Liberal Movement in Theology, and its Sequel, he critically and appreciatively treated of the history of Unitarianism in New England, and of the men who were most important in its development. His taste for historical studies appeared in his Christian History in its Three Great Periods, a work of admirable critical judgment, sobriety of statement, and concise presentation of the essential facts.

Alvan Lamson produced a book of critical value in The Church of the First Three Centuries, which treats of the origin of the Trinitarian beliefs during that period. A work of a similar character was done by Frederic Huidekoper, in whose books were included the results of many years of minute research, and of critical investigation into the origins of Christianity.

Books of a widely different nature were written by Artemas B. Muzzey in his Personal Recollection of the Men in the Battle of Lexington, and Reminiscences of Men of the

Revolution and their Families. He published several volumes of sermons, as well as a number of educational works. Somewhat of a theologian and an ardent student and expounder of philosophy, William R. Alger has made himself widely known by his books on The Genius of Solitude, Friendships of Women, and The School of Life. His fine literary judgments, his artistic appreciations, and his richness of sentiment and imagination show themselves in these attractive volumes. He has also published a Life of Edwin Forrest, with a Critical History of the Dramatic Art. His Critical History of the Doctrine of a Future Life is a work of ripe scholarship and great literary merit, and is everywhere recognized as an authority.

[Sidenote: Unitarians as Historians.]

In the chapter on historians, in his American Literature, Professor Charles F. Richardson enumerates seventeen writers, twelve of whom were Unitarians. It was in Cambridge and Boston, amongst the graduates of Harvard College, that American historical writing began, and that it attained its greatest successes. The same causes that had given the Unitarians pre-eminence in other directions made them especially so in this, where wide learning and sound criticism were of importance. Wealth, leisure, intellectual emancipation, sympathetic interest in all that is human, combined with scholarship and plodding industry, gave the historians an unusual equipment for their tasks.

It may be justly said that historical writing in this country began with Jeremy Belknap, the predecessor of Dr. Channing in the Federal Street Church. When settled in Dover, he wrote his History of New Hampshire; and after his removal to Boston he produced a biography of Watts and two volumes of American Biographies. He first voiced the historical interest that was awakened by the establishment of national independence, and the desire to know of the past of the American people. His chief service to historical studies, however, was in the formation of the Massachusetts Historical Society.

Hannah Adams was not only a Unitarian, but the first woman in this country to enter upon a literary career. Her View of Religious Opinions, first issued in 1784, afterwards changed to a Dictionary of Religions, was the earliest work attempting to give an account of all the religions of the world. It was followed by her History of New England, and by her History of the Jews. She also took part in the religious controversies of the day, her contest with Dr. Jedediah Morse being one of the minor phases of the struggle between the Unitarians and the Orthodox Congregationalists; and her Evidences of Christianity, as well as her letters on the Gospels, were written from the Unitarian point of view. Her books had no literary value, but in their time they helped to foster the growing interest in American subjects.

Alexander Young, minister of the New South Church in Boston, rendered valuable service to historical investigations by his Chronicles of the Pilgrim Fathers of the Colony of Plymouth and his Chronicles of the First Planters of the Colony of Massachusetts Bay, works that were scholarly, accurate, and judicious. Perhaps his most important service was the editing of the Library of Old English Prose Writers, in nine volumes, which appeared from 1831 to 1834, and included such works as Sidney's Defence of Poesie and Sir Thomas Browne's Urn Burial. Of his historical works, O.B. Frothingham has justly said that "they showed extensive and accurate knowledge, extraordinary zeal in research, singular impartiality of judgment, great activity of mind, a strong inclination towards ethical as distinguished from speculative subjects, a passionate love of books and elegant letters."[1]

Of the greater historians, Bancroft, Prescott, Motley, Hildreth, Sparks, Palfrey, Ticknor, Parkman, Higginson, Parton, and Fiske were Unitarians. Three of these men were sons of Unitarian ministers, and four of them prepared for that profession or entered upon its duties. It is not desirable that any attempt should be made here to estimate their historical labors, for their position and their achievements are well known.

It would be interesting to give an account of the Unitarian connections and sympathies of these writers, but the materials are not at hand in the case of most of them. One or two illustrations will suffice for them all, indicating their religious tastes and preferences. In 1829 Prescott made a careful examination of the evidences for belief in Christianity, and his biographer says that "the conclusions at which he arrived were, that the narratives of the Gospels were authentic; and that, even if Christianity were not a divine revelation, no system of morals was so likely to fit him for happiness here and hereafter. But he did not find in the Gospels or in any part of the New Testament the doctrines commonly accounted orthodox, and he deliberately recorded his rejection of them." At a later time he stated his creed in these words: "To do well and act justly, to fear and to love God, and to love our neighbor as ourselves—in these is the essence of religion. To do this is the safest, our only safe course. For what we can believe we are not responsible, supposing we examine candidly and patiently. For what we do we shall indeed be accountable. The doctrines of the Saviour unfold the whole code of morals by which our conduct should be regulated."[2] Prescott was a regular attendant at the First Church in Boston.

In his biography of George Ticknor, George S. Hilliard says that "the strong religious impressions which Mr. Ticknor received in early years deepened as his character matured into personal convictions, the confirmed and ruling principles of his life. He had been brought up in the doctrines of Calvinistic orthodoxy, but later serious reflection led him to reject those doctrines; and soon after his return from Europe he joined Dr. Channing's church, of which he continued through life a faithful member. He was a sincere Liberal Christian, and his convictions were firm, but they were held without bigotry, and he never allowed them to interfere with kindliness and courtesy." It may be added that Ticknor was an active member of the church with which he was connected, that in 1822 he took charge of a class of boys in the Sunday–school, which he kept for eight years. In 1839 and the next year he gave a course of instruction in the history and contents of the Bible to a class of young girls, for which he prepared himself carefully.[3]

The influence exerted by the historians in teaching love of country and a true patriotism may be accounted as very large. That men thoroughly grounded in principles of religious liberty, in high ideals of justice and humanity, in the broadest spirit of toleration and freedom of opinion, should have written our histories, is of no small importance in the formation of American character. That they have made many Unitarians we cannot suppose, but that their influence has been large in the development of a true spirit of nationality we have a right to think. They have indicated concretely the effects of bigotry and intolerance, and they have not failed to point out the defects in the practices of the Puritans. In so far as they have had to deal with religious subjects, they have taught the true Unitarian idea of liberty of conscience and freedom of opinion. They have wisely helped to make it possible for many religions to live kindly side by side, and to give every creed the right of utterance. These ideals had been developed before our historians began to write, but these men have helped to make them the inheritance of the whole nation. All the more effective has been their teaching that it has grown out of the events of our history, and has not been the voice of a merely personal opinion. But we owe much to them that they have seen the true meaning of our history, and that they have uttered it with clearness of interpretation and with vigorous moral emphasis.

[Sidenote: Scientific Unitarians.]

A considerable number of the leading men of science have been Unitarians. Notable among the mathematicians were Nathaniel Bowditch, Benjamin Peirce, and Thomas Hill, who was president of Antioch College and of Harvard University. Among the astronomers have been Benjamin Gould, Maria Mitchell, Asaph Hall, and Edward C. Picketing. Of Maria Mitchell it was said that she "was entirely ignorant of the peculiar phrases and customs of rigid sectarians." Her biographer says she "never joined any church, but for years before she left Nantucket she attended the Unitarian church, and her sympathies, as long as she lived, were with that denomination, especially with the more liberally inclined portion."[4] James Jackson, the first physician of the Massachusetts General Hospital, should be named in this connection. Joseph Lovering, the physicist, and Jeffries Wyman, the comparative anatomist, are also to be included. And here belongs Louis Agassiz, who has had more influence than any other man in developing an interest in science among the people generally. He gave to scientific investigations the largest importance for scientific men themselves. At the same time he was a religious man and a theist. "In religion," says his biographer, "Agassiz very liberal and tolerant, and respected the views and convictions of every one. In his youth and early manhood, Agassiz was undoubtedly a materialist, or, more exactly, a sceptic; but in time, and little by little, his studies led him to belief in a divine Creative Power. He was more in sympathy with Unitarianism than with any other Christian denomination."[5]

[Sidenote: Unitarian Essayists.]

A considerable number of essayists, lecturers, and general writers have been Unitarians. Among these have been Edwin P. Whipple, George Ripley, Mrs. Ednah D. Cheney, John S. Dwight, Professor Charles Eliot Norton, Henry T. Tuckerman, James T. Fields, and Professor Francis J. Child. These writers represent several phases of Unitarian opinion, but they belong to this fellowship by birthright or intellectual sympathies. In the same company may be placed Henry D. Thoreau and John Burroughs, not because they had any direct connection with Unitarianism, but because the religious convictions they expressed are such as most Unitarians accept.

To the Unitarian fellowship belong Margaret Fuller, Lydia Maria Child, Caroline M. Kirkland, Grace Greenwood (Mrs. Lippincott), and Julia Ward Howe. All the early associations of Margaret Fuller were with Unitarians; and her brother, Arthur Fuller, became a Unitarian minister. In her maturer life she was with the transcendentalists, finding in Rev. W.H. Channing and Emerson her spiritual teachers. Writing of her debt to

Emerson, she said, "His influence has been more beneficial to me than that of any American; and from him I first learned what is meant by an inward life."[6] She was a pronounced individualist, an intense lover of spiritual liberty, a friend of those who live in the spirit. This may be seen in what she called her credo, a sentence or two from which will indicate her type of thought. "I will not loathe sects, persuasions, systems," she writes, "though I cannot abide in them one moment; for I see that by most men they are still needed." "Ages may not produce one worthy to loose the shoes of the Prophet of Nazareth; yet there will surely be another manifestation of this word which was in the beginning. The very greatness of this manifestation demands a greater. We have had a Messiah to teach and reconcile. Let us now have a man to live out all the symbolical forms of human life, with the calm beauty of a Greek god, with the deep consciousness of Moses, with the holy love and purity of Jesus."[7]

[Sidenote: Unitarian Novelists.]

Among the novelists have been several who were Unitarian ministers, including Sylvester Judd, William Ware, Thomas W. Higginson, and Edward Everett Hale. Judd's Margaret was of the very essence of transcendentalism, besides being an excellent interpretation of some of the phases of New England character. Ware's historical novels were popular in their day, and are now worth going back to by modern readers, and especially by those who do not insist upon having their romances hot from the press. Catherine M. Sedgwick is another novelist worth returning to by modern readers, and especially by those who would know of New England life in the early part of the nineteenth century. She became an ardent Unitarian, and her biography gives interesting glimpses of the early struggles of that faith in York City. Other Unitarian women novelists were Lydia Maria Child, Grace Greenwood, Helen Hunt Jackson, Louisa M. Alcott, and Harriet Prescott Spofford.

In naming John T. Trowbridge, Bayard Taylor, Bret Harte, William D. Howells, and Nathaniel Hawthorne as Unitarians, no merely sectarian aim is in view. In the common use of the word, Hawthorne was not a religious man; for he rarely attended church, and he had no interest in ecclesiastical formalities. No man who has written in this country, however, was more deeply influenced than he by those spiritual ideas and traditions which may be properly called Unitarian. The same may be said of Howells, who is not a Unitarian in any denominational sense; but his religious interests and convictions bring him into sympathy with the movement represented by Unitarianism.

Unitarianism in America

It may be said of the most popular novels of Edward Everett Hale, such as Ten Times One Is Ten, In His Name, His Level Best, that they are the best possible interpretations of the Unitarian spirit; for it is not merely a certain conception of God that characterizes Unitarianism, nor yet a particular theological attitude. It is the wish to make religion real, practical, altruistic.

[Sidenote: Unitarian Artists and Poets.]

Unitarianism has been as friendly to poetry and the other arts as it has been to philosophy and science. In its early days it fostered the artistic careers of Washington Allston, the painter, and Charles Bulfinch, the architect. It has also nurtured the sculptors, William Wetmore Story, who was also poet and essayist; Harriet Hosmer, whose career shows what a woman can accomplish in opening new opportunities for her sex; Larkin G. Mead and Daniel C. French. To these must be added the actors Fanny Kemble and Charlotte Cushman.

It is as one of the earliest of our poets that Charles Sprague is to be mentioned, and one or two of his poems are deservedly remembered. Jones Very was one of the best of the transcendental poets, and a few of his religious poems have not been surpassed. The younger William Ellery Channing and Edward R. Sill belong to the same school, and deservedly keep their places with those who admire what is choice in thought and individual in artistic workmanship. As a biographer of O.B. Frothingham and as a member of his congregation, it may be proper to add here the name of Edmund C. Stedman.

Among our greater poets, Bryant, Longfellow, Emerson, Holmes, Lowell, Stoddard, and Bayard Taylor were Unitarians. As being essentially of the same way of thinking and believing, Whittier and Whitman might also be so classed. Though Whittier was a Friend by education and by conviction, he was of the liberal school that places religion above sect and interprets dogmas in the light of human needs and affections. If he had been born and bred a Unitarian, he could not have more sympathetically interpreted the Unitarian faith than he has in his poems. Whitman had in him the heart of transcendentalism, and he was informed of its inmost spirit. To the more radical Unitarians his pleas for liberty, his intense individualism, and his idealistic conceptions of nature and man would be acceptable, and, it may be, enthusiastically approved.

William Cullen Bryant early became a Unitarian; and he listened to the preaching of Follen, Dewey, Osgood, and Bellows. "A devoted lover of religious liberty," Bellows said of him, "he was an equal lover of religion itself—not in any precise, dogmatic form, but in its righteousness, reverence, and charity. He was not a dogmatist, but preferred practical piety and working virtue to all modes of faith."[8] It would be difficult to give a better definition of Unitarianism itself; and it was the large humanity of it, and its generous outlook upon the lives of individuals and nations, that made of Bryant a faithful Unitarian.

Henry W. Longfellow was educated as a Unitarian, his father having been one of the first vice–presidents of the Unitarian Association,—a position he held for many years. Stephen Longfellow was an intimate friend of Dr. Channing in his college years, and he followed the advance of his classmate in the growth of his liberal faith. "It was in the doctrine and the spirit of the early Unitarianism that Henry Longfellow was nurtured at church and at home," says his brother. "And there is no reason to suppose that he ever found these insufficient, or that he ever essentially departed from them. Of his genuine religious feeling his writings, give ample testimony. His nature was at heart devout; his ideas of life, of death, and of what lies beyond, were essentially cheerful, hopeful, optimistic. He did not care to talk much on theological points; but he believed in the supremacy of good in the world and in the universe."[9]

Although Oliver Wendell Holmes was educated in the older forms of religious beliefs, he became one of the most devoted of Unitarians. His rejection of Calvinism is marked by his intense aversion to it, shown upon many a page of his prose and poetry. No other prominent Unitarian was so aggressive against the doctrines of the older time. He was a regular attendant at King's Chapel upon the preaching of Dr. F.W.P. Greenwood, Dr. Ephraim Peabody, and Rev. H.W. Foote; but, when he was in Pittsfield, for a number of years he went to the Episcopal church, and at Beverly Farms in his later years, during the summer, he attended a Baptist church. He was, therefore, a conservative Unitarian, but with a generous recognition of the good in other religious bodies. At the Unitarian Festival of 1859 Dr. Holmes was the presiding officer, and in his address he gave a statement of the Unitarian faith that clearly defines his own religious position:—

We believe in vital religion, or the religion of life, as contrasted
with that of trust in hierarchies, establishments, and traditional
formulae, settled by the votes of wavering majorities in old councils

and convocations. We believe in evangelical religion, or the religion
of glad tidings, in distinction from the schemes that make our planet
the ante–chamber of the mansions of eternal woe to the vast majority of
all the men, women, and children that have lived and suffered upon its
surface. We believe that every age must judge the Scriptures by its own
light; and we mean, by God's grace, to exercise that privilege, without
asking permission of pope or bishop, or any other human tribunal. We
believe that sin is the much–abused step–daughter of ignorance, and
this not only from our own observation, but on the authority of him
whose last prayer on earth was that the perpetrators of the greatest
crime on record might be forgiven, for they knew not what they were
doing. We believe, beyond all other beliefs, in the fatherly relation
of the Deity to all his creatures; and, wherever there is a conflict of
Scriptural or theological doctrines, we hold this to be the article of
faith that stands supreme above all others. And, lastly, we know that,
whether we agree precisely in these or any other articles of belief, we
can meet in Christian charity and fellowship, in that we all agree in
the love of our race, and the worship of a common Father, as taught us
by the Master whom we profess to follow.[10]

Educated as a Unitarian, James Russell Lowell felt none of the animosity toward
Calvinism that was characteristic of Holmes; but his poetry everywhere indicates the
liberality and nobleness of his religious convictions. That he was not sectarian, that he
felt no active interest in dogmatic theology as such, is only saying that he was a genuine
Unitarian. Writing in 1838, Lowell said, "I am an infidel to the Christianity of
to–day."[11] In a letter to Longfellow written in 1845, he made a more explicit statement
of his attitude: "Christ has declared war against the Christianity of the world, and it must
down. There is no help for it. The church, that great bulwark of our practical paganism,
must be reformed from foundation to weathercock."[12] These passages indicate his
dissatisfaction with an external religion and with dogmatic theology. On the other hand,
his letters and his poems prove that he was strongly grounded in the faith of the spirit. In
that faith he lived and died; and, if in later years he gave recognition to some of the
higher claims of the older types of Christianity, it was a generous concession to their
rational qualities and their practical results, and in no degree an acceptance of their
teachings. The definite form of Lowell's faith he expressed when he wrote, "I will never
enter a church from which a prayer goes up for the prosperous only, or for the

unfortunate among the oppressors, and not for the oppressed and fallen; as if God had ordained our pride of caste and our distinctions of color, and as if Christ had forgotten those that are in bonds."[13]

Emerson left the pulpit, and he withdrew from outward conformity to the church; but that there came a time when he no longer felt an interest in religion or that he even ceased to be a Christian, after his own manner of interpretation, there is no reason to assume. His radicalism was in the direction of a deeper and truer religion, a religion of the spirit. He rejected the faith that is founded on the letter, on historical evidences, that is a body without a soul. He was not the less a Unitarian because he ceased to be one outwardly, for he carried forward the Unitarian principles to their legitimate conclusion. The newer Unitarianism owes to him more than to any other man, and of him more than of any other man the older Unitarianism can boast that he was its product.

Such a survey as this indicates how great has been the influence of Unitarianism upon American literature. There can be no question that it has been one of the greatest formative forces in its development. "Almost everybody," says Professor Barrett Wendell, "who attained literary distinction in New England during the nineteenth century was either a Unitarian or closely associated with Unitarian influences,"[14] More even than that may be said, for it is the Unitarian writers who have most truly interpreted American institutions and American ideals.

[1] Boston Unitarianism, 168.

[2] George Ticknor, Life of William Hickling Prescott, 91, 164.

[3] George S. Hillard, Life, Letters, and Journals of George Ticknor, 327.

[4] Phoebe Mitchell Kendall, Life, Letters, and Journals of Maria Mitchell, 239.

[5] Jules Marcou, Life of Agassiz, II. 220.

[6] Memoirs, I. 194.

[7] Memoirs, II. 91.

[8] John Bigelow, Life of Bryant, 274, 285.

[9] Samuel Longfellow, Life of H.W. Longfellow, I. 14

[10] Quarterly Journal, VI. 359, July, 1859.

[11] Biography of James Russell Lowell, by H.E. Scudder, I. 63.

[12] Ibid., 169.

[13] Biography of James Russell Lowell, by H.E. Scudder, I. 144, quoted
from Conversations on Some of the Old Poets.

[14] A Literary History of America, 289.

XX. THE FUTURE OF UNITARIANISM.

The early Unitarians in this country did not desire to form a new sect. They wished to remain Congregationalists, and to continue unbroken the fellowship that had existed from the beginning of New England. When they were compelled to separate from the older churches, they refrained from organizing a strictly defined religious body, and have called theirs a "movement." The words "denomination" and "sect" have been repellent to them; and they have attempted, not only to avoid their use, but to escape from that which they represent. They have wished to establish a broad, free fellowship, that would draw together all liberal thinkers and movements into one wide and inclusive religious body.

The Unitarian body accepted in theory from the first the principles of liberty, reason, and free inquiry. These were fully established, however, only as the result of discussion, agitation, and much friction. Theodore Parker was subjected to severe criticism, Emerson was regarded with distrust, and the Free Religious Association was organized as a protest and for the sake of a freer fellowship. In fact, however, Parker was never disfellowshipped; and from the first many Unitarians regarded Emerson as the teacher of a higher type of spiritual religion. Through this period of controversy, when there was much of bitter feeling engendered, no one was expelled from the Unitarian body for opinion's sake. All stayed in who did not choose to go out, there being no trials for, heresy. The result of this method has been that the Unitarian body is now one of the most united and harmonious in Christendom. The free spirit has abundantly justified itself. When it was found that every one could think for himself, express freely his own beliefs, and live in accordance with his own convictions, controversy came to an end. When heresy was no longer sought for, heresy ceased to have an existence. The result has not been discord and distrust, but peace, harmony, and a more perfect fellowship.

In the Unitarian body from the first there has been a free spirit of inquiry. Criticism has had a free course. The Bible has been subjected to the most searching investigation, as have all the foundations of religion. As a result, no religious body shows, a more rational interest in the Bible or a more confident trust in its great spiritual teachings.

The early Unitarians anticipated that Unitarianism would soon become the popular form of religion accepted in this country. Thomas Jefferson thought that all young men of his time would die Unitarians. Others were afraid that Unitarianism would become sectarian in its methods as soon as it became popular, which they anticipated would occur in a brief period.[1] The cause of the slow growth of Unitarianism is to be found in the fact that it has been too modern in its spirit, too removed from the currents of popular belief, to find ready acceptance on the part of those who are largely influenced by traditional beliefs. The religion of the great majority of persons is determined by tradition or social heredity, by what they are taught in childhood or hear commonly repeated around them. Only persons who are naturally independent and self–reliant can overcome the difficulties in the way of embracing a form of religion which carries them outside of the established tradition. For these reasons it is not surprising that as yet there has not been a rapid growth of organized Unitarianism. In fact, Unitarianism has made little progress outside of New England, and those regions to which New England traditions have been carried by those who migrated westward.

The early promise for the growth of Unitarianism in the south, from 1825 to 1840, failed because there was no background of tradition for its encouragement and support. Individuals could think their way into the Unitarian faith, but their influence proved ineffective when all around them the old tradition prevailed as stubborn conviction. Even the influence of a literature pervaded with Unitarianism proved ineffective in securing any rapid spread of the new faith, except as it has found its way into the common

Christian tradition by a process of spiritual infiltration. The result has been that Unitarianism has grown slowly, because it has been obliged to create new traditions, to form a new habit of thought, and to make free inquiry a common motive and purpose.

In a word, Unitarianism has been a heresy; and therefore there has been no open door for it. Most heretical sects have been narrow in spirit, bigoted in temper, and intensely sectarian in method. Their isolation from the great currents of the world's life acts on them intellectually and spiritually as the process of in–and–in breeding does upon animals: it intensifies their peculiarities and defects. A process of atrophy or degeneration takes place; and they grow from generation to generation more isolated, sectarian, and peculiar. Unitarianism has escaped this tendency because it has accepted the modern spirit and because to a large degree its adherents have been educated and progressive persons. Its principles of liberty, reason, and free inquiry, have brought its followers into touch with those forces that are making most rapidly for the development of mankind. Unitarians have been conspicuously capable of individual initiative; and yet their culture has been large enough to give them a conservative loyalty to the past and to the profounder and more spiritual phases of the Christian tradition. While strongly individualistic and heretical they have been sturdily faithful to Christianity, seeking to revive its earlier and more simple life.

A chief value of Unitarianism in the past has been that it has pioneered the way for the development of the modern spirit within the limits of Christianity. The churches from which it came out have followed it far on the way it has travelled. Its most liberal advocates of the first generation were more conservative than many of the leaders are to–day in the older churches. Its period of criticism, controversy, and agitation is being reproduced in many another religious body of the present time. The debates about miracles, the theory of the supernatural, the authenticity of Scripture, the nature of Christ, and other problems that are now agitating most of the progressive Protestant denominations, are almost precisely those that exercised Unitarians years ago. The only final solution of these problems, that will give peace and harmony, is that of free inquiry and rational interpretation, which Unitarians have finally accepted. If other religious bodies would profit by this experience and by the Unitarian method for the solution of these problems, it would be greatly to their advantage.

The Unitarian churches have been few in number, and they have suffered from isolation and provincialism. These defects of the earlier period have now in part passed away, new traditions have been created, a cosmopolitan spirit has been developed, and Unitarianism has become a world movement. This was conspicuously indicated at the seventy–fifth anniversary of the organization of the American Unitarian Association, and in the formation of The International Council of Unitarian and Other Liberal Religious Thinkers and Workers. It was then shown that Unitarianism has found expression in many parts of the world, that it answers to an intellectual and spiritual need of the time, and that it is capable of interpreting the religious convictions of persons belonging to many phases of human development and culture. A broader, more philosophical, and humaner tradition is being formed, that will in time become a wide–reaching influence for the development of a religious life that will be at once more scientific and more spiritual in its nature than anything the past has produced.

The promise of Unitarianism for the future does not consist in its becoming a sect and in its striving for the development of merely denominational interests, but in its cultivation of the deeper spiritual life and in its cosmopolitan sympathy with all phases of religious growth. Its mission is one with philanthropy, charity, and altruism. Its attitude should be that of free inquiry, loyalty to the spirit of philosophy and science, and fidelity to the largest results of human progress. It should always represent justice, righteousness, and personal integrity. That promise is not to be found in the rapid multiplication of its churches or in its devotion to propagandist aims, but in its loyalty to the free spirit and in its exemplification of the worth and beauty of the religion of humanity. As a sect, it will fail; but as a movement towards a larger faith, a purer life, and a more inclusive fellowship, the future is on its side.

While recognizing the Unitarian as a great pioneer movement in religion, it should be seen that its strong individualism has been a cause of its slow growth. Until recently the Unitarian body has been less an organic phase of the religious life of the time than a group of isolated churches held together only by the spontaneous bonds of fellowship and good will. Such a body can have little effective force in any effort at missionary propagandism or in making its spirit dominant in the religious life of the country. As heredity and variation are but two phases of organic growth, so are tradition and individual initiative but two phases of social progress. In both processes—organic growth and social progress—the primary force is the conservative one, that maintains what the past has secured. If individualism is necessary to healthy growth, associative action is essential to any growth whatever of the social body. In so far as individual perfection can be attained, it cannot be by seeking it as an end in itself: it can be reached only by means of that which conduces to general social progress.

It may be questioned whether there is any large future for Unitarianism unless all excessive individualism is modified and controlled. Such individualism is in opposition to the altruistic and associative spirit of the present time. Liberty is not an end in itself, but its value is to be found in the opportunity it gives for a natural and fitting association of individuals with each other. Freedom of religious inquiry is but an instrument for securing spiritual growth, not merely for the individual, but for all mankind. So long as liberty of thought and spiritual freedom remain the means of individual gratification, they are ineffective as spiritual forces. They must be given a wider heritage in the life of mankind before they can accomplish their legitimate results in securing for men freedom from the external bonds of traditionalism. Even reason is but an instrument for securing truth, and not truth itself.

Rightly understood, authority in the church is but the principle of social action, respect for what mankind has gained of spiritual power through its centuries of development. Authority is therefore as necessary as freedom, and the two must be reconciled in order that progress may take place. When so understood and so limited, authority becomes essential to all growth in freedom and individuality. What above all else is needed in religion is social action on the part of freedom—loving men and women, who, in the strength of their individuality, co—operate for the attainment, not of their own personal good, but the advancement of mankind. This is what Unitarianism has striven for, and what it has gained in some measure. It has sought to make philanthropy the test of piety, and to make liberty a means of social fidelity.

Free inquiry cannot mean liberty to think as one pleases, but only to think the truth, and to recognize with submissive spirit the absolute conditions and the limitations of the truth. Though religion is life and not a creed, it none the less compels the individual to loyalty of social action; and that means nothing more and nothing less than faithfulness to what will make for the common good, and not primarily what will minister to one's own personal development, intellectually and spiritually.

The future of Unitarianism will depend on its ability further to reconcile, individualism with associative action, the spirit of free inquiry with the larger human tradition. Its advantage cannot be found in the abandonment of Christianity, which has been the source and sustaining power of its life, but in the development of the Christian tradition by the processes of modern thought. The real promise of Unitarianism is in identifying itself with the altruistic spirit of the age, and in becoming the spiritual interpreter of the social aspirations of mankind. In order to this result it must not only withdraw from its extreme individualism, but bring its liberty into organic relations with its spirit of social fidelity. It will then welcome the fact that freedom and authority are identical in their deeper meanings. It will discover that service is more important than culture, and that culture is of value to the end that service may become more effective. Then it will cheerfully recognize the truth that the social obligation is as important as the individual right, and that the two make the rounded whole of human action.

[1] See pp. 131, 328.

APPENDIX. A. FORMATION OF THE LOCAL

CONFERENCES.

The local conferences came into existence in the following order: Wisconsin and Minnesota Quarterly Conference, organized at Sheboygan, Wis., October 24, 1866; New York Central Conference of Liberal Christians, Rochester, November 21, 1866; Conference of Unitarian and Other Christian Churches of the Middle and Southern States, Wilmington, Del., November 22, 1866; Norfolk Conference of Unitarian and Other Christian Churches, Dedham, Mass., November 28, 1866; New York and Hudson River Local Conference, New York, December 6, 1866; Essex Conference of Liberal Christian Churches, Salem, Mass., December 11, 1866; Lake Erie Conference of Unitarian and Other Christian Societies, Meadville, Penn., December 11, 1866; Worcester County Conference of Congregational (Unitarian) and Other Christian Societies, Worcester, Mass., December 12, 1866; South Middlesex Conference of Congregational Unitarian and Other Christian Societies, Cambridgeport, Mass., December 12, 1866; Suffolk Conference of Unitarian and Other Christian Churches, Boston, December 17, 1866; North Middlesex Conference of Unitarian Congregational and Other Christian Churches, Littleton, Mass., December 18, 1866.

The Champlain Liberal Christian Conference, Montpelier, Vt., January 9, 1867; the Connecticut Valley Conference of Congregational Unitarian and Other Christian Churches, Greenfield, Mass., January 16, 1867; the Plymouth and Bay Conference,

Hingham, Mass., February 5, 1867; the Ohio Valley Conference of Unitarian and Other Christian Churches, Louisville, Ky., February 22, 1867; the Channing Conference, Providence, R.I., April 17, 1867; Liberal Christian Conference of Western Maine, Brunswick, Me., October 22, 1867.

The Local Conference of Liberal Christians of the Missouri Valley, Weston, Mo., March 18, 1868; the Chicago Conference of Unitarian Churches, Chicago, December 2, 1868; Western Illinois and Iowa Conference of Unitarian and Other Christian Churches, Sheffield, Ill., January 28, 1869; Cape Cod Conference of Unitarian Congregational and Other Liberal Christian Churches, Barnstable, Mass., November 30, 1870; Conference of Liberal Christians of the Missouri Valley, Kansas City, Mo., May 3, 1871; Michigan Conference of Unitarian and Other Christian Churches, Jackson, October 21, 1875; the Fraternity of Illinois Liberal Christian Societies, Bloomington, November 11, 1875; Iowa Association of Unitarian and Other Independent Churches, Burlington, June 1, 1877; Indiana Conference of Unitarian and Independent Religious Societies, Hobart, October 1, 1878; Ohio State Conference of Unitarian and Other Liberal Societies, Cincinnati, May, 1879.

Kansas Unitarian Conference, December 2, 1880; Nebraska Unitarian Association, Omaha, November 9, 1882; the Southern Conference of Unitarian and Other Christian Churches, Atlanta, Ga., April 24, 1884; the New York Conference of Unitarian Churches superseded the New York and Hudson River Conference at a session held in New York, April 29, 1885; Pacific Unitarian Conference, San Francisco, November 2, 1885; the Illinois Conference of Unitarian and Other Independent Societies superseded the Illinois Fraternity in 1885; Minnesota Unitarian Conference, St. Paul, November 17, 1887; Hancock Conference of Unitarian and Other Christian Churches, Bar Harbor, Me., August 8, 1889; Missouri Valley Unitarian Conference superseded the Kansas Unitarian Conference, December 2, 1889.

Rocky Mountain Conference of Unitarian and Other Liberal Christian Churches, Denver, Col., May 17, 1890; the Unitarian Conference of the Middle States and Canada, Brooklyn, N.Y., November 19, 1890, superseded New York State Conference; Central States Conference of Unitarian Churches, Cincinnati, December 9, 1891, superseded the Ohio State Conference; Pacific Northwest Conference of Unitarian, Liberal Christian, and Independent Churches, Puyallup, Wash., August 1, 1892; Southern California Conference of Unitarian and Other Liberal Christian Churches, Santa Ana, October 1892.

Four of the early conferences, the New York Central, Champlain, Western Maine, and Missouri Valley, were not distinctly Unitarian. These were union organizations, in which Universalists, and perhaps other denominations, were associated with Unitarians. The New York Central Conference refused to send delegates to the National Conference on account of its union character. In other conferences, such as the Connecticut Valley and the Norfolk, Universalists took part in their organization, and were for a number of years connected with them.

Most of the conferences organized from 1875 to 1885 were within state limits; but those organized subsequently to 1885 were more distinctly district conferences, and included several states. Several of the conferences have been reorganized in order to bring them into harmony with the prevailing theory of state or district limits at the time when such action took place. A few of the conferences had only a name to live, and they soon passed out of existence.

In the local, as in the National Conference, two purposes contended for expression, the one looking to the uniting of all liberal denominations in one general organization, and the other to the promotion of distinctly Unitarian interests. In the National Conference the denominational purpose controlled the aims kept most clearly in view; but the other purpose found expression in the addition of "Other Christian Churches" to the name, though only in the most limited way did such churches connect themselves with the conference. The local conferences made like provision for those not wishing to call themselves distinctly Unitarian. Such desire for co–operation, however, was in a large degree rendered ineffective by the fact that the primary aim had in view in the creation of the local conferences was the increase of the funds of the American Unitarian Association.

B. UNITARIAN NEWSPAPERS AND MAGAZINES.

There was a very considerable activity from 1825 to 1850 in the publication of Unitarian periodicals, and probably the energies of the denomination found a larger expression in that direction than in any other.

In January, 1827, was begun in Boston The Liberal Preacher, a monthly publication of sermons by living ministers, conducted by the Cheshire Association of Ministers, with

Rev. Thomas R. Sullivan, of Keene, N.H., as the editor. It was continued for eight or ten years, and with considerable success.

With November, 1827, Rev. William Ware began the publication in New York City of The Unitarian, a quarterly magazine, of which the last number appeared February 15, 1828.

The Unitarian Monitor was begun at Dover, N.H., October 1, 1831, and was continued until October 10, 1833. It was a fortnightly of four three–column pages, and was well conducted. It was under the editorial management of Rev. Samuel K. Lothrop, then the minister in Dover.

The Unitarian Christian, edited by Rev. Stephen G. Bulfinch, was published quarterly in Augusta, Ga., for a year or two.

In 1823 Rev. Samuel J. May published The Liberal Christian at Brooklyn, Conn., as a fortnightly county paper of eight small quarto pages. He followed it by The Christian Monitor and Common People's Adviser, which was begun in April, 1832, its object being "to promote the free discussion of all subjects connected with happiness and holiness."

The Unitarian, conducted by Rev. Bernard Whitman, then settled in Waltham, Mass., was published in Cambridge and Boston during the year 1834, and came to its end because of the death of Whitman in the last month of the year. It was a monthly magazine of a distinctly missionary character.

Of a more permanent character was The Unitarian Advocate, the first number of which was issued in Boston, January, 1828. It was a small 12mo of sixty pages, monthly, the editor being Rev. Edmund Q. Sewall. He continued in that capacity to the end of 1829, when it was "conducted by an association of gentlemen." The purpose was to make a popular magazine at a moderate price. It came to an end in December, 1832.

With January 1, 1835, was issued in Boston the first number of The Boston Observer and Religious Intelligencer, a weekly of eight three–column pages, edited by Rev. George Ripley. It was continued for only six months, when it was joined to The Christian Register, which took its name as a sub–title for a time. Its motto, "Liberty, Holiness, Love," was also borrowed by that paper.

The Western Messenger was begun in Cincinnati, June, 1835, with Rev. Ephraim Peabody as the editor. It was a monthly of ninety–six pages, and was ably edited. Owing to the illness of Mr. Peabody, it was removed to Louisville after the ninth number; and Rev. James Freeman Clarke became the editor, with Rev. W.H. Channing and Rev. J.H. Perkins as assistants for a time. It was published by the Western Unitarian Association, and was discontinued with the number for May, 1841. Among the contributors were Emerson, Margaret Fuller, William Henry Channing, Christopher P. Cranch, William G. Eliot, who aided in giving it a high literary character. For a number of years the American Unitarian Association made an annual appropriation to aid in its publication.

The Monthly Miscellany of Religion and Letters was begun in Boston with April, 1839. It was a 12mo of forty–eight pages, monthly. The editor was Rev. Ezra S. Gannett, by whom it was "designed to furnish religious reading for the people, treat Unitarian opinions in their practical bearings, and show their power to produce holiness of life; and by weight of contents to come between The Christian Register and The Christian Examiner." It was continued until the end of 1843, when it was absorbed by the latter periodical.

With the first of January, 1844, was begun The Monthly Religious Magazine, to meet the needs of those who found The Christian Examiner too scholarly. The first editor, was Rev. Frederic D. Huntington, who was succeeded by Rev. Edmund H. Sears, Rev. James W. Thompson, Rev. Rufus Ellis, and Rev. John H. Morison. The last issue was that of February, 1874.

A large weekly was begun in Boston, January 7, 1843, called The Christian World, of which Rev. George G. Channing was the publisher and managing editor. He was assisted by Rev. James Freeman Clarke and Hon. John A. Andrew, afterward Governor of Massachusetts, as editors or editorial contributors. The special aims of the paper were "to awaken a deeper religious interest in all the great philanthropic and benevolent enterprises of the day." It was continued until December 30, 1848. George G. Channing was a brother of Dr. Channing, and was settled over two or three parishes. The paper was ably conducted, and while Unitarian was not distinctly denominational.

The Christian Inquirer was started in New York, October 17, 1846, and was a weekly of four six–column pages. It was managed by the New York Unitarian Association; and it was largely under the control of Rev. Henry W. Bellows, who in 1850 was assisted by

Unitarianism in America

Rev. Samuel Osgood, Rev. James F. Clarke, and Rev. Frederic H. Hedge.

In 1846 was begun the publication of the Unitarian Annual Register in Boston by Crosby &Nichols, with Rev. Abiel A. Livermore, then settled in Keene, N.H., as the editor. In 1851 the work came under the control of the American Unitarian Association, and as the Year Book of the denomination it was edited by the secretary or his assistant. From 1860 to 1869 the Year Book was issued as a part of the December number of The Monthly Journal of the American Unitarian Association.

The Bible Christian was begun in 1847 at Toronto by Rev. John Cordner, the minister there, and was continued as a semi–monthly for a brief period.

The Unitarian and Foreign Religious Miscellany was published in Boston during 1847, with Rev. George E. Ellis as the editor. It was a monthly magazine devoted to the explanation and defence of Unitarian Christianity; and its contents were mostly selected from the English Unitarian periodicals, especially The Prospective Review, The Monthly Reformer, Bible Christian, The Unitarian, and The Inquirer.

During this period The Christian Examiner had its largest influence upon the denomination, and came to an end. Its scholarship and its liberality made it of interest to only a limited constituency, and the publisher was compelled to discontinue it at the end of 1869 from lack of adequate support. It was edited from the beginning by the ablest men. Rev. James Walker and Rev. Francis W.P. Greenwood became the editors in 1831, Rev. William Ware taking the place of Dr. Walker in 1837. From 1844 to 1849 Rev. Ezra S. Gannett and Rev. Alvan Lamson were the editors, and they were succeeded by Rev. George Putnam and Rev. George E. Ellis. In July, 1857, Rev. Frederic H. Hedge and Rev. Edward E. Hale became the editors, and continued until 1861. Then the editorship was assumed by Rev. Thomas B. Fox, who was for several years its owner and publisher; and he was assisted as editor by Rev. Joseph H. Allen. The magazine was purchased by Mr. James Miller in 1865, who removed it to New York. Dr. Henry W. Bellows became the editor, and Mr. Allen continued as assistant, until it was discontinued with the December number, 1869.

One of the purposes which found expression after the awakening of 1865 was the establishment of a large popular weekly religious journal that should reach all classes of liberals throughout the country. The Christian Inquirer was changed into The Liberal

Christian with the number for December 22, 1866; and under this name it appeared in a larger and more vigorous form. Dr. Bellows was the editor, and contributors were sought from all classes of Liberal Christians. The effort made to establish an able undenominational journal, of a broad and progressive but distinctly liberal type, was energetic; but the time was not ready for it. With December 2, 1876, the paper became The Inquirer, which was continued to the close of 1877.

There was also planned in 1865 a monthly journal that should be everywhere acceptable in the homes of liberals of every kind. In January, 1870, appeared the Old and New, a large monthly magazine, combining popular and scholarly features. The editors were Dr. Edward E. Hale and Mr. Frederic B. Perkins. In its pages were first published Dr. Hale's Ten Times Ten, and also many of the chapters of Dr. James Martineau's Seat of Authority in Religion. It was discontinued with the number for December, 1875.

The Monthly Religious Magazine was discontinued with the February issue of 1874; and the next month appeared The Unitarian Review and Religious Magazine, edited by Rev. Charles Lowe. When Lowe died, in June, 1874, he was succeeded by Rev. Henry H. Barber and Rev. James De Normandie. In 1880 Dr. J.H. Allen became the editor,—a position he held until the magazine was discontinued, in December, 1891.

In March, 1878, was begun in Chicago the publication of The Pamphlet Mission, a semi–monthly issue of sermons for missionary circulation, with a dozen pages of news added in a supplement. In September the name was changed to Unity; and this publication grew into a small fortnightly journal, representing the interests of the Western Unitarian Conference. A few years later it became a weekly; and it has continued as the representative of the more radical Unitarian opinions, though in 1894 it became the special organ of The Liberal Congress. The chief editorial management has been in the hands of Rev. Jenkin Ll. Jones.

The Unitarian was begun in Chicago by Rev. Brooke Herford and Rev. Jabez T. Sunderland with January, 1886, as the organ of the more conservative members of the Western Conference. In June, 1887, this monthly magazine was removed to Ann Arbor, Mr. Sunderland becoming the managing editor; and in 1890 the office of publication was removed to Boston, and Rev. Frederic B. Mott became the assistant editor. In 1897 the magazine was merged into The Christian Register.

In 1880 The Rising Faith was published at Manchester, N.H., as a monthly, and continued for two or three years.

In August, 1891, The Guidon appeared in San Francisco; and in November, 1893, it became The Pacific Unitarian, a monthly representing the interests of the Unitarian churches on the Pacific coast. Mr. Charles A. Murdock has been the editor.

The Southern Unitarian was begun at Atlanta, Ga., January, 1893; and it was published for five years as a monthly by the Southern Conference.

In December, 1891, was begun at Davenport, Ia., with Rev. Arthur M. Judy as editor, a monthly parish paper, called Old and New. Other parishes joined in its publication, and in 1895 it became the organ of the Iowa Unitarian Association. In 1896 it was published in Chicago, with Rev. A.W. Gould as the editor, in behalf of the interests of the Western Conference. In September, 1898, its publication was resumed in Davenport by Mr. Judy; and a year later it became again the organ of the Iowa Association.

The New World, a Quarterly Review of Religion, Ethics, and Theology, was begun in Boston, March, 1892, and was discontinued with the December number for 1900. Its editors were Dr. C.C. Everett, Dr. C.H. Toy, Dr. Orello Cone, with Rev. N.P. Gilman as managing editor.

The Church Exchange began in June, 1893, and was published as a monthly at Portland, in the interest of the Maine Conference of Unitarian Churches, with Rev. John C. Perkins as editor. In 1896–97 it was published at Farmington, and in 1897–99 Mr. H.P. White was the editor. Since 1899 it has been published in Portland, with Mr. Perkins as editor.

The above list of periodicals is not complete. More detailed information is desirable, and that the list may be made, full and accurate to date.

Printed in the United States
45956LVS00003B/8